WJEC GCSE

GEOGRAPHY

Includes full coverage of
WJEC Eduqas GCSE (9–1) Geography A

- Alan Brown ■ Gregg Coleman ■ Val Davis ■ Bob Digby
- Andy Leeder ■ Glyn Owen

HODDER
EDUCATION
LEARN MORE

This material has been endorsed by WJEC and offers high quality support for the delivery of WJEC and Eduqas qualifications. While this material has been through a quality assurance process, all responsibility for the content remains with the publisher.

Every effort has been made to trace all copyright holders, but if any have been inadvertently overlooked, the Publishers will be pleased to make the necessary arrangements at the first opportunity.

Although every effort has been made to ensure that website addresses are correct at time of going to press, Hodder Education cannot be held responsible for the content of any website mentioned in this book. It is sometimes possible to find a relocated web page by typing in the address of the home page for a website in the URL window of your browser.

Hachette UK's policy is to use papers that are natural, renewable and recyclable products and made from wood grown in sustainable forests. The logging and manufacturing processes are expected to conform to the environmental regulations of the country of origin.

Orders: please contact Bookpoint Ltd, 130 Milton Park, Abingdon, Oxon OX14 4SE. Telephone: +44 (0)1235 827720. Fax: +44 (0)1235 400454. Email: education@bookpoint.co.uk. Lines are open from 9 a.m. to 5 p.m., Monday to Saturday, with a 24-hour message answering service. You can also order through our website: www.hoddereducation.co.uk

ISBN: 978 1 4718 6128 4

© Alan Brown, Gregg Coleman, Val Davis, Bob Digby, Andy Leeder, Glyn Owen 2016

First published in 2016 by

Hodder Education,

An Hachette UK Company

Carmelite House

50 Victoria Embankment

London EC4Y 0DZ

www.hoddereducation.co.uk

Impression number   10 9 8 7 6 5 4 3 2 1

Year   2020 2019 2018 2017 2016

Cover photo © Aurora Photos/Alamy

Illustrations by Aptara, Inc. and Barking Dog Art

Typeset by Aptara Inc.

Printed in Italy

A catalogue record for this title is available from the British Library.

CONTENTS

INTRODUCTION

How to use this book

THEME **2** Rural–urban links
Chapter 3
Global cities

What are the global patterns of urbanisation?

Over half (54 per cent) of the world's population lives in cities. But it's not always been this way. At the start of the twentieth century most of the world's population lived in the countryside or smaller towns. During the second half of the twentieth century the population of the world's cities, and the physical size of their built-up areas, grew – a process known as urbanisation. This process was particularly rapid in the cities of the newly industrialised countries (NICs) of Asia and Latin America. Urbanisation has been due to a combination of:

- migration from rural to urban areas
- the natural increase of the population when there are more births than deaths each year.

Figure 45 shows a list of the world's largest cities. Cities with over 10 million residents are sometimes known as mega-cities. In 2015 there were 28 mega-cities and 16 of these are located in Asia and only three in Europe. There are 498 cities in the world with a population greater than one million. Of these, 101 are in China and 57 are in India. The UK has only five cities with a population of over one million.

Newly Industrialised Countries (NICs)

NICs are characterised by: rapid urban growth; growth of the manufacturing sector of the economy; strong trading relationships with other countries; and the operation of foreign-owned multi-national companies (MNCs) within the country.

◄ **Figure 1** The centre of Mumbai, India. The neighbourhood of Bhendi Bazaar is in the foreground. The low-rise buildings in this neighbourhood are traditional dormitories known as chawls.

86

Each theme has a different colour so you can find your way around the book easily.

Important geographical terms are shown in **bold red font**. You can check the meaning of these words in the glossary at the back of the book and expand your geographical vocabulary.

Geographical concepts are described in tinted boxes. You will find these important concepts are mentioned in more than one chapter of the book.

Photographs show what real places look like. This photograph shows Mumbai – a unique place. But the photograph shows some features that are common in urban landscapes in many NIC cities. You should study the photographs carefully. What can you learn about NIC cities from this image?

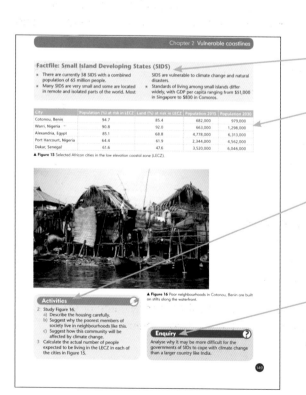

Chapter 2 Vulnerable coastlines

Factfile: Small Island Developing States (SIDS)

- There are currently 58 SIDS with a combined population of 65 million people.
- Many SIDS are very small and some are located in remote and isolated parts of the world. Most
- SIDS are vulnerable to climate change and natural disasters.
- Standards of living among small islands differ widely, with GDP per capita ranging from $51,000 in Singapore to $830 in Comoros.

City	Population (%) at risk in LECZ	Land (%) at risk in LECZ	Population 2015	Population 2030
Cotonou, Benin	94.7	85.4	682,000	979,000
Warri, Nigeria	90.8	92.0	663,000	1,298,000
Alexandria, Egypt	85.1	68.8	4,778,000	6,313,000
Port Harcourt, Nigeria	64.4	61.9	2,344,000	4,562,000
Dakar, Senegal	61.6	47.6	3,520,000	6,046,000

▲ **Figure 15** Selected African cities in the low elevation coastal zone (LECZ).

▲ **Figure 16** Poor neighbourhoods in Cotonou, Benin are built on stilts along the waterfront.

Activities

2 Study Figure 16.
  a) Describe the housing carefully.
  b) Suggest why the poorest members of society live in neighbourhoods like this.
  c) Suggest how this community will be affected by climate change.
3 Calculate the actual number of people expected to be living in the LECZ in each of the cities in Figure 15.

Enquiry

Analyse why it may be more difficult for the governments of SIDS to cope with climate change than a larger country like India.

149

Fact files make it easy for you to learn a few facts and figures about real places.

Maps, graphs and tables of data like this one provide us with evidence about the state of the world. Thinking like a geographer means that you need to look for patterns and trends in this evidence.

The activities will make you think carefully about the geographical information that has been presented in the photographs, maps, graphs and tables on the page. Doing them will help to build your geographical confidence and your ability to describe features, spot patterns and trends and explain why things happen.

Enquiries are longer activities. Some of them require further research, debate or discussion. Many will ask for your opinion and build your skills of analysis, evaluation and decision making. These tasks will encourage you to take an enquiry approach to learning – helping you to think like a geographer.

Fieldwork enquiries are described on pages which have a coloured background with footprints at the top and bottom of the page. Some pages focus on how to use specific fieldwork methods for collecting or representing data – like this page which describes the use of a transect to collect data in a sand dune ecosystem. Other fieldwork pages provide advice on sampling strategies, measuring flows and investigating concepts such as place.

Fieldwork Enquiries	Page numbers
Investigating visitor use of a honeypot site	8–9
Developing an enquiry question	10–11
Investigating downstream changes	16–17
Investigating landscape change	34
Investigating the concept of place	35
Does each town centre need its own distinct identity?	84–85
Bi-polar surveys	104–105
Investigating sand dunes	188–189
Collecting qualitative data	301

Geographical Skills panels describe how to carry out some important skills that are needed by geographers. These panels cover subjects like describing locations, drawing scattergraphs and reading hydrographs.

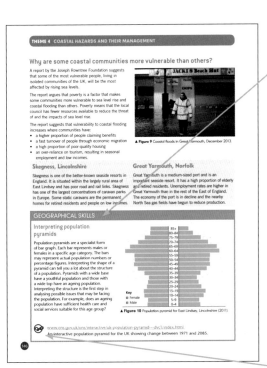

Geographical Skills	Page numbers
Calculating and representing frequency	23
How do you analyse a hydrograph?	38
Calculating percentage of average	44
Diamond ranking	83
Calculating percentages from raw data	93
Describing locations	98
Describing distributions	100
Interpreting population pyramids	146
Locating places on an OS map	259
Using choropleth maps	263
Testing relationships between sets of data	267

Weblinks will allow you to carry out further research or explore interactive maps on sites that use Geographical Information Systems (GIS).

ACKNOWLEDGEMENTS

Text acknowledgements: p.4 Data from www.nationalparks.gov.uk/learningabout/whatisnationalpark/factsandfigures; **p.7** *t and b* Extracts from Clwydian Range AONB: Sustainable Tourism Strategy and Action Plan, the Tourism Company 2009–2014; *m* Data from www.clwydianrangeaonb.org.uk/files/1906706421-Tourism%20Strategy%20Final%20Document.pdf; *b* Shropshire Hills Area of Outstanding Natural Beauty Management Plan 2014–2019; **p.15** Ordnance survey map extract © Crown copyright 2016 Ordnance Survey. Licence number 100036470; **p. 23** Data from British Geological Survey; **p.30** *m* Ordnance survey map extract © Crown copyright 2016 Ordnance Survey. Licence number 100036470; **p.32** Ordnance survey map extract © Crown copyright 2016 Ordnance Survey. Licence number 100036470; **p.34** *br* Data from Gerd Masselink, Plymouth University; p.41 Screenshot from Met Office, © Crown copyright 2016 Met Office; **p. 42** *m* Graph data © Crown copyright 2016 Environment Agency; **p.46** *b* Based on data provided by the UK National River Flow Archive, hosted by the Centre for Ecology and Hydrology, Natural Environment Research Council. http://nrfa.ceh.ac.uk; **p.55** Data from ww.ukcensusdata.com; **p.57** *t* Data from Office for National Statistics; *m* Data from Office for National Statistics; **p.59** Data from Welsh Government; **p.61** Map from Office of National Statistics, © Crown copyright 2016 Office of National Statistics; **p.62** *r* Map from Welsh Government, © Crown copyright 2015 Welsh Government; **p.63** *t* Screenshot from www.neighbourhood.statistics.gov.uk, © Crown copyright 2015 Office of National Statistics; **p.66** r Graph © Crown copyright 2014 Office for National Statistics; **p.74** *tr* Data from www.dannydorling.org/?p+4476; *bl* Map data from Oxford City Council; **p.75** Screenshot from the Environment Agency, © Crown copyright 2016 Environment Agency; **p.79** *m* Graph found on page 5 of 'Vacancy Report H1 2015 summary "Cautious Optimism"' by the Local Data Company, published September 2015; **p. 80** *t* Data from Office of National Statistics; *m and b* Data from Google; **p.87** *all* Data from United Nations Department of Economic and Social Affairs, Population Division, World Urbanizations Prospects: The 2014 Revision; **p.89** *all* Data from United Nations Department of Economic and Social Affairs, Population Division, World Urbanizations Prospects: The 2014 Revision; **p.92** *tr* Data from Census of India; **p.93** *t* Data adapted from National Sample Survey Organization (NSSO), http://timesofindia.indiatimes.com/city/mumbai/70-migrants-to-Mumbai-are-from-Maharashtra/articleshow/16428301.cms; *m* Data from Census of India and www.devinfolive.info/censusinfodashboard; **p.94** *m* Data from http://blogs-images.forbes.com/niallmccarthy/files/2014/09/Bollywood_2.jpg; **p.99** *tl* Data from National Census; **p.101** *r* Data from National Census; **p.102** *l* Ordnance survey map extract © Crown copyright 2016 Ordnance Survey. Licence number 10003647; **p.111** *tr* Diagram courtesy of the USGS; **p.115** *t* Data from World Bank; **p.119** *t* Data from UNSD Demographic Statistics; **p.123** Data from United Nations, Department of Economic and Social Affairs, Population division (2014), World Urbanization Prospects: The 2014 Revision, CD-ROM Edition; **p.124** *tr* Diagram based on Seismic Waves Radiate from the Focus of an Earthquake, University of Waikato; *m* Data from US Geological Survey and World Bank; **p.129** *b* Data from World Bank; **p.131** *b* Graph © Crown copyright 2014 Met Office; **p.137** *l* Ordnance survey map extract © Crown copyright 2016 Ordnance Survey. Licence number 100036470; **p.139** Extract from 'A Simple Life of Luxury' © 2016. All Rights Reserved; **p.140** *m* Screenshot from Natural Resources Wales, © Crown copyright 2016 Natural Resources Wales; *b* Screenshot from Data Shine © Crown copyright 2015; **p.141** *t* Data from Neighbourhood Statistics, 2011; **p.144** *r* Data from Environment Agency; **p.145** Map from 'Safecoast – trends in flood risk', www.safecoast.org (July 2008), reproduced by permission of Rijkswaterstaat-Centre for Water Management; **p.146** Graph from LRO 2011 Census Population Estimates: East Lindsey; **p.147** *l* Data from Office for National Statistics; r Extract from Joseph Rowntree Foundation Report, Summary of 'Impacts of climate change on disadvantaged UK coastal communities' (6 March 2011); **p.148** Map copyright: James Morgan / Panos published by SciDev.Net; **p.149** Data from UN Habitat, State of the World's Cities 2008/2009; **p.150** *bl* Map copyright © 2008, United Nations Environment Programme; **p.151** *r* Maps from 'Impact of sea level rise on the Nile delta' © GRID-Arenday. Used with permission; **p.163** *t* Data from Pakistan Meteorological Department; *b* Data from www.seatemperature.org; **p.166** Map copyright 2015 National Drought Mitigation Center; **p.169** Graph copyright 2015 National Drought Mitigation Center; **p.171** *m* Satellite image © NASA; **p.174** Weather map © Crown copyright 2014 Met Office; **p.187** Quotation from http://www.ceh.ac.uk/news-and-media/blogs/farmland-ditch-management-hydrologist-perspective © NERC Centre for Ecology & Hydrology 2016; **p.196** Data from www.obt.inpe.br/degrad; **p.197** *all* Data from American Soybean Association; **p.200** Data from World Bank; **p.207** Maps © NASA; **p.217** *l* Data from Nike.com; *r* Estimates based on *Washington Post*, 1995 and http://answers.yahoo.com/question/index?qid+20100225152454AACzalP; **p.221** *l* Text extract from http://qz.com/389741/the-thing-that-makes-bangladeshs-garment-industry-such-a-huge-success-also-makes-it-deadly/; *r* Text extract © Institute for Global Labour and Human Rights; **p.224** *b* Data from World Trade Organization Statistics Database; **p.226** *b* Map data from COVAMS Newsletter, No. 1, 29 May 2009; **p.228** Data from UNWTO Tourism Highlights 2015 Edition; **p.230** Data from Datatur; **p.237** *tl and bl* Graphs from The Millennium Development Goals Report by the Inter-Agency and Expert Group on MDG Indicators. Copyright © 2016 United Nations. Reprinted with permission of the United Nations; **p.242** Data from Aquastat; **p.243** Text extract from *Rural Women in the Sahel and Their Access to Agricultural Extension: Overview of Five Country Studies*. 1994. Report No. 13532 AFR. AF5AE. Washington, D.C.: World Bank; **p.245** *t* Map from Food and Agriculture Organization of the United Nations,2016, Proportion of total water withdrawal withdrawn for agriculture, http://www.fao.org/nr/water/aquastat/maps/WithA.WithT_eng.pdf. Reproduced with permission; *bl* Graph © UNESCO 2015; *br* Data from Aquastat; **p.252** *l* Screenshot from World Resources Institute, © World Resources Institute (http://creativecommons.org/licenses/by/4.0/); **p.256** *bl* Screenshot from Annual Survey of Hours and Earnings, © Crown copyright 2015 Office of National Statistics; **p.259** Ordnance survey map extract © Crown copyright 2016 Ordnance Survey. Licence number 100036470; **p.263** Screenshots from Statistics South-Africa; **p.264** *l and r* Data from World Bank; **p.265** Map © www.worldmapper.org; **p.268** Data from ILO; **p.269** Graph from Making Progress Against Child Labour: Global Estimates and Trends 2000–2012, © 1996–2013 International Labour Organization (ILO); **p.270** *b* Extract from Breaking Free from Child Labour © UNICEF India; **p.271** *r* Data from Census of India; **p.272** *l* Graph from The Millennium Development Goals Report by the Inter-Agency and Expert Group on MDG Indicators. Copyright © 2016 United Nations. Reprinted with permission of the United Nations; **p.276** *tr* Graph from The Millennium Development Goals Report by the Inter-Agency and Expert Group on MDG Indicators. Copyright © 2016 United Nations. Reprinted with permission of the United Nations; **p.277** *b* Data from National Statistical Office, Malawi; **p.280** Map data from Adult HIV Prevalence Rate, 2014 The Global HIV/AIDS Epidemic, Kaiser Family Foundation; **p.284** Data from UN Water; **p.286** *m* Data from IMO GHG study, 2009; *b* Data from Eurostat; **p.287** *m* Quotation courtesy of Guardian News & Media; **p.289** Map data from www.oafrica.com; **p.290** Catch of cod in the North Sea (in 1,000s of metric tonnes). Retrieved from: http://standardgraphs.ices.dk/ViewCharts. aspx?key=4121_as © ICES – All Rights Reserved; **p.291** The weight of adult cod (spawning stock) in the North Sea. Retrieved from: http://standardgraphs.ices.dk/ViewCharts.aspx?key=4121_as © ICES – All Rights Reserved; **p.293** Data from FAO Yearbook 2014, Fishery and Aquaculture Statistics; **p.294** *b* Data from www.palmoilextractionmachine.com/FAQ/what-is-palm-oil-used-for.html; **p.295** Data from www.worldpalmoilproduction.com/; **p.296** Screenshot from Future Flooding Report, © Crown copyright 2012 Department for Business Information & Skills; **p.304** Data from www.thetravelfoundation.org.uk; **p.306** *b* Artwork © 1996–2016 Australian Institute of Marine Science; **p.309** This article was first published by the Asian Development Bank (www.adb.org).

Photo credits can be found on page 322.

Upland landscapes of the UK

The **upland** landscapes of the UK are areas of mountain or moorland, high above the enclosed fields of farmland. These regions contain river valleys at lower altitudes where farmland is defined by field boundaries and where people have built settlements. You might think that upland areas are all the same, but each regional upland landscape is slightly different, affected by factors such as:

- geology
- the history of settlement and farming that have affected land use
- natural processes in the past (such as erosion by ice during the last ice age) and now (such as river erosion)
- type of vegetation.

http://mapapps2.bgs.ac.uk/quaternary/home.html – an interactive map of the UK from the British Geological Survey (BGS) showing broad types of landscape.

▲ **Figure 2** Mountain and valley landscape in the Lake District.

▲ **Figure 1** The upland landscape types of the UK and the extent of the ice during the last ice advance 22,000 years ago.

Understanding complex landscapes

Every landscape contains many separate features and landforms. Rather like the pieces of a jigsaw, it is the combination of these different features that creates a distinctive and unique landscape in each place in the UK.

Study Figure 3. It shows the sand dunes at Ynyslas on the west coast of Wales. At first this landscape appears to be quite simple, but look more carefully and you begin to see some complexity. For example, there is a sandy ridge running through the middle of the photograph at A. The ridge is vegetated. In front of the ridge, at B, is a deep trough of bare sand. Beyond the ridge is further detail – a wide estuary and then, beyond that, the hills of north Wales. The sand dunes themselves are not uncommon. Figure 4 shows that a large number of coastal locations have similar landscape features.

▲ **Figure 3** The sand dunes at Ynyslas at the mouth of the River Dyfi.

The landscape of the Dyfi estuary

Seen from above, in Figure 5, the sand dunes are just one small feature in a complex landscape. The sand dunes cover an area of less than one square kilometre, but the river estuary behind is of a much larger **scale**. This area includes a number of river and coastal landforms and a variety of ecosystems. This landscape looks natural but it includes human influences. Much of the boggy land in the estuary has been drained with ditches and is grazed. The landscape is popular with tourists and includes a number of caravan sites and small towns. It is the combination of these different human and physical features that give the estuary of the River Dyfi its unique landscape qualities.

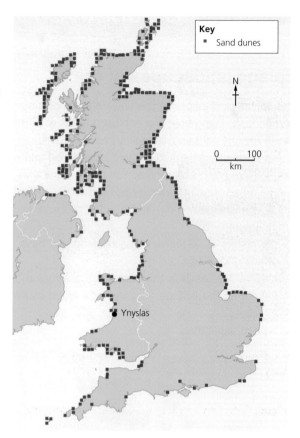

▲ **Figure 4** Distribution of sand dunes in the UK.

Investigating the concept of place

Place is a geographical concept that is used to describe what makes somewhere special, unique or distinct. Each place includes many different features of the human and physical environment, such as landscape features and landmarks, local styles of building, ecosystems and habitats, and local historical and cultural features. Each of these features may be relatively common across the UK; it is the unique combination of these geographical features, however, that creates an identity for any one place.

Activities

1 Describe the distribution of sand dunes shown in Figure 4.
2 a) Match each label to the correct numbered feature of Figure 5.
    b) Explain why the sand dunes in Figures 3 and 5 are an important element of the landscape of the Dyfi estuary that help to give it a sense of place.
3 Describe three different features in Figure 7.

Deciduous woodland ecosystems	Meanders on the River Dyfi	Sand dunes at Ynyslas	Upland grazing and moorland habitat	Features of the estuary including salt marsh and sheep pasture	Small towns such as Aberdyfi	Coastal landforms – beaches and bars

▲ **Figure 5** An aerial view of the Dyfi estuary, Mid Wales.

▲ **Figure 6** The small market town of Machynlleth, about 9 km from the mouth of the River Dyfi.

▲ **Figure 7** Ponds in the valley of the River Dyfi at Ynyshir, about 3 km from the mouth of the river.

Activity

4 a) Make a copy of Figure 8 and use it to calculate a bi-polar score for each photograph.

b) Share your scores with at least four members of your class. Calculate a mean score for each photograph.

	+5	+4	+3	+2	+1	−1	−2	−3	−4	−5	
Attractive											Unattractive
Varied											Monotonous
Rare											Common
Natural											Human

▲ **Figure 8** Bi-polar statements to assess landscape.

Honeypot sites

Millions of people enjoy leisure activities in the countryside. Walking, jogging and cycling are all popular activities that are good for your health. Leisure activities are also good for the rural economy: day visitors spend money at local attractions, in shops and on food and drink; other visitors stay overnight in guest houses. This allows the rural economy to **diversify** – to branch out from farming and invest in tourism-related service industries.

However, too many visitors can cause problems. Litter, parking and footpath erosion are all issues that need careful management. These issues become acute when the number of visitors exceeds the **carrying capacity** of the location and an activity begins to damage the landscape or ecosystem. Carrying capacity is most likely to be exceeded at the UK's **honeypot sites**. Like bees around a pot of honey, these sites attract the largest numbers of people because they are:
- exceptionally beautiful or interesting
- accessible by road and within easy reach of people living in larger towns or cities.

The majority of the UK's natural honeypot sites occur in either one of the UK's Areas of Outstanding Natural Beauty (AONBs) or one of our National Parks.

National Park	Visitor days* each year (millions)	Visitor spend each year (£ millions)
Brecon Beacons	5.0	197
The Broads	15.5	568
Exmoor	2.0	85
Lake District	24.0	1,146
Northumberland	1.7	190
Peak District	11.75	541
Pembrokeshire Coast	13.0	498

▲ **Figure 10** Data on visitor numbers and visitor spend for selected National Parks, 2014.

*The number of days spent by visitors in each National Park.

▲ **Figure 9** The location and distribution of Areas of Outstanding Natural Beauty and National Parks in England and Wales; AONBs are selected because of their exceptional scenic qualities.

Activities

1 Study Figure 9.
   a) Describe the location of Shropshire Hills AONB.
   b) List five urban areas that fall within 100 km of the Peak District National Park.
   c) Which National Park is furthest from any large city?
2 Study Figure 10.
   a) Give two reasons why some National Parks may have more visitors than others.
   b) Calculate the amount of money spent per visitor day in each National Park.
3 Describe how tourism helps the rural economy to diversify.

Enquiry

What are the distinctive landscapes of one National Park?

Research one National Park in the UK.

- Choose five photographs to summarise the distinctive landscapes of this National Park.
- Write a 500-word article that would attract visitors to this National Park.

Repairing footpath erosion in the Brecon Beacons

The Brecon Beacons is a mountainous region of South Wales. It is a popular area for walkers and mountain bikers. Some of the most-used paths are on land owned by public bodies such as the National Park Authority and the National Trust. During the period 2005 to 2015, the National Trust improved 15 km of paths. This work has allowed bare soil to become re-vegetated and areas of stunted vegetation to recover – in all, over 75,000 m² of vegetation has been restored. The National Trust aims to repair a further 10 km of footpaths where erosion is greater than 4 m in width.

▲ **Figure 11** Volunteers repairing a footpath close to Pen Y Fan, Brecon Beacons, Wales.

The restoration work relies heavily on donations and volunteer labour. During the summer of 2015, a section of path at Cefn Cwm Llwch, close to Pen y Fan, was restored. This is a very remote area and the stone needed for the path was delivered by helicopter in 1 tonne bags. In all, 70 bags of stone were flown in from a nearby quarry. The stones are placed upright in the ground and packed tight to make a hard-wearing and natural-looking path. Once the path is built, the area on either side can be re-vegetated. The cost of footpath management in the Brecon Beacons to the National Trust alone is around £100,000 each year.

Key
- Tall plants
- Short plants
- Soil
- Rock
- Stone

Increasing amount of trampling over time

Metres across path

1 2 3 4 5 6 7 8 9 10 11 12 13 14 15 16 17

Plants die

Soil is exposed to rainwater

Soil is eroded by rain splash and gulley erosion

The path becomes wider and wider

Plants are short and stunted where they have been trampled

Walkers avoid the central muddy section of path so walk at the edge

Stones are exposed as soil is eroded

▲ **Figure 12** Causes of footpath erosion.

Managing distinctive landscapes

The UK countryside is managed by landowners. Farmers manage their land to produce food and conserve habitats and wildlife. The UK's National Parks and AONBs are managed carefully to ensure that special and unique qualities of the landscape, wildlife and cultural heritage are recognised and conserved. The work is done by a small team of full-time staff and a large number of volunteers. Each of the UK's AONBs produces a five-year management plan and identifies action points that need to be met.

Managing the Clwydian Range and Dee Valley AONB

The Clwydian Range is a limestone upland area in northeast Wales. It is a popular area for visitors with an estimated 4.5 million people living within a 90-minute drive of it. Its distinctive landscape, seen in Figure 14, shows the importance of its geology. The limestone is resistant to erosion, forming steep escarpments with long scree slopes below them. Above the escarpment, the limestone soils on the plateau are thin and plants are specialised. Limestone landscapes are relatively uncommon in the UK. Their distribution is shown in Figure 15.

▲ **Figure 13** The location of AONBs and biosphere reserves in, and close to, Wales.

◀ **Figure 14** The limestone landscape of Eglwyseg in the Clwydian Range AONB, Wales.

Key
- Limestone, inland cliffs and scree

Activities

1 Write an appropriate label for each of the features, 1 to 6, in Figure 14.
2 a) Describe the distribution of limestone pavements in the UK.
  b) Explain why, although the limestone pavement in Figure 14 occurs in other places, this feature helps to give Eglwyseg a sense of place.

▲ **Figure 15** The distribution of limestone pavements in the UK.

The unique features that attract visitors to the Clwydian Range AONB

The richness of the landscape comes from a combination of undulating upland, including open heather clad moors and rocky outcrops, gently rolling farmland and wooded valleys. The area is blessed with extensive views in all directions. Attractive hedgerows, stone walls and a number of picturesque small villages add to the striking visual appeal.

The rich landscape of the Clwydian Range is the result of geological processes acting over 500 million years. The landscape of heather-clad uplands, ice-carved valleys, rocky limestone, rolling farmland and wooded valleys are a unique and spectacular resource.

Much of the landscape pattern visible today of villages and isolated farmsteads dates from the medieval period. Offa's Dyke is an important heritage feature of the borderland between England and Wales, and Offa's Dyke Path, a designated National Trail, is an important recreational resource.

▲ **Figure 16** Extract from the Clwydian Range AONB Action Plan.

Activity	Mean score
Driving around in attractive countryside	2.41
Taking longer walks (over 2 hours)	2.57
Taking shorter walks (up to 2 hours)	2.61
Exploring small towns and villages	2.64
Visits to attractions	2.83
Cycling (including mountain biking)	3.07
Horse riding	3.53
Fishing	3.61

▲ **Figure 17** Tourist-related businesses were asked to score each activity on a scale of one to five, where one is 'important to most of my visitors' and five is 'not important to any of my visitors'.

Landscape quality and special character	Establish fixed-point photography monitoring of key viewpoints	Work with power companies to put overhead power lines underground in the most sensitive locations	Organise one day per year when local communities are asked to share their wealth of knowledge about the area
Access and recreation	Improve signage by renewing and replacing finger posts	Improve access by reducing the number of stiles or replacing stiles with kissing gates	Monitor footpath erosion in key areas, e.g. around hill forts, and carry out one erosion project per year
Culture and people	Object to development proposals that involve the loss of community facilities, such as local shops and public houses	Explore options to secure consistent mobile phone coverage across the AONB and to overcome existing 'black spots' without harming the character and appearance of the area	Work with local planning and housing authorities to promote affordable housing schemes for local people

▲ **Figure 18** Selected action points in the Shropshire Hills AONB management plan for 2014–19.

Activities

3 Use Figure 16 to describe how geological, geographical and cultural features of the landscape attract visitors to this AONB.

4 Choose an appropriate technique to represent the data in Figure 17.

5 a) Discuss the nine action points in Figure 18.

   b) Make a diamond nine diagram (like the one on page 83) and place the action points in the diagram, putting those that you think are essential at the top of the diagram.

   c) Explain why you have chosen your top three action points. You should explain how your chosen action points will help to conserve or recognise landscapes, wildlife or local communities/heritage.

Investigating visitor use of a honeypot site

The Stiperstones is a rocky ridge in the Shropshire Hills AONB. This AONB is in easy driving distance of the towns and cities of the West Midlands. The hills are not large: the summits of most are around 400 m above sea level. The slopes are not too steep so they are accessible to walkers and cyclists of all abilities and ages.

The soils on the Stiperstones are particularly thin. In fact, rocky outcrops called **tors** stick out along the backbone of the ridge. People walk up to the top to climb over the tors and admire the view. However, trampling along the same routes has damaged the vegetation and led to erosion of the soil. You can see the scars made by footpath erosion in Figure 20.

Sampling strategies

A sample is a set of data that provides us with a good understanding of what is happening without having to record everything. The sample must be representative – a fair reflection of the whole. It is essential that the sample is not biased. There are three main sampling strategies and these are shown in Figure 19. In addition, sampling can sometimes be 'opportunistic'. Opportunity sampling means that the sample has been chosen because it is convenient and easily or safely available. For example, sample points along a river are usually chosen because access into the river is permitted (the landowner has agreed) and safe. The problem with this type of sampling is that it isn't fair or unbiased, so your sample may not be representative.

What's the difference between quantitative and qualitative data?

Geographers can collect all sorts of different kinds of data during a fieldwork enquiry but it will always fall into one of two categories:

Quantitative data is information that can be measured and recorded as numbers. Counting traffic, measuring the width and velocity of a river, or measuring the size of pebbles on a beach are all examples of quantitative data.

Qualitative data is information that is not numerical. You can collect qualitative data in a wide variety of ways such as by taking photographs, field sketches, videos or audio recordings. Interviewing people to find their opinions or perceptions about an issue is also an example of qualitative data collection. The bi-polar technique (page 104) is a way to try to make the collection of opinions more quantitative.

	Random sampling	Systematic sampling	Stratified sampling
What is it?	Every sample point has an equal probability of being sampled.	Data is collected at regular intervals. These intervals can be in time or space (distance).	Proportional samples are taken from separate groups or strata.
How might you use it?	To investigate how busy a country park is you could select a range of locations across the park and carry out pedestrian counts at each of these sites. Put the names of all locations in a bag and pull out five.	To investigate how tourist impact changes as you move further away from a visitor centre, you might carry out litter counts and environmental impact surveys every 100 m away from the centre.	When carrying out a questionnaire, make sure that you sample appropriate numbers from different age groups based on data from the census, i.e., 20% aged 0–18, 25% aged 19–45, 35% aged 45–65 and 20% aged 66+.
Advantages	Removes bias completely in the selection of sites.	Covers a range of locations and provides an even spread over the whole survey area.	Provides a true representative sample.
Disadvantages	Survey sites may be clustered together, so you do not get an even spread of locations.	If samples are too far apart you may miss important variations.	You will need information on the size of each group before you start.

▲ **Figure 19** Sampling strategies.

Using a control to investigate the impact of trampling

Figure 20 clearly shows the difference in vegetation between areas that have been heavily trampled by visitors and areas that have not been walked across. However, as Figure 12 (page 5) suggests, people walk through the vegetation on either side of the path to avoid walking on the uneven stones. This leads to an enquiry question: are some species of plants more vulnerable to damage than others?

Are some species of plants more vulnerable to damage than others?

If so, you might find that there is a lower percentage of some plants growing immediately next to the path because they have been damaged by trampling. To find out you would need to set up a control – an experiment to find the average amount of each species of plant. This is what you would do:

Step 1: Use a quadrat to measure the percentage of various plants in an area at a distance away from the path that appears to be unaffected by trampling. A quadrat is a metal or plastic grid – usually about half a metre across. You can estimate the percentage of each plant in each quadrat. Take at least five control measurements in different places and then calculate the mean percentage of each plant in these areas.

Step 2: Set up a transect (see page 188) across the footpath. You will need to start and end the transect several metres away from the eroded section of path so that you sample the plants on the edge of the trampled area. Each quadrat will need to be 2 m apart along the transect.

	Quadrat				
	1	2	3	4	5
Bilberry	30	10	40	25	55
Heather	60	80	60	60	40
Other plants	10	10	0	15	5
Bare soil/rock	0	0	0	0	0

▲ **Figure 21** Percentage of each type of vegetation in the control quadrats.

	Quadrat									
	1	2	3	4	5	6	7	8	9	10
Bilberry	30	10	0	0	0	0	0	10	20	35
Heather	60	70	70	0	20	0	70	80	80	65
Other plants	10	20	10	0	0	0	30	10	0	0
Bare soil/rock	0	0	20	100	80	100	0	0	0	0

▲ **Figure 22** Percentage of each type of vegetation in each quadrat; each quadrat was 2 m apart.

Activity

1   How does trampling affect different species of plant?
   a) Use the data in Figure 21 to calculate the mean percentage of each plant in the control.
   b) Choose a suitable technique to represent the data in Figure 22. See page 189 to see how to draw a kite diagram.
   c) What conclusions can you draw about the effect of trampling on bilberry and heather plants at the edge of the path?

Enquiry

How would you go about designing an enquiry into what gives your local area a sense of identity? What quantitative and qualitative data could you collect?

◀ **Figure 20** Footpath erosion is not a widespread problem in the Shropshire Hills AONB but it is a localised problem on the Stiperstones ridge.

Developing an enquiry question

Imagine you are about to go on a fieldtrip to the Stiperstones. Your enquiry will need an enquiry question. First you need to get a feel for the place and the issues it faces. Using the internet to read about the Shropshire Hills AONB or using Google Maps or Google Street View are all good places to research the location of your fieldwork before you visit. Then you can pose possible enquiry questions. For example:

What impact do visitors have on the environment at the Stiperstones?

This question can be broken down into smaller sub-questions to help to give it structure:

1 *What do we know about the visitors to the Stiperstones?*
2 *What is the environment of the Stiperstones?*
3 *How have the visitors affected the environment of the Stiperstones?*

Using questionnaires

Questionnaires are a quick way to capture people's opinions or record their behaviour. However, questionnaires are subjective. You cannot guarantee that people have been honest in their response to you. You can either ask closed or open questions. To set closed questions you will need to create some possible answers – people then select one of these responses. Closed questions are quick and easy for people to complete and the results are easy to represent later. However, respondents are limited to the options that you have already chosen on their behalf. Open questions allow people to answer freely in any way they choose. They can be very useful, in that they allow people to respond freely about the subject, but it can be harder to analyse the answers.

Site	Distance from car park (m)	Impact score on a scale of 0–5 (where 0 is low and 5 is high)				Total score
		Footpath erosion	Noise	Litter	Space (busy-ness)	
1	0	5	4	3	4	16
2	100	5	2	4	3	14
3	200	4	1	2	2	9
4	300	3	1	2	2	8
5	400	2	1	1	1	5
6	500	1	0	1	1	3
7	600	1	2	2	3	8
8	700	0	1	0	1	2
9	800	0	0	1	0	1

▲ **Figure 23** Environmental impact assessment scores; sample points were taken every 100 m from the car park below the Stiperstones ridge.

Activities

1 Use Figure 9 (page 4) to describe the location of the Shropshire Hills AONB.
2 Suggest two separate reasons why it so popular with day trippers from Birmingham.
3 Study the following enquiry question about the Stiperstones:
   What impact do visitors have on the environment at the Stiperstones?
   a) Suggest one way the enquiry question could be amended so that you can investigate whether visitors have an impact on businesses in Shropshire Hills AONB.
   b) How would you amend the sub-questions?

Processing and presenting evidence

You can process data in various ways. For example by calculating:
- totals and percentages
- averages (mean, mode or median)
- maximum, minimum and interquartile ranges (see page 17).

Your data needs to be represented using appropriate techniques to help you identify any patterns or trends. Here are some questions to consider when choosing a technique.
- Is the data expressed as actual values or percentages? You could use block charts for actual values and pie charts to show percentages.
- Is the data discrete or continuous? A block graph should be used to represent discrete data whereas a line graph should be used for continuous data.
- Does the data tell you something about different places? If so, could you locate your blocks or pie charts on a base map?
- Have you got two sets of data that are related to one another? If so, would a scattergraph (page 267) show a relationship?

Analysing the evidence

Analysis means studying the data and identifying any patterns or trends. For example:
- Is the data increasing, decreasing or consistent throughout your surveys?
- Is there any data that does not follow the pattern? These are **anomalies**. Can you explain why this might this be?
- How does the data relate to sites on the ground? Does the data show a **spatial** pattern? In other words, can you see patterns that vary over space?

Evaluating your enquiry

Evaluation means assessing the strengths and weaknesses of each step of the enquiry process. Your evaluation could involve taking the following steps:
- **Step 1**: Did you ask the correct question at the beginning? Were you able to collect the right type of data to allow you to draw conclusions?
- **Step 2**: Was your data representative and reliable? If you used questionnaires, did you get enough responses to properly represent the opinions of the public? If you used data from the internet or another source, can the source be trusted, or could the information be biased?
- **Step 3**: Was the enquiry well planned? Be aware that not collecting enough data, running out of time and not putting in appropriate effort is not human error but poor planning. In what ways could you improve your enquiry if you repeated it?
- **Step 4**: Are there any further questions that need to be answered? How might the enquiry be extended?

Activity

4 Study Figure 23.
   a) What type of sampling was used to collect this data?
   b) Suggest a hypothesis linking distance from the car park to environmental impacts.
   c) Represent the data using two different techniques.
   d) What are the strengths and limitations of each technique?

Enquiry

For a honeypot site that you are familiar with:
- Develop a question that you might study.
- What data might you collect?
- What sampling strategies will you use? Why?
- What analysis and presentation techniques might you use?

THEME 1

Landscapes and physical processes
Chapter 2
Landform processes and change

River processes

► **Figure 1** A number of different river processes are evident in this river.

From the moment water begins to flow over the surface of the land, gravity gives it the power to erode the landscape. The gravitational energy of the flowing water enables the river to **transport** its **load** of boulders, gravel, sand and silt downstream. Where energy levels are high, the main river process is erosion. At other times of the year, or in other parts of the river where energy levels are lower, the main process is **deposition**.

Erosion occurs where the river has plenty of energy so, for example, where the river is flowing quickly or when the river is full of water after heavy rain. Rivers that are flowing across gentle slopes (such as the river in Figure 1) tend to flow with greatest force on the outer bend of each curve (or **meander**). Water is thrown sideways into the river bank, which is eroded by both **hydraulic action** and **abrasion**. The bank gradually becomes undercut. The overhanging soil slumps into the river channel where this new load of material can be picked up and transported downstream by the flowing water.

Transportation process	Sediment size or type	Typical flow conditions	Description of the process
Solution	Soluble minerals such as calcium carbonate	Any	Minerals are dissolved from soil or rock and carried along in the flow
Suspension	Small particles e.g. clay and silt	Suspension occurs in all but the slowest flowing rivers	Tiny particles are carried long distances in the flowing water
Saltation	Sand and small gravels	More energetic rivers with higher velocities	The sediment bounces and skips along
Traction	Larger gravels, cobbles and boulders	Only common in high energy river channels or during flood events	The bed load rolls along in contact with the river bed

▲ **Figure 2** The transportation of sediment.

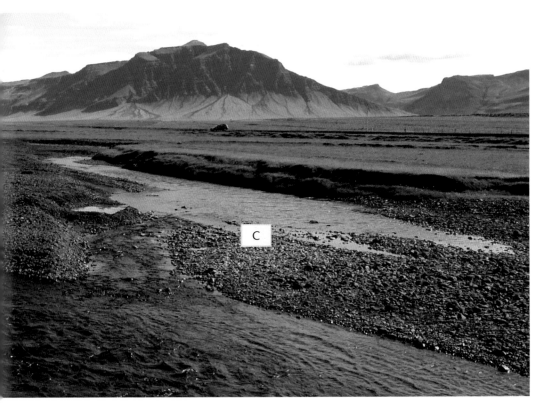

Erosional processes

Hydraulic action – water crashes into gaps in the soil and rock, compressing the air and forcing particles apart

Abrasion – the flowing water picks up rocks from the bed that smash against the river banks

Attrition – rocks carried by the river smash against one another, so they wear down into smaller and more rounded particles

Corrosion – minerals such as calcium carbonate (the main part of chalk and limestone rocks) are dissolved in the river water

▲ **Figure 3** Four processes of river channel erosion.

The process of deposition occurs where the river loses its energy. For example, where a river enters a lake and its flow is slowed by the body of still water. Deposition also occurs in very shallow sections of a river channel where friction between the river bed and the water causes the river to lose its energy and deposit its load. The process of deposition creates layers of sand and gravel that are often sorted by sediment size because the coarsest sediment is deposited first.

▲ **Figure 4** The river channel, which flows from the left, has split into a number of smaller distributaries as it flows into a lake. Derwent Water, the Lake District.

Activities

1 Study Figure 1. Use evidence from the photograph to suggest what river processes are occurring at A, B and C.
2 Draw four diagrams or cartoons to illustrate the ways in which a river transports material.
3 Study Figure 4 and explain how erosion, transportation and deposition have each played a role in the formation of this landform.
4 Study Figures 1 and 4. Use evidence in these photos to explain the difference between abrasion, hydraulic action and attrition.

Meandering rivers

The river in Figure 5 shows typical features of a river flowing over steeper gradients. Much of the force of the water is directed downwards. **Vertical erosion** cuts into the river bed. The river cuts a narrow valley with steep V-shaped sides. The flow of water within the river channel also swings from side to side, creating some sideways erosion. Over time this process means that the V-shaped valley is cut, or incised, into the hillside to form **interlocking spurs** rather like the teeth of a zip.

Rivers flowing over steep gradients can have enough energy to erode and transport a large quantity of material. The load on the river bed here is large and angular. The rocks of the river bed may show evidence of abrasion in the form of smoothly cut potholes or scour holes. As a river flows downstream the process of attrition gradually reduces the overall size of the load.

▲ **Figure 5** Ashes Hollow, Shropshire, is a typical V-shaped valley.

Activity

1 Study Figure 5. Describe how each of the following features was formed:
   a) V-shaped valley sides
   b) large angular boulders in the stream bed
   c) interlocking spurs.

How are river meanders formed?

Rivers flowing over gentle gradients tend to swing from side to side. The water flows fastest on the outside of the bend of each meander. This causes erosion of the banks rather than the bed, a process known as **lateral erosion**. The slower flowing water on the inside of each bend loses energy and deposits its load. The material is sorted, with the larger gravel being deposited first, then the sand and finally the silt. This process creates a **slip-off slope** or **point bar**, which is a pebble beach that slopes down into the river. Meandering rivers such as the Elan, shown in Figure 8, flow across a wide **floodplain**. This flat landform has been created over many thousands of years by the processes of lateral erosion and deposition.

(A) Outside of bank
← Direction of erosion

Inside of bank (B)
Deposition of sand, silt, clay

Point bar

Smallest sediment

Area of highest erosion

Area of fastest flow

Largest sediment

▲ **Figure 6** Processes at work in a meander.

River cliff formed by erosion

Position of fastest flow shifts from side to side

Point bar formed by deposition of sediment

B

A

▲ **Figure 7** Plan view of a meander.

▲ **Figure 8** Meanders on the Afon Elan; the blue arrows show the direction of river flow.

▲ **Figure 9** Detail of the point bar on the Afon Elan at point 3 in Figure 8.

Activities

2 Using Figure 8:
  a) Describe the slopes at points 1 and 2.
  b) Describe the processes at points 3 and 4.
3 Draw a sketch of Figure 9. Use Figures 6 and 7 to add suitable annotations to your diagram that show how this feature has formed.
4 Figure 10 shows the location of the meanders on the Afon Elan.
  a) Use Figures 8 and 10 to estimate the direction the camera was pointing.
  b) In which direction is the river flowing at Pont ar Elan?
5 a) Draw a cross section along the line X–Y on Figure 10.
  b) Describe the differences and similarities between the rivers shown in Figures 5 and 8.

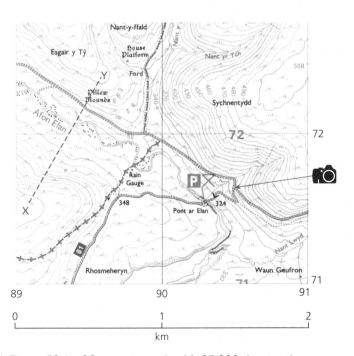

▲ **Figure 10** An OS map at a scale of 1:25,000 showing the meanders on the Afon Elan.

Investigating downstream changes

Rivers can change in shape and character as they flow downstream. It is possible to pose geographical questions about these changes. For example, when investigating change at the small sale:

How does river velocity change across a point bar and how does this affect sediment size?

Or, when investigating change at a larger scale:

How do cross-sectional area and river velocity change as you move downstream?

Choosing sample sites

The UK's rivers vary from just a few hundred metres in length to rivers like the River Severn which, at 369 km, is the UK's longest river. In an enquiry about how a river changes as it flows downstream it is important to make sure that your sample points are far enough apart to show change. For a river that is 10 km long you could collect data at 1 km, 5 km and 10 km, or at 3 km, 4 km and 5 km. The first sampling strategy would provide a representative sample of the whole of the river, whereas the second would only provide evidence of small-scale changes in just one short section of the river.

Activity

1 Explain why sampling at 3 km, 4 km and 5 km would not be representative of change along a whole river that is 10 km in length.

Calculating cross-sectional area

To measure the cross-section of a river channel you will need to set a horizontal line across the river and carefully measure down from this line to the ground. This is shown in Figure 11 where the horizontal yellow line represents the survey line from X to Y and the four vertical lines represent the first four measurements. Collect data when the river is low but take measurements for the dry land on either side of the river. Then, when your results are plotted on a graph, you can estimate the amount of water in the river when the river channel is full and about to flood.

Step 1 Stretch a tape measure at right angles across the river from one bank to the other, keeping it parallel to the surface of the water.

Step 2 Divide the width of the river by 10. This will create 11 equally spaced survey points. For example, in a river that is 4 m wide you will record the depth every 40 cm (1/10th) of the way across. This is an example of systematic sampling (see page 8).

Step 3 At each survey point measure the depth of the river. Make sure that your depth and width readings are both recorded in the same units (for example, both in metres).

Cross-sectional area (CSA) in square metres = width (m) multiplied by mean depth (m).

▼ **Figure 11** Sample sites on a meandering river.

Survey site	1	2	3	4	5	6	7	8	9	10	11
Distance from bank (m)	0	0.4	0.8	1.2	1.6	2.0	2.4	2.8	3.2	3.6	4.0
Distance from survey line to ground (m)	0.25	0.68	0.71	0.65	0.67	0.64	0.58	0.52	0.48	0.33	0.22
Depth of water (m)	0	0.28	0.31	0.25	0.27	0.24	0.18	0.12	0.08	0	0

▲ **Figure 12** Depth measurements taken in the river in Figure 11 at 0.4 m intervals.

Activity

2 Use Figure 12.
   a) Plot the profile of this river on graph paper. Remember to work downwards from your horizontal axis.
   b) What is the mean water depth?
   c) Calculate the cross-sectional area.
   d) If water levels rose by 20 cm, what would be the new cross-sectional area?

How do I calculate range, median and interquartile range?

The flow of water in the river channel has enough energy to transport sediment. As the water speed slows, for example, in shallow water on the point bar, energy is lost and sediment is deposited.

To test whether this process is happening in your river, you will need to sample some pebbles and record their size. Students collected a sample of 11 pebbles from sites A, B and C in Figure 11. Their aim was to discover how the size and range of pebbles changed across the point bar.

To calculate the range, median and interquartile range, you need to put your data into rank order. The data for site A is shown in Figure 14 in rank order.

Site	Pebble sizes (mm)										
A	45	52	12	67	34	75	42	81	65	40	24
B	44	37	28	56	61	43	38	28	35	42	36
C	37	34	26	40	24	35	29	42	38	18	20

▲ **Figure 13** Pebble sizes (mm) collected at random at sites A, B and C in Figure 11.

| 12 | 24 | 34 | 40 | 42 | 45 | 52 | 65 | 67 | 75 | 81 |

The lower quartile (Q1) is the value one-quarter of the way along the range

The median (Q2) is the value half way along the range

The upper quartile (Q3) is the value three-quarters of the way along the range

The interquartile range is the difference between the upper quartile and the lower quartile

▲ **Figure 14** Pebble sizes for site A arranged in rank order.

Activity

3 Use Figure 13.
   a) For each sample site, calculate the:
      i)   range
      ii) median
      iii) interquartile range.
   b) What conclusions can you draw from these results?

How are waterfalls formed?

Waterfalls form along the course of a river where there is a steep change in gradient of the river's channel. Many waterfalls in upland areas of the UK are due to landform processes that occurred at the end of the ice age around 10,000 years ago. During the ice age, ice sheets expanded over large parts of northern and western parts of the UK. The extent of the ice can be seen in Figure 1, page 1. Glaciers flowed from these ice sheets towards the sea – similar glaciers can be seen in southern Iceland today. The glaciers carved deep, steep sided or **U-shaped valleys** into the landscape. Figure 16 shows how this glacial landscape created the tall plunging waterfalls we see in parts of North and Mid Wales today.

▲ **Figure 15** Rhiwargor, in Mid Wales, is an example of a waterfall plunging into a U-shaped valley.

▲ **Figure 16** Glacial landscape and today's landscape.

Waterfalls formed by differential erosion

Waterfalls can occur where the river channel crosses from one rock type to another. If the rate of erosion of each rock type is different, then a waterfall is formed. Waterfalls have been formed in this way on the River Neath and its tributaries in an area of South Wales known as Waterfall Country.

It is the geology of Waterfall Country that is the main factor in the formation of these waterfalls. Carboniferous limestone is overlain by beds of sandstone and mudstone. The sandstone is very resistant to erosion whereas the mudstone is eroded more easily. A series of faults, running across the river channels, has brought the sandstone and mudstones alongside one another, as you can see in Figure 17.

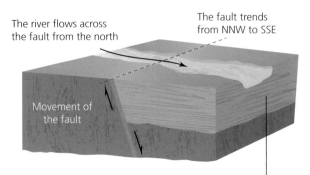

The river flows across the fault from the north

The fault trends from NNW to SSE

Movement of the fault

Mudstones that are easily eroded lie on top of sandstone that is more resistant to erosion

▲ **Figure 17** How the Sgwd yr Eira waterfall on the Afon Mellte was formed.

As the river plunges over the sandstone it pours on to the softer mudstone below. A combination of hydraulic action and abrasion erodes this rock relatively easily, creating a **plunge pool**. Abrasion at the back of the plunge pool undercuts the layers of sandstone. Eventually this overhang will fracture and the rocks will fall into the plunge pool where they are broken up by attrition. So each waterfall is gradually eroded backwards towards the river's source in a process known as **retreat**. Below each waterfall is a narrow valley with almost vertical sides. This feature is known as a **gorge**. The process of retreat has cut the gorge over many hundreds of years.

▲ **Figure 18** The Sgwd yr Eira waterfall on the Afon Mellte.

▲ **Figure 19** River processes at the Sgwd yr Eira waterfall

www.world-of-waterfalls.com/europe.html – an interactive map showing the location of waterfalls across the UK.

1 A 'cap rock' of sandstone is resistant – it erodes relatively slowly	4 Attrition breaks down the eroded rock fragments as they are transported downstream.
2 The overhang is susceptible to collapse and retreat.	5 Pebbles swirl around in hollows to create potholes by abrasion.
3 Abrasion deepens the plunge pool.	6 Beds of resistant rock create an irregular river bed of rapids and smaller waterfalls below the waterfall.

Activities

1 Describe how the faulting of the rocks in Waterfall Country has led to the formation of waterfalls.
2 a) Make a copy of Figure 19.
   b) Add the labels to suitable places on your diagram.
   c) Explain why the retreat of the plunge pool has, over thousands of years, created a gorge.
   d) Draw a series of diagrams to show the formation of the gorge.
3 Explain why we need to understand how natural processes have changed since the last ice age in order to understand the landscape today.

4 Do waterfalls only occur in the upland regions of the UK? Use the weblink on this page to investigate the interactive map.
   a) Describe the location of the UK's waterfalls.
   b) What proportion are located in upland regions? Use Figure 1 on page 1 to help you.

Enquiry

To what extent do you agree with the following statement: 'Geology is the most important factor in the creation of distinctive river landscapes'?

Make use of information on pages 16 to 19 to help you justify your answer.

How do waves erode our coastal landscapes?

Waves provide the force that shapes our coastline. Waves are created by friction between wind and the surface of the sea. Stronger winds make bigger waves. Large waves also need time and space in which to develop. So, large waves need the wind to blow for a long time over a large surface area of water. The distance over which a wave has developed is known as **fetch**, so the largest waves need strong winds and a long fetch.

The water in a wave moves in a circular motion. A lot of energy is spent moving the water up and down. So waves in deep water have little energy to erode a coastline. However, as a wave enters shallow water, it is slowed by friction with the sea bed. The water at the surface, however, surges forward freely. It is this forward motion of the breaking wave that causes the erosional processes described in Figure 22.

Activity

1 Make a copy of Figure 20 and add the following labels in appropriate places.
- Waves in deeper water
- Circular motion
- Breaking wave
- Water thrown forward
- Friction with the sea bed.

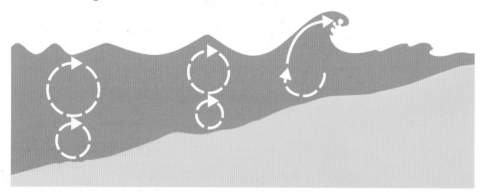

▲ **Figure 20** The motion of water in a wave.

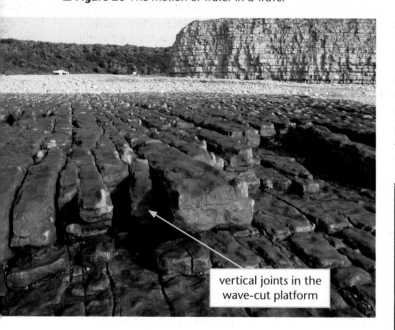

vertical joints in the wave-cut platform

▲ **Figure 21** The rocky wave-cut platform of the Glamorgan Heritage Coast.

The repeated pounding of large waves at the foot of a cliff can cause enormous damage through the process of hydraulic action and abrasion. The repeated hammering effect of the waves on this narrow zone creates a **wave-cut notch**. Cliffs that are already weakened by joints or cracks can suddenly collapse in a rock fall which is a type of **mass movement**. The collapse causes the line of the cliffs to retreat inland. The **wave-cut platform** in Figure 21 has been formed by the gradual retreat of the cliffs.

pothole

Erosional processes

Hydraulic action – waves crash against the cliff, compressing the water and air into cracks and forcing the rocks apart.

Abrasion – waves pick up rocks from the sea bed or beach and smash them against the cliffs.

Corrosion – minerals such as calcium carbonate (the main part of chalk and limestone rocks) are slowly dissolved in sea water.

Attrition – sand and pebbles are picked up by the sea and smash against one another, wearing them down into smaller and more rounded particles.

▲ **Figure 22** Four processes of coastal erosion.

A huge mass of rocks overhang the notch. This will be the next section of cliff to collapse

Horizontal bedding planes and vertical joints in the rock are lines of weakness that can be eroded rapidly by hydraulic action

A recent rock fall. This debris will break the force of the waves so, for a while at least, the cliff behind will be protected from the battering of the waves

Waves use pebbles from the beach to erode a notch at the foot of the cliff through the process of abrasion

▲ **Figure 23** Evidence of erosion in limestone cliffs on the Glamorgan Heritage Coast.

Activities

2 Study Figures 21 and 22.
   a) Use the correct erosion terms to complete the annotations below.
      ▪ Joints in the rock are widened in the process of .... which is when ....
      ▪ Boulders on the beach are rounded because ....
      ▪ This pothole has been scoured into the rock by ....
   b) Make a simple sketch of Figure 21 and add your annotations (above) to the sketch.

3 Consider Figure 23 and its annotations.
   a) Write a list (or draw a timeline) that puts the events acting on this cliff in the correct sequence.
   b) Make another list (or timeline) suggesting what will happen to this cliff in the next few years.
   c) Over the next 100 years this coastline will retreat by about 20–40 m. Draw a story-board to show how this process of retreat creates the rocky wave-cut platform in front of the cliff.

Landslides, rock falls and slumping

The evidence on pages 20 and 21 suggests that wave action is not the only force that shapes our coastline. Wave action at the foot of a cliff can sometimes trigger mass movement of the cliff face above. Rocks, loosened perhaps by winter frosts or heavy rainfall, can fall suddenly to the beach below in a **rock fall**. Large sections of cliff, undermined by erosion at the base, can slide rapidly downwards on to the beach. A **landslide** such as this leaves a concave scar in the upper cliff, like a giant bite mark, and a fan-shaped pile of debris on the beach. A similar process, in loosely compacted rocks such as those found in the Holderness Coast, is called **slumping**. The effects of slumping are much the same as a landslide – bite-shaped chunks are removed from the top of the cliff.

Landslides usually occur in sedimentary rocks and are often triggered by extreme weather events – stormy seas that batter the cliff or heavy rainfall that adds extra weight to the cliff face. But landslides can happen at any time and are dangerous, of course. In June 2015 a young woman was killed by a rock fall at Llantwit Major – the cliffs shown in Figure 23. There have been many landslides and rock falls on this coast, the most recent are shown in Figure 25.

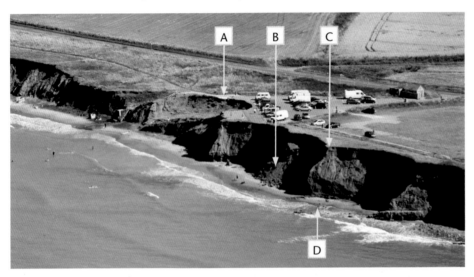

Debris from a landslide forms a fan at the base of the cliff	Beach is too narrow to absorb much wave energy
A narrow headland or arête between two landslides	Concave scarp at the top of the cliff

▲ **Figure 24** Cliffs on the Isle of Wight with numerous landslides.

Activity

1 a) Match the labels to features on Figure 24.
  b) Suggest why these cliffs have no defences.
  c) Suggest why a landslide or rock fall will prevent further wave erosion for a few months. Use Figure 22 to help you.

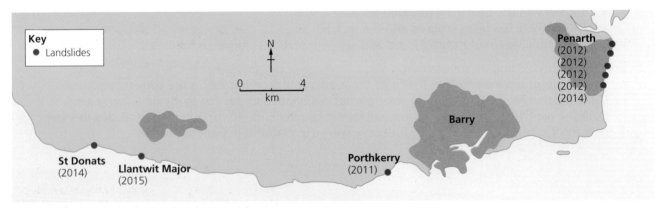

▲ **Figure 25** Recent landslides on the Glamorgan Heritage Coast, South Wales.

GEOGRAPHICAL SKILLS

Calculating and representing frequency

Coastal hazards such as floods, rock falls or landslides are examples of events that happen at random intervals. We tend to record the date and location of such events. Figure 25 shows the location and date of recent landslides on the Glamorgan Heritage Coast in South Wales. Recording such events allows us to see how common or frequent they are. Knowing this may help us to understand the level of risk that is created by the hazard.

Year	Landslides
2005	1
2006	2
2007	0
2008	0
2009	0
2010	0
2011	2
2012	3
2013	1
2014	4
2015	1
Total	14

Frequency describes the recurrence interval of an event. This may be defined as the average time lag between two events. The best way to represent frequency is with a frequency bar graph – with time (usually years) on the x-axis. An example, showing the frequency of landslides on the coast between Lyme Regis and Charmouth in Dorset, is shown in Figure 26.

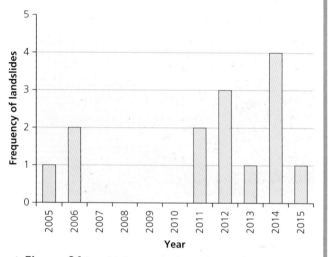

▲ **Figure 26** Landslides on the Lyme Regis–Charmouth coastline, Dorset.

Recurrence interval (T) is simple to calculate. It can be found by dividing the number of years in a record (N) by the number of events (n).

$$T = \frac{N}{n}$$

So, for the data in Figure 26, the recurrence interval (to two decimal places) is:

$$T = \frac{11}{14} = 0.79 \text{ years}$$

Of course, 0.79 of a year isn't very helpful: we usually express parts of a year in months. So, if we multiply 0.79 by the number of months in a year:

$T = 0.79 \times 12 = 9.5$ months

You must remember that what you have calculated is a **mean** time period. The landslides are random events and can occur at any time. Look again at Figure 26. There were no landslides in this location at all for four years, but there were four landslides in 2014.

Activity

2 Using Figure 25:
   a) Represent the frequency of the landslides on the Glamorgan Coast.
   b) Calculate the frequency.
   c) Which is the more hazardous – the coastline in Glamorgan or Dorset?

Enquiry

Which part of the UK coastline has most landslides?

Use the weblink to the BGS site to research the frequency of landslides on the UK coastline.

 http://mapapps2.bgs.ac.uk/geoindex/home. html?theme=hazards – an interactive UK map showing the location of coastal landslides.

Cliffs in unconsolidated rocks

Many kilometres of the UK's coastline are made of layers of sand, silt and clay deposited as ice melted at the end of the ice age. The extent of the ice is shown in Figure 1 on page 1. These young sedimentary rocks have not been compacted as much as older rocks and they are **unconsolidated**, which means the grains of sediment are not 'glued' together very well. This makes them much less resistant to erosion than older sedimentary rocks such as the Carboniferous limestone cliffs seen in Figures 21 and 23 on pages 20–1.

Figure 28 helps to explain why the cliffs at Happisburgh in Norfolk are not very resistant to erosion by waves. Once the toe of the slope has been eroded by the sea, the whole slope becomes unstable. It is then at risk of mass movement – a process by which the whole cliff face can slide or slump on to the beach. The chance of slumping is increased by periods of heavy rain, which adds mass to the cliff. Rain water also erodes small V-shaped notches called **gulleys** in the upper slopes of the cliff.

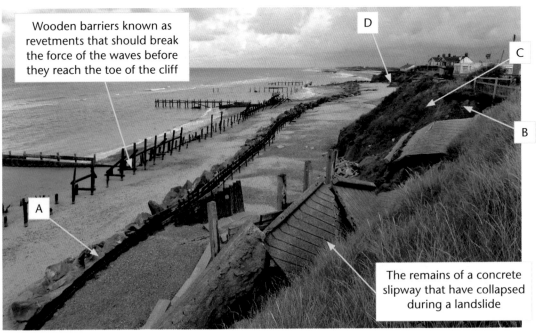

Wooden barriers known as revetments that should break the force of the waves before they reach the toe of the cliff

D

C

B

A

The remains of a concrete slipway that have collapsed during a landslide

▲ **Figure 27** The coastline at Happisburgh, North Norfolk in 2011.

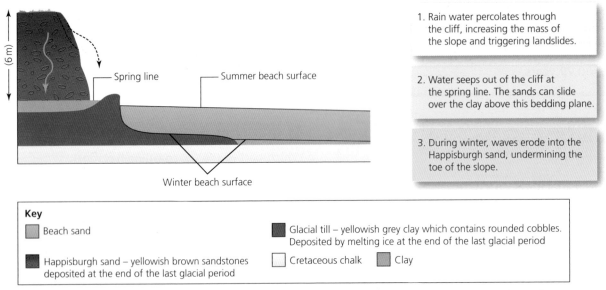

(6 m)

Spring line — Summer beach surface

Winter beach surface

1. Rain water percolates through the cliff, increasing the mass of the slope and triggering landslides.

2. Water seeps out of the cliff at the spring line. The sands can slide over the clay above this bedding plane.

3. During winter, waves erode into the Happisburgh sand, undermining the toe of the slope.

Key

- Beach sand
- Happisburgh sand – yellowish brown sandstones deposited at the end of the last glacial period
- Glacial till – yellowish grey clay which contains rounded cobbles. Deposited by melting ice at the end of the last glacial period
- Cretaceous chalk
- Clay

▲ **Figure 28** Cross section through the cliffs at Happisburgh, North Norfolk; these cliffs are made of loosely compacted layers of sand, silt and clay deposited at the end of the ice age.

Cliff landforms in resistant rock types

We have seen that young sedimentary rocks, such as those at Happisburgh, have a weak structure that makes them vulnerable to erosion. By contrast, older sedimentary rocks are compacted and consolidated, meaning they are more resistant to erosion. Limestone coastlines, like those in Figure 29, tend to form almost vertical cliffs. However, bedding planes and joints in the rock are lines of weakness in these cliffs. These lines are more easily eroded than the massive blocks of stone in-between them. Erosion along these lines can lead to the formation of caves, **sea arches** and **stacks**.

▲ **Figure 29** The Green Bridge of Wales, Pembrokeshire; a natural sea arch formed in a Carboniferous limestone cliff.

Activities

1 Read the following annotations and decide where they fit best on Figure 27.
   - Waves have eroded the toe of the cliff here.
   - The vegetation on this slope proves that it hasn't slumped for several months.
   - Concrete blocks on the beach may protect the cliff from wave erosion.
   - Evidence of gulley erosion by rain water on these slopes.
2 a) Make a copy of Figure 28.
   b) Add the annotations 1 to 3 to suitable places on your diagram.
   c) Use the diagram to explain why the rock type and structure of the cliffs at Happisburgh make them vulnerable to erosion and mass movement.
3 Historical records show that the cliffs here retreated by 250 m between 1600 and 1850. What is the average rate of erosion per year?

4 a) Make a sketch of Figure 29.
   b) Label the following features on your sketch: cave, bedding planes, sea arch, stack.
5 Explain why, even though all of the rocks in Figure 29 are the same, the landscape is so varied.

Enquiry

How might the landscape in Figure 29 evolve over time? Discuss how the processes of wave action and mass movement might affect this coastline. Draw a story board to show how you expect it might change in the future.

Beach and sand dune processes

Beaches are dynamic environments. In other words, the energy of the wind and waves is constantly moving sediment around and changing the shape of the beach. Where the waves approach the beach at an angle, some of the sediment is transported along the coastline in a process known as **longshore drift**. However, most sediment is simply moved up and down the beach. Each wave transports sediment up the beach in the **swash** and back down again in the **backwash**. All of this movement uses a lot of the wave's energy, so a wide, thick beach is a good natural defence against coastal erosion.

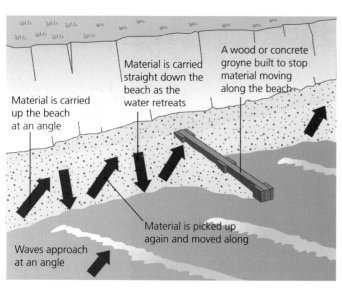

▲ **Figure 30** Transport of sediment by the process of longshore drift.

▲ **Figure 31** The beach at Borth seen from the cliffs to the south of the pebble ridge.

The sand and pebbles on a beach usually come from the local environment. Neighbouring cliffs may supply some sediment if they are being actively eroded by wave action. A lot of finer silts and sands are transported to the coast by rivers. This sediment is then deposited in the estuary or on an **offshore bar** at the mouth of the river. It will be washed onshore by the swash of the waves and deposited on the beach.

At Borth, on the Ceredigion coast, there is a pebble ridge making a **spit** on the southern side of the estuary. These pebbles came from cliffs to the south. Figure 33 shows the processes that are supplying and transporting material on this coastline.

Sediment is swept onto the beach in the swash

Sand is blown onshore and is deposited on the leeward side of the dunes

Offshore bar   Beach   Dunes

X   Y

The river Dyfi supplies sediment from the land and washes it into the estuary or out onto the offshore bar.

Offshore bar

X

Onshore winds blow dry sand off the beach and into the sand dunes where it is deposited.

Swash moves sediment from the offshore bar onto the beach.

Estuary

Sand dunes   Y

Longshore drift moves sediment parallel to the coast.

Pebble ridge

Sea

Backwash drags sediment off the beach. Some is deposited on offshore bars, the rest is moved further along the coast by longshore drift.

Erosion of the cliffs between Aberystwyth and Borth supplies pebbles.

Cliffs

▲ **Figure 33** The transport of beach sediment at Borth and Ynyslas on the Ceredigion coast.

▲ **Figure 32** The sand dunes at Ynyslas seen from Aberdyfi on the north side of the Dyfi estuary.

C

Activities

1 Describe the landforms seen at A, B and C in Figures 31 and 32.
2 Study Figures 30, 31 and 33. Use an annotated diagram to explain the formation of the pebble ridge on which the village of Borth is built.

Enquiry

Interpret the landscape in Figure 32. How have erosion, transportation and deposition all helped to make this landscape? Write a story-board to explain the evolution of this landscape.

What factors affect rates of coastal change?

On a map, the blue line showing the coastline of the UK looks like a fixed and permanent feature. In reality, the coastline is constantly changing, although the rate of change is usually gradual. Rates of landform change depend on three factors:

- the impact of extreme weather events
- geology – the character of local rocks
- the consequences of human intervention.

How does extreme weather affect the UK's coastline?

Sometimes, battered by storms, the coastline and its landforms can change overnight. During the winter of 2014, the UK experienced a series of severe storms that brought widespread damage to many parts of the country. This was probably the stormiest period of weather the country had experienced for at least twenty years.

The power of a storm wave depends on both wind speed and fetch – the distance travelled by wind over open water. The South West of England and parts of Wales were affected by powerful storms approaching from the southwest on 3 and 6 January 2014.

Before

After

▲ **Figure 35** The sea arch at Porthcothan, North Cornwall, before and after the storm of 6 January 2014.

▲ **Figure 34** The amount of energy in a wave depends partly on fetch; waves travelling across the Atlantic towards Porthcothan or Aberdyfi have a fetch of 7,000 km – the longest of any waves approaching the UK.

Activities

1 Using Figure 34:
   a) Calculate the fetch indicated by arrows 2, 4 and 5.
   b) Explain why the coastline at Lyme Regis is more vulnerable to coastal erosion when wind blows from the southwest than when it blows from the south.
   c) Use an atlas to help calculate the fetch affecting Happisburgh, North Norfolk, when the wind blows from the north.

2 a) Describe the differences between the two photographs in Figure 35.
   b) Explain why this change occurred and why it happened suddenly. Make use of Figure 34 in your answer.

The effects of the storms on the Welsh coastline

Aberdyfi is a small town on the north side of the Dyfi estuary on the Gwynedd coast. Its golf course is located at the western end of the village and is protected from the sea by sand dunes. However, in early January 2014 the winter storm and accompanying high tides resulted in considerable damage to the dunes system and to the land to the north of the golf course. Around 3 to 6 m of green on the twelfth hole was lost to the sea and the shingle bank, which protected the dunes to a certain extent, was overtopped by the sea and flooded parts of the course. Other effects of the storms are shown in Figure 36.

Cardigan, 3 January 2014: storm surge floods 30 homes with sea water

Barmouth, 3 January 2014: huge waves demolished sea-wall defences and scattered stones from the sea wall across the promenade; the railway line was covered in pebbles and rail sleepers undermined; fifteen homes were evacuated

Borth, 3 January 2014: one person was rescued from the roof of a building and four people were rescued from a farm by life boat

Aberdaron, 12 February 2014: gusts of 173 kph were recorded – the strongest in Wales; the power of the waves resulted in at least 30 cm of land being taken from these receding cliffs

Pwllheli, 3 January 2014: a lifeboat crew rescued five people from flooded caravans

Aberystwyth, 6 January 2014: all the buildings along the sea front were evacuated; waves damaged the sea wall, demolished part of the promenade and washed pebbles and sand across the main road

▲ **Figure 36** The coastline of West Wales.

Activities

3 a) Make a sketch map of Figure 36.
   b) Use an atlas to add the six labels describing the effects of the storm surge to the correct locations on your sketch.
4 Describe the main effects of the winter storms of 2014 on:
   a) the environment
   b) people.

Enquiry

Which was affected worst by the winter storms of 2014: the east or west coast of the UK?

■ Research the effects of coastal storms and erosion on the east coast of England during the winter of 2014. See pages 130–1.
■ Explain why the impacts on the east coast were severe.
■ Which coastline was affected most? Justify your answer.

How geology affects rates of coastal change

Pen Llŷn (the Llŷn Peninsula) extends about 48 km into the Irish Sea. To the west of Pwllheli, the south coast of the peninsula is made up of a series of headlands and bays created by differential rates of erosion. The headlands consist of outcrops of very resistant (harder) rock. The headland at Llanbedrog (near Abersoch), for example, is composed of the igneous rock granite. Many of the bays, on the other hand, are made up of mudstones and shales. Some of these are covered by layers of loosely consolidated sand, silt and clay deposited at the end of the ice age – similar to the cliffs at Happisburgh in Norfolk (see page 24). Waves are able to erode these areas of less-resistant (softer) rock more rapidly.

Key
- Metamorphic rock
- Igneous intrusions – granite
- Sedimentary rocks – mudstones and shales
- Sedimentary rocks – gritstones
- Igneous extrusions – lava

▲ **Figure 37** A simplified geological map of the western end of the Llŷn Peninsula; the red line shows the area covered by Figure 38.

▲ **Figure 38** OS map extract of Aberdaron and the surrounding area at a scale of 1 : 50 000.

Activities

1. Describe the relief of the coastal area shown in Figure 38.
2. a) Draw an outline map of this coastline.
   b) Label the physical features of this coastline on your map.
   c) Using Figure 37 to help you, explain why bays have formed at:
      i) Aberdaron
      ii) Abersoch.

 http://mapapps.bgs.ac.uk/geologyofbritain/home.html – use this interactive map to discover the geology of a coastline near to you.

Figure 37 shows the extreme western tip of the Llŷn Peninsula. The large headland immediately to the west of Aberdaron is formed of extremely tough metamorphic rocks. These rocks can be seen in the high, almost vertical cliffs on all sides of the headland and on Ynys Enlli (Bardsey Island). The rate of erosion of these headlands depends on rock structure. Faults, vertical joints and cracks within resistant rocks can add distinctive features to cliff coastlines. These lines of weakness can be eroded more rapidly than the rest of the cliff by processes such as hydraulic action. Eventually they are widened to form caves and blowholes.

The largest of the bays is Porth Neigwl (Hell's Mouth). The bay is made of rocks that were easily eroded. The low cliffs along Porth Neigwl are made of loosely consolidated sands. Erosion by waves at the base of these cliffs causes slumping and their collapse onto the beach.

Porth Neigwl lies between two large headlands. In normal weather conditions, the headlands cause waves to slow down and lose energy as they enter the bay, so beach material has accumulated over the years. The beach material itself ranges from very fine sand on the more sheltered western side to coarser shingle and pebbles on the eastern side of the beach, and at low tide vast expanses of sand are exposed. These types of beaches are known as bay-head beaches.

Porth Neigwl was exposed to the full force of winter storms from the Atlantic in 2014. Storm waves eroded the cliffs but they also transported large pebbles and rocks up the beach slope. These were deposited in a steep pile at the top of the eastern end of the beach. This feature is known as a **storm beach**.

▲ **Figure 39** The beach and the cliffs at Porth Neigwl; the headland of Trwyn Cilan can be seen in the background.

Activities

3   Make a sketch of Figure 39.
 a)   Label Trwyn Cilan and explain why it is here in an annotation.
 b)   Annotate the slumped cliff to explain the processes happening here. Make use of Figure 28 (page 24).
4   Summarise two different ways that geology can affect coastal landforms using examples from this page.

How does human activity affect the coastline?

People have managed the coastline for centuries – building flood embankments and draining coastal marshes, for example. The intention is to protect the coastline from flooding and make harbours safer. But engineering strategies such as these can have consequences that were not intended. We saw on page 26 that sediment moves along the coastline by a process of longshore drift. Building a harbour wall or breakwater can trap sediment and prevent its movement along the coast. Beaches further along the coast become starved of new sand and erosion can accelerate.

▲ **Figure 40** The castle headland at Criccieth.

▲ **Figure 41** OS map extract of Criccieth at a scale of 1:25000.

Human intervention at Criccieth (Cricieth)

The town of Criccieth lies on the south coast of Gwynedd overlooking Cardigan Bay. Criccieth Bay is an area of loosely consolidated glacial deposits (or till) and is easily eroded by storm waves. The castle headland, seen in Figure 40, is made up of volcanic rock and is very resistant to erosion.

A number of coastal management strategies have been put in place along Criccieth Bay. These include rock armour at the western end, a recurved sea wall along the promenade and groynes on the beach.

The beach on the western side of the castle is a mixture of sand, shingle and pebbles. The wooden groyne structures positioned along the beach ensure that erosion along the western promenade is minimised, and that sand is trapped between the groynes. As a seaside resort, Criccieth needs to retain the beach to encourage tourists. Beaches also play a vital role in coastal protection as they absorb wave energy, which in turn protects the land behind.

Activities

1 Explain why people manage the coast.
2 Use Figure 41 to:
   a) give a six-figure grid reference for the castle headland
   b) estimate the length of the western beach that is protected by groynes.

There are also two large groynes within Criccieth Bay, at the eastern end of the beach. One of these is very large, and Figure 43 shows how successful the groynes are at trapping sediment.

To the east of the two large groynes is a section of glacial till cliff. This can be seen in Figure 44. Beach material in front of this cliff is limited. As a result the cliff face is easily eroded by large storm waves. Are the groynes responsible for this? There are some places along the cliff where obvious collapses of material have occurred. This, however, adds material at the foot of the cliff and acts as a natural defence by increasing the size of the beach again.

▲ **Figure 42** Wooden groynes at the western side of Criccieth Beach.

Enquiry ?

Should the coastline around Criccieth be protected in the future?

■ Use map evidence to argue the case for coastal defences.
■ Research current defences here.
■ Should more be done to manage the coastline?

▲ **Figure 43** One of the two large groynes on the eastern side of Criccieth Bay (grid reference 505381 in Figure 41).

▶ **Figure 44** The glacial till cliff at the far eastern end of Criccieth beach after the 2014 storms.

Activities

3 a) Draw a sketch of Figure 42.
  b) Annotate your sketch to describe the management strategies that have been used along this stretch of coastline.
4 Study Figure 43.
  a) Explain why beach material is thicker to the right of the photograph.
  b) Is this an intended consequence? If so, why?
  c) Use Figures 41 and 43 to give the direction of longshore drift on this coastline.
5 Describe the features of Figure 44. Explain why erosion here may be an unintended consequence of human activity.

Investigating landscape change

The coastline is a constantly changing landscape. Change can be very gradual and occur over many decades. Change over long periods can be measured by comparing primary fieldwork data with historical photographs or maps. However, the shape of a beach profile (its cross-sectional shape) can sometime change overnight. For example, rapid change occurs when beach sediment is eroded or deposited by an extreme storm event. Rapid change to a beach profile may be recorded by comparing measurements taken on two separate days.

Collecting primary evidence of a beach profile

The size and shape of beaches can be recorded by taking beach profile measurements, as shown in Figure 45.

- Person A stands at a safe distance from the edge of the sea holding a ranging pole.
- Person B stands holding a second ranging pole further up the beach. They must stand at the **break in slope** where there is a change in the angle of the beach.
- The distance between the two ranging poles is measured using a tape measure.
- The angle between markers at the same height on each ranging pole is measured using a clinometer.

Repeat this process at each break of slope until the top of the beach is reached.

When all the data has been collected you can plot the distances and angles for each break on a graph to show the profile of the beach. Data collected on different dates can then be compared.

▲ **Figure 45** How to carry out a beach profile.

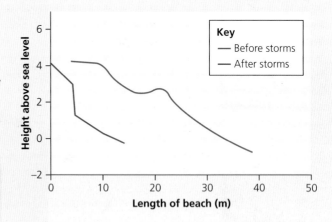

▲ **Figure 46** Beach profiles for different dates at Slapton Sands, Torcross.

Activity

1 Use Figure 46.
  a) Describe how the beach profile changed after the storms. You will need to refer to the height and length of the beach.
  b) How might you calculate the area of the beach by using several profiles?

Investigating the concept of place

Coastal locations provide an opportunity to investigate how people think about the environment – whether it be the physical environment of a natural coastal landscape, or the human environment of a seaside resort. This will involve collecting qualitative data (see page 8) by using, for example:

- bi-polar surveys (see page 104)
- and questionnaires (see page 10).

Place

Place is a geographical concept which is used to describe what makes somewhere special, unique or distinct. Each place includes many different features of the human and physical environment such as landscape features and landmarks, local styles of building, ecosystems and habitats, or local historical and cultural features. Each of these features may be relatively common across the UK. However, it is the unique combination of these geographical features that creates an identity for any one place.

Posing questions for an enquiry

Study Figure 47, it shows the seaside resort of Rhyl on the North Wales coast. How do people of different ages think about this place: what features do they like and dislike? What words would they use to describe the unique or special features of this place? How many would be positive and how many would be negative? Do tourists to Rhyl have the same ideas about this place as local people? You could use a mixture of open and closed questions to investigate these ideas. If you record the approximate age of each person you could then sort your results to see whether younger people have a different view of the place than older people. Or whether tourists have a different view to local people.

▲ **Figure 47** Like many UK seaside resorts, Rhyl has an ageing population and suffers from the decline of tourism, seasonal employment and a shortage of high-paid jobs.

Activities

2 Study Figure 47.
   a) List the human and physical features of this environment.
   b) How do these features compare to other seaside towns?
   c) Create a bi-polar survey that could be used to assess people's views about this environment. Test it on colleagues in your class.

Enquiry

Design an enquiry for Rhyl.

a) Create an over-arching enquiry question about place.
b) Describe how you would collect the qualitative data you need and design data collection sheets.

THEME 1

Landscapes and physical processes
Chapter 3
The flooding issue

How are river landscapes affected by geology?

Climate, geology and human activity all play an important role in the river landscapes of the UK. The **porosity** and **permeability** of the rocks beneath our feet helps to determine how much water we see in the UK landscape. **Porous** rocks have tiny spaces known as pores between the grains of rock. Porosity is a measure of how much water can be stored in these pore spaces. Rocks such as sandstones can hold water in their pore spaces as a **groundwater store**. Permeability is a measure of how easily water can travel through a rock. **Permeable** rocks allow water to pass through them. Water travels easily through the vertical and horizontal joints and cracks that are common in

permeable rocks such as sandstone and limestone. **Impermeable** rocks have few pores spaces or joints, so water tends to flow over them on the surface of the land. Most igneous rocks, such as granite, and metamorphic rocks, such as slate, are impermeable. Clay, which is a sedimentary rock, is also impermeable. In regions where the geology is impermeable, water can be stored at the surface. Lakes and rivers are natural **surface stores** of water. Rivers can be dammed to control flooding and create reservoirs for water supply. There are 168 large dams (defined as being more than 15 m high and holding at least 3,000,000 cubic metres of water) in the UK.

▲ **Figure 1** The Afon Elan flows through an upland area of Wales, where rocks are impermeable and soils are thin; the closest weather station to this drainage basin is at Cwmystwyth.

▲ **Figure 2** The Penygarreg reservoir and the Craig Goch dam in the Elan Valley.

	Jan	Feb	Mar	Apr	May	Jun	Jul	Aug	Sep	Oct	Nov	Dec
Aberystwyth	97	72	60	56	65	76	99	93	108	118	111	96
Cwmystwyth	192	139	158	108	97	116	116	135	151	187	206	213
Birmingham	74	54	50	53	64	50	69	69	61	69	84	67
Norwich	55	43	48	41	42	58	42	54	47	68	70	53

▲ **Figure 3** Monthly precipitation totals for UK weather stations along a west–east transect through Wales and England.

Activities

1. Using Figures 1 and 2, suggest **two** different ways that human activity has affected the landscape of the River Elan.
2. Describe the landforms visible in Figure 1 or 2 and the processes that formed them (see page 13).
3. Study Figure 3.

a) Draw four precipitation graphs.
b) Describe how precipitation changes from west to east across Wales and England.
c) Give two reasons why the Elan Valley may have been chosen to build the Craig Goch dam.

Where are the water stores and flows in a drainage basin?

Very little precipitation falls directly into rivers. Most falls elsewhere within the **drainage basin**, which is the area of land that is drained by the river and its **tributaries**. Figure 4 shows flows of water through a typical drainage basin. Water either flows over the surface as **overland flow** or flows into the soil – a process known as **infiltration**. Once in the soil, water moves slowly downhill as **throughflow**. Some water percolates deeper into the ground and enters the bedrock where it continues to travel as **groundwater flow**. Rates of infiltration, throughflow and groundwater flow depend on a number of factors, including the:

- size and shape of the drainage basin and the steepness of its slopes
- amount of rainfall throughout the year and the intensity of rain storms
- amount and type of vegetation cover
- permeability and porosity of the soil and underlying rocks.

Enquiry ?

What makes the landscape of the Elan Valley distinctive?

Study the combination of features and landforms seen in Figures 1 and 2. The photos in Figures 8 and 9 on page 15 were also taken here – make use of these photos too.

▼ **Figure 4** Stores and flows of water in a natural drainage basin.

Activities

4 Use Figure 4 to name:
   a) three surface stores of water
   b) two places water is stored below the surface.

5 Suggest why precipitation falling into a drainage basin of impermeable rock is likely to reach the river much more quickly than rainwater falling in an area of porous rock.

Why do rivers flood?

In the UK we experience two types of flood:

- **Flash floods**, like the Boscastle flood event of 2004, when high volumes of rain fall in a very short period of time, causing a sudden rise in river levels. Flash floods sometimes occur in the summer in the UK when the ground is hard and baked dry. With these soil conditions, the rainfall is so intense that it cannot soak into the ground quickly enough so runs overland instead.

- Seasonal floods, like the Somerset Levels flood event of 2014, when river levels rise due to seasonal variations in rainfall. These types of flood usually occur after a long period of rain, when the ground is already saturated and cannot absorb any more water. Floods may also occur in the UK when snow melts but the ground is frozen so water cannot infiltrate the soil.

Do human actions increase flood risk?

Flooding occurs when water cannot infiltrate the soil. Paving over the soil creates an impermeable surface and reduces infiltration, so the growth of urban areas increases the risk of flooding. It is thought that paving over front gardens to create parking spaces may increase the risk of flash floods in urban areas. Vegetation helps to remove water from the soil before it reaches a river so cutting down trees or leaving fields bare in winter can increase the risk of seasonal floods. On the other hand, replanting upland areas with trees, a process known as **afforestation**, may help to reduce the risk of floods further downstream. It is thought that afforestation in mid Wales could help to reduce floods at Shrewsbury or Bewdley (see pages 50–1).

GEOGRAPHICAL SKILLS

How do you analyse a hydrograph?

A flood **hydrograph** shows the discharge of a river over the period of a flood. The example in Figure 5 shows how a small river might respond to a flood event. The blue bar represents a sudden downpour of rain, like the one at Boscastle in 2004. In this example it takes two hours for overland flow from the drainage basin to reach the river channel. At this point the amount of water in the channel rises rapidly and reaches its maximum or **peak discharge**. The time between the peak rainfall and the peak discharge is known as **lag time**. The lag time and height of the peak discharge depend on the features of the drainage basin. In drainage basins where infiltration is reduced, the lag time will be shorter and the peak discharge larger. For example, urban drainage basins have a lot of tarmac and concrete which are impermeable surfaces. Artificial storm drains have to be installed to quickly remove surface water otherwise urban streets would flood after each rainfall event. Some of these factors are illustrated in Figures 6 and 7.

▲ **Figure 5** A simple flood hydrograph.

Activity

1 Use Figure 6 to explain how cutting down a large forest could affect lag time and peak discharge in a nearby river.

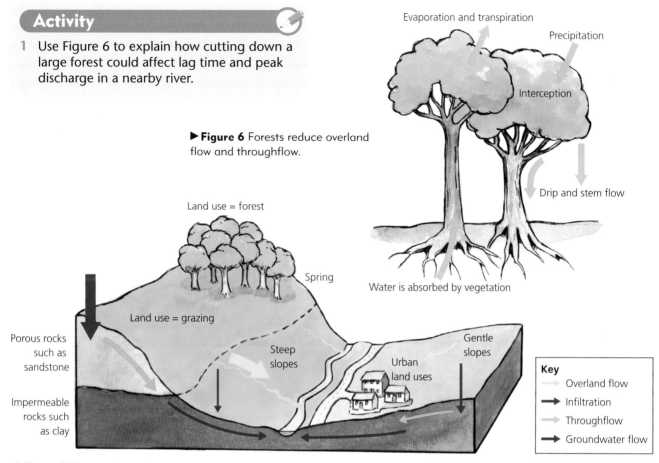

► **Figure 6** Forests reduce overland flow and throughflow.

Evaporation and transpiration

Precipitation

Interception

Drip and stem flow

Water is absorbed by vegetation

Land use = forest

Spring

Land use = grazing

Porous rocks such as sandstone

Impermeable rocks such as clay

Steep slopes

Urban land uses

Gentle slopes

Key
- Overland flow
- Infiltration
- Throughflow
- Groundwater flow

▲ **Figure 7** Factors that influence infiltration and overland flow in the drainage basin.

Activities

2 Study Figure 5.
   a) Use times and discharge figures from the hydrograph to describe:
      i) the shape of the rising limb and the lag time
      ii) the shape of the falling limb and baseflow.
3 Use Figures 4, 5, 6 and 7 to help you copy and complete the following table.

Drainage basin factor	Impact on infiltration	Impact on overland flow and throughflow	Impact on lag time
Steep slopes			
Gentle slopes			
Porous rocks			
Impermeable rocks			
Urban land uses			
Planting more trees			

Enquiry

Can you predict the response of different drainage basins to a sudden downpour of rain?

- Sketch a pair of flood hydrographs to show the difference between similar sized drainage basins – one of which has urban land uses and one of which has lots of forests
- Draw a second pair of hydrographs to compare the response of rivers in a drainage basin that has porous rocks compared with one that has impermeable rocks.
- Discuss your hydrographs with a colleague. Justify the shapes on your hydrographs. Make sure you can explain why you have predicted the shape of the rising and falling limbs and the possible length of the lag time.

How does geology affect flows and stores of water in the drainage basin?

Geology is a major influence on how quickly water flows through a drainage basin. It also influences the amount of water that can be stored within the drainage basin. The amount of water in a river is its **discharge** and this is measured in cubic metres per second, or **cumecs**. The annual pattern of a river is known as its **annual regime**. Study Figures 8 and 9. They show the annual regime in 2004 for two rivers that have similar sized catchment areas. However, the geology of the two drainage basins is quite different and this affects the flow of water through each basin.

29 January–4 February. Low pressure brought storms and heavy rain, especially to north and mid Wales (see Figure 32)

October had more than 1.5 times the average rainfall

▲ **Figure 8** Hydrograph for the River Dyfi, Wales (2004).

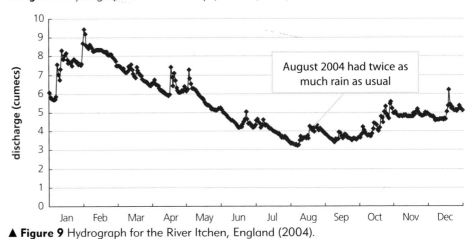

August 2004 had twice as much rain as usual

▲ **Figure 9** Hydrograph for the River Itchen, England (2004).

Factfile: The River Dyfi and River Itchen

River	River Dyfi	River Itchen
Location	West Wales	South East England
Total average rainfall	1,834 mm	838 mm
Geology	100% impermeable rocks	90% chalk
Size of drainage basin (above the gauging station)	471 km²	360 km²
Landscape	Steeply sloping hills and mountains reaching a maximum of 907 m above sea level	Rolling hills. Maximum height 208 m above sea level
Land use	60% grassland (sheep pasture); 30% forest; 10% moorland	Mainly arable (cereal) farmland with some grassland
Human factors affecting run-off	There are virtually no human influences on run-off	Run-off is reduced by some abstraction for water supply. Some water is used to recharge groundwater in the chalk aquifer

Activities

1. Compare Figures 8 and 9. Describe:
   a) one similarity
   b) three differences.
2. Use the Factfile to suggest how each of the following factors may have affected the flow:
   - rainfall
   - total geology
   - landscape
   - land use.
3. Imagine you work for a water company. Suggest how each river could be used for water supply.

How does extreme weather affect flows and stores of water?

Parts of the UK experienced record-breaking levels of rainfall during November and December 2015. A number of low-pressure systems brought wet weather across the UK. The warm, moist air masses came from the Azores – a warm region of the Atlantic to the west of Portugal. They were brought by the jet stream (see page 167), which stayed stuck in a southerly loop to the west of the UK for several weeks.

After weeks of rain the ground was saturated – meaning that further rainfall could not soak into it. River levels rose and a series of floods affected communities across North Wales, Northern England and Scotland.

4–5 December	Storm Desmond arrives. More than a month's rain falls in parts of Cumbria. Flooding in Carlisle, Appleby and other parts of Cumbria.
12 December	Environment Agency issues more than 70 flood warnings, mainly in Cumbria and Lancashire.
22 December	Storm Eva arrives. Cumbria receives more rain and some communities flood again.
26–27 December	People are evacuated from their homes in Lancashire and Yorkshire, including in Hebden Bridge, Leeds, Greater Manchester and York. There is also flooding in Llanrwst in North Wales.

▲ **Figure 10** The timeline of events in December 2015.

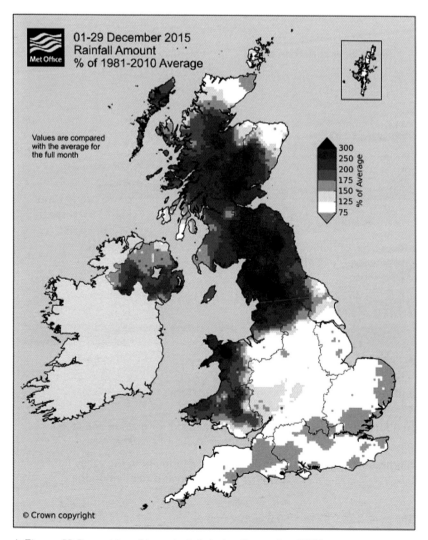

01-29 December 2015
Rainfall Amount
% of 1981-2010 Average

Values are compared with the average for the full month

300
250
200
175
150
125
75

% of Average

© Crown copyright

▲ **Figure 11** Record-breaking rain fell during December 2015.

They were brought by the jet stream (see page 167),

Activities

4 Explain why the UK suffered flooding in late 2015.
5 Use Figures 10 and 11, and an atlas, to label an outline map of the UK showing the main areas affected by flooding.
6 Describe the pattern of rainfall shown on Figure 11. Use an atlas to help you:
   a) name three upland regions that had more than 250 per cent of usual rainfall
   b) name three regions that had less than 75 per cent of usual rainfall.

The impacts of the 2015 floods

During December 2015 rivers were in flood across parts of Wales, northern England and Scotland. Rivers behave very differently when they are in flood. Water levels are not just higher – the discharge is many times greater than during normal flow. During such extreme events rivers can make sudden and dramatic changes to the shape of the river channel. With so much extra energy the river is able to erode and transport huge quantities of material. Banks are undermined and even more rock falls into the torrent. Trees too can be swept into the swollen river. The Raise Beck, a mountain stream in Cumbria, widened its channel by several metres, eroding part of the A591. A similar stream flooded at Glenridding, Cumbria. The force of its flow washed hundreds of tonnes of gravel and large pebbles across the streets.

▲ **Figure 12** Hydrographs for the River Eden at Carlisle (Cumbria) and River Calder at Hebden Bridge (Yorkshire); the blue lines indicate levels recorded on each day; the green line is the typical high level for the month of December.

Factfile: The River Eden and the River Calder

	River Eden at Carlisle	River Calder at Hebden Bridge
Size of catchment (km²)	2,286	171
Geology	Limestone to east and impermeable gritstones to west of catchment	Impermeable gritstones
Land uses	Mainly moorland used for grazing	Mainly moorland used for grazing and steep, wooded slopes
	Towns of Carlisle, Penrith and Appleby in valleys	A lot of urban development in the valley floors; towns of Todmorden and Hebden Bridge
Mean flow (cumecs)	53.3	4.1
Max discharge before 2015	988 cumecs when the river was 5.52 m deep	59.6 cumecs when the river was 3.09 m deep

▲ **Figure 13** The Raise Beck eroded part of the A591 between Ambleside and Keswick; this stream runs off the steep hills of the Lake District in a V-shaped valley and then runs alongside the road.

How were people affected?

Roads were closed either due to flood water or because bridges were in a dangerous condition. Transporting rocks and trees downstream, the river battered the piers of bridges – several bridges collapsed during the December floods. Trees and branches got stuck under bridges, preventing the flow of water. Bridges can begin to act like dams and the extra weight of water behind them can cause structural damage. Road and bridge closures caused delays for drivers and many got stuck in flood water, damaging engines beyond repair. In early January 2016, one month after the floods began, Cumbria had:

- fifteen sections of road closed because the road was washed away or covered by a landslide
- eight footbridges closed and waiting for safety inspections
- twenty bridges closed due to damage and a further three awaiting inspection.

An electricity substation on the River Lune near to Lancaster was flooded, leaving the whole of Lancaster without power for almost three days. Emergency generators were used to keep the power on in Lancaster Hospital and for 19,000 people in the area. The University of Lancaster was closed and students sent home one week before the end of term.

40 bridges were closed due to flooding or damage

341 mm of rain fell at Honister, Cumbria, in 24 hours (between the 4th and 5th of December)

500 homes were flooded in York by storm Eva

5,200 homes were flooded in Cumbria and Lancashire by storm Desmond

20,000 homes were without power over Christmas – mainly in Yorkshire

55,000 homes were without power in the Lancaster area during storm Desmond

▲ **Figure 14** The floods in numbers.

Activities

1 a) Compare the flood hydrographs for the two rivers shown in Figure 12. Use page 38 to help you.
  b) Suggest reasons for the main differences you have identified.
2 Describe the changes that occurred in the channel of the Raise Beck. Use pages 12 and 13 to add detail to your description.
3 Describe the impacts of the flooding on:
  a) infrastructure
  b) the environment.
4 Suggest how each of the following groups of people may have been affected:
  a) elderly people living alone
  b) people living in remote rural areas.

How did flood defences cope in 2015?

The town of Carlisle in Cumbria is built at the confluence of three rivers – the Eden, Petteril and Caldew. In January 2005 it was badly flooded with almost 2,000 homes damaged, foul water from the sewers mixed with the flood water, and the fire service had to borrow wooden rowing boats to reach people trapped by flood water. Following these floods:

- The Environment Agency spent £38 million on improving flood defences for Carlisle. Flood embankments 6.2 m high and 10 km long were built alongside the river and 30 flood gates installed.
- United Utilities replaced 4 km of old sewers at a cost of £13 million.
- The fire service was equipped with inflatable boats and dry suits, and trained to rescue people from fast-flowing water.

During the 2005 flood, some water became trapped by the existing flood defences and couldn't flow back into the river. Ten larger drains were installed to stop that happening again.

▲ **Figure 15** The fire service rescuing residents of flooded homes in Carlisle, December 2015.

Do flood defences work?

Despite all of the investment, why did the town flood again in 2015? The Environment Agency argues that the flood defences in Carlisle were good value for money, but local people were angry that their homes were flooded, and not everyone agrees that this is the best way to defend our towns from flooding.

> Floods threatened Carlisle in 2009 and again in 2012. On each occasion, Carlisle's flood defences worked well. It is estimated that £180 million of flood damage was avoided. The flood defences cost £38 million, so they have more than paid for themselves. I think that's good value for money.

Mike Harper – Environment Agency

> This has been an exceptional period of rainfall but we must acknowledge that, with our changing climate, such weather events are happening more frequently. This is why flood and coastal risk management remains a key priority for this [Welsh] government.

Carwyn Jones – First Minister for Wales

▲ **Figure 16** Two points of view on the 2015 floods.

Year	Flooding event
1963	Flooding
1968	Flooding
1979	Flooding
1980	Flooding
1984	Flooding
2005	Flooding
2009	Floods prevented
2012	Floods prevented
2015	Flooding

▲ **Figure 17** Recent flood events in Carlisle.

GEOGRAPHICAL SKILLS

Calculating percentage of average

Average rainfall figures for each month can be calculated by recording actual rainfall figures over long periods of time (usually at least twenty years) and then finding the mean value. December 2015 was a record breaker – the wettest month ever on record for the UK. To calculate how much wetter than average, you need to divide the actual amount for any month by the average for that month. So, for November 2015 at Hazelrigg:

$249.8 \div 114.7 = 218\%$

	2015	Previous wettest	Average (mean)	2015 % of average
November	249.8	244.8 (2009)	114.7	218
December	306.4	234.5 (1986)	112.8	
November and December	556.2	357.5 (1986)	227.4	

Figure 18 Rainfall (mm) for Hazelrigg in Cumbria, 2015, compared to previous wettest figures and averages for November and December.

Activities

1 Using Figure 15, describe two risks created by flooding.
2 Describe three ways that flood defences in Carlisle were improved after 2005.
3 Calculate the frequency of flooding (see page 23) in Carlisle:
   a) with flood defences
   b) if flood defences had not been built after 2005.
4 Use Figure 18 to calculate the 2015 rainfall for Hazelrigg as a percentage of average for:
   a) December
   b) November and December
5 Use Figures 16, 17 and 18 to suggest two reasons why the floods occurred, despite the flood defences.

What alternative strategies could we use to protect ourselves?

George Monbiot, an environmental author, argues that flood defences are being built in the wrong places. Instead of defending our towns in the valley floors, we should be spending money managing rivers in the upper catchments. He argues that dredging and straightening rivers to protect farmland makes the flood risk worse because water moves down river faster and rushes into the nearest town. He gives the River Liza in Ennerdale as an example. This river used to be dredged – but not anymore. Instead it has been allowed to meander and deposit stones and logs in the river channel, creating a **braided** shape – like plaited hair. The river now looks much more natural. During a flood event, like the one in 2009, the wide braided channel of the River Liza stores flood water and releases it slowly – protecting places downstream from the sudden rush.

▲ **Figure 19** The flood storage basin at Thacka Beck, Penrith.

Penrith is another Cumbrian town that is vulnerable to river flooding. A small stream, the Thacka Beck, runs under the town in a culvert. If the culvert became blocked, the town flooded. A flood defence scheme was completed in the town in 2010 at a cost of £5.6 million. The scheme protects 263 homes and 115 shops, and other businesses. It has two parts:

1 A total of 675 m of culverts were replaced so that water will not back up into the streets.
2 A flood storage reservoir was constructed before the Beck enters the culvert. The reservoir is simply a hollow in a field. In normal weather conditions the pond is just 12 cm deep, but it is capable of storing 76,000 cubic metres of water until flood levels in the river have gone down.

Activities

6 a) Explain why some argue that dredging and straightening has the unintended consequence of increasing the risk of floods.
   b) Describe how flood storage schemes could help protect towns. Give two different examples.
7 The construction of the Thacka Beck flood storage scheme was supported by Cumbria Wildlife Trust. Suggest the benefits of this scheme for local residents and wildlife.

Enquiry

Should higher embankments be built alongside the River Eden in Carlisle?

What should be done in the future? Should alternative schemes be tried? Give reasons for your answer.

The distinctive landscape of the Somerset Levels

The Somerset Levels is a distinctive flat landscape covering 250 square miles. The Levels are only 8 m above sea level and much of this landscape would be flooded twice a month by high spring tides if it wasn't for flood defences at the coast. The Romans built flood defences and they dug ditches to improve the drainage. Over the years, rivers have been dredged and water pumped out, changing the wetland into productive farmland used for livestock and arable crops. Some wetland remains and is conserved as nature reserves. The flat land of the Somerset Levels is vulnerable to:

- coastal flooding by high tides and storm surges, for example in 1919
- river flooding after prolonged periods of rain, for example in 2014.

What caused the 2014 floods?

High rainfall totals over the winter of 2013–14 saturated the soils with water. More rainfall during January and February 2014 ran overland into the already flooded rivers. At each high tide, the rivers backed up because flood water couldn't escape quickly into the Bristol Channel. Local people claimed that the rivers and drainage ditches of the Levels hadn't been cleared of silt and mud since the 1990s. This reduced the capacity of the river channels to hold water. Overhanging trees slowed down the rivers' discharge.

Key
- Somerset Levels
- Area underwater

▲ **Figure 20** Map showing the location of the Somerset Levels and the flooding of 2014.

www.metoffice.gov.uk/public/weather/climate-historic/#?tab=climateHistoric

This website gives access to historic weather data from 40 weather stations across the UK including Yeovilton in Somerset.

http://nrfa.ceh.ac.uk

This is the National River Flow Archive. You can view and download discharge data for many UK rivers. Use this data to create hydrographs like Figure 21.

◀ **Figure 21** Discharge in the River Tone at Bishops Hull (December 2013 to end March 2014).

Activity

1 Use Figure 20 to:
   a) Describe the drainage patterns in the Somerset Levels
   b) Estimate the proportion of the Levels that were flooded in 2014.

Year	Tidal/ coastal	River
1885	✓	
1919	✓	
1968		✓
1981	✓	
1990	✓	
2005		✓
2007		✓
2008		✓
2012		✓
2014		✓

▲ **Figure 22** Historic flood events in the Somerset Levels.

▲ **Figure 24** Large areas of the Levels were under water for weeks in 2014.

Year	Month	Precipitation (mm)
2013	Jun	25.7
	Jul	40.4
	Aug	15.2
	Sep	67.6
	Oct	115.8
	Nov	42.9
	Dec	121.4
2014	Jan	166.4
	Feb	131.2
	Mar	38.4
	Apr	62.2
	May	59.6
	Jun	79
	Jul	56.8
	Aug	74.6
	Sep	3.2
	Oct	99.8
	Nov	108
	Dec	34.8
2015	Jan	75.4
	Feb	41.8
	Mar	22
	Apr	25.8
	May	55.2

▲ **Figure 23** Monthly precipitation totals at Yeovilton (2013–15).

Activities

2 a) Explain why the 2014 floods happened. You should be able to identify physical and human factors.
   b) Study Figure 22. What is happening to the frequency of floods in the Levels?
   c) Suggest two different reasons that might explain this frequency pattern.
3 Use Figure 21 to describe the discharge pattern of the River Tone.
4 a) Draw a graph to represent the monthly precipitation patterns at Yeovilton shown in Figure 23.
   b) How unusual was the rainfall pattern during the period November 2013 to February 2014?
   c) Compare your completed graph to Figure 21. Use these two graphs and your understanding of tidal movements to suggest reasons for the peaks in discharge.

Enquiry

Analyse winter discharge patterns of rivers in the Somerset Levels. Use the National River Flow Archive website for your investigation. How do patterns in the last winter compare to Figure 23? Suggest reasons for any similarities or differences.

How should we react to the Somerset floods?

During January and February 2014, the local authorities, Environment Agency and UK Government reacted to protect people from the floods. The immediate responses to the flooding were:

- Thirteen large pumps from Holland were used to remove 7.3 million tonnes of water per day from the flood plain. The pumps worked day and night for six weeks. The fuel to run the pumps cost £1.5 million per month.
- Residents of flood-damaged homes were given emergency help and insurance advice.
- Teams were brought in to start emergency repairs to infrastructure such as rail and road networks, electricity supplies, telephone systems and sewers.
- Livestock was rescued and moved to other areas.

In mid-2014 the UK Government announced a £100 million recovery programme for the Somerset Levels. The aims of the Somerset Levels and Moors Flood Action Plan are shown in Figure 26.

▲ **Figure 25** Pumps from Holland were used to pump water back into Somerset's rivers from the floodplain.

▶ **Figure 27** Dredging and bank stabilisation on the River Parrett.

The Somerset Levels and Moors Flood Action Plan

Medium term aims – up to 2020

- A dredging operation on the Rivers Parrett and Tone costing £6 million.
- Embankments will be built around vulnerable villages. £180,000 was spent protecting the ten houses in Thorney. Ten other sites will be identified and protected by the year 2020.
- Raising the height of the A372 road and repairing 44 km of damaged roads.
- Better preparation and planning to protect residents and business owners. Ideas such as stored sand bags, knowledge of the location of vulnerable people, emergency livestock movement and improved communication systems would be developed.

Longer-term aims – up to 2035

- Building a flood barrier at Bridgwater by 2024. The estimated cost is £32 million. This would reduce the impact of high tides that prevent flood water from escaping from the Levels.
- Investigate the costs and benefits of building a £16 million flood storage scheme upstream from Taunton. This would capture and hold back rainwater from draining into the River Tone. A large-scale tree-planting programme in the upper catchment would be part of this scheme.

▲ **Figure 26** The Somerset Levels and Moors Flood Action Plan.

Factfile: Impacts of the floods

- Half of all businesses in Somerset were affected either directly or indirectly by flooding.
- Damage to residential property cost up to £20 million.
- Costs to local government, the police and rescue services totalled £19 million.
- The rail line between Taunton and Bridgewater was closed for four weeks, costing the local economy £21 million.
- Over 80 roads were submerged for weeks with a cost of £15 million to the local economy.

Enquiry

Who should pay for the Somerset Levels and Moors Flood Action Plan? Discuss the responsibility of the following groups before making your recommendation:
- Those directly affected by flooding
- All the residents of Somerset
- The tax payers of the UK.

Activities

1 Draw and label a sequence of simple cross-sectional diagrams to show how dredging of the rivers would make them more efficient and reduce the risk of flooding.
2 Evaluate the arguments for and against continued dredging of rivers in the Levels.
3 Use the information on these pages to analyse the Somerset Levels and Moors Flood Action Plan. Do this by completing a table like the one below:

	Advantages	Disadvantages
Economic		
Social		
Environmental		

> Our computer models suggest that the dredging programme will make the rivers 90% effective in flushing out flood water. Currently the silt build up since 2009 makes them only 60% efficient.

Ashley Gibson, Somerset Water Management Partnership

> Part of the blame must be down to the Environment Agency. Why on earth did they cut back on the dredging programme in the first place?

Ian Liddell-Grainger, MP

> Dredging has an impact on the habitat in and around the river. The fish are severely disturbed during dredging and the water is murky for days after. Reed beds alongside the river are ripped up so birds and small mammals lose habitat.

Royal Society for the Protection of Birds

> It would have been cheaper to maintain the rivers properly instead of cutting back the dredging process in 2009. The clean-up and all the repairs will cost the tax payer millions.

National Farmers Union

> I would urge the authorities not to take dramatic action until they have considered the impact of climate change and sea level rise. A 12 cm rise in sea level could easily make the proposed Bridgwater barrage a waste of money.

Lord Krebs, Climate expert

> I object to paying an extra £25 a year in local taxes to fund flood prevention. The council should not allow building on flood plains. I have heard that over 900 homes have been built on vulnerable land in Somerset since 2001.

Resident of Glastonbury not affected by the flood

> The Environment Agency are taking a lot of the blame for reducing the dredging programme in recent years but government cutbacks in public spending required them to lose 1,700 jobs. We can't have it all ways.

Western Morning News

> We must allow the rivers to flood naturally. Some of the wetland habitats are unique. Sometimes nature needs to come before economics and people.

The Somerset Wildlife Trust

▲ **Figure 28** Different views from stakeholders on what should be done.

How is the River Severn managed?

The River Severn is Britain's longest river. A serious flood in 2000 prompted flood defences to be built at Frankwell, Shrewsbury. These included earth embankments, concrete flood walls and demountable flood barriers. These flood defences were completed in 2004 at a cost of £4.6 million. The demountable barriers (seen in Figure 29) are made of aluminium panels. They can be slotted together before the flood arrives. The demountable barriers successfully held back 1.9 m of flood water during a flood in February 2004 and 74 properties were protected. But not everywhere is protected. Land uses in Shrewsbury have been zoned. Land uses that have a low value, such as car parks and playing fields, are not protected. These zones provide safe areas for water to be 'stored' during a flood event, as shown in Figure 29.

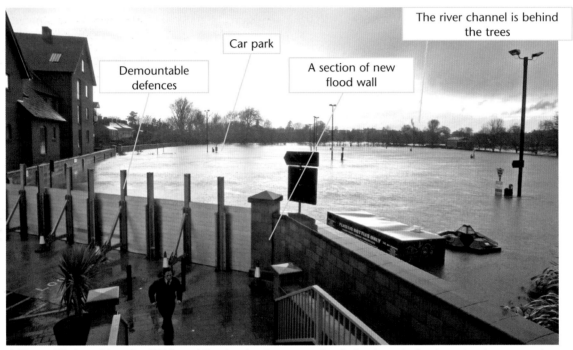

▲ **Figure 29** A total length of 700 m of flood embankments and walls has been built where the river enters the town to prevent floods in Shrewsbury. A further 155 m of river bank is protected using demountable defences.

▲ **Figure 30** Guildhall and Frankwell car park, SY3 8HQ, the same location as shown in Figure 29.

Shrewsbury: Flood damage in 2000 (severe), 2002, 2004 and 2007 (severe) and in 2014. Major flood defences were constructed in the spring of 2004. A further £20 million for extended flood defences for Shrewsbury was announced in February 2015, the work will be completed by 2020.

Bewdley: Flood damage in 2000 and 2002. Severe flooding was avoided in 2004 and again in 2014 by the use of demountable flood barriers.

Tewkesbury: Both Tewkesbury and **Gloucester** were badly affected by floods in 2000 and 2007. A five year multi-million pound flood prevention scheme protected both towns when the River Severn rose to dangerous levels in 2012. Only isolated villages downstream from Tewkesbury suffered any damage in 2012 and 2014.

◀ **Figure 31** Historic floods (2000–15) on the River Severn.

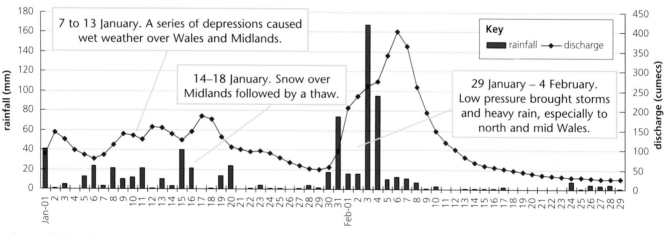

▲ **Figure 32** Flood hydrograph for the River Severn at Bewdley (January–February 2004). Rainfall data is for Capel Curig, North Wales.

Activities

1 Describe the course of the River Severn.
2 Suggest why planners might prevent the building of new homes on the flood plain of the River Severn.
3 Suggest why local residents might prefer demountable barriers to walls and embankments.
4 Explain why flood zoning is used in Shrewsbury. Consider the economic and environmental benefits.

Enquiry

How do weather events affect seasonal flood patterns?
■ Carefully describe the shape of the flood hydrograph between 29 January and 29 February. Use Figure 5 on page 38 to help your description.
■ Describe how each of the three weather events described in the labels affected the flow of the river. Focus on the time lag as well as the gradient of each rising limb.
■ Suggest how the Environment Agency uses rainfall data from Wales to warn householders in Bewdley about future flood events.

What should be done to reduce the risk of future floods?

▶ **Figure 33**
Alternative points of view on solving the flood problem.

Planner

Householders should be encouraged not to pave over their gardens. Paving and tarmac are impermeable. Rainwater goes straight down into storm drains and into the river rather than soaking slowly into the soil. Advice needs to be given so that gravel and permeable surfaces are used instead of tarmac. We also need to replace old storm drains which are too old and small to cope with heavy rain storms. However, motorists won't like that because it will mean digging up urban roads!

Spokesperson for RSPB

The scientists who wrote the 'Futures Report' into flooding identified that poor land management had increased the risk of river floods. For example, over the last 50 years farmers in upland areas of England and Wales have added drains to their fields to improve the amount of grass that can be grown. However, these field drains have had an effect on the flow of rivers further downstream. We are involved in a scheme to restore the old peat bogs in upland Wales. Between 2006 and 2011 we are going to block a total of 90 km of old land drains on the hills close to Lake Vyrnwy. We are using bales made from heather to block the drains. This will slow down the overland flow and force water to soak back into the soil. Not only will this help reduce the risk of floods but it will also improve the moorland ecosystem and will help to protect rare birds of prey like the merlin and hen harrier.

River scientist

Hard engineering schemes, like the flood walls and embankments in Shrewsbury, speed up the flow of water. These schemes may funnel water along to the next community living further downstream and actually increase their risk of flooding. What we need to do is to return river valleys to a more natural state. We should use floodplains as temporary water stores so that flooding can occur away from built-up areas.

House builder

Homes can be made more flood proof with measures such as putting plug sockets higher up the walls and replacing wooden floors and carpets with tiles.

Resident in Shrewsbury

I'm really pleased with the new flood defences. My property has flooded in the past but was protected during 2007. The Shrewsbury flood defence scheme cost £4.6 million but I think it was worth it.

Government housing minister

We need to build an extra 3 million homes in the UK by 2020. Almost half of them are in the Midlands and the south of England, which are the same areas hit by flooding in 2007. Some of these houses will have to be built on greenfield sites. However, we should restrict building on floodplains in the future.

▼ **Figure 34** The movement of water through upland drainage basins in mid Wales was altered when field drains were added. The size of the arrows is in proportion to the amount of each flow.

a) The natural system

Rainfall

Some overland flow occurs when the ground is saturated with water

A lot of water infiltrates into the soil store. Thick layers of peat are able to store large quantities of water

Throughflow: water moves slowly through the soil and enters the river several hours or days after the rainfall

b) Field drains were added to improve drainage

Rainfall

Field drains

Activity

1 Study Figure 34.
    a) Make a copy of the second diagram.
    b) Add labels that explain water flows at 1, 2 and 3.

    c) Explain how the differences in the two diagrams would affect the flow of water in the river downstream.

Enquiry

You have been asked to advise Tewkesbury Council on flood prevention. What do you think should be done to prevent future floods in the town?

- Use what you have learned in this chapter, and the points of view in Figure 33 to complete a copy of the table.

Possible solution	Short-term benefits and problems	Long-term benefits and problems	Who might agree and disagree with this solution
Building flood defences like those in Shrewsbury			
Restoring bogs and moorland in mid Wales by blocking drains			
Tighter controls on building on floodplains and paving over gardens			
Allowing rivers to flow naturally and spill over onto the floodplain			

- Now you need to recommend your plan. What do you think should be done and why do you think your plan will work? Use the following table to plan your answer.

Key questions to ask yourself	My answers
Is my plan realistic and achievable?	
Which groups of people will benefit from my plan?	
How will the environment be affected?	
Why is this plan better than the alternatives?	

Where do people live in the UK?

Urban places are busy **built environments**. People live close together at a high **population density**. In contrast, rural places have more open space. Rural population densities are lower or sparse. Within rural areas there is a **hierarchy** of settlements – hamlets, villages and small towns – but these settlements tend to be smaller than in urban regions.

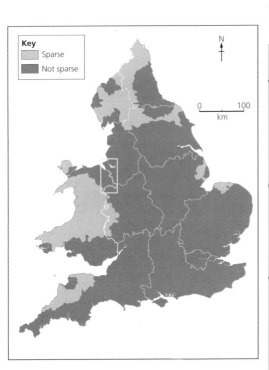

▲ **Figure 1** Sparse populations in England and Wales; the yellow box outlines the shape of Figure 2.

Chester – population 329,608. Shops in Chester attract customers from a huge area across Cheshire, North Shropshire and North Wales. Chester University has 15,000 students.

Broughton – population 6,000. A small rural town in Wales within easy commuting distance of Chester. Airbus has a factory here that makes aircraft wings and employs 6,000 people. People commute to the factory from Chester, Birkenhead and North Wales.

Wrexham – population 42,000. Wrexham is the largest town in North Wales and is the administrative centre of Wrexham County Borough. Wrexham has three secondary schools.

Llangollen – population 4,000. A small rural town popular with tourists visiting the Clwydian Range AONB.

Glyn Ceiriog – population 800. The Ceiriog Valley is a sheep farming community with a population density of 0.2 people per hectare. The village has one shop, which includes the post office.

▲ **Figure 2** Urban and rural places on the northern border between England and Wales.

Urban spheres of influence

Rural and urban areas are closely linked. Cities such as Liverpool or Chester act as a kind of hub. They provide a central place for employment, shops and entertainment for people living in surrounding rural areas. If a city is a hub, then roads and railways are the spokes that connect the city to its surrounding region. These road and rail links allow a daily flow of commuters into and out of the city. Cities contain a high density of business services such as banks, IT firms and lawyers. These services support other businesses that are located in the city and in the surrounding region.

So, a complex web links each city to its surrounding rural region. This web includes infrastructure such as roads, bus services, railways and airports. It also includes flows of people, ideas, business contacts and money. We say that the city has a **sphere of influence** – a region within which the city provides an important economic and social influence. This influence is strongest in places closest to the city and gets weaker with increasing distance. Large cities have a larger sphere of influence than a small town. Indeed, the largest cities have connections with cities in other parts of the world – as you will see in Theme 2 Chapter 3.

My wife and I live in a small hamlet close to Llangollen. We both used to work in Wrexham but are now retired from full-time work. We usually do our shopping in Oswestry or Wrexham. The nearest theatre is in Mold and our closest airports are in Liverpool and Manchester. The closest premier football clubs are Liverpool and Everton.

Activity

1 Describe the distribution of sparse populations in:
   a) Wales
   b) England.

▲ **Figure 3** The rural town of Llangollen.

	Rural places (%)			Urban places (%)		England and Wales
Age	Glyn Ceiriog	Llangollen	Broughton North East	Garden Quarter, Chester	Upton, Chester	
75+	9.6	12.5	8.3	2.8	11.3	7.8
65–74	11.3	12.6	9.9	3.2	9.5	8.6
45–64	31.9	31.1	24.8	11.8	24.0	25.4
30–44	18.0	16.2	20.9	14.4	20.4	20.6
20–29	7.0	9.2	12.7	45.1	10.2	13.7
16–19	5.3	4.3	5.4	17.6	4.3	5.1
10–15	7.1	5.4	7.0	1.5	7.4	7.0
0–9	9.8	8.7	11.0	3.6	12.9	11.9

▲ **Figure 4** Population data for rural and urban places in the region of Llangollen and Chester.

Activities

2 Use evidence from Figures 1 and 2 to identify the one place labelled on Figure 2 that has a sparse population.
3 Study Figures 2 and 3 to help you suggest the different spheres of influence of:
   a) Glyn Ceiriog village shop
   b) Chester University
   c) Airbus at Broughton
   d) Liverpool Football Club.
4 Use evidence from Figures 2 and 3 to suggest why people might want to retire to Llangollen.
5 Explain why people living in rural places such as Llangollen have to travel longer distances and more frequently than people who live in urban places such as Liverpool.

Enquiry

How does the population structure vary between urban and rural places?

■ Analyse the data in Figure 4 and suggest a possible hypothesis.
■ Represent the data in Figure 4 using a suitable style of graph.
■ What conclusions do you reach?
■ Investigate Garden Quarter, Chester. Why does it have an unusual population structure?

The urban–rural continuum

Rural and urban may seem to be opposites but, in reality, there is an **urban–rural continuum** – a sliding scale between urban places and the most remote rural regions. Some rural places are easily accessible to large cities. The rural communities of Kent and South Oxfordshire in England, for example, are close to major transport routes into London. This makes **commuting** and access to shops and entertainment easy. The population of accessible rural areas such as these is growing – a process known as **counter-urbanisation**. At the other end of the continuum are some remote and very sparsely populated rural areas. It is not possible to commute easily from these remote places. The population here is ageing as younger people leave the countryside to seek work in the city.

Different types of rural places

Rural places have common features, such as open spaces and village communities, but they also have other features that can be used to classify them into different types. Figure 6 shows examples of four very different types of rural place:

- *Deep green*: These are remote and isolated rural places with poor road networks. They have lots of open space and very sparse populations.
- *Rapid change*: These rural areas are less densely populated and include some larger towns. Many people living here are commuters who work in urban areas rather than the countryside.
- *Leisure and amenity*: Some of the UK's most beautiful scenery and National Parks are contained in these rural places. They are in remote parts of the UK.
- *Coastal retirement*: The population of these seaside towns includes a significant proportion of people who moved here when they retired.

Key
- Leisure amenity
- Rapid change
- Deep green
- Coastal retirement
- Large urban areas

Gwynedd
Powys
Cardiff
South Oxfordshire London
East Devon

0 ___ 100 km

▲ **Figure 6** The location and distribution of different types of rural place in England and Wales.

Activities

1. Describe the distinctive features of the landscape shown in Figure 5.
2. Study Figure 6.
   a) Describe the distribution of each type of rural area.
   b) Suggest reasons for the distribution of deep green and rapid change areas.

▲ **Figure 5** The 'deep green' sparsely populated region of Powys, Mid Wales.

What are the strengths and challenges of rural life?

Each of the types of rural place shown in Figure 6 has its own strengths and challenges. For example, the very sparse population of deep green places makes it difficult for small rural businesses and services to stay open. These rural places face the challenge of the closure of village shops, schools and post offices. Public transport is poor, so those who cannot drive are worst affected when such services close.

Area	Population density (persons per hectare)	Retired population (%)
East Devon	1.63	22.36
South Oxfordshire	1.98	13.9
Powys	0.26	17.9
Gwynedd	0.48	16.4
Riverside, Cardiff	53.3	7.5

Figure 7 Population features of different rural areas of England and Wales; the figures for Riverside, an inner-urban area of Cardiff, are provided for comparison.

Area	Financial occupations (%)	Professional occupations (%)	Farming, forestry and fishing (%)	Accommodation and food (%)
East Devon	2.35	6.19	3.06	7.25
South Oxfordshire	2.80	11.29	1.03	4.42
Powys	1.43	4.44	8.67	6.42
Gwynedd	1.13	3.66	3.46	9.82

Figure 8 Selected occupations for different rural areas of England and Wales (per cent).

Sparse local services

Ageing populations   Poor mobile coverage

Poor road links   Young adult population increasing

Commuters can use rail services to London

Beautiful scenery   Strong, safe communities

▲ **Figure 9** Strengths and challenges of rural life.

 www.ukcensusdata.com – this site provides easy access to data from the Office for National Statistics. You can search by postcode or place name.

Enquiry

How well do rural places match the types described in Figure 6?

Use the weblink, or any other site that uses census data, to research the population and work characteristics of each of the following rural places. Which rural type does each best match?

- East Lindsey in Lincolnshire
- South Lakeland in Cumbria
- North Norfolk
- Pembrokeshire

Activities

3 Study Figures 7 and 8. They show data for specific places within each of the four types of rural areas shown on Figure 6.
   a) Represent the data to summarise the main similarities and differences.
   b) Use the data to draw conclusions about the people and occupations that typify each of these rural places.
4 a) Sort the statements in Figure 9 into strengths and challenges.
   b) For four of these statements:
      i) decide which of the rural types it best describes
      ii) describe the consequences for rural residents.

How does commuting link urban and rural areas?

Towns and cities are closely linked to their surrounding rural areas by daily flows of commuters. Many commuters live in the region surrounding the city and travel into it each day to work. A smaller number of commuters travel in the opposite direction, leaving their home in the city to work in a nearby town. Almost 11.3 million people in the UK travel between their home in one local authority and their workplace in a different local authority each day of the working week.

Large cities, such as London, Liverpool or Cardiff, have many more jobs available than their surrounding region, and a particularly large sphere of influence. It's often cheaper to live in a smaller town and commute into the city – even if the commute is quite long. Other people only commute occasionally, preferring to **telework** from their rural home. Teleworkers use mobile technology and the internet to use their home as an office.

Commuting factfile

- Average commuting times in the UK are going up: in 2003 it was 45 minutes; by 2015 it had risen to 54 minutes.
- 616,000 people commute into the city of London each weekday.
- 1.8 million people in the UK (one in ten UK commuters) travel for over 3 hours a day. These are so-called 'extreme commuters'.

Area of UK	Average commuting time (minutes)
London	74.2
South East	56.4
East of England	56.0
South West	44.8
Wales	41.0

Figure 10 Average UK commute times.

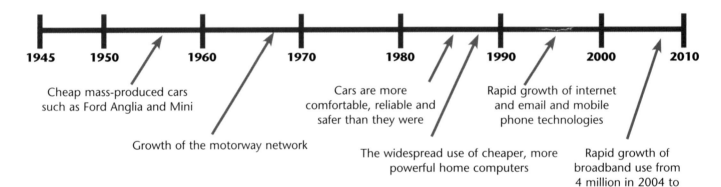

▲ Figure 11 Technological changes have increased the connections between rural and urban places.

1945 1950 1960 1970 1980 1990 2000 2010

Cheap mass-produced cars such as Ford Anglia and Mini

Growth of the motorway network

Cars are more comfortable, reliable and safer than they were

The widespread use of cheaper, more powerful home computers

Rapid growth of internet and email and mobile phone technologies

Rapid growth of broadband use from 4 million in 2004 to 11 million in 2006

The difference in house prices between a city and its surrounding region
Fast rail links
The rising cost of fuel and the rising cost of rail fares
The availability of good 3G and 4G signals and free wi-fi on train services
The affordability of fuel-efficient cars
Flexible working hours that allow workers to begin the working day any time between 7 a.m. and 10 a.m.

▲ Figure 12 Factors that affect commuting.

Activities

1 Study Figure 11. Use it to explain why:
   a) the number of commuters has increased since the 1960s
   b) more people are able to work from home now than before 1980.
2 For each factor in Figure 12, suggest how it may affect patterns of commuting.
3 a) Suggest why London has the longest commute times in the UK.
   b) Suggest two different reasons why the length of the average commute in the UK is increasing.

Patterns of commuting in southeast Wales

Cardiff has a very wide sphere of influence – people from all over Wales occasionally travel to Cardiff for its shops, to attend concerts and sporting events, and to visit its museums. This sphere of influence is felt most strongly across southeast Wales. People in this region regularly commute into and out of Cardiff, as shown in Figure 13.

Cardiff city region factfile

- Cardiff has a population of 350,000.
- Half the population of Wales, 1.49 million people, live within 32 km of Cardiff city centre.
- The city has a workforce of 189,000.
- Almost 78,000 people commute into Cardiff, and 33,900 people commute out of Cardiff, each weekday.

Local council	Total workplace population	Daily commuters to Cardiff	Daily commuters from Cardiff
Vale of Glamorgan	37,300	20,600	4,700
Rhondda Cynon Taf	71,500	20,400	3,800
Caerphilly	56,500	15,100	3,200
Newport	70,200	6,900	6,700
Bridgend	62,900	5,400	ND
Merthyr Tydfil	21,900	2,300	ND
Torfaen	35,400	1,900	1,900
Monmouthshire	43,200	1,700	ND
Swansea	111,400	1,600	ND
Neath Port Talbot	45,200	1,500	ND
Blaenau Gwent	19,200	1,000	ND
Cardiff	217,000	0	0
Other		4,500	13,700

Figure 13 Commuting patterns in and out of Cardiff; ND means there is no data for these commuter flows (they are likely to be small).

Enquiry

How are commuter patterns affected by transport infrastructure?

Use the internet to find the main road and rail links into Cardiff. How do these transport routes help explain any patterns shown in Figure 13?

Key

1. Aberdare
2. Abertillery
3. Porth
4. Caerphilly
5. Cwmbran
6. Cowbridge
7. Penarth
8. Newport

Activity

4 a) Make a simple copy of Figure 14.
   b) Use the data in Figure 13 to make a choropleth map of daily commuters to Cardiff.
   c) Describe the patterns shown by your map.
   d) Describe another technique that could be used to represent this data.

▲ **Figure 14** Map of Cardiff and the surrounding local councils.

Issues created by commuting

Almost 63,000 people commute into Cardiff each weekday by car. Queues on the A470, from the north, and on the A48, from the east, can cause traffic delays of up to an hour to get into Cardiff. Most other commuters arrive by train. Once in the city, they rely on bus, cycle or pedestrian routes to get them safely to their place of work. But cycling, and even walking, can be dangerous when streets are packed with commuter traffic.

▲ **Figure 15** The Taff Trail; a green corridor of parks provides a safe environment for commuters to walk or cycle through Cardiff from north to south.

| Cardiff has three park-and-ride schemes |
| The Taff Trail |
| Cycle routes |
| Bus lanes |
| Car share schemes |
| Integrated systems where bus routes connect with train stations and cycle routes |
| Flexi hours so that businesses start and finish at different times |
| Locating major employers, such as the BBC, close to train stations |
| Water taxis take passengers from Cardiff Bay, up the River Taff to the city centre |

▲ **Figure 16** Nine solutions to Cardiff's traffic problems.

Cardiff Central Square to be redeveloped as integrated transport hub

An area of central Cardiff is being regenerated at a cost of £400 million. The site outside the Central Train Station will be transformed as buildings are demolished and new offices are built. As many as 10,000 jobs could be created by the project. The plan includes a new building for the BBC, which should be open in 2019. The regeneration also includes other new office buildings, a 150-bedroom hotel, shops, 200 residential homes and a new central bus station. All will be within minutes' walking distance of the city centre.

The new bus station is planned to be open by the end of 2017. It will link to the existing train station on wide, flat pavements with no steps to allow easy pedestrian movement. The design of the new station will include: live information screens; facilities for travellers to include assistance points, toilets and restaurants; safe storage for bicycles; pleasant waiting areas; and protection from the rain by overhangs from the new office buildings.

▲ **Figure 17** The regeneration of Central Square will include an integrated transport hub.

Enquiry

'The regeneration of Central Square will solve all of Cardiff's transport problems.'

To what extent do you agree with this statement? Use evidence from the factfile on page 59 and Figure 17 to support your view.

Activities

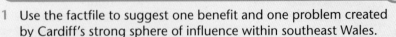

1 Use the factfile to suggest one benefit and one problem created by Cardiff's strong sphere of influence within southeast Wales.
2 a) Discuss the nine solutions to Cardiff's traffic problems in Figure 16.
 b) Make a diamond nine diagram (like the one on page 83) and place the solutions in the diagram, placing those that you think are essential at the top of the diagram.
 c) Explain why you have chosen your top three solutions.

The issue of second homes

Around 1.6 million people in England and Wales own a second home in the countryside that they use at the weekends or for holidays. Many of these are in the most picturesque parts of the countryside, such as the Lake District in England or Pen Llŷn (the Llŷn Peninsula) in Wales. The lack of affordable housing in Gwynedd, Wales, is linked by some to the sale of rural houses as second homes. Holiday homes are empty for long periods of time. As regular demand for services falls, village pubs close and are converted to homes, bus services are axed, and local shops and banks may also close. The rise of internet banking has also led to the closure of high street banks in rural places.

▲ **Figure 18** Rural housing issues.

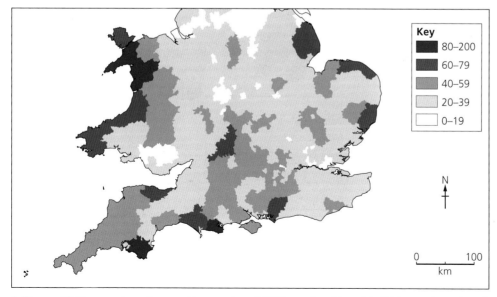

▲ **Figure 19** The number of second homes (per 1,000 usual residents) in Wales and southern/central England.

Activities

3 Study Figure 18.
  a) Identify three main reasons for the lack of affordable housing in rural places.
  b) Explain why the sale of houses as holiday homes may lead to the closure of village shops and other services.

4 Compare Figure 19 to the map of National Parks, Figure 10 on page 4, and Figure 6 on page 56. What conclusions can you reach?

Issues facing remote rural places

Remote rural places can be affected by a number of problems:

- low incomes and part-time work
- lack of services, especially health services, schools and adult education
- infrequent public transport and high transport costs.

Poor roads, isolation and sparse populations are all factors that can lead to a decline in rural jobs and rural services. These problems are examples of rural **deprivation**. The lack of jobs, leisure facilities and shops in the countryside are all push factors for younger adults. In addition, the high cost of buying a house may prevent young families on lower incomes from staying in a rural area. This leads to a falling birth rate. As a result, the population of some rural areas is both ageing and decreasing – a process known as rural **depopulation**.

Deprivation

Communities are described as being deprived if they lack features that are usually regarded as necessary for a reasonable standard of living. Low wages are a cause of deprivation in some urban places. Lack of public transport, health care and education services are reasons for deprivation in some rural places.

▲ **Figure 20** How rural depopulation creates unsustainable communities.

Too few rural jobs and opportunities.

Rural to urban migration is greater than migration into the rural area.

Declining rural populations.

Reduced demand for schools, shops and other services.

Collapse of rural services.

Further rural depopulation.

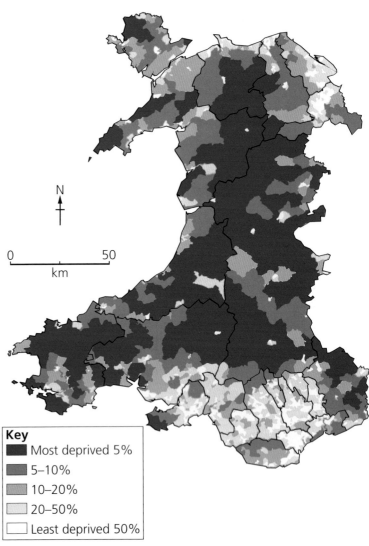

Key
- Most deprived 5%
- 5–10%
- 10–20%
- 20–50%
- Least deprived 50%

▲ **Figure 21** Rural deprivation: local authorities in Wales have been ranked by their isolation from important services (including education, health and post offices); those coloured red have the worst access to these services.

Isolation from health services

Cities provide an important range of health and education services to the surrounding rural region – this is an important function of their sphere of influence (see page 54). Hospitals, located in the city, provide specialist care that is available to people across very large rural regions. We saw on pages 56–7 that many rural places have an **ageing population**. This creates issues:

- Elderly people are more likely to have long-term (or chronic) health issues. These include diabetes, reduced mobility due to arthritis, and dementia.
- The sparse population usually means that specialist treatment or care is not locally available – patients have to travel long distances. For example, there are currently only three health centres serving the whole of Pen Llŷn (the Llŷn Peninsula) in northwest Wales. Two of these are in the larger settlements of Pwllheli and Nefyn. The main hospital, however, is some 40 km away in Bangor.

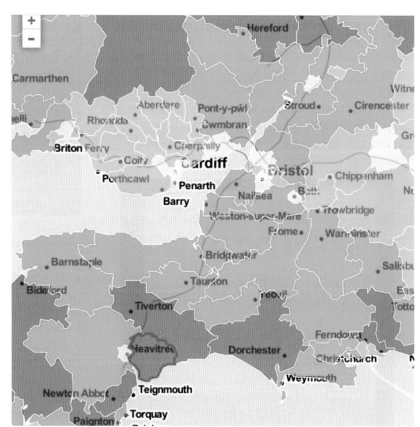

▲ **Figure 22** The percentage of the population aged over 65 in southeast Wales and southwest England.

Key
Per cent
- <12.5
- 12.5–16.6
- 16.7–20.2
- 20.3–24.3
- 24.4+
- No data

	Powys		Cardiff	
Population	132,976	–	346,090	–
Population aged over 65	a	22.7%	c	13.16%
Population aged over 75	b	10.5%	d	6.6%
Population density (per hectare)	0.2567	–	24.6534	–
Area (hectares)	518,037	–	14,038	–

Figure 23 Comparing the population over 65 in rural and urban areas of Wales.

Activities

1 Give two main reasons for rural depopulation. Use Figure 20 to help you.
2 Use Figure 21 to describe the distribution of the:
   a) most deprived places
   b) least deprived places.
3 Compare Figure 21 to Figure 1 on page 54 and Figure 6 on page 56. Suggest reasons for the patterns shown on Figure 21.
4 a) Make a copy of Figure 23.
   b) Calculate the missing population figures and add them to cells a, b, c and d.
5 a) Describe the patterns shown on Figure 22.
   b) Use Figure 6 on page 56 to help explain these patterns.

Enquiry

'The issue created by the ageing population is greater in rural areas than in urban ones.'

To what extent do you agree with this statement? Use evidence from Figures 22 and 23 to help your answer.

Are rural communities sustainable?

Sustainable communities are places that are able to support the needs of all residents – providing a decent quality of life in the present and for the foreseeable future. This means that people living in a sustainable rural community will have access to the services they need, and feel safe and secure. The features of sustainable communities are examined in more detail on page 72.

▲ **Figure 25** The mobile library takes books to rural communities.

▲ **Figure 24** Does better broadband help create sustainable rural communities?

Economic investment in rural tourism in Pen Llŷn

In 2015 the £9 million Welsh National Sailing Academy and Events Centre, Plas Heli, was opened in Pwllheli. Welsh and international sailing championships are held here. In the first month after opening over 32,000 visitors were attracted to Pwllheli. These extra visitors help to boost the local rural economy. Visitors stay in local hotels, guest houses and caravan parks in the peninsula. Plas Heli employs people to run the restaurant, meeting rooms and hall, which is available for concerts, conferences and exhibitions. Jobs were also created in the Hafan Marina workshops and in the shops that sell sportswear and sailing equipment located in Pwllheli. In this way, the investment should create a positive multiplier effect (see page 218) in the local rural economy.

▲ **Figure 26** Plas Heli sailing academy and a view across the marina.

How can secondary education services be more sustainable?

The education issues in sparsely populated rural areas are complex. The birth rate in many remote rural areas is declining and the number of children attending schools is falling. Schools with fewer students receive less income, so they have to make teachers redundant. However, secondary schools still need to offer a wide range of subjects. They can only do this by having larger class sizes or by having some subjects taught by non-specialist teachers.

In Powys, the county council are reviewing secondary school provision across the county. In 2015 they made two controversial recommendations:

- two secondary schools in the south of the county should be closed and replaced with the Beacons Learning Campus: one large 11–18 school and sixth form
- two secondary schools in the middle of the county should be closed and replaced with one larger school, probably in Builth Wells.

Local authority spokesperson

For schools to provide the broadest range of subjects they need at least 600 students aged eleven to sixteen. In an 11–18 school the sixth form needs to have at least 150 students. Where we have several small schools, these should be closed and replaced by one larger one so that students get specialist teaching across a range of subjects.

Parent

Travelling long distances to and from school is not something I want for my child. It means a really early start. In the winter months it will involve a ten-minute walk down a dark lane to catch the bus and then a journey of 40 minutes. He won't be able to take part in after-school clubs, or see his friends who live on the other side of the school catchment.

Head teacher

By having fewer, larger schools, we would have at least two classes per year group learning through the medium of Welsh. This will allow schools to provide a wide range of subjects through the medium of Welsh.

Local resident

The local school is an important part of our community. Many local people were students here. It's part of who we are – our identity. The school buildings are sometimes used in the evening by the community. We have already lost the post office and pub in our village. We don't want to lose our school.

▲ **Figure 27** Views on changes to secondary school provision in Powys.

Activities

1 Explain why each of the following factors could be a challenge for a rural community:
   a) the closure of a village shop
   b) infrequent bus services
   c) an ageing population.
2 How might each of the ideas shown in Figures 24, 25 and 26 contribute to a sustainable rural community? Use the ideas on page 73 to help you.
3 a) Explain why the investment in Plas Heli is likely to create positive multiplier effects in the local economy.
   b) Suggest why this type of investment will not work for every rural place. Use Figure 6 on page 56 to help your answer.
4 Explain why population change in rural areas can lead to issues for local schools.
5 Summarise the arguments for and against closing rural schools.

Enquiry

'Investment in leisure and tourism are the best way to solve the problems of remote rural areas.'

How far do you agree with this statement? Make use of examples from this chapter and Theme 1 Chapter 1 to help your answer.

How and why is the UK population changing?

Since 1964 the population of the UK has grown by over 10 million. The population is now around 65 million and is slowly increasing. Changes to the size of the UK's population are due to a number of factors:

- An increase in the age that people live to, known as **average life expectancy**. Improving health care has led to fewer deaths and longer average lifespan. Better health care also means lower infant mortality rates. In 1980 there was an average of eleven deaths per thousand live births. This had fallen to four deaths in 2014.

- Migration both in and out of the UK, especially from Commonwealth countries and members of the EU. European migration laws allow movement of workers between members of the EU. For example, 50,000 EU migrants came from Bulgaria and Romania in the year ending June 2015. Of these, 84 per cent came to the UK for work-related reasons.

- The changing birth rate. The **birth rate** in the UK has been relatively low since the 1980s. Women choose to have small families so that they can concentrate on a career. However, the birth rate has increased slightly since 2004 as young adults have moved into the UK and had families of their own.

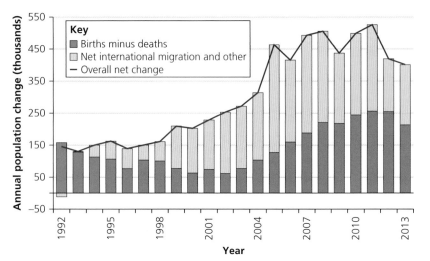

▲ **Figure 1** Annual UK population change; the line graph shows the number (in thousands) of extra people in the UK population each year; the bars show whether they are due to natural change (births minus deaths) or migration.

Year	Aged 0–15 (%)	Aged 16–64 (%)	Aged 65 and over (%)
1984	21	64	15
1994	21	63	16
2004	20	65	16
2014	19	64	18
2024	19	61	20
2034	18	58	24
2044	17	58	25

▲ **Figure 2** The UK's ageing population – actual and predicted figures.

Activities

1. a) Identify three main reasons why the UK population is growing.
    b) Discuss these reasons. Can you classify them as economic, political or social?
2. Study Figure 1. In which period of years was growth of the population:
    a) slowest
    b) fastest
    c) due mainly to natural change
    d) due mainly to migration?
3. a) Choose a suitable technique to represent the data in Figure 2.
    b) What conclusions can you reach?
4. Study Figure 3.
    a) Copy the statements in the green boxes.
    b) Match the statements in the blue boxes and connect them with a suitable phrase.
5. Discuss each statement in Figure 4. Explain why each of these ideas might help to respond to the issues created by an ageing population.

How should the UK prepare for an ageing population?

People in the UK are living longer. In 1995 there were less than 9 million people aged over 65 in the UK. Forecasts vary but it seems likely that by 2030 there will be about 13 million. Not only are more people living into retirement, many more people are living into old age. In 1951 there were only about 300 people over 100 years old. By 2030 there could be as many as 36,000 centenarians. The ageing of the population will have consequences for UK society, shown in Figure 3. Government, businesses and individuals all need to prepare for these consequences, and possible responses are shown in Figure 4.

 www.neighbourhood. statistics.gov.uk/HTMLDocs/ dvc174/index.html – for interactive census maps of England and Wales.

Many older people have valuable work skills and experience	Valuable contribution to business, education and training
There are a growing number of wealthy older people	Commitment to support local communities through voluntary work
The proportion of people of working age is shrinking while the proportion of people who are retired is growing	Feelings of isolation and lack of value
The number of older people who live alone is increasing	Create and maintain jobs when they spend money on holidays or leisure activities
The number of older people who have complex or long-term health issues is growing	Require expensive health care or support from family and carers
People who are retired have flexibility about when and how often they work	The government receives less money but pays more in state pensions

▲ **Figure 3** Some consequences of the UK's ageing population.

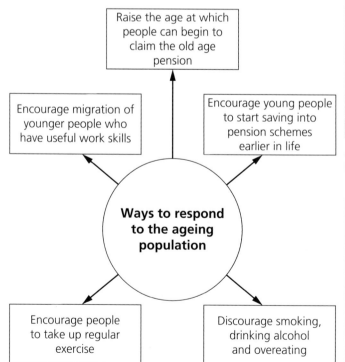

▲ **Figure 4** Ways to respond to the ageing population.

Area	Area type	Over 65 (%)
Bristol West	Urban	
Cardiff Central	Urban	
Cardiff South	Urban	
Bristol East	Urban	
Vale of Glamorgan	Rural – commuter	
Monmouth	Rural – commuter	
Brecon and Radnor	Deep rural	
West Dorset	Coastal retirement	

▲ **Figure 5** The percentage of the population aged over 65 in southeast Wales and southwest England.

Enquiry

How does the pattern of the ageing population vary across the UK?

- Make a copy of Figure 5.
- Use the weblink to investigate the population aged over 65. Focus on the areas around south Wales and the southwest of England to find the data for each area in Figure 5.
- What implications does this have for health care in these different places?

Why is there migration into the UK?

London, 4 August 2012, during London's 2012 Games. The cheering in London's Olympic Stadium reaches a deafening roar, as Team GB wins its sixth Olympic Gold medal that day. The winner is Mo Farah, Somalian by birth but a British citizen. Earlier, Jessica Ennis-Hill also won gold, daughter of a Jamaican-born father and British mother. It's one of the upsides of globalisation. The UK is lucky enough to be the home of choice for migrants who contribute to its sporting and cultural history.

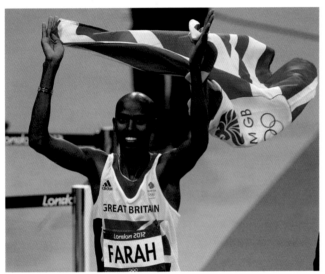

▲ **Figure 6** Mo Farah, Somalian by birth, but winning gold for Team GB in London's 2012 Games.

Year	Population (millions)
1965	54.3
1970	55.6
1975	56.2
1980	56.3
1985	56.6
1990	57.2
1995	58.0
2000	58.9
2005	60.4
2010	62.8
2014	65.0

▲ **Figure 7** The UK's increasing population.

The impacts on the UK population

Globalisation has brought a migration revolution to the UK. In 2014, 15 per cent of the UK working population was born overseas, and net migration into the UK was 318,000. By July 2015, the UK's population had reached 65 million, an increase of 6 million in 14 years, and the fastest growth in UK population history.

There have been two causes of this growth:
- **Net immigration**, mostly of young working adults aged 18–35. This is partly caused by the UK's membership of the EU, whereby anyone in the EU is free to move to and work in any EU member state.
- A higher **birth rate**, partially caused by immigration of women of childbearing age (15–44) and also due to rising fertility among UK-born women.

The UK Government believes that immigration benefits the UK. Like many HICs, the UK has an ageing population, with a smaller proportion of people of working age. Ageing populations are expensive because of pension and health costs. Governments need increased taxation from working people to pay for these.

Activity

1 a) Draw a line graph using Figure 7 to show the UK population. Extend the x-axis to 2050.
   b) Using the graph, calculate:
      i) when the UK population will reach 70 million
      ii) the size of the UK population in 2050.

 www.ons.gov.uk/ons/interactive/uk-population-pyramid---dvc1/index.html

An interactive population pyramid for the UK showing change between 1971 and 2085.

▲ **Figure 8** Canary Wharf in London, where the knowledge economy is most concentrated.

The impacts on the UK economy

The globalised UK economy has led to higher immigration. Its manufacturing economy declined in the 1970s and 1980s, and was replaced by a growing service economy. Now, two groups of workers migrate to the UK for jobs here. Half of these are **highly skilled**.

- Many come to take up well-paid jobs in the UK's **knowledge economy**. These are jobs requiring expertise in, for example, finance and banking, law, and IT. Between them, people in these jobs produce 35 per cent of all UK exports.
- The majority of these jobs are in the city of London, where banks, law firms, shipping and biotechnology companies need employees recruited from the world's most highly qualified people.
- London now 'imports' experts from overseas, as there are not enough in the UK.

The other half are **unskilled workers**. There is plenty of work:

- Many dirty, difficult and dangerous jobs are rejected by UK workers.
- The lifestyle of many British families is sustained by unsocial hours jobs ranging from childcare to house cleaning and pizza delivery.
- Jobs are filled by immigrants in sectors such as farming, construction, hotels, restaurant and tourism, which suffer from seasonal shortages of labour.

The social and cultural impacts of immigration

With 37 per cent of its population born overseas, London has the world's second largest urban immigrant population, after New York. Immigration is much debated by politicians and newspapers.

- Some journalists and politicians claim there are too many migrants: that migrants take jobs from local people and strain services such as schools and housing. In fact, the impact on services is more than made up by taxes paid by migrants.
- Others emphasise benefits of immigration. Many believe that the UK is improved by migrant skills and cultural contributions. They claim that diverse friendships, varied restaurants and the cultural impact on British sport, music and media more than make up for any problems.

Activities

2 Suggest the likely reasons why UK manufacturing jobs declined after the 1980s.
3 Draw a spider diagram to show economic benefits to the UK of:
   a) skilled migrants
   b) unskilled migrants.
4 Draw and complete a table to show possible benefits and problems for the UK economy if:
   a) the UK reduced immigration
   b) the UK left the EU.

Does the UK need to build more new homes?

In the financial year 2012–13 there were 135,500 new homes built in the UK. That was the lowest amount since 1945. It's not enough. As the population of the UK increases we need more homes. If too few are built, demand is greater than supply and the price of buying a new home rises faster than people's wages. The government wants to see an extra 240,000 homes being built every year. But where should these new homes be built? The greatest demand is in the South East of England. The economy is strongest in the South East, so this is an area where many younger people are moving to from other parts of the UK and from other EU countries.

Activities

1 Study Figure 9.
  a) Draw proportional bars on graph paper to represent the growth of population in each region.
  b) Cut out the bars and stick them onto an outline map of the UK.
  c) Explain why this representation of Figure 9 is more useful than a simple bar graph.
2 Describe the location of the Thames Gateway development.

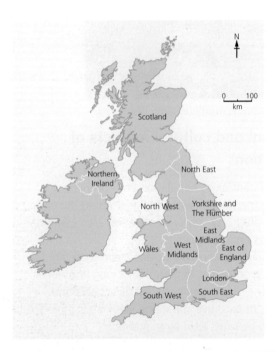

Region of the UK	Population increase (1,000s)
Northern Ireland	135
Scotland	247
Wales	163
North East	63
North West	307
Yorkshire and The Humber	336
West Midlands	355
East Midlands	374
East of England	491
London	955
South East	683
South West	384

◄ **Figure 9** Population increase in the regions of the UK (2001–12).

▲ **Figure 10** The key areas for new homes in the South East of the UK.

Are new garden cities the answer?

In 2014 the UK Government announced that three new **garden cities** would be built in England. Each would have about 15,000 new homes. The first garden cities were built in the 1930s at a time when there was a lot of new housebuilding. These towns had a lot of open space – hence the name. The new garden cities will feature high quality homes, lots of green space and access to local jobs and services. They will be built at:

• Bicester, near Oxford
• Northstowe, in Cambridgeshire
• Ebbsfleet, in the Thames Gateway (Kent).

Ebbsfleet, in Kent, is part of the Thames Gateway region. This region is well connected to London – it is only 20 minutes by rail from Ebbsfleet. The UK Government is keen to see new housebuilding in the Thames Gateway – perhaps as many as 90,000 new homes by 2030. It has committed £200 million to help fund the Ebbsfleet Development Corporation that will oversee the project and pay for new infrastructure in Ebbsfleet, such as roads.

The proposed garden city of Ebbsfleet will be designed as though it were a cluster of smaller traditional villages. Each 'village' will have its own primary school that is within walking distance of all homes in its catchment. Each 'village' will also have green open space, allotments, sports pitches and a community building for the use of groups of local residents. Building at Ebbsfleet has begun. It is expected that between 3,000 and 5,000 homes will be built between 2015 and 2020.

The Thames Gateway is low lying and at risk of coastal flooding (see pages 144–5). The cost of new sea defences could be £500 million.

Much of the development land in the Thames Gateway is brownfield. Part of Ebbsfleet will be built on a disused quarry.

Neighbouring small villages will become part of the new, larger town. They may lose their distinctive character.

A new bus service, called Fastrack, will run every 5–10 minutes during the day between Ebbsfleet and other towns in the Thames Gateway.

The government wants the Thames Gateway to be a low-carbon region. It hopes that people will work locally.

▲ **Figure 11** Aspects of development in the Thames Gateway.

▲ **Figure 12** Existing homes on the edge of an area of scrubland that has been identified as the possible site of the new Ebbsfleet garden city. Part of this site is a disused quarry.

Activity

3 Use information about the Thames Gateway and Ebbsfleet to complete a table like the one below. You will write more in some boxes than others.

	Arguments for building new homes in Ebbsfleet	Arguments against building new homes in Ebbsfleet
Economic		
Environmental		
Social		

Enquiry

Do the new garden cities sound as though they will be sustainable communities?

Use Figure 15 (page 73) to help you to justify your ideas.

How can we create sustainable urban and rural communities?

Planners want to create **sustainable communities** in the towns and countryside of the UK. This means they have to consider how new housing, roads or other developments can be planned so that people and the environment benefit both now and in the longer term. It's relatively easy to see how new houses can be made more environmentally sustainable. Figure 13 shows some features of modern eco-housing.

▼ **Figure 13** Eco-homes at the Beddington Zero Energy Development (BedZED) in Surrey. BedZED was the first and largest carbo-neutral eco-community in the UK

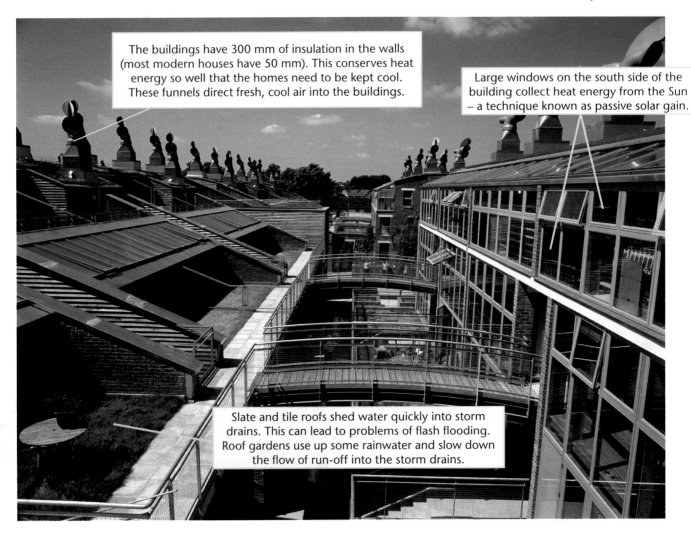

The buildings have 300 mm of insulation in the walls (most modern houses have 50 mm). This conserves heat energy so well that the homes need to be kept cool. These funnels direct fresh, cool air into the buildings.

Large windows on the south side of the building collect heat energy from the Sun – a technique known as passive solar gain.

Slate and tile roofs shed water quickly into storm drains. This can lead to problems of flash flooding. Roof gardens use up some rainwater and slow down the flow of run-off into the storm drains.

some affordable housing for people on lower incomes

a brownfield site rather than a greenfield site

jobs available locally

public transport available to everyone

A sustainable community has …

some buildings designed for elderly or disabled people with wide doorways for wheelchair users and ground-floor bedrooms and bathrooms

local facilities for people of all ages, e.g. crèche, youth group, community centre

green technologies to reduce heating costs and carbon emissions

schemes to reduce car ownership such as increased parking costs

▲ **Figure 14** Possible features of a sustainable community.

Egan's Wheel

However, to build a sustainable community we need to consider other features of the urban or rural environment, as well as housing. Figure 15 explains the concept of the Egan Wheel. It shows the criteria we can use to judge a sustainable community.

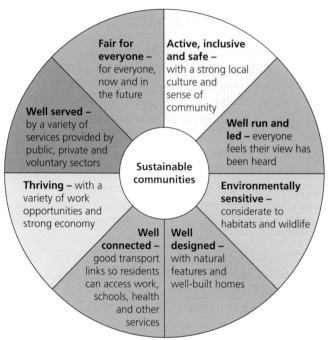

▲ **Figure 15** Egan's Wheel.

▲ **Figure 16** Evidence of sustainable urban communities in Cardiff.

Should we build on the green belt?

A lot of new housebuilding took place after the Second World War. New suburban homes were built on the edges of UK cities and the term 'suburban sprawl' is used to describe the resulting rapid growth of the suburbs. UK planners at the time were so concerned about the loss of countryside that they prevented further loss by creating wide **green belts** around many UK cities. Green belts currently occupy 13 per cent of total land area in England. They contain smaller towns and villages, farmland and countryside. The building of new homes is restricted on green belt land.

The population of the UK is growing and there is demand for new homes. Should these new homes be built on **greenfield sites** – land that has not been used for building before? Or should homes be built on **brownfield sites** – land that has had a former use such as a factory, warehouse, dock or quarry and which is now unused or derelict? New housebuilding on greenfield sites may be opposed by local people who are concerned that new housing will spoil the rural character of their local community. Protests about local planning issues are commonly called **NIMBYism** – which stands for Not in My Back Yard.

City	Ratio
Oxford	15.0
Cambridge	14.8
London	14.0
Brighton	12.2
Reading	10.1
Milton Keynes	8.0
Birmingham	7.3
Nottingham	6.8
Swansea	6.7
Derby	6.2
Liverpool	5.8

▲ **Figure 18** The cost of housing compared to average local wages (2014).

Oxford's employers, who include BMW Mini, schools, hospitals and the university, are finding it difficult to recruit workers because of the high cost of housing.

Over 50 per cent of the workforce commute into the city. In Oxford, new building on greenfield sites leap-frogs the green belt. This means that families who occupy the new housing in places like Bicester have a particularly long commute to work into Oxford. The pressure on our roads and public transport is not sustainable.

Oxford's universities have an international reputation for excellence in both research and teaching. We need cheaper housing so we can recruit the best research workers. These researchers are the reason for so many high-tech firms locating here.

▲ **Figure 19** Members of Oxford City Council explain why building on the green belt may be necessary.

New homes in Oxford?

Where demand for houses is greater than supply, the price of homes has risen rapidly. Research in 2014 suggests that house prices are particularly high in Oxford. In 2014, average wages in Oxford were £26,500 per year. At the same time, the average cost of a house was £426,720, which is 15 times the average wage.

Oxford City Council believes that Oxford needs between 24,000 and 32,000 homes to be built by 2031. Controversially, it would like to build many of these within the green belt. South Oxford District Council has opposed the plan. It recognises that new homes are needed but doesn't want them built on green belt land.

▲ **Figure 17** Development areas suggested by Oxford City Council that are within Oxford's green belt.

Map legend

Click on the map to see what Flood Zone (National Planning Policy Guidance definitions) the proposed development is in.

☐ ☑ Flood Map for Planning (Rivers and Sea) ⓘ

Flood Zone 3

Flood Zone 2

Flood defences (Not all may be shown*)

Areas benefiting from flood defences (Not all may be shown*)

☐ ☑ Main River Line ⓘ

✎ Main River Line

☐ ☑ Other national environmental organisations ⓘ

Natural Resources Wales Area of responsibility

Scottish Environment Protection Agency Area

Oxford, Oxfordshire at scale 1:40,000   Other maps ◗ Data search ◗ Text only version ◗

▲ **Figure 20** A screenshot from the Environment Agency website. The city centre is in the bottom right corner of the shot. Notice the open space to the north-west of the city which forms a green corridor along the River Cherwell.

Activities

1 Write a 200-word press release which explains why Oxford City council thinks it is necessary to build in the green belt. Use Figure 19.
2 Study Figure 18.
   a) Choose a suitable technique to represent this data.
   b) Use an atlas to analyse the pattern shown by this data.
3 a) Describe the location of the development site at Wheatley. Use Figure 17.
   b) Use Figure 21 to list two reasons why you think the development should go ahead.
   c) Give two reasons why you think the development should not go ahead.
   d) Suggest two different groups of people who might object to this development.
4 a) Use Figure 20 to describe the areas of Oxford that are vulnerable to flooding.
   b) Explain why it is important to maintain green corridors of land that have not been developed within cities like Oxford.

The development will extend the village of Wheatley. The village will lose its distinctive character.

The site is alongside the A40 so access into Oxford is easy.

The land is open countryside and has never been built on before.

The land is sloping and poor quality farmland used for grazing.

Steep slopes on some of the site will make the building of homes expensive.

▲ **Figure 21** Features of the proposed development site at Wheatley.

Enquiry

How important is the green belt?

Design a survey to investigate people's views of house building on green belt land. How could you design the sampling strategy (see page 8) to ensure that the views of different groups of people are included?

Urban renewal

During the 1970s and 80s, it became unfashionable to live in the inner urban areas of many UK towns and cities. People didn't really want to live in areas of older inner-city housing, especially in the docks and waterfront areas of the UK's ports like Butetown in Cardiff or Salford Quays in Manchester.

However, these once run-down or derelict brownfield sites have been redeveloped with new homes and businesses. People are moving back into the inner-city – a process known as re-urbanisation.

Urban renewal in Ipswich

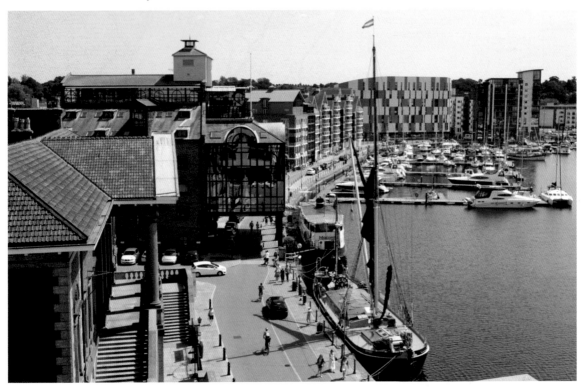

▲ **Figure 22** A view of Ipswich waterfront from one of the blocks of flats.

Ipswich is one of the fastest growing towns in the UK. Like many of the towns and cities in the South East, Ipswich is partly growing through natural population increase but also through significant inward migration of people.

Ipswich Waterfront development is the biggest urban renewal project in the East of England. The site was formerly an industrial dock area with warehouses and factories, but it had become increasingly derelict since the 1970s. Ipswich Borough Council worked in partnership with a number of developers to renew this brownfield site. Old warehouses have been refurbished and turned into shops, restaurants and flats. A range of new buildings has been constructed for homes, leisure use and education. Sadly, due to the economic crash of 2009, the project has not been entirely

successful. Cranfield Mill, a 23-storey block remained unfinished in 2015. The development company owed money to the banks and could not afford to complete the building. Ipswich Council hopes to buy the building and work with a new building firm to complete the project. When finished, it will contain 300 flats, offices, shops and restaurants.

Activities

1 Study Figure 22. Write a 100-word description of this distinctive urban landscape.
2 a) Represent the data shown in Figure 23.
   b) What factors create the need for so many new dwellings in Ipswich?

	Population			Estimated number of new dwellings required
	2001 Census	2021 (predicted)	Change	
Suffolk as a whole	670,200	733,600	+ 63,400	61,700
Ipswich	117,400	138,700	+ 21,300	15,400

▲ **Figure 23** Population growth of Ipswich and housing need.

Some derelict sites were contaminated by waste from their former industrial use. For example, the Orwell Gasworks Quay was the site of a town gasworks where coal had been converted to gas. The land was polluted and it cost up to £270,000 per hectare to remove the waste and make it safe.

Anglo-Saxons lived here in the seventh century so archaeological surveys had to be carried out. Remains of historical value had to be conserved. This cost £1.2 million per hectare.

The ground is mainly soft sands and gravels deposited at the end of the ice age. This means that the foundations for new buildings had to be driven deep into the ground, which was expensive.

The site is next to a tidal estuary. Flood defences had to be built to protect central Ipswich from tidal floods. These cost £53 million. They protect 10 hectares of brownfield land which could not have been redeveloped without these flood defences.

Buildings of historical interest, such as old warehouses, had to be conserved and modernised. This was more expensive than building new homes and offices.

Building on greenfield sites on the edge of Ipswich may have been cheaper but it leads to urban sprawl. As our towns grow larger, this creates more transport problems as people have to commute further to work.

If we fill in the empty spaces in our towns and cities with pockets of new housing then the city doesn't grow any larger and people can live close to their work and leisure facilities in the city centre.

▲ **Figure 24** Advantages and disadvantages of developing the waterfront sites in Ipswich.

The location is superb. I can walk to my office in the town centre in minutes and I no longer need to use my car during the week.

I have all the entertainment I need on my doorstep. The bars are lively at night and on a sunny day you can sit and watch the activity in the marina while enjoying a coffee with friends.

▲ **Figure 25** The views of residents.

▲ **Figure 26** The medieval street pattern, narrow roads and old sewers are under pressure as the waterfront development has created more traffic in this area of the inner city.

Activities

3   Study Figures 24, 25 and 26. Use information from these resources to complete a table like the one below. You will write more in some boxes than others.

	Advantages of using brownfield sites	Disadvantages of using brownfield sites
Economic		
Environmental		
Social		

4   Use Figure 15, page 73, to explain why developing a brownfield site is often more sustainable than developing a greenfield site.

Enquiry

For a new housing or other urban development close to your school, design a table which has two columns featuring positive and negative aspects of the scheme. Try to consider social, economic and environmental factors when you review the successes and failures of the scheme.

Where does retailing occur in UK towns and cities?

The **Central Business District (CBD)** is the traditional town centre location for a wide range of shops and services. Roads spread out from the CBD like arteries in the human body. These arterial roads give shops in the CBD access to a large catchment area and threshold population. By comparison, district shopping centres located in the suburbs of a larger city tend to have a much smaller range of shops. These are usually convenience stores such as small supermarkets, cafés or hairdressers whose catchment area is the immediate neighbourhood. Two other shop locations are common in the UK:

- Shopping centres, or malls, are usually located in the town or city centre. Covered shopping centres have a variety of shops under one roof.
- Retail parks are usually located in out-of-town locations close to arterial roads or the ring roads that circle our towns and cities.

- Consumers can visit several shops, usually chain stores, while under one roof.
- Large department stores may be a feature of this location.
- Limited parking can be a problem, especially on busy roads.
- Parking close to the shops may be expensive or difficult to find.
- Large surface car parks are usually free.
- Good road links makes access easy.
- Shops cater for ethnic groups.
- Large supermarkets and superstores selling furniture or electrical items are common.
- Newsagents, off-licences and takeaways are all common.
- There may be a lot of 'pound shops' and charity shops.

▲ **Figure 27** Features of retail locations in UK towns and cities.

▲ **Figure 28** Map of retail locations in the cities of Stoke-on-Trent and Newcastle-under-Lyme.

Activity

1 Study Figure 28.
   a) Describe the distribution of (i) Tesco and (ii) Sainsbury's supermarkets.
   b) Suggest reasons for these locations.
   c) Tesco has a number of smaller 'Express' stores in this area. Predict where they might be located. Justify your prediction.

www.aldi.co.uk/storelocator

This page on the Aldi supermarket site allows customers to search for their nearest store using an interactive map. Tesco, Morrisons, Sainsbury's and Asda have similar sites. Use a search engine to search for the supermarket and add the words 'store locator'.

▲ **Figure 29** Festival Park, an out-of-town retail park in Stoke-on-Trent.

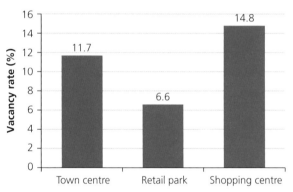

▲ **Figure 30** UK shop vacancy rates. This graph shows the percentage of empty shops in three different locations (2015).

Activities

2 Consider how the site and location of Festival Park might give advantages to retailers there.
 a) Use Figure 28 to consider the advantages of this location.
 b) Use Figure 29 to consider the advantages of this site.

3 Discuss the advantages and disadvantages for the consumer of each retail location before completing the following table. Figure 27 will give you some ideas.

Retail location	Advantages	Disadvantages
Town centre high street locations		
Town centre shopping centres		
District/suburban shopping centres		
Out-of-town retail sites		

4 Use Figure 30 to compare vacancy rates across these three locations. Can you suggest why they might vary so much?

Enquiry

How well are the smaller towns, such as Burslem and Tunstall, served by the supermarket chains?

■ Use the Aldi, Asda and Morrisons store locators on the internet to find the location of other supermarkets in the area covered by Figure 28. You could create a sketch map to show all supermarket locations.

■ Analyse the pattern made by the supermarkets on your sketch map. How well do you think independent grocers and butchers are coping in this urban area?

How is technology changing how and where we shop?

In the past ten years there has been a rapid increase in the number of people who buy their clothes, furniture, groceries, music or books online. Clothes are the most popular item that is bought online, followed closely by household goods such as furniture, computers or TVs. However, it's not just the online sales of goods that affect our high street shops. We also like to pay for our train journeys, flights and holidays online, with 37 per cent of all travel arrangements now being made online rather than in a high street travel agent. Managing your bank account online is easy and more convenient than visiting a high street bank. Consequently, as more people bank online, more high street banks have closed their branches.

Factfile: Online shopping

In 2014 almost three-quarters (74 per cent) of all adults reported buying goods or services online. This has risen from 53 per cent in 2008.

About 50 per cent of online browsing for retail items in 2015 was on mobile devices (up from 42 per cent in 2014) and about 25 per cent of purchases are made using mobile devices.

	2011	2012	2013	2014
Food	74.4	86.8	97.8	109.2
Department stores	34.1	41.6	54.1	60.7
Textiles, clothing and footwear	62.8	75.1	85.4	100.1
All online sales	483.0	556.9	643.0	718.7

▲ **Figure 31** Weekly online sales (£ million).

I run a small business selling antiques. I have a shop in a small town and I also have a website. Sales in the shop and website have declined over the last 10 years. I have noticed that a lot of the antique shops that I visit to buy items for my business have closed. I think the main reason is the rise of online auction websites. It's so easy to sell second hand items on one of these sites. You don't need to pay the bills for a shop like rent, electricity or business rates.

I live in a rural area of mid Wales. I was really quite annoyed when my bank closed its local branch. It forced me to start banking online. I admit that banking online is convenient. I can check my account whenever I want. But I worry about online security and the internet connection where I live isn't brilliant. Also, if I need advice, it's a 25 mile round trip to see my bank manager!

▲ **Figure 32** Points of view on the rise in online services.

Activities

1 Study Figure 31. Draw a series of graphs to show how each type of shopping has changed.
2 List the positive and negative impacts of online shopping for goods and services. Consider the social, economic and environmental impacts.
3 Use Figures 33 and 34.
   a) Describe each graph and compare the similarities and differences.
   b) Suggest how Tesco might use this information.
   c) Suggest how you could use this information if you were doing fieldwork into consumer shopping patterns.

1 a.m.   3 a.m.   6 a.m.   9 a.m.   noon   3 p.m.   6 p.m.   9 p.m.

▲ **Figure 33** Footfall in Tesco Extra in Hanley on Fridays.

1 a.m.   3 a.m.   6 a.m.   9 a.m.   noon   3 p.m.   6 p.m.   9 p.m.

▲ **Figure 34** Footfall in Tesco Extra in Hanley on Saturdays.

 www.google.co.uk

Use the Google search engine to search for 'Tesco' and the name of your nearest town. The search engine will display footfall for each day of the week for its stores that are open for 24 hours a day.

24-hour opening and online groceries

The way we shop is changing. We expect to be able to go shopping 24/7 – either from the comfort of home, or by visiting a large store that is open 24 hours a day. The rise of 24-hour shopping for groceries has created a new set of logistical problems for the supermarkets. How do you get perishable goods to the customer quickly and efficiently? The answer is to have effective distribution services that can take advantage of the UK's motorway network. Morrisons has a total of 143 acres of warehouse space – similar in size to 81 football pitches.

Morrisons' expansion into the south of the UK

Morrisons is the UK's fourth largest supermarket chain. It has 500 supermarkets and 150 smaller 'M' convenience stores. The company began in Yorkshire and up until 2004 most of its stores were in the north of England. At that point the company bought Safeway and expanded its stores into locations in the south of England. It needed to improve its distribution system so that it could supply its new stores. Two new distribution centres were built in Sittingbourne (in the South-East) and Bridgwater (in the South West).

Factfile: Morrisons

1889 – William Morrison begins selling eggs and butter on a market stall in Bradford.

1961 – Morrisons' first supermarket opens in Bradford.

1988 – The first distribution centre opens close to Junction 41 of the M1 motorway to allow Morrisons to expand beyond Bradford.

2004 – Morrisons buys Safeways.

2011 – Morrisons opens a new distribution centre at Bridgwater in Somerset.

▲ **Figure 35** Morrisons regional distribution centres and manufacturing plants.

Activities

4 Use Figure 35 to compare the pattern made by Morrisons' distribution centres and its manufacturing plants.
5 Using Figure 35:
 a) Describe the location of the Bridgwater Distribution Centre.
 b) Explain why Morrisons chose this location for a new distribution centre after 2004.

Enquiry

Conduct a survey within your class and at home to find out the online shopping habits in your area. Discuss the questions you need to ask collectively, to enable you to build up a picture of who is buying online and what they are buying.

The high street fights back

The past twenty years have seen high streets in UK towns and cities undergoing rapid change. Town planners and high street retailers have had to adapt to threats from both out-of-town retailing and online shopping. The high street has fought back to improve the quality of the urban environment for shoppers. A variety of strategies have been used to win back high street shoppers. Some schemes have provided safer streets for pedestrians by restricting access for cars or adding more CCTV cameras. Local councils have worked with developers to create covered shopping malls where it doesn't matter if it's raining outside!

The city centre of Lancaster has recently been improved with new paving in some pedestrianised streets and better street furniture using high quality, strong materials. Changes to road layouts meant that old signposts were confusing. New wayfinding (or signage) information has been installed for shoppers and visitors to the town. A camera was also installed to measure footfall – the number of pedestrians in key locations. It proves that 185,000 people use the city centre each week and that Wednesday is the most popular day – which is market day. This would seem to prove that people still like to shop from independent traders as well as the big chain stores.

▲ **Figure 36** New wayfinding information was installed in Lancaster in 2015.

Activities

1 Study Figure 37 carefully. Write an annotation for each of the features that has a number. Use your annotation to explain how this improves the environment for shoppers.
2 Explain how the features shown in Figures 37 and 38 can improve the quality of the retail environment.

▲ **Figure 37** The high street environment in Lancaster.

▲ **Figure 38** French market in Oswestry.

GEOGRAPHICAL SKILLS

Diamond ranking

Diamond ranking, or diamond nine, is a useful technique to use when you have been asked to make a decision. Sometimes it's not easy to try to rank or prioritise ideas when there is no obvious answer. Use this technique to group your ideas, putting your favourite ideas near the top, and the ones you think are less convincing at the bottom of the diamond.

> ### Enquiry
>
> What are the best strategies for improving the retail environment?
>
> Study the strategies in Figure 39.
>
> a) Make a diamond nine diagram and place the strategies in the diagram, putting those that you think are essential at the top of the diagram.
> b) Justify your choice of the top three strategies by explaining how they will benefit the experience of shoppers and improve the economy of the high street.

Pedestrianised shopping streets	Traffic calming such as ramps and pinch points	Permitting street entertainment such as buskers
Improving signs and wayfinding information for pedestrians	Providing street furniture such as flower beds and benches	Reducing the cost of short-stay parking
Creating park-and-ride schemes	Special high street events such as French or Christmas markets	Allowing pop-up shops to sell from vacant shops

▲ **Figure 39** Strategies to improve the high street.

Does each town centre need its own distinct identity?

Each town's identity is created by the mixture of features that give it its own character. A town's identity is what gives it its unique sense of place. Many are concerned that a town loses its identity when locally owned independent shops are replaced by shops that are part of a national chain.

Bailey Street (left side)
Timpson – dry cleaning and key cutting
Radio – café
VACANT
Shades – curtains/fabrics
The Flower Gallery – florists
The Oak Furniture Shop – beds and furniture
Polka Dot – travel agent
RJ Christian – jewellers
The Works – book shop

Bailey Street

Bailey Street (right side)
Bailey's – café and bakery
Age UK – charity shop
Cascade – amusement arcade
Pound Stretcher – discount shop
Card Factory – greeting cards
Specsavers – opticians

▲ **Figure 40** A simple way to record shops. Note that the photographs in Figure 42 were taken in the same street.

Clone town

The clone town survey is part of a national survey to identify the number of independent shops that are left in the UK's high streets. It is a measure of the range of different types of shop (diversity) and of the proportion of independent shops compared to chain stores (identity). Follow these steps to calculate a 'clone town' score.

Step 1 Use a recording sheet like Figure 43 to survey between 40 and 60 shops.

Step 2 Find the total number of **types** of shop in your survey and the total number of **independently** owned shops in your table.

Step 3 Multiply the total number of independently owned shops by 75, then divide this by the total number of shops in your survey.

Step 4 Add the total number of types of shop to the figure you found in Step 3. This gives your clone town score. Scores below 50 are clone towns. Scores above 65 have a good diversity of shops and enough independent shops to give the town identity.

▲ **Figure 41** Clone town score.

▲ **Figure 42** Shops on Bailey Street, Oswestry, Shropshire. Bailey Street is pedestrianised. It has not been photographed on Google Street View.

Type of shop	Independently owned ✓	Part of a chain ✓
Food (butcher, baker, supermarket)		
Newsagent/tobacconist		
Books/stationery		
Department/catalogue store		
Pub/bar		
Off-licence		
Professional e.g. insurance/accountancy		
Estate agent		
Healthcare/pharmacy/optician		
Household goods (furniture, kitchen)		
Clothes/shoes		
Cinema/theatre		
Electronic/IT, e.g. phones, computers		
Pets/pet supplies/vet		
Hair salon/beauty treatment		
Toys/sports/cycling/outdoor leisure		
Car accessories/petrol		
Builders merchant/DIY store		
Florist/garden centre		
Dry cleaning/launderette		
Travel agent		
Camera/photo processing		
Post Office		
Other, e.g. betting, amusements, antiques, charity shops, jewellers		
TOTAL		

▲ **Figure 43** Clone town survey recording sheet.

Activities

1 Study Figure 42.
   a) Identify one feature that gives this street an identity.
   b) Use Figures 40 and 43 to help you create a tally chart for the shops in Figure 42. In your tally chart, you should identify:
      i) the number of independently owned shops
      ii) the number of different types of shop.
2 Use Google Street View to complete a virtual clone town survey of Oswestry. You can add your results to Figure 43. This means that you will need to classify between 25 and 45 shops.
3 Discuss the features that give your local town centre an identity of its own.
   a) List three features of the built environment and three features of the human environment that create identity.
   b) To what extent do you agree that it is important for town centres to have their own identity? Why does this issue seem to be important?

Enquiry

Create an enquiry that could be used to investigate perceptions of identity in your own town centre. Your plan should include:

■ an overarching enquiry question
■ your sampling strategy
■ ideas for how you would gather both quantitative and qualitative data (see page 8).

What are the global patterns of urbanisation?

Over half (54 per cent) of the world's population lives in cities. But it's not always been this way. At the start of the twentieth century most of the world's population lived in the countryside or smaller towns. During the second half of the twentieth century the population of the world's cities, and the physical size of their built-up areas, grew – a process known as **urbanisation**. This process was particularly rapid in the cities of the **newly industrialised countries** (NICs) of Asia and Latin America. Urbanisation has been due to a combination of:

- migration from rural to urban areas
- the natural increase of the population when there are more births than deaths each year.

Figure 2 shows a list of the world's largest cities. Cities with over 10 million residents are sometimes known as **mega-cities**. In 2015 there were 28 mega-cities and 16 of these are located in Asia and only three in Europe. There are 498 cities in the world with a population greater than one million. Of these, 101 are in China and 57 are in India. The UK has only five cities with a population of over one million.

Newly industrialised countries (NICs)

NICs are characterised by: rapid urban growth; growth of the manufacturing sector of the economy; strong trading relationships with other countries; and the operation of foreign-owned multi-national companies (MNCs) within the country.

◀ **Figure 1** The centre of Mumbai, India. The neighbourhood of Bhendi Bazaar is in the foreground. The low-rise buildings in this neighbourhood are traditional dormitories known as chawls.

1990		2015		2030	
Tokyo, Japan	32.53	Tokyo, Japan	38.00	Tokyo, Japan	37.19
Osaka, Japan	18.39	Delhi, India	25.70	Delhi, India	36.06
New York–Newark, USA	16.09	Shanghai, China	23.74	Shanghai, China	30.75
Ciudad de México (Mexico City)	15.64	São Paulo, Brazil	21.07	Mumbai, India	27.80
São Paulo, Brazil	14.78	Mumbai, India	21.04	Beijing, China	27.71
Mumbai, India	12.44	Ciudad de México (Mexico City)	21.00	Dhaka, Bangladesh	27.37
Kolkata, India	10.89	Beijing, China	20.38	Karachi, Pakistan	24.84
Los Angeles–Long Beach-Santa Ana, USA	10.88	Osaka, Japan	20.24	Cairo, Egypt	24.50
Seoul, South Korea	10.52	Cairo, Egypt	18.77	Lagos, Nigeria	24.24
Buenos Aires, Argentina	10.51	New York–Newark, USA	18.59	Ciudad de México (Mexico City)	23.86

▲ **Figure 2** The world's ten largest mega-cities, population in millions.

What will happen next?

The world's urban population is expected to rise from 3.9 billion (in 2014) to 6.0 billion by 2045. The largest urban growth is expected to be in India, China and Nigeria where an extra 404 million, 292 million and 212 million urban dwellers will be added respectively by 2050. The fastest growing cities are not mega-cities but those with a population under 500,000. Many of the world's fastest growing cities are expected to be in sub-Saharan Africa and Asia.

Region	1990–95 (%)	2015–20 (%)	2045–50 (%)
Sub-Saharan Africa	4.09	3.83	2.78
East Asia (including China)	3.28	1.91	-0.06
South Asia (including India)	2.95	2.40	1.37
Western Europe	0.78	0.47	0.12
South America	2.43	1.16	0.36

▲ **Figure 4** Average annual rate of change of the urban population (per cent).

Year	Mumbai, India	Kinshasa, DRC
1950	2.86	0.20
1960	4.06	0.44
1970	5.81	1.07
1980	8.66	2.05
1990	12.44	3.68
2000	16.37	6.14
2010	19.42	9.38
2020	22.84	14.12
2030	27.80	20.00

▲ **Figure 3** Population (millions) of Mumbai, India and Kinshasa, Democratic Republic of Congo (DRC), which is one of Africa's fastest growing cities.

Enquiry

What is the geographical future for urban areas around the world?
- Represent the data in Figure 4. A good way to do this would be to draw proportional bars on an outline map of the world.
- Use your map to write a 200-word report. Make sure that you contrast the rates of urban growth in different regions of the world.

Activities

1 Write definitions for the following terms:
   urbanisation   mega-cities   NICs
2 Study Figure 2.
   a) Choose a suitable graph to present this data.
   b) Describe what has happened to the distribution of the world's largest cities.
3 Study Figure 3.
   a) Draw a pair of line graphs to represent the growth of these two cities.
   b) Describe the similarities and differences of these two graphs.
4 Is rapid urbanisation a good thing? Predict the possible consequences of rapid population growth in a city such as Kinshasa, which is in a Low Income Country (LIC). You should consider the advantages and disadvantages.

So what are global cities?

All cities have a regional influence. They interact with the area that surrounds them, for example:

- attracting daily commuters to work
- providing specialist services such as hospitals and universities
- acting as transport hubs for rail networks or regional airports.

However, some cities have greater influence than others. **Global cities** are those cities which interact with other places at the global scale. Figure 5 illustrates some of these global connections. The Globalisation and World Cities Research Network has identified over 300 cities that have inter-connections with other parts of the globe. The UK has 13 global cities. London is ranked first but the next highest in the UK is Manchester at 78th. Cardiff is in 248th place. Figure 6 shows those Global Cities that have the most important global connections.

Globalisation

The process of **globalisation** connects places economically, socially, politically or culturally. Global cities play an important role in this process. Cities have always been connected by trade and migration. However, as communications and transport improve, the process is accelerating. It is as though the world is shrinking as it becomes better connected and places become less isolated.

Migration and culture:
Global cities attract economic migrants from all over the world. Migration leads to cultural diversity. More than 100 languages are spoken in 30 of London's 33 boroughs. The 2011 Census showed that 22 percent of London's residents do not speak English as their main language. That's just over 1.7 million people.

Finance and trade:
The world's most important global cities are financial centres. Banks have their head offices here. Dealers working at financial markets like FTSE buy and sell commodities on the world markets.

Transport hubs:
The top global cities are all well-connected to the rest of the world by major airports or ports. These allow the flow of people, tourists and trade. About 1,400 flights take off or land at London's Heathrow airport every day.

Governance and decision making:
Business managers in one city can make decisions that affect people worldwide. For example, Tata is an Indian TNC with its headquarters in Mumbai and businesses in over 100 countries. Politicians and civil servants can also have worldwide decision-making roles. The UN employs 41,000 people. 6,389 are based in their headquarters in New York.

Ideas and information:
Many of the world's global cities are the home for major broadcasting companies. Newspapers, TV stations and filmmakers are based in global cities. BBC World News is an international TV channel broadcasting 24 hours a day to over 300 million households in 200 countries.

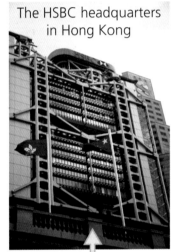

The HSBC headquarters in Hong Kong

Global cities

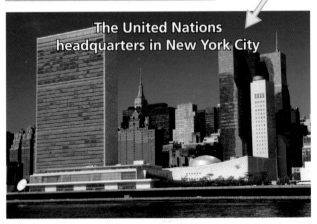

The United Nations headquarters in New York City

New Broadcasting House in London

▲ **Figure 5** How global cities connect to the rest of the world.

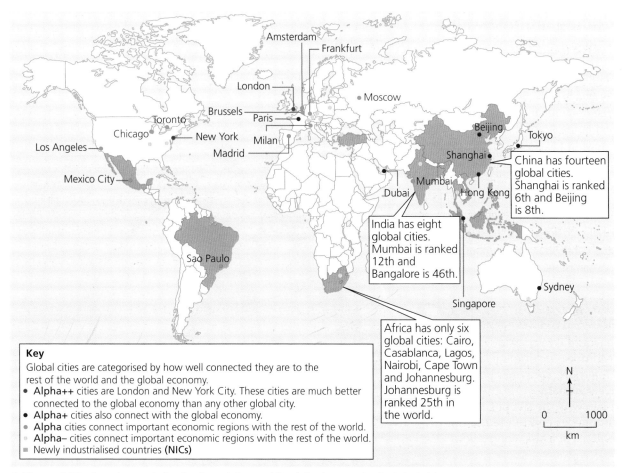

Key

Global cities are categorised by how well connected they are to the rest of the world and the global economy.

- **Alpha++** cities are London and New York City. These cities are much better connected to the global economy than any other global city.
- **Alpha+** cities also connect with the global economy.
- **Alpha** cities connect important economic regions with the rest of the world.
- **Alpha–** cities connect important economic regions with the rest of the world.
- Newly industrialised countries (**NICs**)

Map labels: Amsterdam, Frankfurt, London, Brussels, Paris, Toronto, Chicago, New York, Milan, Los Angeles, Madrid, Mexico City, Moscow, Beijing, Tokyo, Shanghai, Mumbai, Dubai, Hong Kong, Sao Paulo, Singapore, Sydney

China has fourteen global cities. Shanghai is ranked 6th and Beijing is 8th.

India has eight global cities. Mumbai is ranked 12th and Bangalore is 46th.

Africa has only six global cities: Cairo, Casablanca, Lagos, Nairobi, Cape Town and Johannesburg. Johannesburg is ranked 25th in the world.

N
0   1000
km

▲ **Figure 6** The location and distribution of the world's alpha (top-ranked) global cities.

Year	Population
1950	8.36
1960	8.19
1970	7.51
1980	7.66
1990	8.05
2000	8.61
2010	9.70
2020	10.85
2030	11.47

▲ **Figure 7** Population (millions) of London, the top-ranked global city.

Activities

1 Explain the difference between mega-cities and global cities. Make sure that you give examples of cities that fall into both categories by using Figures 2 and 6.

2 Study Figure 6.
   a) Describe the distribution of the world's alpha++ and alpha+ cities.
   b) What percentage of global cities shown on Figure 6 are located in NICs?
   c) Suggest why there are so many global cities in India and China.

3 a) Use the data in Figure 7 to draw a line graph of London's population growth.
   b) Use your graph to estimate the year in which London became a mega-city.
   c) Compare and contrast London's population growth to that of Mumbai and Kinshasa (shown in Figure 3 on page 87).

Enquiry

Why do you think London is the world's most important global city? Make a list of ten ways that London is:

- connected to other parts of the UK
- interconnected with other parts of the world.

Introducing Mumbai: an Indian mega-city

Mumbai is India's largest city with a population of 18.4 million in 2015. The city of Greater Mumbai is built on a low-lying island in the Arabian Sea. As the city has grown it has sprawled northwards and eastwards across Thane Creek to form a large metropolitan region. 465 km of suburban railway links Central Mumbai to its suburbs on the mainland. However, there are only four rail crossings onto the island and this creates congestion for Mumbai's daily 7.5 million commuters.

Activities

1 Use Figure 8 to draw a sketch map of Mumbai. Include the city centre, CST, airport, container port and Navi Mumbai.
2 Explain why the site of Greater Mumbai has contributed to the problems of traffic congestion.

Key

- Densely populated urban areas
- Areas into which Mumbai is expanding
- Railway lines

▲ **Figure 8** The Metropolitan Region of Mumbai.

◄ **Figure 9** Crowded platforms in Chhatrapati Shivaji Terminus (CST) in Mumbai's city centre. Double platforms allow passengers to board trains quickly from each side.

Transport issues – an inevitable consequence of rapid growth?

Large cities like Mumbai need efficient **mass transit** or (rapid transit) systems so that commuters can get into work quickly and safely. Mumbai's rail system is one of the busiest in the world. At peak times trains carry three times the number of passengers they were designed for. People hang from doorways and even ride on the train's roof. Overcrowding is more than just uncomfortable – it is dangerous. People die when they fall from trains or are hit when they are crossing the tracks. At least nine people are killed every day on Mumbai's railways. How can the system be improved? Trains run every three minutes at peak times. It may not be possible to add any more trains without risking accidents.

Encourage businesses to offer flexi-hours instead of regular 9a.m.–5p.m. hours.
Reserve more seats on trains for elderly passengers.
Improve toilet facilities.
Prevent people from travelling on the roofs of trains.
Remove fast food kiosks and other vendors from all platforms.
Increase platform length.
Improve ventilation in carriages.
Demolish informal housing next to railway tracks.
Fit proper doors to all trains so passengers cannot travel half-in and half-out.

▲ **Figure 10** Possible ways to improve Mumbai's rail system.

◄ **Figure 11** Many people live dangerously close to Mumbai's railways in informal housing.

Activities

3 a) Discuss the ideas in Figure 10. Explain the best ways to improve the following:
   i)   rail safety
   ii) passenger comfort
   iii) train times.
   b) Use a diamond nine technique (see page 83) to rank all nine ideas. Which three do you think should be given the highest priority to improve services? Justify your choice.

4 Explain why demolishing informal housing next to railway lines could:
   a) improve rail safety
   b) improve train times.

5 Study Figure 11.
   a) Describe the buildings in this neighbourhood.
   b) Suggest three ways that people who live here are affected by the quality of their environment.

Why has Mumbai grown?

We saw on page 87 how quickly Mumbai's population has grown. Like other Indian cities, Mumbai has grown due to a combination of **natural increase** and **rural to urban migration**.

Natural increase of Mumbai's population

Natural increase is the growth of population that occurs when there are more births than deaths. Natural increase has been the main reason for Mumbai's growth during the twentieth century. One simple way to investigate this is to examine average family size, a statistic which is known as **fertility rate**. If women, on average, have more than two children, then the population will grow. Fertility rates in Mumbai tend to be slightly lower than in rural areas of Maharashtra. In 2007, the fertility rate was:

- 2.2 in rural areas of Maharashtra
- 1.8 in urban areas of the state.

Year (or period)	Fertility rate
Average 1974–82	4.03
Average 1984–90	3.45
Average 1994–2000	2.60
2004	2.20
2010	2.00
2013	1.80

▲ **Figure 12** Changing fertility rates in Maharashtra.

What push/pull factors explain rural to urban migration in Maharashtra?

India's rail system has some of the lowest fares in the world. It costs only 250 rupees (about £2.50) to travel from Kolkata to Mumbai. Cheap rail travel is one **pull factor** that encourages migration to Mumbai. People living in rural areas of India are attracted by the jobs and better training opportunities available in cities such as Mumbai. Poverty, the poor standard of housing, health care and sanitation are all **push factors** that can force people to move away from rural areas.

◀ **Figure 13** Migrant flows into Mumbai from other Indian states.

Factfile: Why do people move to Mumbai?

Out of 1,000 people who were interviewed about why they moved to Mumbai:

- 538 moved because of marriage
- 187 moved because a family member/parent moved
- 173 moved to find work
- 35 moved to improve their education/attend university
- 62% of males gave work or business-related reasons
- 80% of females moved to marry or accompany a family member.

◄ **Figure 14** Where do migrants to Mumbai come from?

from rural areas within Maharashtra

from rural areas outside Maharashtra

from urban areas within Maharashtra

from urban areas outside Maharashtra

Name of Indian state	Number of households	Number of households with no bathroom	Number of households with a computer
Maharashtra	23,830,580	3,478,681	3,174,031
Uttar Pradesh	32,924,266	14,761,001	2,664,447
Gujarat	12,181,718	3,967,358	1,077,510
Karnataka	13,179,911	1,807,662	1,692,253
Rajasthan	12,581,303	5,595,753	869,923
Bihar	18,940,629	11,849,779	1,334,565
Tamil Nadu	18,493,003	6,625,321	1,956,630
Andhra Pradesh	21,024534	6,910,308	1,763,555
Kerala	7,716,370	1,097,456	1,214,644
West Bengal	20,067,299	12,869,502	1,668,757

▲ **Figure 15** Selected data for the Indian states which are the source of Mumbai's migrant population.

GEOGRAPHICAL SKILLS

Calculating percentages from raw data

The census data in Figure 15 is **raw data**, meaning data that has not been processed. It would be interesting to see whether poverty in Uttar Pradesh is a push factor. For example, are there more households in Uttar Pradesh than Maharashtra that do not have a bathroom? To make a comparison we need to process the raw data to find the percentage of homes that have no bathroom. You do this by dividing the number of households with no bathroom by the total number of households in that state and then multiplying by 100. For Uttar Pradesh this would be:

$14,761,001 \div 32,924,266 = 0.4483$

$0.4483 \times 100 = 44.83\%$

Activities

2 a) List five facts about the origin of Mumbai's migrants.
   b) In African countries, most migrants only move short distances. To what extent is this true in India?

3 Describe the main push and pull factors for migration to Mumbai.

Enquiry

Is poverty a push factor in rural to urban migration?

- Process the data in Figure 15 into percentage figures.
- Draw a scattergraph to show the percentage of migrants (shown in Figure 13) on the vertical axis and the percentage of households with no bathroom on the horizontal axis.
- Comment on the trend shown by your scattergraph. What conclusions can you draw?

Why is Mumbai a global city?

Mumbai's economy is well connected to other locations both within India and abroad:

- The Hindi film industry, known as Bollywood, is based in Mumbai and is thought to employ 175,000 people.
- Tata Steel, which employs people in over 100 countries, has its headquarters in Mumbai.
- Nhava Sheva is India's largest container port. Goods made in India can be shipped to Felixstowe, via the Suez Canal, in nineteen days. Container ships from Kolkata, on India's east coast, take 28 days. This gives Mumbai a clear advantage in its global rankings.
- Mumbai International Airport is well placed to fly businessmen and women between Europe, the Middle East and Asia. London is nine hours, Dubai three hours and Hong Kong six hours by air.

Activities

1 a) Use a suitable technique to represent the data in Figure 16.
   b) Suggest what this tells you about the value of Bollywood to people living and working in Mumbai.
2 Explain why the location of Mumbai has given the city an economic advantage over Kolkata and Chennai in its global rankings.

Film producer	Gross box office revenue (US$ billion)	Number of films produced per year	Number of tickets sold per year (millions)
USA	10.8	476	1,358
China	2.74	745	470
Japan	2.45	554	155
India	1.59	1,602	2,641

▲ **Figure 16** Global film: figures for the world's four largest film-making nations.

▲ **Figure 17** Rohit Suri, Vice President of Jaguar and Land Rover India, a subsidiary company owned by Tata Steel; he is posing with a Jaguar F-type in Mumbai when the car was launched in 2013.

Key
- ● Headquarters and main offices
- ● Sales office
- ○ Projects
- ● Plants and mines

Tata employs 40,000 people making steel at Jamshedpur

▲ **Figure 18** The location and distribution of Tata Steel in India.

Mumbai: formal or informal occupations?

An **emerging middle class** of young, professional, well-paid men and women is creating urban and economic change in India. Many are young graduates who left rural lives behind when they went to university in a city like Mumbai. They take jobs in central and state government, banking and financial industries, the IT industry, textile manufacturing, jobs related to the sea port, and the Hindi movie industry. These are all **formal occupations** that receive a regular wage. However, Mumbai's economy also has a very large **informal sector**. Street vending, rickshaw driving and recycling waste are all examples of informal jobs. These jobs are not regulated by the state. You don't necessarily need a qualification to do them and you probably don't pay tax. However, informal jobs have no paid holidays, pensions or sickness benefits, and there are no rules to protect your health and safety at work.

Mumbai is a city of huge contrasts between rich and poor. It is said to have the third most expensive office space in the world. It is also home to millions of people living in poverty. Informal housing occupies seven per cent of Mumbai but houses 60 per cent of its population, so it is extremely overcrowded. These slums develop on unwanted land: marshland that is vulnerable to flooding during the monsoon or alongside busy railway tracks. Dharavi is on such an informal settlement – it recycles Mumbai's rubbish.

▲ **Figure 19** A young ragpicker in Dharavi, one of Mumbai's slums. Sorting recycled plastics is an example of an informal occupation; ragpickers recycle 80 per cent of Mumbai's waste and together contribute around £700 million to Mumbai's economy each year.

Activities

3 Suggest how each of the following is creating urban and economic growth in India:
   a) low wages in rural occupations
   b) university education
   c) demand for consumer goods
   d) the emerging middle class.
4 Study Figure 20. Explain why poverty in the informal sector may prevent India from:
   a) developing greater wealth in the economy
   b) improving education, training and health care facilities
5 Using Figure 19 to help you, suggest how the informal sector helps to support Mumbai's growing economy.

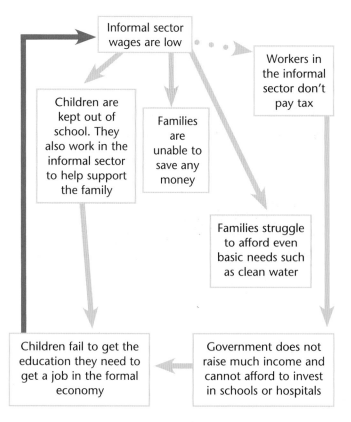

Informal sector wages are low

Workers in the informal sector don't pay tax

Children are kept out of school. They also work in the informal sector to help support the family

Families are unable to save any money

Families struggle to afford even basic needs such as clean water

Children fail to get the education they need to get a job in the formal economy

Government does not raise much income and cannot afford to invest in schools or hospitals

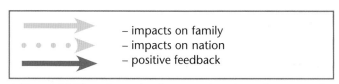
– impacts on family
– impacts on nation
– positive feedback

▲ **Figure 20** The relationship between the informal sector and the wider economy.

What are Mumbai's housing problems?

Overcrowding, poor sanitation and homes that are in danger of collapse, flooding or fire – these are some of the issues facing the urban poor of Mumbai. There are three types of housing where occupants are at risk because of the poor conditions:

- **Chawls** are a type of four- or five-storey tenement building. Families live in single rooms arranged along a corridor. Basic toilet facilities are shared by the tenants on each corridor. Many chawls were built between 1920 and 1956. They are overcrowded and poorly ventilated. But they are affordable.

- **Squatter homes**, also known as **slums** in India, are simple single or two-storey buildings built without planning control. Sanitation is very poor: 73 per cent of residents share communal latrines.
- **Pavement dwellers**, many of whom are children, live in huts which narrow the pavement. Pavement dwellers pay rent to criminals who control the pavements. The structures are illegal and may be demolished by the authorities.

Opinions vary about how these issues can be solved. Some people believe that **self-help** projects can improve housing or sanitation. Others think that **wholesale clearance** and redevelopment are the best solutions. Which is the most sustainable solution?

◀ **Figure 21** Traditional chawl tenements in Bhendi Bazaar that will be demolished.

▼ **Figure 22** Market traders in Bhendi Bazaar.

Activities

1 Use Figure 8 on page 90 to describe the location of Bhendi Bazaar.
2 Suggest how each of the following might affect the safety and health of local residents:
   a) overcrowding in the chawls
   b) having to share toilet facilities
   c) insecurity of tenure for pavement dwellers.
3 Study Figure 15 on page 73. It shows Egan's Wheel. Explain how each of the following elements of sustainability might be met by the redevelopment of Bhendi Bazaar:
   a) housing and built environment
   b) social and cultural
   c) economy.

Is wholesale clearance and redevelopment the answer?

Bhendi Bazaar is a mixed area of chawls and 1,250 shops and stalls. It is estimated that 20,000 people live here. The chawls are old and overcrowded. There is no proper waste disposal system and water is only supplied for a few hours each day. An ambitious plan will demolish 250 buildings and replace them with 17 high-rise tower blocks. Work started in 2010 and some families have already been moved temporarily into a new tower block in a neighbouring district.

The new development is planned to be sustainable:
- There will be a mixture of houses and shops so people can continue to work locally.
- Wide roads and tree-lined pavements will replace narrow alleyways.
- There will be open spaces for parks, green spaces and play areas.
- Mosques will be retained and enhanced.
- Car parking and connections to public transport are planned.

The aspect of the buildings will make the best use of natural light and ventilation in each home

Solar panels will be used to generate electricity

◀ **Figure 23** Sustainable features of the new multi-storey buildings at Bhendi Bazaar.

Rainwater harvesting

Sewage treatment and water recycling to flush toilets

Air-source heat pumps will use natural heat in the atmosphere to heat water in the tower-block

CCTV will improve safety for tenants

Wide, tree-lined pedestrian areas

Good lighting of communal areas

Activity

4 a) Discuss the strengths and limitations of this redevelopment scheme.
   b) Can you suggest three different ways it could be improved?

My home in Bhendi Bazaar has already been demolished and I now live in the 'transit' housing while I wait to be permanently rehomed. Life is much better here. We have moved into a furnished room. It has a carpet, curtains and a cupboard. There is a small kitchen with hot water and a washing machine. It is so much cleaner and quieter here! My children can play cricket in the open space in front of the tower block. We even have internet connection.

Mariya, tenant of the temporary 'transit' block

I am a street vendor and I sleep in front of one of the shops. Tenants will get a new home. But I am fearful that I will get nothing. There are thousands of pavement dwellers like me who make a living in the street market. If I can no longer live and work here I may have to go back to my village in Uttar Pradesh.

Taha, a second-hand wristwatch seller

Large fire engines cannot get into districts with chawls like Bhendi Bazaar or squatter settlements like Dharavi. We need to buy mini-fire tenders to get into the narrow, congested alleyways. We also need to build new fire stations across the city. Mumbai has only 33 fire stations. It needs at least 100 fire stations to meet global standards.

Aziz, city planner

In 2015 a fire quickly spread through Kalbadevi which is another congested neighbourhood of chawls. Widening of roads is crucial to make the area safer. I understand that the clearance of Bhendi Bazaar will allow them to widen the roads from the current width of 6 to 8 metres to up to 16 metres.

Mohammed, a firefighter

▲ **Figure 24** Opinions on the redevelopment of Bhendi Bazaar.

Introducing Cardiff

Cardiff is the largest city in Wales. We saw on pages 59 and 60 that Cardiff has a strong local sphere of influence. A population of 1.49 million people live within 32 km of Cardiff city centre. Many use the city regularly for work, shopping or entertainment. However, Cardiff's sphere of influence is larger – it also has national and global links. Cardiff is home to the Welsh Government, which has responsibilities for education, health and the economy for the whole of Wales. Cardiff is well connected by rail to London, and flights from Cardiff's airport fly to several European destinations. The Principality (Millennium) Stadium is a world-class sporting and music venue that has hosted international events including the Rugby World Cup in 2015. One large multinational – Admiral, the insurance company – has its main office here. Several BBC TV programmes, including Sherlock and Doctor Who, are filmed on location here and in film studios based in Cardiff. These TV programmes are sold all around the world. These media and cultural links help to place Cardiff on the list of global cities.

Cardiff's growth

Like many cities in the UK, Cardiff went through a period of rapid growth between around 1850 and 1920 as people moved into the city to find work in industries related to the sale of coal from Cardiff Docks. Terraced houses were built to provide homes for these dock workers and many of these homes can still be seen today in the **inner-urban** areas close to the city centre.

During the period from 1930 to the mid-1980s Cardiff went through a phase of **suburban** growth. Better public transport and more widespread car ownership meant that people could live further from their place of work. New housing was built, filling in the spaces between the edge of the city and existing small villages such as Radyr and Whitchurch. These villages are now part of the urban area of Cardiff.

Between the mid-1980s and today, Cardiff has gone through a phase of **re-urbanisation**. This time new housing was built on the brownfield sites once occupied by the dock-related industries in Butetown next to Cardiff Bay.

▲ **Figure 25** The location of Cardiff.

GEOGRAPHICAL SKILLS

Describing locations

To describe a location means to be able to pinpoint something on a map. Describing a location on an Ordnance Survey (OS) map is easily done by giving a grid reference. However, describing a location on a map that has no grid lines requires a different technique.

First, you need to give a broad indication of the location by describing in which part of the map the viewer should be looking. Always use geographical terms such as 'in south Wales' rather than 'at the bottom of the map' or 'near to the Bristol Channel'.

Then, to describe the exact location, you should use another significant place on the map and give:
- the distance from that other place in kilometres
- the direction using points of the compass.

For example, on Figure 25, Bridgend is 28 km to the west of Cardiff.

Enquiry ?

How important is Cardiff as a global city?

Compare Cardiff's global sphere of influence with that of at least one other city in the UK and with Mumbai (page 94). Put these cities into rank order. Explain your decision.

Year	Population
1801	1,870
1851	18,352
1861	48,965
1871	57,363
1881	96,637
1891	128,915
1901	164,333
1911	182,259
1921	222,827
1931	226,937
1941	No data
1951	243,632
1961	283,998
1971	293,220
1981	285,740
1991	296,900
2001	305,353
2011	346,000

▲ **Figure 26** Population of Cardiff.

In 1841, 87,000 tonnes of coal was being shipped from Cardiff Docks. By 1862, the docks were exporting 2 million tonnes of coal each year and, by 1883, this figure had risen to 6 million. The maximum figure was 10.7 million in 1913. By 1946 it had fallen to 1 million tonnes. In 1970, Bute East Dock was closed. In 1980, the M4 was completed to the north of Cardiff.

▲ **Figure 27** Some significant dates in Cardiff's development

Activities

1 a) Identify five links that Cardiff has with the rest of the UK and/or the rest of the world.
   b) Classify these links as economic, political or social.
2 a) Select a suitable method to represent the information in Figure 26.
   b) Describe the changes in Cardiff's population carefully. In which decades did Cardiff's population rise most rapidly and in which did it decrease?
   c) Use the information in Figure 27 to create four labels for your graph. Your labels should help explain why Cardiff's population changed.
3 Study Figure 28. Describe how Cardiff changed between 1920 and the present day. Use the following specialist terms in your answer: suburban sprawl, inner urban and re-urbanisation.

▲ **Figure 28** Cardiff's built-up area; the named neighbourhoods are described in later pages.

Ethnic minorities in Cardiff

Cardiff is a multicultural city. Between 1800 and the 1930s **economic migrants** moved from other European countries and the countries of the British Empire to Cardiff. Many were sailors who worked on the ships that exported coal from South Wales. Most settled in Butetown, close to the docks, in an area that was then called Tiger Bay. Today, a total of 8 per cent of Cardiff's population are members of ethnic minorities. People have settled in the city from over 50 different countries. The two largest communities are descended from South Asian (India, Pakistan and Bangladesh) and Somali migrants.

The Somali population in Cardiff has a population estimated to be a little under 10,000. Most of them live in a relatively small neighbourhood within the inner urban area in the wards of Grangetown and Riverside. Somalis choose to live in this district to be close to other family members. The area has many shops that cater for the Muslim population such as halal butchers and fast food shops that sell food prepared using halal meat. The area has a number of mosques and Muslim cultural centres. This district has a wide variety of different sized houses and flats for rent and sale at a variety of prices.

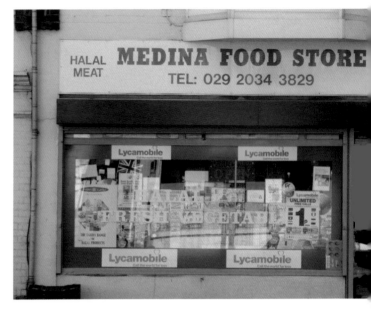

▲ **Figure 29** A shop in Riverside, Cardiff, selling halal meat.

GEOGRAPHICAL SKILLS

Describing distributions

To describe a distribution is to describe how similar things are spread across a map. Geographers are interested in the distribution of natural features such as glaciers, coral reefs and volcanoes; as well as human features such as settlements, hospitals or sporting facilities.

Describing a distribution requires you to do two things.

1 You need to describe where on the map the features are located. For example, of the ten parks marked on Figure 31, the majority are in the northern suburbs of the city and only four are within the inner urban area.
2 Describe any pattern the features might make. Distribution patterns usually fall into one of three types:
   ■ Regular, where the features are more or less equally spaced.
   ■ Random, where the features are scattered across the map at irregular distances from each other.
   ■ Clustered, where the features are grouped together into only one part of the map.

▲ **Figure 30** Distribution patterns.

In addition to this, some features make a **linear** pattern if they all fall along a line. Several parks in Cardiff make a linear pattern. The largest park follows the line of the River Taff as it enters the city in the north and flows southwards towards the city centre. The park makes a green corridor running north-south through the city.

▲ Figure 31 Map showing the distribution of mosques in Cardiff. The white lines show the ward boundaries.

The history of Somali migration to Cardiff

Somali migrants first arrived in Cardiff in the period 1880 to 1900. Many of them worked in the ships that were exporting coal from the docks in Butetown (which was then known as Tiger Bay). At this time Somali seamen settled in other UK ports, as well as Cardiff, such as the London docklands, Bristol, Hull and Liverpool. By 1945 there were around 2,000 Somali sailors and their families living in Cardiff. In 1991 a long civil war began in Somalia. Refugees from this conflict moved first to refugee camps in other African countries such as Kenya and Ethiopia. Eventually some of these people migrated to the UK where they joined the existing Somali community.

Ward	Black	Asian	Mixed ethnicity
Adamsdown	3.4	5.8	3.5
Butetown	13.4	8.1	8.3
Canton	0.8	4.7	1.8
Grangetown	4.2	13.2	3.8
Plasnewydd	1.5	9.5	1.7
Riverside	2.8	15.6	2.4
Splott	1.8	3.3	2.9

Figure 32 Wards with significant ethnic populations.

Activities

1 Match the four distribution patterns shown in Figure 30 to the following terms:
   - random
   - regular
   - linear
   - clustered
2 a) Match the following geographical features to one of the four distribution patterns shown in Figure 30:
   - motorway service stations
   - high street banks in a large town
   - primary schools in a city.
   b) Suggest why these features are distributed in this way.
3 Use Figure 31 to describe the distribution of mosques in Cardiff. Suggest what this map tells you about the distribution of the Muslim population of Cardiff.
4 Use the text on these pages to draw a timeline of Somali migration to Cardiff.
5 Explain why the Somali population of Cardiff is found in a relatively small area of the city. Make sure you give one historical reason and one social reason.

Enquiry

How does Cardiff's growth compare to that of Mumbai?

Consider the importance of natural increase and migration patterns in both cities.

Zones of wealth and poverty

Like all other UK cities, Cardiff has some neighbourhoods where residents have, on average, high incomes while other neighbourhoods have residents with much lower average incomes. Sometimes, these neighbourhoods exist very close to one another. One example is Riverside, an inner urban area which stretches down the western bank of the River Taff in Figure 34.

▲ **Figure 33** Houses in Pontcanna in RIV04, opposite Llandaff Fields (grid reference 164773).

◄ **Figure 34** Extract from an Ordnance Survey map. Scale 1:25,000.

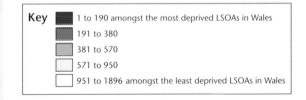

Key
- 1 to 190 amongst the most deprived LSOAs in Wales
- 191 to 380
- 381 to 570
- 571 to 950
- 951 to 1896 amongst the least deprived LSOAs in Wales

▲ **Figure 35** Deprivation in Riverside (2011). There are 1896 Lower Super Output Areas (LSOAs) in Wales. The Welsh Government has put all of these small districts into rank order of deprivation. The map shows five categories of deprivation (by rank order).

ACTIVITY

Activity

1 Study Figure 34.
   a) Match the following grid references to leisure features (i – iii) on the map:
   163776   178766   174770
   i) sport/leisure centre
   ii) Llandaff Fields (public park)
   iii) Bute Park (public gardens).
   b) Suggest how residents of Riverside may be affected by the sphere of influence of each of these features.

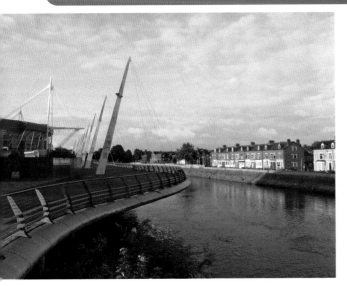

▲ **Figure 36** Houses in lower Riverside overlooking the River Taff and Millennium Stadium (in RIV02 grid reference 177763).

LSOA	Post code	Percentage of residents in:		
		very good health	*professional occupations*	*elementary occupations*
RIV01	CF11 6EW	46.5	15.8	18.2
RIV02	CF11 6AH	43.0	17.2	17.7
RIV03	CF11 6JQ	39.4	17.0	16.6
RIV04	CF11 9QJ	55.0	39.6	3.6
RIV05	CF11 9PW	57.6	38.3	4.4
RIV06	CF11 9DQ	56.1	36.0	6.2
RIV07	CF11 9LJ	57.4	40.6	6.2
RIV08	CF11 6LR	49.2	20.1	19.2

Figure 37 Selected factors that indicate standard of living or deprivation in Riverside (2011).

LSOA	% Muslim faith
RIV01	33.2
RIV02	42.2
RIV03	20.8
RIV04	2.1
RIV05	3.4
RIV06	5.8
RIV07	7.8
RIV08	32.4

Figure 38 Percentage of the population of the Muslim faith in Riverside.

Ways of measuring wealth and poverty

Standard of living is a measure of the relative wealth of individuals or families. It can be measured using household income figures. A person's level of qualifications or job type can also be an indicator of income. Professional jobs, such as accountants or doctors tend to be well paid. Elementary jobs, such as labouring on a building site, tend to be low paid. In neighbourhoods where unemployment figures are high, or jobs are part time or low paid, the number of households living in poverty can be high.

Deprivation is a more complex way of measuring poverty. It takes into account factors such as income and job type. However, it also takes into account other factors such as people's health, community safety and the physical condition of the local environment.

Activities

2 Describe the urban environment in Figures 33 and 36.
3 a) Use Figure 35 to describe the pattern of deprivation in Riverside.
    b) Use evidence from Figures 33, 34 and 36 to help explain the pattern on Figure 35.
4 Use the evidence in Figure 37 to investigate patterns of deprivation further.
    a) Select a graphical or mapping technique to display one or more of the columns of data.
    b) Compare your map or graph to Figure 35. What are the main similarities or differences?
5 Use the evidence in Figure 38 to investigate the distribution of the Muslim population within Riverside. Most Muslims in this neighbourhood are of South Asian or Somali descent.
    a) Represent the data in Figure 38 using a map or graph of your choice.
    b) Use evidence from pages 99–103 to suggest reasons for this pattern.

Enquiry

How do patterns of inequality compare in Cardiff and Mumbai?

What are the main similarities and differences between the two cities when it comes to patterns of wealth and poverty?

Bi-polar surveys

Some features of the urban environment are easy to count and quantify. An example would be the number of cars passing along a street in ten minutes. However, fieldwork enquiries sometimes involve features that cannot be quantified so simply. People's perceptions of the urban environment are one example of something we might want to measure. Because perceptions vary a lot from one person to another we say they are subjective. So how do we assess perceptions?

▲ **Figure 39** Flats and neighbourhood shops in RIV07 (grid reference 169765) on Figure 34.

Activity

1 Study the urban environments in Figures 33, 36, 39 and 41.
   a) Use the bi-polar assessment in Figure 40 to calculate a score for each urban environment in these four photographs.
   b) Share your scores with at least four members of your class. Calculate a mean score for each photograph.
   c) Create a sketch map of Riverside using information from Figure 34. Plot the location of Figures 33, 36, 39 and 41 on your map. Choose a suitable method to represent your mean scores on this map.

Creating a simple bi-polar survey

Step 1 Choose categories for the bi-polar statements. These will depend upon the specific focus of your study, but may include factors such as presence/absence of natural vegetation, street lighting, upkeep of building and condition of pavements. In some cases more personal attitudes may be investigated such as fear of crime or feelings of safety. Pairs of opposing statements are put at either end of a scale as can be seen in Figure 40. A bi-polar scale has a range of values, for example, from -5 to +5. The positive and negative values indicate a person's perception of an environment. The zero is usually removed from the middle of the scale to discourage people from choosing the safe middle option.

Step 2 Choose the location for your survey. Your choice of location may be the result of a pilot study, having previously visited the area, or as a result of some previous knowledge of your study area. If you are unfamiliar with your site then you might use aerial photography (Bing Maps, Google Earth, for example) or an application such as Google Street View to help you choose your sites before going on the field trip. You could use secondary data (like Figures 37 or 38) from http://www.neighbourhood.statistics.gov.uk to help select your sites. If so, you would want to make sure that you visited at least eight sites in Riverside, Cardiff. This is at least one in each LSOA.

Step 3 Collecting the bi-polar scores. The simplest method is to complete the survey yourself. However, in order to investigate differing perceptions you will need to compare your score with other people. These could be members of your class or members of the public. You can combine scores together to create a 'class score' or by calculating the mean score for each location. If so, these mean scores could then be represented on a base map of the area that you visited.

	+5	+4	+3	+2	+1	–1	-2	–3	–4	–5	
Attractive urban environment											Unattractive urban environment
Safe for pedestrians											Unsafe for pedestrians
Natural features nearby											No natural features nearby
Thriving communities with job opportunities											Declining communities with few job opportunities

▲ **Figure 40** An example of bi-polar statements.

Creating a more sophisticated bi-polar assessment

Here are three suggestions to try. In each case, think about the strengths and weaknesses of these assessments compared to a standard bi-polar survey.

1 **Different perceptions** Conduct a standard bi-polar survey as yourself – a teenager. Then imagine what it might be like to perceive the urban environment as though you were someone else. Try doing the bi-polar survey again but imagining yourself as someone with limited mobility, for example, or as a single parent with a very young child. How would your perception change?

2 **Photo surveys** Decide on five categories, or features, for your bi-polar survey. For example, open spaces, building design, pedestrian safety, leisure features and road traffic. Don't write opposing statements. Inspect your area carefully, taking as many photographs as you can. Make sure you record where each photo was taken. Then choose the pair of photos that represent the best and worst examples of each category or feature.

3 **Weightings** Not all of the categories or features recorded by a bi-polar survey have equal importance to people when they think about the quality of the environment. For example, you may decide that open space is a more important feature than road traffic or litter. Try ranking or weighting your bi-polar statements. For example, if you think the amount of open space is twice as important as litter then you should multiply your bi-polar scores for open space by a two. Discuss these weightings to get an agreement as a class or group. How might your weightings be different if you were an OAP rather than a teenager?

▲ **Figure 41** Flats and neighbourhood shops in RIV02 (grid reference 179759) on Figure 34.

Enquiry

Write four new pairs of bi-polar statements. Use them to survey the neighbourhood around your school.
- Conduct the survey as yourself.
- Now imagine how another person might perceive this neighbourhood. Imagine yourself as:
  i) a single parent with a young child
  ii) an elderly resident.
- What are the strengths and limitations of this more sophisticated style of bi-polar survey in trying to collect different perceptions?

THEME 3

Tectonic landscapes and hazards
Chapter 1
Tectonic processes and landforms

What are the largest scale tectonic processes?

The Earth's crust may appear to be a stable and unchanging place but, in fact, it is constantly changing and in motion. In 1835 Charles Darwin said: 'Nothing, not even the wind that blows, is so unstable as the crust of this earth.' His visit to the volcanic Galapagos Islands inspired him to think about the forces that shape the Earth. We now understand that the Earth's crust is made up of several very large **plates** that move relative to one another. Plates move towards each other on **destructive plate margins** and away from each other on **constructive plate margins**.

▲ **Figure 1** The crater of Villarica and Lanín (a stratovolcano) in Chile; this tectonic landscape is typical of the fold mountains in the Andes, South America.

Why do the plates move?

Heat from deep within the Earth causes molten rock, or **magma**, to rise up through the **mantle**, which is the thick layer beneath Earth's thin, solid crust. It is this rising magma that causes volcanic eruptions in places like Iceland in the Mid-Atlantic. Magma rising through the mantle may also explain the movement of the plates that make up our crust. There are two theories: slab pull and convection.

Slab pull is one explanation for plate movement. Plates are immensely heavy. In this theory, it is gravity, acting on these heavy plates, that pulls them apart. As magma rises beneath a constructive plate margin it heats the rocks of the crust and forces them to bend upwards. The crust is raised, forming the **mid-ocean ridge**, which is about 2,500 m higher than the ocean floor. Gravity pulls the crust and it slides down the slope away from the centre of the mid-ocean ridge, allowing further eruptions. An even greater gravitational force pulls at the crust at the other end of the plate. This occurs where the oldest and densest ocean crust bends downwards and slides back into the mantle. This process is known as **subduction**. The huge mass of the subducting slab pulls the rest of the ocean plate away from the mid-ocean ridge.

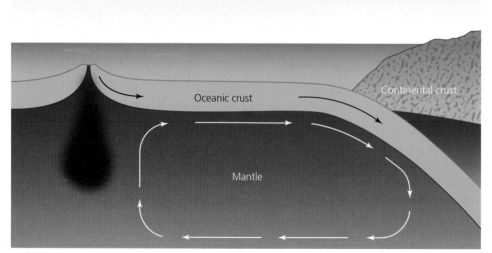

| A plume of hot magma rises through the mantle |
| The oceanic crust is warmed and forced upwards by the magma, creating a mid-ocean ridge |
| The ocean crust cools, becomes denser and slides away from the ridge under gravity |
| A deep ocean trench is formed where the oceanic crust flexes downwards under the continental crust |
| The immense weight of the oceanic crust pulls the plate as it subducts into the mantle |

Oceanic crust

Continental crust

Mantle

▲ **Figure 2** The processes that drive plate movement.

Convection is an alternative explanation for plate movement. It is a process that transfers heat energy. You can see it in a boiling saucepan: the contents of the pan are heated by the hob beneath; the heat rises through the contents of the pan and you see bubbles burst at the surface, which is a little cooler; the cooler fluids sink back into the pan towards the heat source, and the whole process starts again. This creates a circular convection current. It is thought that a similar process may be happening in the mantle. The Earth's core is the heat source and magma rising through the mantle transfers this heat energy away from the source. If convection currents exist within the mantle then they may help to explain the movement of the plates seen in Figure 2.

Activities

1 Make a copy of Figure 2.
   a) Add the labels to suitable places on your diagram to describe the process of slab pull.
   b) Add your own labels in a different colour to explain the process of convection.
2 a) Which of the two theories that explain plate movement do you think is the best explanation? Justify your choice.
   b) Why are explanations for plate movement described as theories?

Large-scale features of destructive plate boundaries

Oceanic trenches are formed where the ocean crust bends downwards and slides back into the mantle on destructive plate margins. Oceanic trenches are long, narrow, deep features in the seabed. Most are deeper than 6 km. The Mariana Trench, in the western Pacific Ocean, is 11 km deep, 2,500 km long and has an average width of just 70 km. Subduction is not a smooth process. Friction locks the plates together. As pressure increases, friction is finally overcome and the plates move with a violent jerk. These large earthquakes can have huge impacts. It was this type of subduction zone earthquake that caused the 2011 tsunami in Japan (see page 128).

Fold mountain ranges, such as the Andes of South America, are another large-scale feature of destructive plate margins. The Andes are 7,000 km long and several peaks rise to over 6,000 m. They are formed as continental crust is squashed together and folded upwards. Heat from the mantle and friction caused by subduction melt the oceanic plate beneath the Andes. The resulting magma rises through the crust above and forms a chain of large volcanoes, like those in Figure 3.

Activities

3 a) Describe the landscape in Figure 1.
   b) Use Figure 3 to describe the processes responsible for this landscape.
4 Explain why scientists need to understand the process of subduction.

Enquiry

Are all sections of the mid-ocean ridge system similar?

■ Research these two sections:
   a) Mid-Atlantic Ridge
   b) East Pacific Rise.
■ Describe the similarities and differences between these two sections of the mid-ocean ridge system.

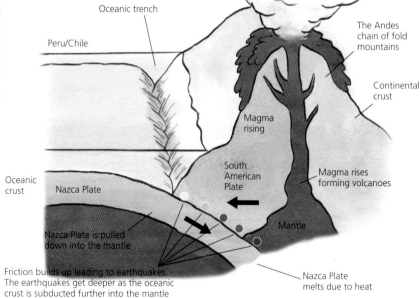

▲ Figure 3 How oceanic trenches and fold mountains are formed in South America.

What large tectonic features are found at constructive plate margins?

Constructive plate margins (also known as **divergence zones** or divergent plate boundaries) are where plates are pulling apart. One example occurs in the middle of the Atlantic Ocean where the Eurasian Plate and North American Plate are moving away from each other. Earthquakes occur along these plate boundaries caused by the wrenching apart of plates and the movement of magma forcing its way through **fractures** in the crust. These earthquakes are usually of a small to medium magnitude but they are felt strongly as they occur close to the surface. However, as most constructive plate boundaries are in mid-ocean, these earthquakes usually pose little threat to people.

Activities

1 Use Figure 4 to name pairs of plates that form:
   a) constructive plate margins
   b) destructive plate margins.
2 Use Figure 4 and an atlas to name:
   a) four countries that are on destructive plate boundaries
   b) four countries that are on constructive plate boundaries.
3 a) Make a sketch of Figure 5.
   b) Match the labels to the five numbered features in the photograph.

▲ **Figure 4** Plate margins and the direction of plate movement.

The mid-ocean ridge system

The mid-ocean ridge system is a huge mountain chain formed along the Earth's constructive plate boundaries. The ridge is an average of about 2,500 m high (about twice the height of Snowdon) and over 65,000 km long. It wraps itself around the world a little like the seam on a cricket ball. The central region of the ridge is deeply cracked and fissured where the crust is pulling apart. Volcanic eruptions are common along the ridge. Most of the mid-ocean ridge is about 2,500 m beneath sea level, but the ridge is visible in a few places where volcanic activity has created islands, such as in Iceland.

The formation of rift valleys

Iceland sits astride the Mid-Atlantic Ridge on a **volcanic hotspot**. Iceland is being gradually torn in two and this can be clearly seen in Thingvellir National Park. Over time a giant fissure, 7.7 km long, has opened in the Earth's surface. As the fissure has widened, the land at the centre has gradually collapsed downwards. This process has formed a **rift valley** (or **graben**) with a flat valley floor and steep **escarpments** along either side. The rift continues to grow. The valley walls are pulling apart at an average of about 7 mm per year and the valley floor is subsiding at about 1 mm per year.

1 2 3 4 5

The flat rift valley floor is formed by subsidence

Steep escarpments on the western edge of the rift

The gentle slopes of a shield volcano

Deep fissures in the valley floor indicate further divergence

Tilted slabs of crust subside along the edge of the rift

◀ **Figure 5** A view northwards from the western escarpment of the rift valley at Thingvellir, Iceland.

North American Plate ▲ ← → Eurasian Plate

N

Krafla

ICELAND

Thingvellir

Reykjavik

0   100
km

Atlantic Ocean

Key
▨ Divergence zone
☐ Ice caps
▲ Active volcanoes
● Earthquake

▲ **Figure 6** Map of Iceland showing where the divergence zone crosses the country.

Steep escarpments

7.7 km

Slab of crust sinks downward

Hot springs

Lake Thingvallavatn

North American Plate

Eurasian Plate

Mantle

▲ **Figure 7** Formation of the rift valley at Thingvellir, Iceland.

Activity

4 a) Use Figure 7 to describe the location of the divergence zone.
   b) Suggest a hypothesis that explains the pattern made by volcanoes and earthquakes in Iceland.
   c) Where would you expect to find the oldest rocks in Iceland and why?

Enquiry

Where else can constructive plate margins be found on land?

Research the features of the African Rift Valley. Create a poster describing the tectonic features found here. Include:

■ a sketch map showing plate boundaries and the direction of plate movement
■ a description of the rift valley and one active volcano in this region.

Features of volcanic landscapes

Volcanoes are created on both constructive and destructive plate boundaries when magma is forced to the surface. The shape of the volcano depends on the type of magma and its gas content.

▲ **Figure 8** The Erta Ale shield volcano in Ethiopia has a summit at 613 m and gentle slopes; it is famous for having a lava lake in its crater.

Shield volcanoes

Magma from constructive plate boundaries tends to have a low **viscosity** and low gas content. The lava spreads out across wide, almost flat, **lava fields** rather than building steep-sided cones. Volcanoes formed in this way are called **shield volcanoes** because of their gentle slopes and circular shape. Examples of shield volcanoes include Erta Ale in Ethiopia, Skjaldbreidur in Iceland and Mauna Loa in Hawaii. Mauna Loa is the world's largest volcano. It is 9,170 m high from the seabed to its summit and 125 km across its base.

Stratovolcanoes

A **stratovolcano** (or composite volcano) is a large, steep-sided, conical-shaped volcano. They are made up of layers of ash and lava from a large number of eruptions. They are formed where the magma contains a lot of gas. This gives the lava a high viscosity, making it less able to flow freely. During an eruption the sticky lava may make a steep-sided dome.

Stratovolcanoes are commonly found on destructive plate boundaries – Mount Merapi in Indonesia (Figure 9, and page 120) and the Soufrière Hills on the Island of Montserrat (page 118) are examples. However, they can also occur on mid-ocean ridges, such as Mount Pico in the Azores (page 112). Some stratovolcanoes occur close to large populations and their explosive style of eruption makes them dangerous. Vesuvius in Italy and Merapi in Indonesia are examples.

▲ **Figure 9** Mount Merapi in Indonesia is a stratovolcano; notice the deeply eroded river valleys that have been cut through layers of soft ash from numerous eruptions.

Volcanic hotspots

Some locations on the Earth's crust seem to be particularly active. These locations are known as volcanic hotspots. It is thought that hotspots occur where super-hot plumes of magma rise through the mantle. The plume finds a weakness in the crust and breaks through to create volcanic activity. Some hotpots are on plate boundaries. One example is Iceland, which is a hotspot on the Mid-Atlantic Ridge. Hotspots can also occur in the middle of plates.

The shield volcanoes of Hawaii

The Hawaiian Islands are a chain of very large mountains formed by volcanic activity, but they are not close to a plate boundary. The Hawaiian Islands have formed over a volcanic hotspot in the middle of the Pacific Plate. The nearest plate boundary is 3,200 km away. Figure 10 shows that, as the Pacific Plate moves slowly across the hotspot, magma rises through the crust forming a volcanic island. As time passes, the plate moves but the hotspot stays in the same place, so that new shield volcanoes are formed behind a line of increasingly older islands that contain extinct volcanoes.

Geysers

In many volcanic regions, water interacts with heat in the ground to create thermal features such as **geysers**, hot springs, fumaroles and mud pots. These small-scale features are formed when rainwater or snowmelt percolates downwards and meets hot rocks. The water is heated and expands. This increases the pressure and forces a mixture of boiling water and steam back up through fissures in the ground. It sometimes emerges in spectacular hydrothermal explosions that send columns of steam high into the air. Repeated explosions of a geyser can create a small crater, a few metres in diameter.

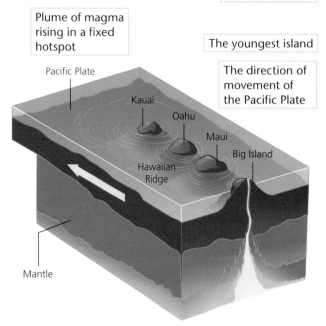

The oldest island

Plume of magma rising in a fixed hotspot

Pacific Plate

The youngest island

The direction of movement of the Pacific Plate

Kauai

Oahu

Maui

Big Island

Hawaiian Ridge

Mantle

▲ **Figure 10** Hotspot formation of volcanic island chains, such as the Hawaiian Islands.

Activities

1 Describe the main similarities and differences between shield and stratovolcanoes.
2 Why are stratovolcanoes considered more dangerous than shield volcanoes? What damage could shield volcanoes cause?
3 a) Make a copy of Figure 10.
   b) Add the labels to suitable places on your diagram.
4 Draw a simple labelled diagram or flow chart to show how a geyser works.

Enquiry

Create a hierarchy of volcano types according to their size and danger. Describe any problems you had deciding on places.

◀ **Figure 11** Steam, in the centre of the image, forcing a bulge of water out of a small hydrothermal crater; this geyser, at Strokkur in Iceland, erupts every 8–10 minutes.

Understanding volcanic landscapes

Shield and stratovolcanoes are large volcanic features, but volcanic landscapes contain many separate landforms of different scales. It is the combination of these different landforms that creates a distinctive and unique landscape.

◀ **Figure 12** A view of Pico, in the Azores, from Faial; both are volcanic islands located on the Mid-Atlantic Ridge.

A small rift valley (graben)

A 2,351 m high stratovolcano with a typical steep-sided conical shape

A group of at least three cinder cones, each about 100–250 m high

Gently sloping lava fields on the lower slopes of the stratovolcano; lava tubes have been discovered here

A small lava cone that grew within the crater of the stratovolcano during its last eruption

Cinder cones

The smallest, most common type of volcano is a **cinder cone**. These cone-shaped hills can be found on their own (such as Parícutin, Mexico) or on the slopes of other, larger volcanoes. They are made from cinders (or **scoria**) created when lava is ejected into the air from a single vent. The lava spray cools very quickly as it is thrown through the air, falling to the ground as hot cinders. These build up around the vent to form a steep-sided, circular cone. Cinder cones usually form during a single eruption. This explains why they don't reach the size of composite volcanoes, which evolve over many eruptions.

Lava tubes

Figure 5, page 116, shows a lava flow in Hawaii. The surface of the lava has been chilled by the air and is solidifying. This layer insulates the lava below, which remains liquid – you can see red-hot lava at over 1,000 °C in the centre of the photo. Underground rivers of lava can flow just below the surface of the ground as far as 50 km from the volcano's crater before cooling enough

to solidify. When the eruption stops, the liquid lava drains away and an empty **lava tube** is left. These lava tubes are typically oval in cross section, 5–10 m wide, 1–5 m high and hundreds of metres in length. Some tubes have branching patterns where tributary rivers of lava have joined one another.

▲ **Figure 13** A lava tube on the lower slopes of Mount Pico, the Azores; notice the formations on the roof where hot lava has solidified as it dripped from the ceiling of the tube.

Calderas

In some violent eruptions, so much lava and ash is ejected that the **magma chamber** that supplies the volcano empties. The upper part of the volcano collapses into the empty space below creating a circular depression which is larger than a typical volcanic vent. These features are called **calderas** (from the Spanish word for caldron). Calderas vary greatly in size. The caldera on Faial, in the Azores, shown in Figure 14, is 2 km across and 400 m deep. The Yellowstone caldera, in North America, was formed by a much more explosive eruption and, consequently, is much larger. This caldera is 55 km by 72 km across.

▲ **Figure 14** A view into the caldera on Faial, the Azores.

▲ **Figure 15** Formation of a caldera.

The steeply sloping wall of the caldera is 400 m high

A small cinder cone with a central vent is at the bottom of the caldera

A recent landslide on the steep slope has removed all vegetation

Piles of scree at the foot of the caldera wall from old landslides

Why do geographers talk about scale?

Scale is an important geographical concept. Landscapes are often a complex mix of different features and landforms. Scale helps geographers to break the landscape down into its different parts and describe the relative size of these geographical features and the processes that create them. Tectonic features vary greatly in size from huge mid-ocean ridges to tiny cinder cones.

Activities

1 a) Make a sketch of Figure 12.
   b) Add the correct label to each of the numbered points.
2 a) Make a copy of Figure 15.
   b) Add your own labels to the diagrams to describe the formation of a caldera.
3 a) Match the correct label to each of the numbered points in Figure 14.
   b) Which of the features in Figure 14 is the most recent and why?
   c) Why must the formation of the cinder cone be more recent than the last large eruption of this volcano?
4 Explain why an understanding of scale is important when trying to interpret the landscape in Figures 12 and 14.
5 Draw a series of three diagrams to show the formation of a lava tube.

THEME
3
Tectonic landscapes and hazards
Chapter 2
Vulnerability and hazard reduction

Why are some communities more vulnerable to tectonic events than others?

Tectonic processes create a variety of potentially dangerous events, which include volcanic eruptions, earthquakes and tsunami. The threat to people created by these events depends on a number of factors:

- the strength or **magnitude** of the event
- the number of people who may be affected – an underwater volcanic eruption on a mid-ocean ridge is not a hazard, but a volcanic eruption close to a large city would pose a huge threat
- the **vulnerability** of the people affected by the event; vulnerability is linked to factors such as poverty.

Activity

1 Use Figure 1 to describe the location of the world's most active volcanoes.

Vulnerability

Vulnerability is a measure of someone's inability to cope with, or recover from, a disaster such as an earthquake or other tectonic hazard. Some groups of people are more vulnerable to hazards than others. Poverty, age, gender and disability are all factors that can affect vulnerability. For example, someone's poverty may mean that their house is badly built and unable to withstand ground shaking during an earthquake.

Capacity

Capacity is the opposite of vulnerability. It describes someone's ability to survive a hazard or recover from it quickly. Capacity is increased where individuals or communities have the resources they need to cope with the hazard. Resources can be financial or material, such as strong building materials. But capacity can also be improved by factors such as education, technology and disaster preparedness and planning.

Key

	Pacific Ring of Fire
Bold	Active volcanoes mentioned in this chapter
Unbold	Selected active volcanoes close to large centres of population

▲ **Figure 1** The location of the world's most active volcanoes.

Country	Number of active volcanoes	Cities with a population greater than 300,000	Gross national income (GNI) per person (US$)	Number of people living on less than US$1.90 per day (million)
Chile	108	7	14,910	0.16
DR Congo	6	15	380	50.71
Iceland	35	0	46,350	0
Indonesia	147	28	3,630	38.27
Japan	118	19	42,000	0
Papua New Guinea	67	1	2,240	2.70
Philippines	53	18	3,500	12.68

▲ **Figure 2** Selected countries that have a significant number of active volcanoes.

How can we reduce vulnerability to tectonic events?

Across the world there are 67 large cities (with a population greater than 100,000) that are close to active volcanoes. These include Tokyo in Japan, Manila in the Philippines and Mexico City, which all have populations greater than 10 million. The number of large cities at risk from earthquakes is even greater. There are 38 major cities at risk from earthquakes in India alone. To reduce vulnerability to a tectonic event, organisations need to:

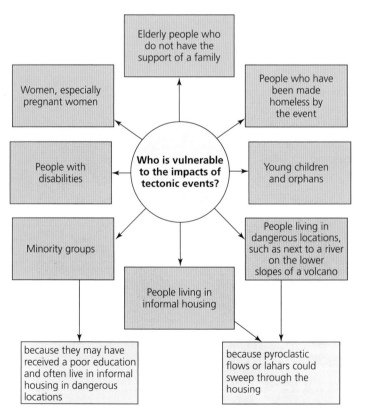

▲ **Figure 3** Why are some groups of people more vulnerable than others to natural disasters?

- *Reduce the impact of the hazard*: it is possible to reduce the impact of a volcanic hazard by monitoring volcanic activity, making predictions about possible eruptions and evacuating people. In the longer term, risk can be managed by mapping the hazards and restricting the movement of people in zones that are at risk. This has been attempted on the volcanic island of Montserrat in the Caribbean.
- *Build capacity to cope with the tectonic hazard*: for example, educating people about what to do during an earthquake so that they are more likely to survive, or creating a disaster plan so that emergency services, hospitals and local authorities all know what to do during and after a major earthquake. In Japan and California, USA, a lot of money is spent on the organisation of disaster plans in the event of an earthquake.
- *Tackle the root causes of vulnerability*: this means that governments need to reduce poverty and inequality in society so that everyone has the same opportunities and the same level of protection during a disaster.

Activities

2 Study Figure 2.
   a) Explain why volcanoes pose a greater threat in Japan than in Iceland.
   b) Suggest which two countries may have the greatest vulnerability to volcanic activity. Justify your choice.
3 Choose four different groups of people in Figure 3.
   a) For each group explain why they may be more vulnerable to natural disasters.
   b) For one of these groups, suggest how their capacity could be improved to cope with an earthquake.

Volcanic hazards

The magnitude of volcanic eruptions is measured using the **Volcanic Explosivity Index (VEI)**. It measures the height and volume of the plume of material ejected from a volcano. Each point on the scale is ten times the magnitude of the one before it.

VEI	Amount of material ejected	Height of plume	Example
0	<10,000 m³	<100 m	
1	>10,000 m³	100 m–1 km	Nyiragongo, DR of the Congo (2002)
2	>1,000,000 m³	1-5 km	
3	>10,000,000 m³	3-15 km	Soufrière Hills, Montserrat (1995)
4	>0.1 km³	>10 km	Calbuco, Chile (2015)
5	>1 km³	>20 km	
6	>10 km³	>20 km	Pinatubo, Philippines (1991)
7	>100 km³	>20 km	
8	>1,000 km³	>20 km	

▲ **Figure 4** The Volcano Explosivity Index (VEI).

Lava flows

Lava flows rarely cause death or injury. They usually move slowly and people can simply move out of their way. A lava flow will, however, destroy anything in its path, including buildings, roads and crops. Blocked roads can hamper aid efforts or prevent evacuation.

Kilauea, one of Hawaii's five volcanoes, has been erupting since 1983. Lava from this eruption has destroyed 214 buildings, covered over 100 km² of land and buried 14 km of roads, but has not directly caused a single fatality. It is possible to divert lava flows but this isn't generally done in Hawaii for spiritual reasons. The Mauna Loa volcano observatory in Hawaii is protected by barriers as it contains very expensive and important equipment. It is the only lava barrier in Hawaii.

Lava flows often threaten towns and villages on the slopes of Mount Etna in Italy. Diverting these flows is costly, and deciding which land to save and which to sacrifice raises complex legal, political and social issues. There are a number of successful methods that can be used to divert lava flows, including:

• spraying lava with water to cool and solidify it, so it acts as its own barrier to the molten lava behind
• creating earth embankments to channel the direction of the lava flow
• dropping concrete blocks via helicopter to divert the flow
• blowing up lava tubes to widen them and spread out the flow so it solidifies quicker and doesn't travel as far.

▲ **Figure 5** A slow-moving lava flow on Big Island, Hawaii.

Ash clouds

Calbuco is a stratovolcano in Chile. It erupted violently in April 2015 creating a huge **ash cloud** that can be seen in Figure 7. Ash clouds form when an explosive eruption throws a mixture of gas, fractured rock and tiny lava droplets high into the air. The lava droplets cool rapidly and solidify into tiny fragments of glass-like ash. These ash particles are sharp and abrasive. If sucked into the engine of a passenger jet it can cause its engines to stall. In 2010 the eruption of Eyjafjallajökull in Iceland caused an ash cloud that rose up to 10 km high. The cloud spread over much of Northern Europe, forcing the cancellation of around 100,000 flights at a cost of around US$2.6 billion to the aviation industry.

Falling ash collects on power and communication lines as well as on buildings. When rain falls the ash becomes heavier, causing structural damage and power blackouts. Ash can have health effects too. It can pollute water supplies, and inhalation of volcanic ash can lead to lung damage. Crops can also be damaged by ash, leading to food shortages and higher food prices.

▲ **Figure 6** Map showing the extent of Calbuco's ash cloud on 25 April 2015.

▲ **Figure 7** The Calbuco volcano in southern Chile erupted in 2015 after lying dormant for 43 years.

1893–94	1895	1906	1907	1909	1911–12	1917	1929	1961	1972	2015

▲ **Figure 8** Years in which Calbuco, Chile, has erupted.

Factfile: Eruption of Calbuco, Chile, 22 April 2015

- The ash plume rose higher than 15 km.
- Pyroclastic flows travelled up to 7 km.
- Lahars (volcanic mud flows) travelled 15 km; people were warned to keep at least 200 m from rivers.
- International flights were delayed or cancelled.
- The town of Ensenada (population 1,600) was covered in 50 cm of ash; some houses collapsed from the weight of the ash on their roofs.
- Several roads and bridges were blocked by ash.
- Schools in the area around the volcano were closed.
- About 5,000 people were evacuated from the area.

Activities

3 Use the Factfile to describe:
   a) the magnitude of the Calbuco eruption in 2015
   b) the economic and social impacts of the event.
4 a) Plot a frequency graph using the data in Figure 8.
   b) Calculate the frequency of eruptions of Calbuco.
5 Use Figure 6 to describe:
   a) the location of Calbuco
   b) the approximate area and location of the ash cloud.
6 a) Explain why flights across Europe were cancelled during the Eyjafjallajökull eruption in 2010.
   b) Suggest how this may have affected business travellers and tourists.

Why are pyroclastic flows so hazardous?

Pyroclastic flows are fast-moving clouds of super-heated gas, ash and rock. They are caused by the collapse of a column of ash. Alternatively, they occur when a dome of cooling lava collapses. This triggers the release of energy from the magma chamber beneath, causing the sudden and violent eruption of ash and gas.

Pyroclastic flows are deadly. The British Geological Survey, which monitors Soufrière Hills in Montserrat, has recorded temperatures between 100 and 600 °C inside the flows.

Pyroclastic flows on Montserrat typically travel at around 110 kph down the volcano, carrying rock fragments ranging in size from fine ash to boulders the size of a small car. It can demolish buildings and the high temperatures start fires. Even on the edges of the flow, people are in danger from burns and the inhalation of hot, choking gases. Although pyroclastic flows are clouds of solid material they move like a liquid, hugging the ground and following contour patterns downwards much like an avalanche. However, they also have enough mass and energy to travel uphill on the lower slopes of a volcano. This makes their paths difficult to predict.

▲ **Figure 9** The collapse of an ash column can trigger pyroclastic flows.

Ash rises in a column up to 20 km into the atmosphere; as pressure is released from the magma chamber, the gas in the rising column expands; it's like shaking a bottle of pop before you take the lid off

The weight of the ash cannot be sustained by the eruption; it collapses due to the effect of gravity

The pyroclastic flow is a mixture of heavier rock fragments, ash and gas; It rolls down the slopes, hugging the ground

Lighter rock fragments and ash billow upwards above the main part of the flow

▲ **Figure 10** A pyroclastic flow on Soufrière Hills, Montserrat.

Activities

1 Describe how pyroclastic flows could affect:
   a) people
   b) the economy
   c) the environment.
2 a) Make a copy of Figure 9.
   b) Add the annotations to suitable points on your diagram.
3 Suggest suitable labels or annotations for each of the three points in Figure 10.

How can hazard mapping help reduce the threat?

The level of threat of tectonic events, such as pyroclastic flows, increases not only with the magnitude of the event but also with the vulnerability of local communities. If communities can be removed from these areas, then the threat disappears. **Hazard mapping** allows local authorities to do two things:

- limit access to hazardous areas, for example, allowing people to only have access during daylight hours or only allowing scientists to enter the most dangerous zones

- control the development of areas considered to be at risk from tectonic events, for example, preventing the building of new homes in hazard zones.

The Soufrière Hills volcano in Montserrat has been erupting since 1995 to date. The southern part of the island has been divided into six zones, shown in Figure 11. A hazard level system that restricts access

 www.mvo.ms – website of the Montserrat Volcano Observatory.

to certain areas is used depending on how active the volcano is according to measurements made by the Montserrat Volcano Observatory (MVO). Zone V is out of bounds except to scientists, although daytime access to some areas of this zone is permitted when volcanic activity is low. There are also maritime exclusion zones because pyroclastic flows can reach the coast and travel out to sea. Many residents have left the island since the 1995 eruption began – many moved to the UK.

Year	Population
1951	14,100
1961	11,900
1971	11,600
1981	11,900
1991	10,800
2003	4,500
2011	5,000

▲ **Figure 12** The population of Montserrat.

Activities

4 Study Figure 11.
   a) Estimate the percentage of the island which is in the safe zone.
   b) How might the maritime exclusion zones affect local people?
   c) The old capital city Plymouth and WH Bramble airport had to be abandoned. What problems would this have caused for the people of Montserrat?

5 a) Represent the data in Figure 12 in a suitable graph.
   b) Describe what has happened to the population since the eruption began in 1995.

Enquiry

What is the hazard level in Montserrat today?

- Use the weblink to the Montserrat Volcano Observatory.

- Make a sketch map of Figure 11. Colour code your map to show the present level of hazard.

- What level of activity is permitted in each zone under this level?

Key
- - - Zone boundary
ℂ Zones
W Maritime Exclusion Zones

▲ **Figure 11** Hazard map for Montserrat; only the northern part of the island is the safe zone.

Volcanic hazards of Mount Merapi

Mount Merapi is a stratovolcano located in Central Java. This is one of the most densely populated areas of Indonesia. Mount Merapi is Indonesia's most active volcano, producing pyroclastic flows and ash clouds. It is formed by the subduction of the Indo-Australian Plate beneath the Eurasian Plate at a destructive plate boundary.

Activities

1 Use Figure 13 to describe:
   a) the location of Mount Merapi
   b) the distribution of volcanoes in this region.
2 a) Plot a frequency graph using the data in Figure 14.
   b) Calculate the frequency of eruptions of Mount Merapi.
3 Describe the effects of the 2010 eruption. Consider the effects on:
   a) people
   b) the economy.

▲ **Figure 13** The location of Mount Merapi, Indonesia.

1933–35	1939–40	1944–45	1948–49	1953–58	1961	1967–69	1971
1972–90	1992–98	2001–2	2006	2007	2010–11	2012	2013

▲ **Figure 14** Frequency of eruptions of Mount Merapi, Indonesia, since 1933.

Impacts of the October 2010 eruption

Mount Merapi's 2010 eruption was magnitude VEI 4. The blast destroyed homes and crops, with pyroclastic flows travelling up to 10 km from the summit. Thousands were left homeless. Ash falls of 30 cm were recorded in villages up to 20 km away and caused breathing difficulties. Planes were grounded in Western Australia because of the risk of damage to aircraft and hundreds of international flights had to be cancelled to and from Indonesia. Financial losses have been estimated at around US$700 million.

In the weeks after the eruption, the price of food rose and thousands had difficulty affording the increase in food prices. The 700 emergency shelters provided were cramped and there wasn't enough clean drinking water or toilets. This led to poor sanitation and the risk of outbreaks of disease such as cholera.

20 km exclusion zone

353 deaths

26,00 hectares of crops covered in ash

27 million cubic metres of ash and rock deposited in the River Gendol

320,000 people evacuated

1,900 livestock killed (mainly dairy cattle)

▲ **Figure 15** The 2010 eruption of Mount Merapi in numbers.

How might the risks associated with volcanic eruptions be reduced?

Active volcanoes are constantly monitored to try to predict when the next eruption will take place. Accurate prediction gives people enough time to evacuate. Data from monitoring stations on Mount Merapi is sent to the Merapi Volcano Observatory in Yogyakarta City. The data is processed and the alert level of the volcano is adjusted on a daily basis.

Six observation posts around Mount Merapi take regular photographs to show the evolution of the lava dome and record rock fall activity. Scientists can attempt to predict the direction of future pyroclastic flows based on the changing shape of the dome. Satellites provide high-resolution images of visible changes while thermal infrared images show increases in temperature due to rising magma. **Tiltmeters** analyse ground movements and five observation stations send a laser beam to mirrors placed around the volcano to measure the smallest change in ground shape.

Mount Merapi has eight **seismometers** – instruments that record earthquakes. **Geomagnetic** monitoring is carried out by four stations: they take measurements of geomagnetic intensity once every minute. There are also several fixed-point **geochemical** monitoring sites, which sample gas emissions.

▲ **Figure 16** Search and rescue teams look for survivors in a riverside community that was home to 200 villagers, about 8 km from Mount Merapi, Indonesia.

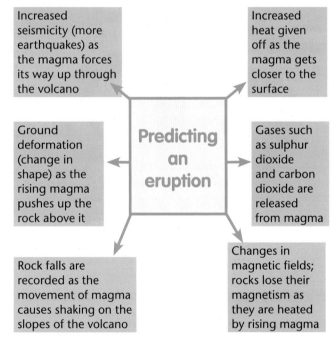

Increased seismicity (more earthquakes) as the magma forces its way up through the volcano

Increased heat given off as the magma gets closer to the surface

Ground deformation (change in shape) as the rising magma pushes up the rock above it

Predicting an eruption

Gases such as sulphur dioxide and carbon dioxide are released from magma

Rock falls are recorded as the movement of magma causes shaking on the slopes of the volcano

Changes in magnetic fields; rocks lose their magnetism as they are heated by rising magma

▲ **Figure 17** Scientists monitor volcanoes to try to predict when an eruption will take place.

Activities

4 Describe the landscape in Figure 16. How has the volcanic eruption affected the environment?
5 What is the cause of the observable changes in a volcano before an eruption?
6 Describe three different ways that volcanoes are monitored. For each one:
   a) describe what is monitored
   b) explain why it is monitored.

Enquiry

What processes formed Mount Merapi?

Draw an annotated sketch to show how Mount Merapi formed. Use Figure 3 on page 107 to help you.

Coping with the threat from lahars on Mount Merapi

Pyroclastic flows deposit layers of loose rock and ash. After a large eruption these deposits can be hundreds of metres thick. When mixed with water they create a destructive type of mudflow known as a **lahar**. Lahars can be formed in two different ways:
- Snow and ice on the upper slopes of the volcano can be melted by the eruption. The melt water mixes with the ash deposits creating the lahar.
- Rainfall, during or after the eruption, mixes with pyroclastic deposits.

Lahars can travel at 65 kph, which is faster than a river in flood. The mixture of ash, rock and water has the consistency of wet concrete. The density of a lahar causes far more damage than water alone. People, buildings, roads and bridges are simply swept away or buried. Farmland is ruined, putting a strain on local food supply. Lahars can travel long distances from the volcano. Lahars can continue to be created long after the volcano has stopped erupting, every time heavy rain mixes with rock and ash deposited in river valleys.

	Jan	Feb	Mar	Apr	May	Jun	Jul	Aug	Sep	Oct	Nov	Dec
Precipitation (mm)	353	335	310	211	127	89	41	5	30	94	229	340
Temperature (°C)	26	26.5	26.5	27	27	26	25	25.5	26.5	27	27	26.5

▲ **Figure 18** Average precipitation and temperature for Yogyakarta, Indonesia.

▲ **Figure 19** Local people remove sand from a river during the eruption of Mount Merapi, Indonesia, to make sand bags to try to prevent flooding.

Why do people continue to live here?

Mount Merapi erupts frequently but most eruptions are relatively small. The average eruption is of magnitude VEI 3, so effects are usually localised. Volcanic ash is rich in minerals. Once it has weathered it creates fertile soil for agriculture. The area between the volcano and the city of Yogyakarta is a National Park that is popular with tourists. Some local people work in the tourist industry as guides, taking tourists into the new conservation areas where it is considered too dangerous to live.

Activities

1 a) Describe how a lahar can be formed during an eruption.
   b) Explain why the risk of lahars continues for many months after an eruption.
2 Describe the similarities and differences between a lahar and a river flood.
3 a) Use Figure 18 to plot a climate graph for Yogyakarta.
   b) Label the months in which lahars would have been a hazard following the October 2010 eruption.
4 a) Describe two positive impacts of volcanic activity in Yogyakarta.
   b) Suggest one other reason why people live close to this active volcano, despite the frequent eruptions.

Sector of the economy	(%)
Agriculture	16
Manufacturing	14
Tourism	21
Other service industries	49

▲ **Figure 20** Economic sectors and their value to Yogyakarta's economy.

Reducing the vulnerability of riverside communities

Indonesia is a newly industrialised country (NIC) with a rapidly growing urban population. Planners have struggled to keep up with the demand for affordable new housing. It is estimated that as much as 80 per cent of all new housing is in informal settlements. Much of this housing is built in locations that are not really suitable or safe, for example, riverside communities that are at risk of flooding in Indonesia's wet season. After volcanic eruptions, these communities are at deadly risk from lahars.

One non-governmental organisation (NGO) that is trying to help the situation is Arkomiogia – a group of community architects working in the riverside community of Kali Jawi in Yogyakarta. This project was begun by a group of women who started a **micro-credit** scheme so they could make regular savings. The women's group met with architects, planners and local government officials regularly to plan a new community centre. This centre can be used for village meetings and as a shelter during a flood or lahar. The new community centre has several features to make it practical and sustainable, which can be seen in Figure 21.

1 Concrete stilts raise the building above flood height	2 The bamboo construction uses three species of bamboo that are all commonly found in Java

3 Steel bolts firmly hold the flexible structure together

4 Community members were able to be involved in the simple construction

5 The traditional style of building fits in with local architecture

6 The large roof provides shade and shelter from rain; open spaces provide ventilation

▲ **Figure 21** The new hazard-resistant community centre in Kali Jawi.

Activities

5 Suggest why people living in informal housing in Yogyakarta are most vulnerable to ash falls and lahars.
6 Study Figure 21. Describe how one or more features of the building are designed to:
   a) be sustainable
   b) suit the climate of the region
   c) improve the capacity of Kali Jawi to cope with flooding and lahars.

Enquiry

Which of the cities in Figure 22 is most at risk of lahars?

- Use an interactive world map, such as Google Maps, to find the distance of each city from Mount Merapi.
- Describe the drainage pattern of rivers in this region.
- Use this information to put the three cities in rank order of risk. Justify your choice.

Year	Yogyakarta	Semarang	Surakarta
1970	343,000	627,000	408,000
1980	397,000	1,009,000	468,000
1990	412,000	1,243,000	503,000
2000	397,000	1,427,000	491,000
2010	388,000	1,558,000	499,000
2020	402,000	1,761,000	533,000
2030	503,000	2,188,000	668,000

▲ **Figure 22** Population of cities close to Mount Merapi.

The earthquake hazard

Earthquakes are measured on the **moment magnitude scale** (M_w). It measures the product of the distance moved by a fault and the force needed to move it. Each number on the scale is ten times more powerful than the one before it.

The strength of ground shaking during an earthquake is reduced with distance from its origin – a point underground known as the **focus**. This means that earthquakes close to the Earth's surface will be felt more than an equally strong earthquake with a deeper focus. Similarly, ground shaking is reduced with distance from the **epicentre**, the point on the surface that is immediately above the focus.

The amount and strength of ground shaking during an earthquake is affected by the hardness of the rock the seismic waves travel through. Earthquake waves travel quickly through hard rock. When they reach softer ground they slow down and the amount of shaking becomes amplified.

 http://earthquaketrack.com – this interactive website plots recent earthquakes on to a world map.

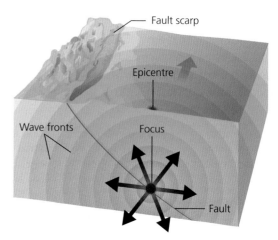

▲ **Figure 23** Cross section through a fault showing the features of an earthquake.

Date	Country	Magnitude (M_w)	Deaths	Depth (km)	GNI per capita (US$)*
02/02/2015	Argentina	6.3	0	172	13,480
27/02/2015	Indonesia	7	0	552	3,630
25/04/2015	Nepal	7.8	8,964	8	730
12/05/2015	Nepal	7.3	218	15	730
04/06/2015	Malaysia	6	18	10	11,120
03/07/2015	China	6.4	0	20	7,400
16/09/2015	Chile	8.3	14	25	14,910
20/10/2015	Vanuatu	7.1	0	135	3,160
26/10/2015	Afghanistan	7.5	398	231	680
17/11/2015	Greece	6.5	0	10	22,680
24/11/2015	Peru	7.6	0	600	6,360

▲ **Figure 24** Magnitude, location and depth of selected large magnitude earthquakes (2015).

*World Bank latest figures

 Activities

1 Study Figure 23. Describe the difference between the focus and epicentre of an earthquake.
2 Explain why people living in homes built on soft ground are more vulnerable to earthquakes.
3 a) Using Figure 24, roughly how much greater was the magnitude of the Nepal earthquake (12/05/2015) than the one in Greece?
  b) Explain why the shallow depth of the two earthquakes in Nepal was significant.

 Enquiry

Why are some earthquakes more deadly than others?

■ Study Figure 24. Suggest a hypothesis linking the number of deaths to one of the other factors in the table. Make a prediction.
■ Use evidence from the table to investigate your hypothesis.
■ What conclusion can you reach? What are the limitations of this enquiry?

Can technology be used to reduce the impacts of earthquakes?

The capacity to survive an earthquake is increased where individuals or communities have the resources or technology they need to cope with the hazard. Japan is a high income country (HIC) that has financial resources it can invest in technology and hazard preparedness. Many aseismic buildings have been constructed, such as the Yokohama Landmark Tower, to withstand earthquakes. These structures are flexible and strong rather than being rigid and brittle like concrete. Infrastructure, such as roads, can also be built to flex and withstand earthquakes.

So, as countries become more economically developed, do they become safer? Not necessarily. In many NICs, such as India or China, economic development does not guarantee that everyone has a reduced risk from earthquakes. Vulnerability is not reduced for everyone in society.

Shillong is a city in northeast India. In 1897 an earthquake of magnitude 8.3 M_W killed about 1,500 of the 50,000 people who lived there. It has been estimated that an earthquake of similar size today could perhaps kill 90,000 people of the current 400,000 population. Why are so many more people at risk today? The reason is technology. In 1897 most people lived in traditional single-storey bamboo homes. These were flexible and lightweight, like modern steel-frame structures. Now, most people live in cheaply constructed multi-storey buildings constructed from concrete. Many are on steep slopes. During an earthquake, these buildings could collapse, crushing and killing people inside.

Disaster planning

After an earthquake people face a number of further hazards, for example:
- from unstable buildings, which have been weakened by the earthquake
- the need of medical attention for their injuries
- risks associated with exposure because they have lost their homes
- risks associated with the lack of basic resources, such as food, clean water and sanitation

A swift and targeted response is needed to minimise these effects. This is harder to achieve when:
- the area is very remote
- the country does not have enough money to invest in disaster planning and preparation.

Specialist emergency teams trained to use equipment specifically designed to locate survivors buried under rubble are found in most HICs at risk of tectonic disasters, such as Japan, Italy and the USA. In these countries, educational programmes in schools and workplaces teach people how to react during an earthquake, tsunami or volcanic eruption. Annual events like the 'Great ShakeOut' in California involve whole communities in raising awareness of what to do during and after a major earthquake. In Japan, coastal towns have tsunami escape routes clearly signposted.

Activities

4   a) Give two reasons why a large-magnitude earthquake in Shillong could be deadly for so many people. Use evidence from Figure 25.
    b) Suggest why some groups of people in India remain vulnerable to earthquakes despite the rapid economic growth of the country. Use Figure 3, page 115, to help you.
    c) How might the capacity of vulnerable communities in Shillong be improved?

▲ **Figure 25** Housing in Shillong, India, today.

The Nepal earthquake of April 2015

On 25 April 2015, a 7.8 M$_w$ earthquake occurred in the Gorkha district of Nepal. The epicentre was close to the Nepalese city of Kathmandu, but people in India, China and Bangladesh were also affected by the powerful quake. A number of powerful aftershocks caused further damage and injuries, including one of 7.3 M$_w$ close to Mount Everest on 12 May.

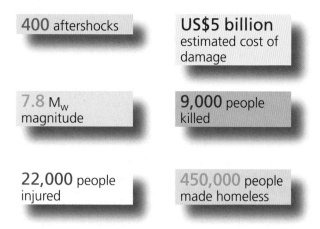

400 aftershocks	**US$5 billion** estimated cost of damage
7.8 M$_w$ magnitude	**9,000** people killed
22,000 people injured	**450,000** people made homeless

▲ **Figure 26** The 2015 Nepal earthquake in numbers.

▲ **Figure 27** The location of the 2015 Nepal earthquakes. Larger earthquakes are represented by larger circles.

What were the effects of this earthquake?

The earthquake was caused by the Indian Plate moving under the Eurasian Plate in a sudden movement. As a result, Kathmandu is now 3 m further south than it was before the earthquake.

The violent shaking of the ground during the earthquake caused a lot of damage to buildings and infrastructure. Whole villages were destroyed as buildings collapsed. Many roads were fractured by the Earth's movement. Others were blocked by landslides that slid down the steep mountain slopes because of the earthquakes. Hundreds of people were killed by avalanches of snow and ice that were triggered by ground shaking. One of these avalanches was over 2 km wide.

Aid workers struggled to reach people who needed help because of the mountainous terrain and damaged roads. Much of the help had to come by helicopter. This meant that smaller amounts of supplies could be delivered and fewer people could be rescued in each trip. Many medical centres were destroyed and medical supplies hard to access. Fresh food and clean water were scarce. Many tourists were stranded on the mountains. Priority was given to the wounded and communities without food and water. Six months later, many people were still suffering with respiratory diseases and infected wounds. Nepal is a low income country (LIC); its economy generates about US$20 billion each year. The cost of rebuilding is estimated to be at least US$5 billion.

Activities

1 Look at Figure 27.
   a) Describe the location of the epicentre of the earthquake.
   b) Describe the area affected by severe ground shaking. Use the scale line to estimate its area.
2 Describe how the Nepal earthquake affected:
   a) people
   b) the economy.
3 Explain why it was difficult to get aid to some communities after the earthquake.
4 India's economy is worth about US$2,180 billion a year. Suggest why it will take longer for Nepal to recover from this earthquake than India.

How can technology help reduce risk?

Electricity and telephone lines were broken during the earthquake. This damaged communications, which could have slowed down the relief effort. However, a mixture of old and new technologies allowed the public to help. Amateur radio operators, using radios running on solar power and batteries, were able to give information about conditions in remote areas to the Nepalese police. This was made possible by the US chapter of the Computer Association of Nepal, who supplied the equipment needed to relay the radio messages. People also used social media to describe conditions in remote areas. Humanity Road, an NGO, kept a log of social media messages to relay important information to the rescue teams.

Other projects are in place to reduce the damage caused by future earthquakes. Traditional Nepalese houses use alternating bands of stone and wood; the wooden bands stitch the buildings together and allow some flexing during an earthquake. However, cut stone is expensive and many of the trees in Nepal have been cut down for firewood, so poorer people have built cheap concrete houses. These houses have no flexibility and many collapsed during the earthquake. Abari is a project that aims to revive traditional building techniques along with the benefits of modern technology. Specially treated bamboo is used instead of wood, and people are taught the traditional methods, thus making the buildings more affordable and sustainable.

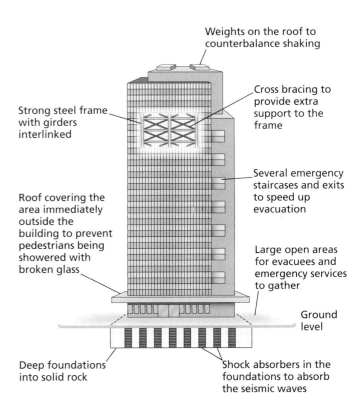

Weights on the roof to counterbalance shaking

Cross bracing to provide extra support to the frame

Strong steel frame with girders interlinked

Several emergency staircases and exits to speed up evacuation

Roof covering the area immediately outside the building to prevent pedestrians being showered with broken glass

Large open areas for evacuees and emergency services to gather

Ground level

Deep foundations into solid rock

Shock absorbers in the foundations to absorb the seismic waves

▲ **Figure 28** Features of an earthquake-resistant building.

▲ **Figure 29** A stone and bamboo school built by Abari and Learning Planet, which survived the earthquake in Gorkha.

Activities

5 Describe how technology was used to help the relief effort in Nepal.
6 Study Figure 28. Suggest how three of the features of this building improve its safety during an earthquake.
7 Compare the features of the Abari project (in Figure 29) with the Kali Jawi project (page 123). What are the similarities and differences?

Enquiry

'In a low income country, like Nepal, people in densely populated urban areas are more vulnerable than people in remote rural areas during a powerful earthquake.'

To what extent do you agree with this statement? Consider why the effects of an earthquake could be worse in a densely populated urban area. What advantages would an urban area have over a rural area during the hours and days after the earthquake?

Tsunami

Tsunami are caused by violent movements of the ocean floor, such as those during an earthquake. This movement displaces huge amounts of water upwards, which creates a series of waves. Tsunami waves travel at 25 m per second in deep water. As a tsunami reaches shallow water it slows down and increases in height in a process called shoaling. Debris carried in these large, powerful waves can be carried far inland across coastal plains and up river valleys, causing injury to people and severe damage to buildings. The danger can last for several hours after the first wave.

The 2011 Tōhoku earthquake and tsunami

The 11 March 2011 undersea earthquake off the coast of Tōhoku, Japan, had a magnitude of 9.0 M_w. Less than half an hour later the coast was hit by the subsequent tsunami. Waves reached heights of up to 10 m and travelled up to 10 km inland. The number of confirmed deaths was just under 20,000. Most were caused by drowning. The massive surge overtopped Japan's sea defences and destroyed three-storey buildings where people believed they were safe. Fukushima Daiichi, a

nuclear power plant to the south of Sendai, had lost power to its cooling rods during the earthquake and was running on back-up power. When the tsunami struck it destroyed this back-up power, eventually causing a full meltdown of a number of reactors and releasing harmful radiation. Thirty-six nuclear reactors across the country were closed after the earthquake, resulting in electrical blackouts across much of the country.

How are tsunami monitored?

The Pacific Tsunami Warning System (PTWS) was set up after the 1960 Chile earthquake. This earthquake caused a tsunami responsible for the deaths of hundreds of people across the Pacific region. There was no warning. The PTWS uses a network of seismographs and ocean buoys to detect earthquakes that might create tsunami and changes in sea levels that may indicate the formation of a tsunami. Once a tsunami is detected, warnings can be given to local centres around the Pacific region. These centres can then warn local people by radio or text message, giving them time to evacuate the area. A similar system was set up in the Indian Ocean in 2006 following the Boxing Day tsunami of 2004, which killed over 230,000 people.

	Tōhoku, Japan	Solomon Islands, South Pacific
Date	11 March 2011	01 April 2007
Magnitude (M_w)	9.0	8.1
Depth (km)	30	10
Distance from shore (km)	129 km east of Sendai	45 km south-southeast of Gizo
Deaths	20,000	52

▲ **Figure 31** Comparing two tsunami events.

 www.timeanddate.com/worldclock/distances. html – use this tool to find the distance from anywhere to other significant places.

Activities

1 How much greater in magnitude was the 2011 Tōhoku earthquake than the Nepal earthquake of April 2015 (page 126)?
2 Describe the impacts of the Tōhoku earthquake. Use Figure 30 to help you.
3 Explain why the magnitude and scale of this event had such an impact.

▲ **Figure 30** Damage in Kesennuma, Miyagi Prefecture, after the March 2011 earthquake and tsunami.

The 2007 Solomon Islands tsunami

The Solomon Islands are a group of 492 islands in the Pacific Ocean to the northeast of Australia. On 1 April 2007, a powerful earthquake created a tsunami; it was detected by the PTWS but the wave struck the island of Ghizo before the warning could be issued. The small coastal town of Gizo was swamped by waves several metres high, which flooded 50–70 m inland, destroying a number of timber-framed buildings. Aid workers struggled to reach the scene, which is 370 km from the capital, Honiara. Australia sent US$54.1 million in aid. The nearest major airport in Australia is Darwin, which is 2,887 km away.

▲ **Figure 32** An informal settlement on Ghizo built to replace houses lost in the 2007 tsunami.

Factfile: Small Island Developing States

- There are currently 58 small island developing states (SIDS) with a combined population of 65 million people.
- Many SIDS are very small and some are located in remote and isolated parts of the world. Most SIDS are vulnerable to climate change and other natural disasters, such as earthquakes and tsunami.
- Standards of living among small islands differ widely, with GNI per capita ranging from US$830 in Comoros to US$51,000 in Singapore.

Activities

4 Use Figure 31 to compare the two tsunami events.
5 Using Figure 33 and the Factfile, suggest three reasons why many SIDS are vulnerable to natural hazards.
6 a) Explain why people in Ghizo were vulnerable to the tsunami of 2007.
   b) Describe the buildings in Figure 32.
   c) Suggest why people in Ghizo remained vulnerable to other natural hazards after the tsunami.

SIDS	Volcano?	Earthquake?	GNI per person (US$)	Poverty (% below US$1.90 a day)
Cape Verde	Yes	Yes	3,450	17.6
Comoros	Yes	Yes	790	13.5
Fiji	Yes	Yes	4,870	3.6
Haiti	No	Yes	820	53.9
Papua New Guinea	Yes	Yes	2,240	39.3
Saint Lucia	Yes	Yes	7,260	35.8
Solomon Islands	Yes	Yes	1,830	45.6

▲ **Figure 33** Hazards in selected small island developing states (SIDS).

Enquiry

Why are some coastal communities more vulnerable than others?
- Research two of the SIDS in Figure 33.
- Describe the tectonic hazards each country faces.
- Explain why these communities are vulnerable and suggest ways of building capacity.

THEME
4

Coastal hazards and their management
Chapter 1
Managing coastal hazards

Erosion and coastal flooding during extreme weather events

The UK's coast is at risk of a variety of coastal hazards including:

- erosion, landslips and rock falls (see pages 20 to 23)
- storm surges during severe weather events
- flooding due to sea level change.

The coastline of the UK is densely populated. Cities such as Newport, Hull and London are all located on estuaries that are at risk of coastal flooding. England alone has 3.1 million people living in seaside towns, such as Blackpool or Bournemouth. Consequently, large parts of the UK population can be affected by coastal hazards. These hazards become more likely during severe weather events.

▲ **Figure 1** Rapid coastal erosion of the cliffs at Hemsby during the 2013 storm caused the collapse of seven homes.

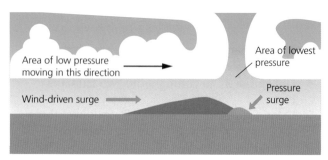

▲ **Figure 2** Storm surge due to low pressure.

The storm surge of December 2013

Low pressure in the atmosphere has the effect of raising sea levels. When air pressure falls by 1 millibar (mb), sea levels rise by 1 cm. So, a deep depression of 960 mb will cause sea levels to rise by 50 cm. Strong winds create large waves that are pushed in front of an advancing area of low pressure creating even higher water levels. This effect is known as a **storm surge**, and is shown in Figure 2. If a storm approaches the coast at high tide, an event that happens twice a day, then the risk of flooding is increased. The UK's North Sea coastline is particularly vulnerable to storm surges. The southern part of this sea is shallow and shaped like a funnel. When low pressure travels southwards across the North Sea, the bulge of the storm surge can increase in height as water is forced through this shallow funnel.

During December 2013 coastal communities along the North Sea Coast faced the worst storm surge since 1953. Erosion is more rapid during extreme weather events, as you can see in Figure 1. Other effects of the storms are shown in Figure 3. Nevertheless, the Environment Agency said 800,000 homes had been protected by:

- accurate weather forecasts that gave people time to evacuate their homes
- coastal defences that held back some of the storm surge.

1,000 sandbags were distributed to home-owners in Aldeburgh, Suffolk.

In the Humber region, 400 homes were affected by flood water.

Seven houses were destroyed in Hemsby, Norfolk when the cliff beneath them collapsed into the sea.

In Great Yarmouth, Norfolk, residents of 9,000 homes were advised to evacuate overnight.

The sea wall was breached at Jaywick, Essex. Firefighters and 10 rescue boats helped to evacuate 2,500 homes.

Boston, Lincolnshire was flooded; 223 people were evacuated from their homes.

In Kent, 200 homes were evacuated in Faversham and another 70 in Seasalter.

The sea wall at Scarborough, Yorkshire, was damaged.

▲ **Figure 3** The locations affected by the 2013 storm surge.

▲ **Figure 4** The course of the December 2013 North Sea storm.

Key

- Area of low pressure and strongest winds at 00 hours 05/12/2013
- Area of low pressure and strongest winds at 12 hours 05/12/2013
- Area of low pressure and strongest winds at 00 hours 06/12/2013

▲ **Figure 5** Sea levels at Lowestoft, Suffolk, during the storm surge.

Enquiry

How did the 2013 storm surge compare to the 1953 event?

Use the internet to research the main causes and effects of the 1953 North Sea storm surge.

- Compare the causes.
- Compare the effects.

How do we manage our coasts?

The usual way to manage coastlines has been through a combination of hard and soft engineering strategies. **Hard engineering** means building structures that prevent erosion and fix the coastline in place. The concrete sea wall and boulders in Figure 6 are a typical example. Wide beaches soak up a lot of wave energy and are a natural defence against coastal erosion. **Soft engineering** strategies mimic this by encouraging natural deposition to take place along the coastline. In Figure 8 you can see that an artificial rock reef has been built parallel to the coastline. This encourages deposition on the beach behind.

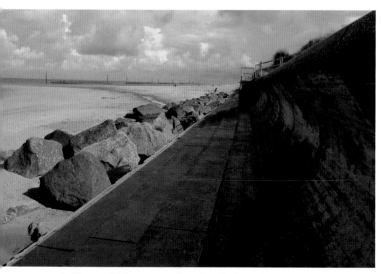

▲ **Figure 6** The sea wall at Sea Palling, Norfolk is an example of hard engineering.

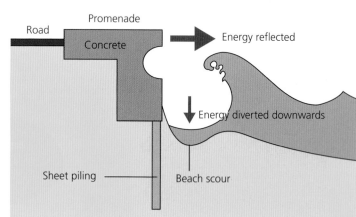

▲ **Figure 7** Sea walls can cause erosion of sediment from the beach.

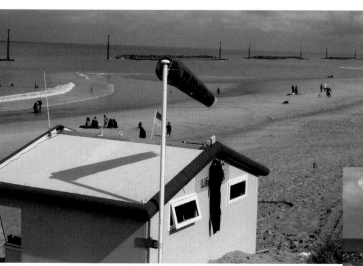

▲ **Figure 8** There are a total of nine artificial reefs at Sea Palling. Notice how sand has been deposited behind the reef, joining it to the beach.

Activity

1 a) Make a sketch of Figure 6.
   b) Label two hard engineering features on your sketch.
   c) Explain why boulders have been positioned at the top of the beach.

The importance of the inter-tidal zone

Estuarine landscapes, such as the one in Figure 9, contain many tidal creeks, salt marshes and mud banks. These features are exposed at low tide but at high tide they can store huge quantities of water. This is the **inter-tidal zone** and it acts as a natural buffer during storms – soaking up wave energy during a storm surge before the waves can reach more valuable land further inland.

Why is there a need for managed realignment?

There is a much narrower inter-tidal zone in the UK than there used to be:

- Many salt marshes were reclaimed in the past to create new farm land. Old earth embankments have kept the sea off these low-lying fields for centuries.
- Some salt marshes are being eroded by the sea. This is a particular problem along the Essex and Thames gateway coastlines where the land is subsiding so sea levels are rising faster than elsewhere in the UK.

Managed realignment can be used to create new inter-tidal zones of salt marsh. The process begins by punching holes through the old earth embankment. The invading sea water moves slowly across the land at high tide. As it flows in, it deposits mud. As it flows out, it creates tidal creeks like those in Figure 9. This process recreates natural mudflats and salt marshes that will store water and act as a buffer to erosion in future flood events.

▲ **Figure 9** The inter-tidal zone of the Lune estuary, Lancashire. Tidal creeks and mud flats, here at low tide, can store huge quantities of water and help prevent flooding and erosion.

Before

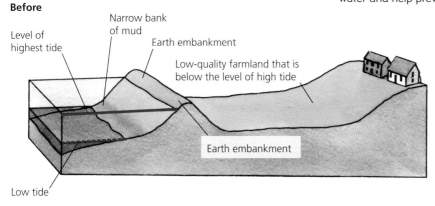

Level of highest tide

Narrow bank of mud

Earth embankment

Low-quality farmland that is below the level of high tide

Earth embankment

Low tide

After

3. The new layers of mud absorb wave energy. The mudflats act as a buffer zone, protecting homes and farm land from future erosion.

1. The old embankment is breached.

2. Sea water floods the reclaimed land at high tide and deposits mud.

Level of highest tide

Low tide

Key

—— Level of highest tides

▪▪▪▪▪ Low tide

▲ **Figure 10** How managed realignment creates wide inter-tidal zones that act as natural stores for flood water at high tide.

Activity

2 a) Make a sketch of Figure 9.
   b) Annotate your sketch to explain why the inter-tidal zone is an important natural defence against erosion and flooding.

Enquiry

Should we create more inter-tidal zones along the UK's coastline? Outline the arguments for and against managed realignment.

Is everyone in favour of managed realignment?

Managed realignment is an example of 'retreating the line' which is an option available in all **Shoreline Management Plans**, but it is a controversial choice. In 2014 the UK's largest realignment sea defence scheme was completed at Medmerry, West Sussex. This scheme has effectively redrawn the coastline 2 km further inland! The scheme began with the destruction of the existing sea wall, allowing some land to flood naturally at high tide. The newly flooded area will be able to absorb the energy of the waves and will reduce the risk of coastal flooding. A new 7 km sea wall has been built further inland. The Environment Agency says homes are much better protected as a result. However, at £28 million, the scheme was not popular with everyone.

▲ **Figure 11** The location of the Medmerry realignment scheme.

The old sea defenses have been breached here to allow sea water to flood the land to the left and create new salt marshes.

▲ **Figure 12** Medmerry seen from the air.

Has the Medmerry scheme been successful?

During the winter of 2014–15, weeks of rain and fierce storms lashed the south coast. Allan Chamberlain, estate director at the adjacent Medmerry Holiday Village, was shocked by how successful the scheme was. 'It's the first winter in years we haven't had to deal with surface flooding. The rainwater drains into the new marsh beautifully.' The bonus for the Holiday Village and the nearby Bunn Leisure Homes complex is that the new nature reserve is attracting even more tourists. Bookings are up and the tourist attractions can stay open for longer now that the area is largely flood free. Other, somewhat unexpected gains relate to farming. Cattle will be grazed on the salt marsh. This produces a flavour of beef that is highly prized. It is worth more to farmers than the beef usually sold in supermarkets. Also, there are plans for a fish nursery in the new estuarine environment. This could boost the fishing economy in neighbouring Selsey.

> Once you give land back to the sea, there's no getting it back, so if this doesn't work, we will have given up that land for nothing. I would like to see the Environment Agency look at other alternatives such as constructing rock barriers out in the ocean in front of the coast to break wave energy.

Ben Cooper – a resident of nearby Selsey

> Three productive farms producing oilseed rape and winter wheat will have to be sacrificed to the sea. The UK is not self-sufficient in food. The idea of letting perfectly good agricultural land disappear into the sea is wasteful and short-sighted.

Local farmers

> We already have to close for a number of months each year due to coastal flooding. It could get even worse if the sea wall is breached.

Bunn Leisure Holiday Homes

> We have had to endure terrible flooding this winter and we are quite upset about the whole thing. Why is the Environment Agency spending £28 million on creating a coastal nature reserve at Medmerry when they could use the money to dredge rivers and reduce the risk of flooding where we live instead?

Somerset residents badly affected by floods in 2013/14

▲ **Figure 13** Opposition to the Medmerry scheme.

Activities

1. Use Figure 11 to describe the location of Medmerry.
2. Summarise the benefits of realignment at Medmerry for:
   a) local homeowners and businesses
   b) the environment including wildlife.
3. Explain why some local people may have opposed realigning the coast here.

Enquiry

How sustainable is the decision to realign the coast at Medmerry?

Explain how the sustainability of this scheme could be measured over the next 50 years.

Shoreline Management Plans

Coastal communities expect the government to help protect them from erosion and coastal floods. However, managing the coastline is very expensive. Furthermore, there is no legal duty for the government to build coastal defences to protect people or their property. It is the responsibility of the local councils of England and Wales to prepare a Shoreline Management Plan (SMP) for their section of coast. In deciding whether or not to build new coastal defences (or repair old ones), the local council needs to weigh up the benefits of building the defences against the costs. They may consider factors such as:

- How many people are threatened by erosion and what is their property worth?
- How much would it cost to replace infrastructure such as roads or railway lines if they were washed away?
- Are there historic or natural features that should be conserved? Do these features have an economic value, for example, by attracting tourists to the area?

Option	Description	Comment
Do nothing	Do nothing and allow gradual erosion.	This is an option if the land has a lower value than the cost of building sea defences, which can be very expensive.
Hold the line	Use hard engineering such as timber or rock groynes and concrete sea walls to protect the coastline, or add extra sand to a beach to make it more effective at absorbing wave energy.	Sea walls cost about £6000 per metre to build. Sea-level rise means that such defences need to be constantly maintained, and will eventually need to be replaced with larger structures. For this reason hard engineering is usually only used where the land that is being protected is particularly valuable.
Retreat the line	Punch a hole in an existing coastal defence to allow land to flood naturally between low and high tide (the inter-tidal zone).	Sand dunes and salt marshes provide a natural barrier to flooding and help to absorb wave energy. They adapt naturally to changing sea levels through a process of erosion at the seaward side and deposition further inland.
Advance the line	Build new coastal defences further out to sea.	This requires a huge engineering project and would be the most expensive option. The advantage would be that new, flat land would be available that could be used as a port or airport facility.

▲ **Figure 14** The options available to local councils when they prepare a Shoreline Management Plan.

◀ **Figure 15** Wooden groynes on Borth beach in 2009.

Activity

1 Use Figures 15 and 16.
  a) Describe these structures.
  b) Suggest how they helped to protect Borth from erosion and flooding.

Management at Borth, Ceredigion

The village of Borth is built on the southern end of a pebble ridge, or spit, that sticks out into the Dyfi estuary. Sand is trapped on the beach by wooden groynes. The sand absorbs wave energy and prevents waves from eroding the pebble ridge. However, the groynes are in poor condition and are at the end of their working lives. What should be done?

The Ceredigion SMP divides the coast up into small management units (MU). Figure 17 shows the extent of five of these MUs.

▲ **Figure 16** The wooden sea wall at the top of the pebble ridge (2009).

◄ **Figure 17** An Ordnance Survey extract of Borth. Scale 1:50,000.

Activities

2 Work in pairs.
Use Figure 17 to provide map evidence which suggests that this coast is worth protecting. Copy and complete the table below and add at least five more pieces of evidence.

Management Unit	Map evidence
16.2	Railway station at 609901 would be expensive to replace
16.3	
16.4	The campsite in 6192 provides local jobs
17.1	

3 Which is the best SMP option for Management Unit (MU) 16.2? Use information from Figure 14 and evidence in Figure 17 to help you make your choice.

What coastal management is appropriate for Borth?

Ceredigion Council decided that there were two possible options for Management Unit (MU) 16.2 that needed further consideration. Read the points of view in Figure 19 before deciding what you would do.

Do nothing	Loss of property and economic loss in the short term. Change to Borth Bog.	Consider further
Hold the line	Current policy which protects property and businesses. Coastal processes disrupted with reduced longshore drift.	Consider further
Retreat	Retreat would affect homes that are immediately behind the existing line of defence.	Not considered further
Advance	No need to advance the line except to improve the tourist facilities.	Not considered further

▲ **Figure 18** The initial decision of the Ceredigion Council for MU16.2.

Sand from the southern end of the beach is gradually being eroded by longshore drift, moving it northwards. This process is happening faster than new sand is being deposited. The beach is getting thinner and is less able to protect the pebble ridge (on which Borth is built) from erosion. If the council does nothing then the pebble ridge will be breached by storm waves and the town of Borth, and Borth Bog (Cors Fochno) will be flooded by the sea. This could happen in the next ten to fifteen years. The peat bog at Cors Fochno will be covered in sea water at high tide and its existing ecosystem lost. Over the next few years erosion will punch more holes through the pebble ridge. A new spit of pebbles will eventually form further to the east. The sand dunes at Ynyslas will probably be cut off and form a small island.

Scientist

The beach and landscape of the spit, including the sand dunes at Ynyslas, are an important economic asset to the village. It's this natural environment that attracts thousands of holidaymakers each year. If the council does nothing then my home and many others will be flooded and local people will lose their livelihoods.

B&B owner

Scientist

The peat bog at Cors Fochno should be protected from flooding. It is a nationally and internationally important ecosystem. It has protection as a Special Area of Conservation and is also recognised by UNESCO. 'Do nothing' is an unacceptable option.

We calculate that property in Borth village is worth £10.75 million. On top of this there are many local businesses which would lose their income from tourism if we do nothing. The cost of holding the line is around £7 million. However, we are concerned that building new groynes will prevent longshore drift. We need to consider the impact of that. Currently the sediment moves to Ynyslas where it provides a natural defence to the whole estuary (including the larger village of Aberdyfi) from south-westerly storms.

Local councillor

▲ **Figure 19** Views on the future management of MU16.2.

Activities

1 Using a table, summarise the economic, social and environmental impacts of doing nothing or holding the line in Management Unit 16.2.
2 State which option you would recommend. Explain why you think your option is best for this stretch of coast.

Enquiry

Which is the best SMP option for Management Unit 17.1?

Analyse information from Figure 17 and evaluate the views in Figure 19 to help you justify your choice.

What happened next in Borth?

A decision was made to 'hold the line' and continue to protect the community at Borth. The old wooden groynes (seen in Figure 15) were constructed in the 1970s. These were badly worn so they were removed as four new rock groynes were built. These will trap sediment moved by longshore drift and maintain a wide beach in front of the town. A rock reef, parallel to the shore, was constructed at the southern end of the spit. The reef will help to break the force of the waves. As waves wash around each end of the reef they will lose energy, encouraging the deposition of sand and shingle behind the reef. The reef has been described as multi-purpose. As well as defending the coastline it should improve wave conditions for surfing. If the reef works, Borth's tourist economy could benefit.

The new coastal defences at Borth also include:

- replacing the wooden sea wall at the top of the beach
- adding new shingle to widen the beach.

The scheme was completed in 2015 at a cost of £18 million. Of this, £5 million came from the European Regional Development Fund – funding from the EU designed to promote growth in deprived regions. All of the rock was purchased from a local quarry.

▲ **Figure 20** The rock reef at the southern end of the spit at Borth, 2015.

Borth's sea defences a success

Some of the large boulders within the defences have moved slightly. The pebble banks that were extended and built up as part of the defences have also been reshaped by the waves, but the damage to houses and other properties was minimal. Some were flooded and there was plenty of debris in the road behind them, but along the stretch of beach where the defences are situated there was certainly less damage.

Flooding and storm damage along this stretch was quite a common occurrence too, and that was during storms that were much less ferocious than the one we've just expe-

rienced, so I'm almost certain that without the new sea defences the damage would have been much worse.

This recent storm was the first real test of the sea defences in Borth and it looks as though they have proved their worth. They may require a little reshaping and work to restore the banks following this storm, but surely that is better than rebuilding homes. They may not be the prettiest of things and they may not have worked as a surf reef, but they do seem to have fulfilled their primary purpose of acting as a sea defence in this instance.

▲ **Figure 21** A local resident comments on the reef in his blog on 11 January 2014 after a severe winter storm.

Coastal hazard mapping

Flood preparedness can help save lives and prevent injury. The ability of coastal communities to cope during a storm surge can be improved when:

- a warning of an extreme weather event is given
- people know which areas will be affected, what to do and how to protect themselves
- the emergency services and hospitals have a plan of action in the event of disaster.

The UK has sophisticated services that provide weather forecasts and warnings of extreme weather and flooding. Forecasts are provided by the Flood Forecasting Centre at Exeter, which provides a service 24 hours a day, seven days a week. Their forecasts are passed to the Environment Agency (England) and Natural Resources Wales, who inform the public. Each of these bodies provides two types of online **hazard map**:

- One showing areas that are prone to river and coastal flooding. This type of map can be used to plan an evacuation route long before the flood happens.
- A live map that uses warning symbols in places where floods are likely. The Met Office also has a live weather map that uses warning symbols. A red weather warning means there is danger to life.

Online hazard maps alert the public to the danger of coastal flooding. Hazard mapping also allows local authorities to control the development of areas considered to be at risk, for example by preventing the building of new homes in areas at risk of erosion or coastal flooding.

 https:// naturalresources. wales/ This site displays interactive flood maps for Wales.

▲ **Figure 22** Screenshot of the Natural Resources Wales flood hazard map for Kinmel Bay and West Rhyl.

 http://datashine. org.uk This site displays interactive maps for the 2011 census.

▲ **Figure 23** Screenshot from Data Shine. It shows the proportion of people aged 65–75 in Kinmel Bay and West Rhyl. Green colours are above the national average.

Kinmel Bay – a community at risk of coastal flooding

Natural Resources Wales calculate that 80,000 properties are potentially at risk of flooding around the coastline of Wales. Towyn, Kinmel Bay and Rhyl in North Wales are all examples. This area was badly affected by coastal flooding in 1990 and again in 2013. The storm surge of 5 December 2013 caused coastal flooding: 400 people were evacuated from their homes to Rhyl Leisure Centre. RNLI crews and the fire service rescued 25 residents from flooded bungalows in Rhyl, while caravan sites in Kinmel Bay were flooded and a number of caravans, which were empty for the winter season, were destroyed. At least 400 homes were without power. Two severe warnings – meaning there was a danger to life – were given. People were alerted by phone, text, email and Twitter. Volunteer flood wardens in the area helped with the evacuation.

Activities

1 a) Describe two different uses of hazard mapping in coastal flood zones.
   b) Explain why people living in flood zones should have a personal evacuation plan.
2 Describe the extent of the potential flood zone in Figure 22.
3 Compare the patterns shown on Figures 22 and 23.
4 a) Represent the data in Figure 24 using a suitable technique.
   b) Compare the health of people living in the flood zone in North Wales with those living in Cardiff.
   c) Suggest why residents in the flood zone in North Wales may be at greater risk from floods than other people.

	Towyn	Kinmel Bay	Rhyl West	Cardiff	Wales
Very good health	34.0	40.9	38.8	50.4	46.7
Good health	31.2	30.3	29.9	31.1	31.1
Fair health	21.1	17.6	18.4	12.1	14.6
Bad health	10.6	8.5	9.9	4.8	5.8
Very bad health	3.1	2.7	3.0	1.6	1.8
One person in household with long-term health problem or disability (no dependent children)	31.8	27.3	35.0	21.5	25.2

▲ **Figure 24** Selected health data for the flood zone in North Wales compared to Cardiff and Wales as a whole. The 2011 census asked people to describe their general health over the preceding twelve months as 'very good', 'good', 'fair', 'bad' or 'very bad'. Figure 24 shows the percentage who responded in each category.

Towyn	Kinmel Bay	Rhyl West
LL22 9HW	LL18 5BB	LL18 1LP
LL22 9LR	LL18 5AS	LL18 3AH
LL22 9LX	LL18 5EQ	LL18 3ET

▲ **Figure 25** Selected postcodes.

 https://naturalresources.wales/flooding – follow the link from this page to the river level flood map, which also shows coastal flooding.

Enquiry

How vulnerable is Kinmel Bay and the surrounding area to coastal flooding?

- Use an online UK atlas (such as Google Maps or Bing Maps) to find the businesses located at each postcode in Figure 25.
- Which of these businesses is in the flood zone shown in Figure 22? You could use the weblink to Natural Resources Wales to check the map.
- Summarise the economic and social impacts of flooding at the postcodes you have researched.

THEME 4 — Coastal hazards and their management
Chapter 2
Vulnerable coastlines

Why are some coastal communities more vulnerable than others?

Coastal environments pose a number of potential hazards, such as landslides, flooding and sea level rise. The level of risk depends on a number of factors:

- the strength or **magnitude** of the event
- the number of people who may be affected
- the vulnerability of the people affected by the event; vulnerability is linked to factors such as poverty.

▲ **Figure 1** Fishermen's stilt houses, Luzon, Philippines.

Vulnerability

Vulnerability is a measure of someone's inability to cope with, or recover from, a disaster such as coastal flooding. Some groups of people are more vulnerable to hazards than others. Poverty, age, gender and disability are all factors that can affect vulnerability. For example, someone's poverty may mean that their house is badly built and unable to withstand flooding.

Capacity

Capacity is the opposite of vulnerability. It describes someone's ability to survive a hazard or recover from it quickly. Capacity is increased where individuals or communities have the resources they need to cope with the hazard. Resources can be financial or material, such as strong building materials. But capacity can also be improved by factors such as education, technology and disaster preparedness and planning.

How can we reduce vulnerability to coastal hazards?

To reduce vulnerability to a coastal hazard, organisations need to:

- Reduce the impact of the hazard. Examples include building flood walls and other coastal defences.
- Build capacity to cope with the hazard. Examples include educating people about what to do during a cyclone or storm surge so that they are more likely to survive, and creating a disaster plan so that emergency services, hospitals and local authorities all know what to do during and after a major disaster.
- Tackle the root causes of vulnerability. This means that governments need to reduce poverty and inequality in society so that everyone has the same opportunities and the same level of protection during a disaster.

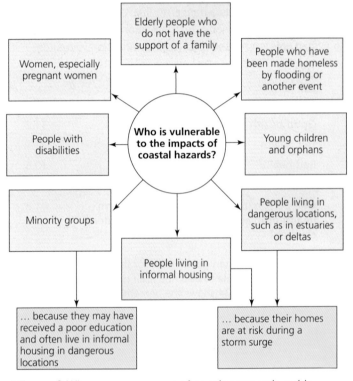

▲ **Figure 2** Why are some groups of people more vulnerable than others to coastal hazards?

Activities

1 a) Describe the housing in Figure 1.
   b) Why are people living here particularly vulnerable? What hazards do they face?
2 Choose four different groups of people in Figure 2.
   a) For each group explain why they may be more vulnerable to natural disasters.
   b) For one of these groups, suggest how their capacity could be improved to cope with coastal flooding.

How will climate change affect coastal communities in the UK?

Rising sea levels will increase the rate of coastal erosion. More farmland will be lost and more expensive sea defences will be needed to 'hold the line' against erosion of our towns and cities. Climate change also means a warmer atmosphere, which means more storms like the devastating storm surges that flooded Jaywick in 1953 and 2013.

Year	2007	2032	2057	2082	2107
Rise in sea level (cm)	0	13	35	65	102

▲ **Figure 3** Predicted sea level rise at Jaywick, Essex.

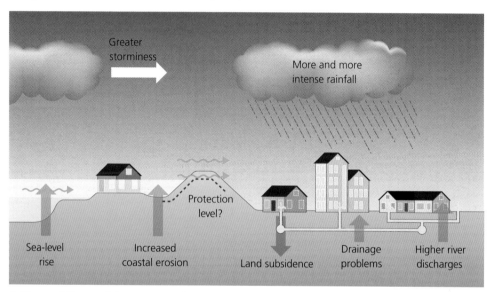

▲ **Figure 4** Some of the impacts of climate change on our coastline by 2050.

Activities

3 Use Figure 4 to describe five different impacts of sea-level rise on coastal communities in the UK.

4 Use Figure 5 and an atlas to name:
  a) five counties in England facing problems of extreme coastal erosion
  b) three counties in Wales facing very high rates of erosion.

5 a) Use Figure 3 to draw a graph of the predicted sea level rise at Jaywick.
  b) Give two reasons to explain why sea levels are rising here.

▶ **Figure 5** Coastal erosion if carbon dioxide emissions continue to increase and sea levels rise.

How could climate change affect London and the Thames Gateway?

One of the most vulnerable coastlines in the UK is the estuarine landscape of the River Thames to the east of London. This coastline, known as the Thames Gateway, is at risk from storm surges (like those in 1953 and 2013) that push sea into the narrow funnel-like coastline between Essex and Kent. This coastline has been sinking ever since the end of the ice age in the UK about 10,000 years ago – a process called **postglacial rebound**. As a result, the Thames Gateway is sinking at about 2 mm a year relative to current sea levels. Climate change means that sea levels in the Thames estuary are rising at about 3 mm a year. So the combined effect of sea level rise and postglacial rebound means that sea levels here are rising at 5–6 mm per year.

Year	Type of risk that caused closure		Total closures
	Tidal	River flood	
1983	1	0	1
1984	0	0	0
1985	0	0	0
1986	0	1	1
1987	1	0	1
1988	1	0	1
1989	0	0	0
1990	1	3	4
1991	2	0	2
1992	0	0	0
1993	4	0	4
1994	3	4	7
1995	2	2	4
1996	4	0	4
1997	1	0	1
1998	1	0	1
1999	2	0	2
2000	3	3	6
2001	16	8	24
2002	3	1	4
2003	8	12	20
2004	1	0	1
2005	4	0	4
2006	3	0	3
2007	8	0	8
2008	6	0	6
2009	1	4	5
2010	2	3	5
2011	0	0	0
2012	0	0	0
2013	0	5	5
2014	7	41	48

▲ **Figure 7** Closures of the Thames Barrier to protect against storm (tidal) surges (1983–2014).

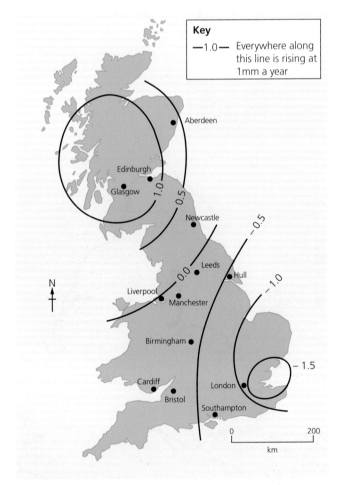

Key

—1.0— Everywhere along this line is rising at 1mm a year

▲ **Figure 6** The amount of postglacial rebound (mm per year). Positive numbers mean the land is rising relative to the sea and negative numbers mean the land is sinking.

Activities

1 Use Figure 6 to describe the parts of the UK where:
   a) land is rising fastest
   b) land is sinking fastest.
2 a) Use the data in Figure 7 to produce a graph of closures.
   b) Describe the trend of your graph.
   c) Explain why this graph could be seen to be more evidence for climate change.

Holding the line

The Thames flood barrier was completed in 1982. It is situated to the east of the City of London so protects large parts of London from tidal surges coming up the river from the North Sea. It protects 1.25 million people from tidal floods. However, it is now thought that the barrier is not large enough to protect London from future floods. The Thames Estuary 2100 Plan (TE2100) suggests that, by 2100, London needs to be protected from a possible flood that would be 2.7 m higher than current flood levels.

Factfile: Property at risk of tidal flooding on the Thames floodplain

- Over 500,000 homes
- 40,000 commercial and industrial properties
- 400 schools
- 16 hospitals
- 35 tube stations
- Over 300 km of roads

The TE2100 Plan uses three strategies to protect London and the Thames Gateway:

- Continue to renew and replace existing embankments, sea walls and sluices in the Thames Gateway.
- Increase the amount of inter-tidal habitat in the Thames estuary by 876 hectares. These salt marshes will help to store flood water as it moves up the estuary during a tidal surge. These storage areas would be created by managed realignment projects like the one at Tollesbury, Essex.
- Consider building a new, larger barrier at Long Reach to the east of the existing barrier. The construction of this new barrier would cost between £6 billion and £7 billion.

Activities

3 Use Figure 8 to describe:
   a) the distribution of breaches
   b) the amount and value of flooded land.
4 Explain why the cost of flood damage in Essex would be lower than that in London.

Legend
- 0 €/m²
- 0 - 1 €/m²
- 1 - 10 €/m²
- 10 - 100 €/m²
- 100 - 200 €/m²
- 200 - 1000 €/m²
- 1000 - 2000 €/m²
- 2000 - 5000 €/m²
- 5000 - 10.000 €/m²
- > 10.000 €/m²
- ● Breach location

▲ **Figure 8** The cost of flood damage in 2050 after a flood similar to the 1953 storm surge if sea levels continue to rise and flood protection is not improved. Red dots show where coastal defences would be breached.

Enquiry

How should London and the Thames Gateway be protected in the future? Some people are sceptical about managed realignment. Justify why the TE2100 Plan proposes to combine a new flood barrier with managed realignment.

Why are some coastal communities more vulnerable than others?

A report by the Joseph Rowntree Foundation suggests that some of the most vulnerable people, living in isolated communities of the UK, will be the most affected by rising sea levels.

The report argues that poverty is a factor that makes some communities more vulnerable to sea level rise and coastal flooding than others. Poverty means that the local council has fewer resources available to reduce the threat of and the impacts of sea level rise.

The report suggests that vulnerability to coastal flooding increases where communities have:

- a higher proportion of people claiming benefits
- a fast turnover of people through economic migration
- a high proportion of poor-quality housing
- an over-reliance on tourism, resulting in seasonal employment and low incomes.

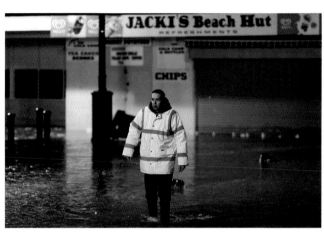

▲ **Figure 9** Coastal floods in Great Yarmouth, December 2013.

Skegness, Lincolnshire

Skegness is one of the better-known seaside resorts in England. It is situated within the largely rural area of East Lindsey and has poor road and rail links. Skegness has one of the largest concentrations of caravan parks in Europe. Some static caravans are the permanent homes for retired residents and people on low incomes.

Great Yarmouth, Norfolk

Great Yarmouth is a medium-sized port and is an important seaside resort. It has a high proportion of elderly and retired residents. Unemployment rates are higher in Great Yarmouth than in the rest of the East of England. The economy of the port is in decline and the nearby North Sea gas fields have begun to reduce production.

GEOGRAPHICAL SKILLS

Interpreting population pyramids

Population pyramids are a specialist form of bar graph. Each bar represents males or females in a specific age category. The bars may represent actual population numbers or percentage figures. Interpreting the shape of a pyramid can tell you a lot about the structure of a population. Pyramids with a wide base have a youthful population and those with a wide top have an ageing population. Interpreting the structure is the first step in analysing possible issues that may be facing the population. For example, does an ageing population have sufficient health care and social services suitable for this age group?

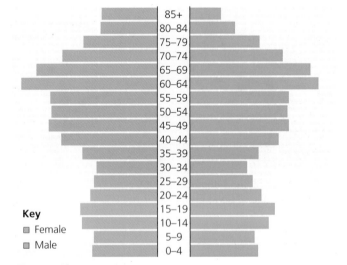

▲ **Figure 10** Population pyramid for East Lindsey, Lincolnshire (2011).

 www.ons.gov.uk/ons/interactive/uk-population-pyramid---dvc1/index.html

An interactive population pyramid for the UK showing change between 1971 and 2085.

Llanelli, Gwent

Unemployment in Llanelli is higher than the national average and the town has been particularly hard hit by the economic recession of 2008–09. Derelict industrial sites along the coastline are now the focus of several regeneration schemes. The town has a higher than average proportion of elderly residents. A high number of migrants from Eastern Europe have settled in the town.

Indicator	Skegness	Lincolnshire	England
% of working population in professional/ management jobs	14	18	23
% of working population claiming work-related benefits	18	13	13
% of adult population with no academic qualifications	33	26	22
% of the adult population who are in very good health	38	43	47

▲ **Figure 11** Socio-economic statistics for Skegness.

Benbecula, Outer Hebrides

With a population of 1,200, the population and economy of this remote Scottish island have been in decline since the mid-1970s because of the closure of a military base. The lack of jobs for younger people has also contributed to the decline and to the ageing of the island's population. The island's coastal drainage system was built in the 1800s and is not very efficient. It struggles to cope with the combined effects of heavy rainfall and high tides.

▲ **Figure 12** Skegness has a large concentration of static caravans.

In such communities, local people may lack the funds to make structural changes to their homes (e.g. to make them flood resistant). They may not be able to afford to move away. Coastal local authorities with areas of high deprivation may not be able to afford the resources for climate change preparation. Government policy means that there is an ever-increasing expectation that individuals and communities should help themselves to prepare for the likely increase in sea level rise. For disadvantaged residents, the threat of sea level rise is simply not a major issue at this moment in time. They have other things to focus on.

▲ **Figure 13** An extract (adapted) from the Joseph Rowntree Foundation Report, Summary of 'Impacts of climate change on disadvantaged UK coastal communities' (2011).

Activities

1 Compare the four communities described on these pages. Describe three similarities that link at least two of these communities.
2 a) Describe the structure of the population structure for East Lindsey.
  b) Use the Weblink to compare this population structure to that of the UK.
  c) What does this suggest is needed in East Lindsey?
3 Explain why every local authority may not be able to afford the resources needed to prepare for sea level rise.
4 a) Use Figure 11 to identify the overall pattern shown in the table.
  b) The figures in the table date from the National Census in 2011. The worst impact of sea level rise is not expected to happen until 2050. Should the local authority use the data to appeal for additional outside help when planning for sea level rise? Justify your answer.

Enquiry

Who should be responsible for protecting communities in the UK from the effects of sea level rise?

Government policy means that there is an ever-increasing expectation that individuals and communities should help themselves to prepare for the likely increase in sea level rise. How far do you agree with this statement? Discuss this in groups.

How might climate change affect coastal communities around the world?

By 2030 it is estimated that 950 million people around the world will live in the **Low Elevation Coastal Zone (LECZ)** – that is, coastal areas that are less than 10 m above sea level. Climate change presents a triple threat to people living in LECZs:

• Sea level rise increases the risk of coastal flooding at high tide.
• Heavier rainfall increases the risk of flash floods in urban areas with poor drainage.
• More violent storms and hurricanes increase the risk of coastal erosion and storm surges.

The worst-affected coastal communities could be those living on the world's major river deltas. People living here are affected by subsidence of the soft land as well as by sea-level rise. Millions of people live on deltas in Bangladesh, Egypt, Nigeria, Vietnam and Cambodia.

In 2013 the World Bank identified 136 of the world's coastal cities that were at greatest risk from climate change. Mumbai, home to 18.4 million people, is one.

Built on a low-lying island, much of Mumbai is only 10 m above sea level. Other cities, like New York, Singapore and New Orleans, are also at risk. Many cities are in developing countries where the poorest members of society are at most risk of natural hazards. This is because the poorest neighbourhoods, like those in Figure 15, are often in low-lying areas and built alongside waterways or seafronts that are vulnerable to flooding. As sea levels rise, some people may have to leave their homes. They will become **environmental refugees**.

Activity

1 Use Figure 14 to describe:
   a) the distribution of SIDS
   b) the location of:
      i) the Maldives
      ii) the Marshall Islands.
   c) Suggest why people living in isolated places like these are vulnerable to natural hazards.

▲ **Figure 14** Small Island Developing States (SIDs) such as the Maldives in the Indian Ocean and the Marshall Islands in the pacific are very low lying. A 1 m rise in sea level by 2100 would flood up to 75 per cent of the land in each of these two nations.

Factfile: Small Island Developing States (SIDS)

- There are currently 58 SIDS with a combined population of 65 million people.
- Many SIDS are very small and some are located in remote and isolated parts of the world. Most

SIDS are vulnerable to climate change and natural disasters.
- Standards of living among small islands differ widely, with GDP per capita ranging from $51,000 in Singapore to $830 in Comoros.

City	Population (%) at risk in LECZ	Land (%) at risk in LECZ	Population 2015	Population 2030
Cotonou, Benin	94.7	85.4	682,000	979,000
Warri, Nigeria	90.8	92.0	663,000	1,298,000
Alexandria, Egypt	85.1	68.8	4,778,000	6,313,000
Port Harcourt, Nigeria	64.4	61.9	2,344,000	4,562,000
Dakar, Senegal	61.6	47.6	3,520,000	6,046,000

▲ **Figure 15** Selected African cities in the low elevation coastal zone (LECZ).

▲ **Figure 16** Poor neighbourhoods in Cotonou, Benin are built on stilts along the waterfront.

Activities

2 Study Figure 16.
   a) Describe the housing carefully.
   b) Suggest why the poorest members of society live in neighbourhoods like this.
   c) Suggest how this community will be affected by climate change.
3 Calculate the actual number of people expected to be living in the LECZ in each of the cities in Figure 15.

Enquiry

Analyse why it may be more difficult for the governments of SIDs to cope with climate change than a larger country like India.

Communities vulnerable to climate change and sea level rise in Egypt

The International Organization for Migration suggests that climate change will displace 200 million people by 2050. Rising sea levels, drought, food and water insecurity and increased health risks are the main reasons. Egypt is one country that could be affected.

Egypt is a desert country. It has a population of 85 million. Most urban areas and farmland are squashed into just 15 per cent of the nation's landmass – mainly along the length of the River Nile and in the Nile Delta. Climate change will create a number of challenges for Egypt:

- Rising temperatures and less frequent rain will increase the current problems of water stress. This will affect the urban poor and it will mean that farmers will have to find new efficient techniques to irrigate crops.
- Water-borne diseases and malaria will become more common. There is also likely to be a huge increase in parasitic diseases, skin cancer, eye cataracts, respiratory ailments and heat stroke.
- Sea level rise may erode and flood the Nile Delta, displacing as many as 8 million people.

Alexandria, in the Nile Delta, is Egypt's second largest city. This Mediterranean port handles 80 per cent of Egypt's imports and exports. The wealth of the city attracts migrants. Natural population increase adds to pressure on space. Houses and flats are often built without proper planning permission or building regulation. In fact, it is estimated that 50 per cent of Alexandria's population live in informal housing. The urban poor are perhaps at greater risk of climate change than others because they:

- have few savings so cannot afford to lose their jobs or their homes
- often rely on boreholes that are polluted by human waste so are at risk of water-borne disease or they have to buy water from street vendors at great cost
- often live in locations that are dangerous to human health, for example near to stagnant water where mosquitoes that carry malaria breed
- live in badly built multi-storey buildings that are at risk of collapse during earthquakes.

Key
Population density (per km²)

- <25
- 26–100
- 101–250
- 251–500
- 500–1,000
- >1,000
- Urban extents

Mediterranean Sea

Alexandria

Cairo

EGYPT

Gulf of Suez

N

0   50
km

◀ **Figure 17** Population density of the Nile Delta.

Year	Population
1950	1.04
1960	1.50
1970	1.99
1980	2.52
1990	3.06
2000	3.55
2010	4.33
2020	5.23
2030	6.31

▲ **Figure 18** The population of Alexandria (millions). Figures after 2010 are predictions.

Alexandria is built on Egypt's Low Elevation Coastal Zone (LECZ) (see page 148) so is vulnerable to permanent flooding if sea levels rise. If this happens, Egypt will find it difficult to re-house the huge number of environmental refugees. Presumably, many people who currently live in informal housing in Alexandria will move into the poorest, most overcrowded districts of Cairo.

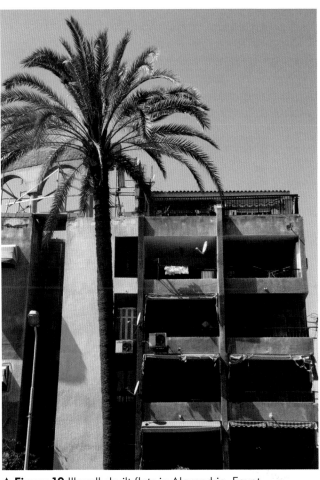

▲ **Figure 19** Illegally built flats in Alexandria, Egypt.

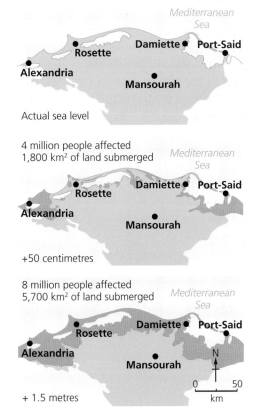

▲ **Figure 20** Predicted changes to Egypt's coast-line as the sea level rises.

Activities

1 Describe the location of Alexandria.
2 a) Use Figure 18 to draw a line graph of population growth.
  b) Describe the trend of your graph.
  c) If this trend continues, what might be the population of Alexandria in 2040?
3 a) Outline three different problems that will be created for the people of Egypt by climate change.
  b) Explain why the urban poor are most at risk. Give two different reasons.
4 Describe the possible loss of land in the Nile Delta. How big is the potential environmental refugee problem?
5 a) Use Figure 17 to describe the distribution and density of Egypt's population.
  b) Why is this a significant problem for the Egyptian government if sea levels rise as predicted?

Enquiry

'Solving the problems caused by climate change refugees is the responsibility of all nations.' How far do you agree with this statement? Justify your answer.

Is it too late to save the Maldives?

The Republic of Maldives, in the Indian Ocean, is made up of 1,190 islands. It has a population of 350,000. Most of the islands are uninhabited, with over one-third of the population living in Malé, the capital city. Eighty per cent of the land area is under 1 m above sea level. Nowhere is above 3 m. No place on earth is more vulnerable and threatened by sea level rise. The GDP of the Maldives ranks the country as 165th out of 192 nation states (2013).

For more than three decades politicians from the country have tried to persuade world leaders to take climate change more seriously. In the 2015 Geneva Climate Change Conference, Dunya Maumoon, the minister of foreign affairs for the Maldives, asked the global community to take concrete action. He said, *'2015 should be remembered, not for stories about sea level rise, but ones about how we rose up together to stop it.'* The fact is, it's probably already too late.

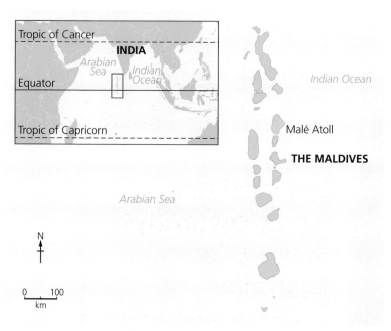

▲ **Figure 21** The location of the Maldives.

▲ **Figure 22** Is this the future for the Maldives?

▲ **Figure 23** The capital city of the Maldives, Malé, is surrounded by sea.

Factfile: The effects of sea level rise on the Maldives

- A rise in sea level of 0.5 m by the year 2100 would mean that 77 per cent of the land surface of the Maldives will be underwater.
- A rise in sea level of 1 m by the year 2100 would make the islands uninhabitable by 2085.

Chapter 2 Vulnerable coastlines

How is sea level rise already affecting the islands?

Frequent flooding of the islands over the past 30 years has caused ongoing problems for the Maldives. Most of the problems occur when the highest spring tides coincide with storms across the northern India Ocean.

| The impact of flooding across the Maldives |

Male – a capital city surrounded by sea walls:
In 2008 Japan offered $60 million in aid to fund a 3 m sea wall for Male. The sea wall has been completed and will hold back the advance of the sea for the medium term. All the other islands remain vulnerable. The sea wall needs constant repair and the cost has to be paid for through local tourist taxes.

Drinking water is in short supply:
Sea level rise is already beginning to put stress on the scarce freshwater resources of the Maldives; 87% of the population can currently be supplied by collecting rainwater. Groundwater sources across the chain of islands have been contaminated by salt-water intrusion and are now undrinkable. Bringing in supplies from abroad is unsustainable.

The tourist industry under threat:
Tourism is by far and away the most important industry. It accounts for 90% of government tax revenue. The damage caused by the 2004 tsunami-related sea surge destroyed many prize beaches and ruined some luxury resorts. For a year, tourist numbers dropped dramatically as the islands implemented a recovery programme. Tourist numbers have since recovered, but the industry may have been given a taste of what's to come.

▲ **Figure 24** The impact of flooding across the Maldives.

Islands that float

Floating islands will be moored to the seabed using cables to minimise environmental impact. This idea has been put forward by a Dutch company. One of the islands will be used to create an artificial golf course. Golfers will access the floating 'golf island' by a tunnel on the seabed. There will be a spectacular underwater clubhouse for golfers to relax in after their game. The artificial islands will be built in India or the Middle East and towed to the Maldives.

▲ **Figure 25** How might the Maldives develop tourism in the future?

Sea level rise forces castaways to move to Australia

The Maldivian President said his government was considering Australia as a possible new home if the Maldives disappear beneath rising seas. He explained that Maldivians wanted to stay but moving was an eventuality his government had to plan for. Australia may need to prepare for a mass wave of climate refugees, seeking a new place to live.

▲ **Figure 26** Sea level rise may create environmental refugees.

Activities

1 Describe the location of the Maldives.
2 Study the two newspaper headlines shown in Figures 25 and 26. Both were published in 2012. They offer very different radical solutions to the problems faced by the Maldives.
   a) Discuss how sustainable each idea would be.
   b) Discuss which is the most likely to be turned into reality.

Enquiry

What should the Maldives Government do?

- List five different ideas for action – place your ideas in priority order.
- Justify why you think ideas one and two need to be put into action as soon as possible.

THEME
5
Weather, climate and ecosystems
Chapter 1
Climate change during the Quaternary

Why has climate changed?

The Quaternary, sometimes called the Pleistocene, is the most recent period of geological time. It is a period of Earth's history that has been dominated by cold climates and ice shaping the land. At the beginning of the Quaternary, the polar ice sheets were far bigger than they are today, as you can see in Figure 1. Throughout the 2.6 million years of the Quaternary the climate has changed constantly. There have been periods, known as **glacials**, when the polar ice has reached much further south, covering large parts of the Earth. At other times, known as **inter-glacials**, the polar ice retreated. Scientists have evidence of 60 different cycles of ice advance and retreat. The ice sheets retreated about 10,000 years ago and the Earth is currently experiencing an inter-glacial period. However, the ice has not totally disappeared. Technically, we are still living in an ice age!

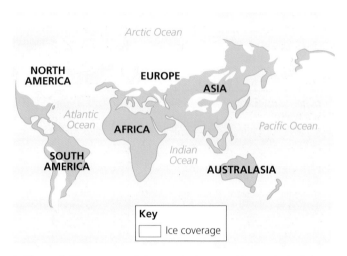

▲ **Figure 1** The extent of the ice during a colder period of the Quaternary period.

What are the natural causes of climate change?

There is much debate about the cause of the change from glacial periods to inter-glacial periods. The most commonly accepted theory is based on the work of a scientist called Milankovitch. He suggested that the warmer and cooler periods are caused by a combination of two things:

- The natural wobble of the Earth as it moves around the Sun. This affects the tilt of the Earth and the amount of energy it receives from the Sun.
- The fact that the Earth does not have a circular orbit around the Sun. The orbit is eccentric: sometimes it is closer to the Sun, and sometimes it is further away.

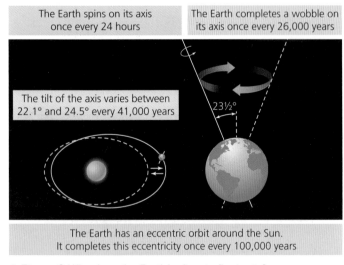

The Earth spins on its axis once every 24 hours

The Earth completes a wobble on its axis once every 26,000 years

The tilt of the axis varies between 22.1° and 24.5° every 41,000 years

23½°

The Earth has an eccentric orbit around the Sun. It completes this eccentricity once every 100,000 years

▲ **Figure 2** Why does the Earth's climate fluctuate?

Activities

1 Study Figure 1.
   a) Describe the amount and distribution of the ice sheets.
   b) Study the Mediterranean region carefully. Suggest why the Mediterranean Sea appears to be smaller than it is today.
   c) To what extent are we still living in an ice age? Use an atlas or the internet to compare the amount and distribution of permanent ice today with that shown in Figure 1.

2 Why does the surface temperature of the Earth change when:
   a) its tilt varies due to the natural 'wobble'
   b) due to its eccentric orbit?

How do volcanic eruptions affect climate?

Large volcanic eruptions can eject dust and sulphur dioxide (SO_2) into the lower stratosphere – a layer in the atmosphere that is 15 to 25 km above the Earth. At this altitude the jet stream is able to carry the volcanic material in a belt right around the globe. The mixture of ash and SO_2 form an **aerosol** – tiny droplets that scatter sunlight back into space. This can have the effect of reducing the amount of solar energy that reaches the Earth's surface, so average temperatures can be reduced. The largest volcanic eruption of the last 100 years was the eruption of Mount Pinatubo in the Philippines in 1991. This eruption had a magnitude of VEI-6. It ejected enough ash and SO_2 to block out about ten per cent of the sunlight reaching the northern hemisphere, reducing temperatures by 0.4 to 0.6°C for two years. However, the very largest volcanic eruptions could have much greater effects.

The eruption of Tambora in Indonesia in 1815 had a magnitude of VEI-7, making it ten times larger than Pinatubo's eruption. Temperatures in the northern hemisphere fell. Crops failed in North America and Europe during the cold, wet weather of 1816 and thousands died of starvation. Dust in the stratosphere scattered sunlight creating spectacular sunsets – an effect captured by the British artist JMW Turner as you can see in Figure 3.

▲ **Figure 3** Sunset over Chichester Canal, painted by JMW Turner.

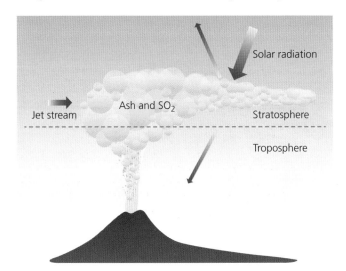

▲ **Figure 4** How volcanic eruptions can reduce global temperatures.

Activity

3   Make a copy of Figure 4. Add annotations to explain how a large volcanic eruption can reduce global temperatures.

Enquiry

How significant is the effect of large volcanic eruptions on climate?

Research the Toba eruption (75,000 years ago) – perhaps the largest eruption during the Quaternary period. What were its effects on climate? How might this compare to other natural reasons for warming or cooling?

▲ **Figure 5** Wildfires in San Marcos, California (May 2014). 13,000 people had to be evacuated.

What is the greenhouse effect?

The greenhouse effect is a natural process of our atmosphere. Without it, the average surface temperature of the Earth would be −17° Celsius rather than the 15° Celsius we currently experience. At these temperatures, life would not have evolved on Earth in its present form and we probably wouldn't exist!

The greenhouse effect, shown in Figure 6, means that Earth's atmosphere acts like an insulating blanket. Light (short-wave) and heat (long-wave) energy from the Sun passes through the atmosphere quite easily. The Sun's energy heats the Earth and it radiates its own energy back into the atmosphere. The long-wave heat energy coming from the Earth is quite easily absorbed by naturally occurring gases in the atmosphere. These are known as **greenhouse gases**. They include carbon dioxide (CO_2), methane (CH_4) and water vapour (H_2O). Carbon dioxide is the fourth most common gas in the atmosphere. It occurs naturally in the atmosphere as a product of respiration from all living things. So carbon dioxide has existed in the atmosphere for as long as there has been life on Earth. Methane and water vapour have been in the atmosphere for even longer, so the greenhouse effect has been affecting our climate for thousands of millions of years.

Activity

1 Use Figure 6 to explain the greenhouse effect. Make sure that you use technical terms such as long-wave and short-wave energy in your answer.

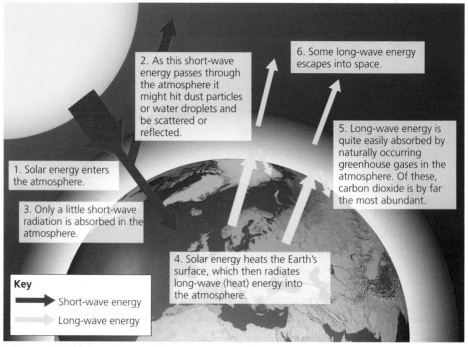

▲ **Figure 6** The greenhouse effect.

How have people's actions affected the greenhouse effect?

Carbon is one of the most common elements in the environment. It is present in:

- all organic substances, i.e. all living things
- simple compounds such as CO_2, which exists as a gas in the atmosphere and is dissolved in the oceans
- complex compounds, for example, hydrocarbons found in fossil fuels such as oil, coal and gas.

Carbon is able to transfer from one part of the environment to another through a series of biological processes, such as respiration, and chemical processes such as solution. These transfers take place between parts of the environment that release carbon, known as sources, and parts of the environment that absorb the carbon over long periods of time, known as **carbon sinks**. The transfer between sources and sinks is shown in the carbon cycle diagrams, Figures 7 and 8.

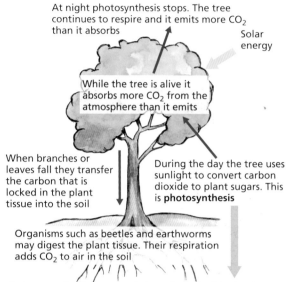

At night photosynthesis stops. The tree continues to respire and it emits more CO_2 than it absorbs

Solar energy

While the tree is alive it absorbs more CO_2 from the atmosphere than it emits

When branches or leaves fall they transfer the carbon that is locked in the plant tissue into the soil

During the day the tree uses sunlight to convert carbon dioxide to plant sugars. This is **photosynthesis**

Organisms such as beetles and earthworms may digest the plant tissue. Their respiration adds CO_2 to air in the soil

Rainwater dissolves some of the carbon dioxide that has come from soil organisms. This water may carry the dissolved CO_2 into a river and eventually to the sea.

▲ **Figure 7** A simplified carbon cycle.

Respiration releases CO_2

Photosynthesis absorbs CO_2

Decomposition

Burning releases CO_2

Vegetation

Fire

Fossil fuel

Key
Speed of transfer of carbon between stores
→ Very fast (less than 1 year)
→ Fast (1 to 10 years)
→ Slow (10 to 100 years)
→ Very slow (more than 100 years)

Soil

Absorption   Degassing

Surface water

Deep water

Sediment

▲ **Figure 8** The carbon cycle, showing fast and slow transfers.

Activities

2 Study Figures 7 and 8.
   a) Describe the human actions that release CO_2 into the atmosphere.
   b) Explain the processes that allow forests to act as a carbon sink.
   c) Give two reasons why the burning of tropical rainforests will increase the amount of CO_2 in the atmosphere.

3 Use Figure 8.
   a) Describe the difference in the speed of transfer of carbon in the natural part of the cycle compared with the part of the cycle affected by human action.
   b) Explain what difference this makes to the amount of carbon stored in the atmosphere compared with the long-lasting carbon sinks. Explain why this is alarming.

How conclusive is the evidence for climate change?

In 1958 a team of scientists began to take regular measurements of carbon dioxide concentrations from the atmosphere. They realised that local levels of CO_2 could be higher if the sampling took place close to industry or traffic congestion, so they decided to conduct their tests on Mauna Loa, Hawaii. They thought that this would give them readings that would represent average CO_2 levels in the atmosphere. The sampling has been conducted regularly ever since and the graph, known as the Keeling Curve, is shown in Figure 9.

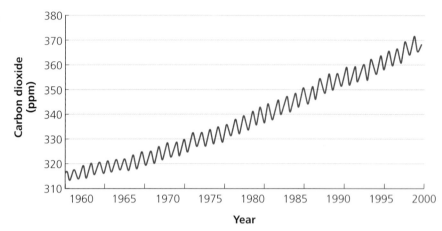

▲ **Figure 9** The Keeling Curve shows the rise of carbon dioxide in the atmosphere since monitoring began in 1958 (ppm = parts per million).

Evidence from the ice cores

We have already seen that scientific evidence from Hawaii proves that carbon dioxide levels have been rising steadily since 1958. However, can we be certain that this isn't part of a natural cycle? Perhaps carbon dioxide levels vary over long periods of time and the recent rise is part of one of those cycles.

Scientists working in both Greenland and Antarctica have been investigating information trapped in the ice to uncover evidence of past climate change. The snowfall from each winter is covered over and compressed by the following winter's snowfall. Each layer of snow contains chemical evidence about the temperature of the climate. Each layer also contains trapped gases from the atmosphere that the snow fell through. Gradually the layers turn to ice. Over thousands of years these layers have built up and are now thousands of metres thick. By drilling down into the ice, scientists can extract older and older ice cores. Chemical analysis of these ice layers and the gases they contain reveal a record of the climate over the last 420,000 years. This evidence suggests that the climate has indeed gone through natural cycles of colder and warmer periods known as glacials and inter-glacials. They also show that levels of carbon dioxide in the atmosphere have also gone up and down as part of a natural cycle.

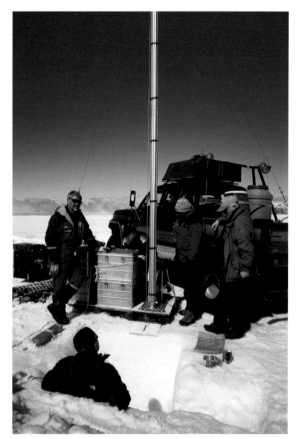

▲ **Figure 10** Scientists taking ice core samples from the ice sheet in Iceland.

Activity

1 a) Describe and explain the trend of the Keeling Curve.
   b) Explain why the scientists chose Hawaii as a good place to collect their samples.

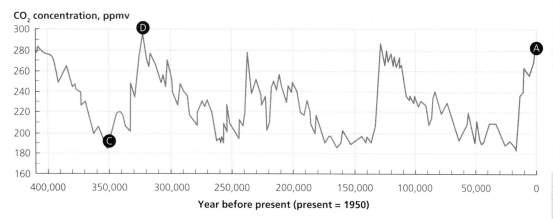

CO₂ concentration, ppmv

Year before present (present = 1950)

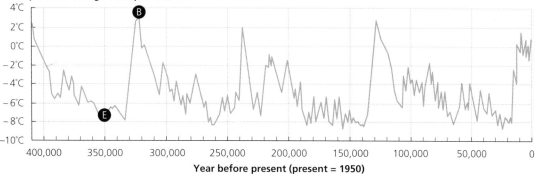

Temperature change from present, °C

Year before present (present = 1950)

Carbon dioxide concentrations reached a maximum of 300 ppm in the warmest periods.

Carbon dioxide concentrations dropped to 180 ppm during the coldest periods

Narrow peaks in the temperature record represent short warm episodes (interglacials)

Broad dips in temperature represent glacial periods

Carbon dioxide concentrations were at about 280 ppm in 1950

▲ **Figure 11** Temperature and CO_2 concentration (ppm) in the atmosphere over the past 420,000 years.

Activities

2 Use Figure 11.
   a) Match the five statements to the correct place on the graph shown by the letters A, B, C, D and E.
   b) Use the graph to copy and complete the following statement:
   The graph shows natural cycles of .... periods and .... periods. Average temperatures were higher than present on *three/four/five* occasions. These are known as .... periods. The current interglacial period appears to have lasted much *longer than/shorter than* previous periods.

3 Use your understanding of the greenhouse effect to explain why reduced levels of carbon dioxide in the atmosphere might be linked to cooler periods of climate.

4 Compare Figure 11 with Figure 9.
   a) How many times in the last 420,000 years have CO_2 levels been as high as in 2000?
   b) Based on the ice core data, do you think that the Keeling Curve fits into a similar natural cycle of carbon dioxide concentrations? Explain your answer fully.

Enquiry

How conclusive do you find the evidence for:
- natural cycles of climate change over the last 420,000 years?
- an unusual rise in carbon dioxide levels since 1958?

Investigating global patterns of extreme weather

In March 2015, the Pacific Island of Vanuatu was devastated by the destructive power of a **cyclone**. Homes and crops were destroyed by the extreme winds and rain. Eleven people lost their lives. At the same time in California, USA, farmers were managing limited water supplies during the third consecutive year of **drought**. The hot, dry weather caused wildfires that burnt out of control. How can such extremes of weather exist at the same time? What causes them?

Activity

1 Study Figure 1.
  a) Describe the location of cyclones that affect:
     i)   Australasia
     ii) North and South America
     iii) South East Asia.
  b) Compare the direction of storm tracks in the northern and southern hemispheres.
  c) Name two countries that are at risk of both cyclones and drought.
  d) Describe the location of areas affected by drought in the northern hemisphere. How are these areas different to those that are vulnerable to cyclones?

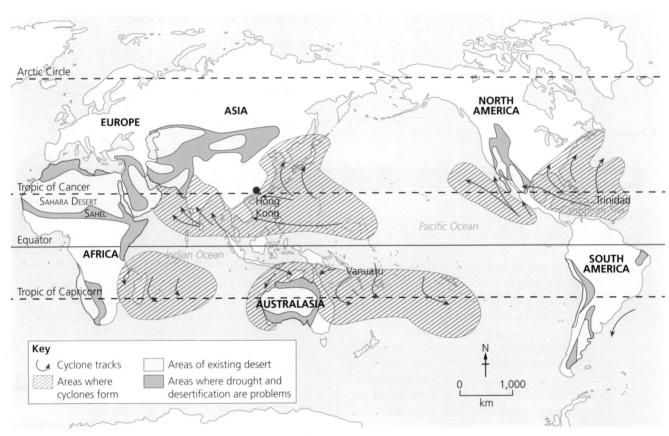

Key
- ⤸ Cyclone tracks
- ▨ Areas where cyclones form
- ☐ Areas of existing desert
- ▨ Areas where drought and desertification are problems

N
0   1,000
      km

▲ **Figure 1** The global distribution and location of areas affected by cyclones and drought.

Activity

2 a) Make a copy of Figure 2 on page 161. Use the text boxes to annotate your diagram. Place your annotations in appropriate places on the diagram.

  b) Use your completed diagram to explain why there is rainforest at the Equator and desert at latitudes 30° to the north and south.

What is happening in our atmosphere to cause extreme weather?

We can begin to understand extreme weather by considering the intensity of the Sun's heat on the ground at different latitudes on the Earth. The climate close to the Equator (within 5° of latitude) is hot throughout the year. The Sun heats the Earth and the Earth heats the air above, which becomes **unstable** and rises. This creates a band of low pressure in the atmosphere, known as the **intertropical convergence zone (ITCZ)**, which circles

the equatorial region of the Earth. The position of the ITCZ is shown in Figure 3. Notice that its position varies throughout the year. This is because of the tilt of the Earth's axis. The northern hemisphere leans towards the Sun in June and July so the ITCZ is slightly north of the Equator. The ITCZ migrates to south of the Equator in December and January when the southern hemisphere leans towards the Sun.

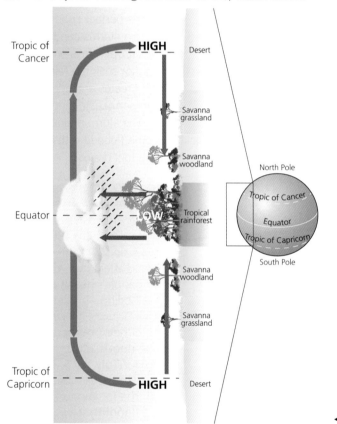

The Sun heats the Earth and the Earth heats the air above, which becomes unstable and rises creating an area of low pressure.

The air circulates back towards the equator in the lower atmosphere creating the trade winds.

At about 30 °N and 30 °S the air descends creating an area of high pressure. This air is dry. It seldom rains.

The air reaches a boundary layer in the atmosphere called the tropopause which is about 17 km above the equator. The air spreads outwards towards the poles.

◀ **Figure 2** How solar heating at the Equator creates the ITCZ.

Activity

3 a) Using Figure 3, describe the position of the ITCZ:
   i) over the Pacific Ocean in January and July
   ii) over Central America in July.
   b) Compare the location and distribution of cyclones on Figure 1 to the position of the ITCZ in Figure 3. What conclusion do you come to?

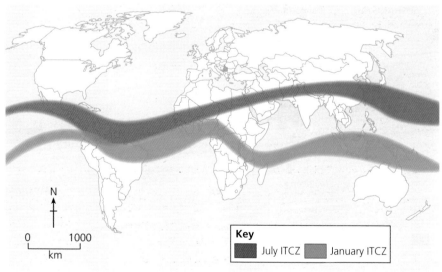

Key

July ITCZ   January ITCZ

▲ **Figure 3** The location of equatorial and tropical low-pressure systems (ITCZ).

How low pressure causes extreme weather

In late July 2015, India and Pakistan were badly affected by **monsoon** rains that caused flash floods and landslides. More than 120 people were drowned in India. It is thought that 116 people died in Pakistan and almost one million people had to leave their homes temporarily because of the floods. At the same time, West Bengal, Bangladesh and Myanmar were hit by flooding after a tropical storm caused heavy rainfall. Villagers in West Bengal said 'We have seen floods, but never anything like this before. This year is the worst.' Why did these extreme weather events take place?

▲ **Figure 4** People struggle to get around after flash floods in Lahore.

Why does South Asia have a monsoon season?

The flash floods of July 2015 were not the first time this region has suffered extreme weather. The monsoon rains occur each year across South Asia. These rains are formed as the ITCZ moves northwards across India during July (see Figure 3 on page 161). Figure 7 shows how the position of the ITCZ creates the perfect conditions for a month during which heavy rain storms can happen on any day. When the rain comes it often falls on hard, dry, baked earth. The ground cannot soak the rainwater up fast enough so it runs off and creates a sudden flash flood. In cities the rain falls on impermeable tarmac or concrete and cannot soak away. The storm drains cannot cope so the streets quickly become flooded with a mixture of rainwater and sewage from the foul drains.

Activities

1 Study Figure 4. Apart from drowning, list five ways floods of this sort could affect everyday life or people's health and well-being.
2 Use Figure 5 to write a brief news report about the floods across South Asia in July 2015. Make sure you describe:
   a) the location of the flooding
   b) the cause and effects of the flooding.

Key
- Tropical storm
- Areas affected by severe flooding
- Disputed territory

◀ **Figure 5** Map of South Asia showing areas affected by flooding during July 2015.

Day	1	2	3	4	5	6	7	8	9	10	11	12	13	14	15	16
Rainfall (mm)	0	0	1.6	0	0	0	9	0	0	0.1	0.1	42	4	0.1	0	0
Day	17	18	19	20	21	22	23	24	25	26	27	28	29	30	31	
Rainfall (mm)	119	0.1	75	5	2	0.1	2	17	0.1	17	2	0	0	0	1	

▲ **Figure 6** Rainfall in Lahore for each day of July 2015.

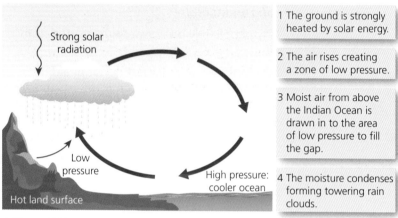

1 The ground is strongly heated by solar energy.

2 The air rises creating a zone of low pressure.

3 Moist air from above the Indian Ocean is drawn in to the area of low pressure to fill the gap.

4 The moisture condenses forming towering rain clouds.

▲ **Figure 7** Circulation of the atmosphere over South Asia during July.

Activities

3 a) Use the data in Figure 6 to draw a suitable graph.
  b) Use your graph to explain the flash floods you can see in Figure 4.
4 Make a copy of Figure 7. Annotate your diagram in appropriate places to show why the ITCZ's position creates such a large quantity of rainfall during the monsoon.

How do cyclones form?

Cyclones, known as hurricanes in America and typhoons in Asia, are more violent than tropical storms. They are seasonal events caused by extreme low pressure when the ITCZ is overhead. The destructive energy of a cyclone is created when warmth from the sea is transferred to the air above. Sea temperatures need to be at 27°C or above for several weeks before a cyclone will form. The warm water heats the air above it which rises rapidly creating an area of very low pressure in the atmosphere. This causes towering clouds to form and torrential rain to fall. At sea level, the rising air is replaced by more warm moist air coming in from the outside. As the air moves toward the centre of the low pressure it spirals upwards into the atmosphere. The spiral effect comes from the rotation of the Earth, a process known as the **Coriolis Effect**.

	Jan	Feb	Mar	Apr	May	Jun	Jul	Aug	Sep	Oct	Nov	Dec
Vanuatu	29.1	29.5	29.5	29.3	28.4	27.7	27.0	26.5	26.6	27.0	27.4	28.2
Trinidad	27.6	27.3	27.3	27.6	28.1	28.2	28.3	29.3	29.4	29.0	28.4	27.9
Hong Kong	19.1	18.9	20.1	22.7	26.8	28.5	29.1	28.6	28.3	26.5	24.3	21.0
Cornwall, UK	10.4	10.0	9.7	10.6	12.0	14.2	16.5	17.1	16.5	14.8	13.2	11.7

▲ **Figure 8** Average sea temperatures for selected locations (°C).

Activity

5 Use Figure 8 to draw two graphs to represent average sea temperatures in Hong Kong and Cornwall. Use your graphs and Figure 1 to explain why Hong Kong is at risk of cyclones but Cornwall is not.

Enquiry

Predict when cyclones are most likely to threaten each of the following islands. Use the information in Figures 1, 3 and 8 to justify your answer:
- Trinidad
- Vanuatu.

Cyclone Pam, March 2015

In March 2015 Cyclone Pam tore through the island chain of Vanuatu in the Pacific causing a trail of destruction. Cyclones are placed in different categories according to the strength of the wind. These categories are described in Figure 10. Pam was a Category 5 cyclone. The cyclone was at full strength as it crossed several islands. Winds were at around 250 km per hour with some gusts reaching 320 km per hour. Many homes were destroyed and crops flattened by the wind. The cyclone had been forecast and many people took shelter in evacuation centres. Eleven people lost their lives.

Factfile

- Vanuatu is a group of 83 volcanic islands in the Pacific Ocean.
- The population is 272,000.
- GNI is US$3,090 making Vanuatu one of the Lower Middle Income Countries.
- The main forms of employment are farming, fishing and tourism.
- Many people rely on rainwater harvested from roofs.
- Australia is Vanuatu's largest donor of aid. It gave A$60.7 million (£31.45 million) in 2013–14.

▲ **Figure 9** The track of Cyclone Pam.

Activities

1 Describe the track of Cyclone Pam. Use the North arrow and scale line.
2 Identify one social, one economic and one environmental problem faced by islanders.
3 Identify one social, one economic and one environmental problem caused by Cyclone Pam.

Key

🌀 Cyclone track

Numbers - Cyclone strength

🌀(TS) - Tropical storm

Category	Strongest gusts of wind (km/h)	Air pressure at the centre (millibars)	Typical damage
1	Less than 125	> 980	Minimal damage to houses, but there is some damage to crops and trees. Some boats may drag their moorings.
2	125–164	965–980	Storm winds cause minor damage to houses but significant damage to road signs, trees and some crops. There is a risk of power failure. Small boats break from their moorings.
3	165–224	945–964	Very destructive winds cause damage to roofs. Many crops and trees are damaged. The risk of power failure is high.
4	225–279	920–944	Very destructive winds cause damage to roofs, walls and windows. Widespread power failures. Debris is blown by the wind, creating risk of injury.
5	More than 280	< 920	Extremely destructive winds cause widespread damage to property and vegetation. Severe disruption to infrastructure such as roads, telephone lines and power lines.

▲ **Figure 10** Cyclone categories.

What were the effects of Cyclone Pam?

Villages in Vanuatu rely on two types of water supply:
• Rainwater is collected from streams or from the roofs of buildings and fed into over-ground tanks.
• Groundwater is collected from shallow wells.
Both types of supply were damaged by Cyclone Pam. The strong winds tore off roofs and blew down the storage tanks. Sea water from the storm surge flooded coastal areas and contaminated freshwater wells. It is estimated that 68 per cent of rainwater harvesting structures and 70 per cent of wells were damaged.

The destructive winds damaged up to 90 per cent of homes on islands that lay directly in the path of the storm, such as Erromango. In all, 90,000 people had their homes damaged. The winds also damaged hospitals and schools, affecting more than 35,000 pupils. The winds destroyed up to 80 per cent of subsistence crops, such as vegetables, and cash crops such as coffee. Damage to farming was estimated to be US$2.5 million.

How did the world respond to the emergency in Vanuatu?

Australia, Fiji, France, New Zealand, Solomon Islands, Tonga and the UK all sent emergency aid using military aircraft and personnel. Vanuatu is a very remote group of islands. The steep volcanic slopes mean that there are very few long airstrips and the islands have very few harbours capable of taking large ships. Emergency aid was flown into Port Vila. The government then set up an 'air bridge' using smaller planes and boats to take the aid to where it was most needed.

▲ **Figure 11** United Nations personnel on board an RAF plane carrying emergency aid to Port Vila, Vanuatu.

21,000 people received supplies of safe drinking water

92,500 blankets

26,000 repairs made to water supply systems

20 foreign medical teams

153 temporary schools created

95,000 people received medical care

67,000 tarpaulin sheets

19,000 children vaccinated against measles

▲ **Figure 12** Emergency aid in numbers, July 2015.

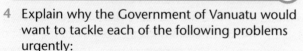

Activities

4 Explain why the Government of Vanuatu would want to tackle each of the following problems urgently:
   a) repairing water supplies
   b) providing medical care
   c) setting up temporary schools.
5 Suggest how countries, such as Australia, might provide effective long-term aid for the people of Vanuatu. Justify your ideas.

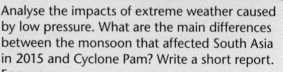

Enquiry

Analyse the impacts of extreme weather caused by low pressure. What are the main differences between the monsoon that affected South Asia in 2015 and Cyclone Pam? Write a short report. Focus on:
■ causes
■ the scale of the event (area and people affected)
■ the duration of the event (length of time)
■ the social and economic impacts.

Heat wave and drought in California

In July 2015, wildfires in California hit the news headlines in the UK. In one fire, near Clear Lake, over 3,000 acres of land burnt out of control. People had to be evacuated from their homes. In another wildfire, shown in Figure 17 (on page 168), cars stuck in roadworks on Interstate 15 had to be abandoned as a wildfire swept across the road. What was causing this extreme weather?

The wildfires were a result of a three year-long drought that affected California between 2012 and 2015. A drought is when significantly less rain falls than usual over a prolonged period of time. During the period 2012–15, the winter rainfall totals in California were much lower than usual and it doesn't normally rain much in the summer months anyway. The result was a drought and dry vegetation that easily burns in the hot summer months.

Activities

1 Use Figure 13 to describe:
   a) the location of Los Angeles
   b) the distribution of states affected by exceptional drought conditions.
2 Suggest how the drought and wild fires might have affected farmers, consumers, homeowners and firefighters.
3 Use Figure 15 and an atlas.
   a) Forecast the weather in each of the following places. You should be able to comment on the temperature and precipitation.
      i) Los Angeles
      ii) Ottawa
      iii) Mexico City.
   b) The jet stream has a wave-like motion as it swerves to the north and south, as shown in Figure 14. Explain why the winter weather of the USA would be different if the jet stream followed a more normal pattern.

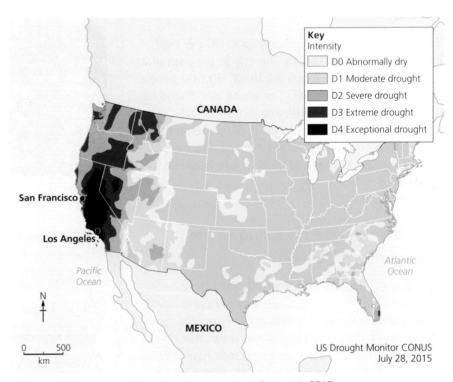

▲ **Figure 13** The extent of the drought across the USA in July 2015.

What caused the drought in California?

The low winter rainfall has been caused by the position of the **jet stream**. The jet stream is a strong ribbon of winds that circle the globe between 9 and 16 km above the surface of the Earth. These winds separate the cold polar air masses to the north from the warmer tropical air masses to the south. The jet stream usually curves further south than in Figure 14. It normally pushes rain-bearing low pressure air masses across California during the winter months. However, between 2012 and 2015, it was wrapped around a huge area of high pressure in the north-eastern Pacific. Dry air to the west of California had remained stationary for long periods of time. The United States Weather Service nicknamed this pressure system the 'Reluctant Ridge' of high pressure because of its reluctance to break down or move. Meanwhile, low air pressure and cold air from Canada was dragged down into the central and eastern areas of the USA, as you can see in Figure 15.

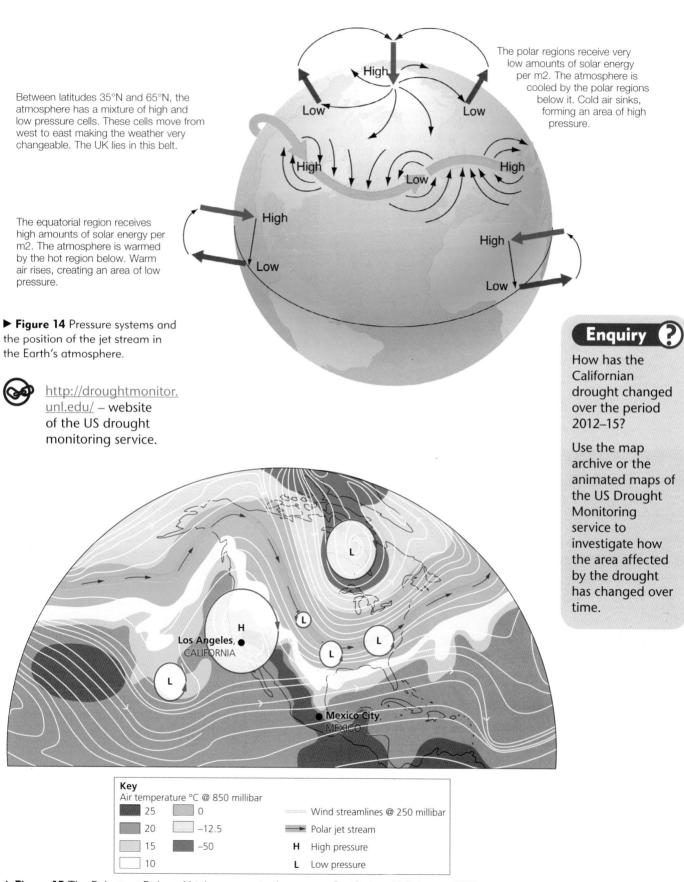

Between latitudes 35°N and 65°N, the atmosphere has a mixture of high and low pressure cells. These cells move from west to east making the weather very changeable. The UK lies in this belt.

The polar regions receive very low amounts of solar energy per m2. The atmosphere is cooled by the polar regions below it. Cold air sinks, forming an area of high pressure.

The equatorial region receives high amounts of solar energy per m2. The atmosphere is warmed by the hot region below. Warm air rises, creating an area of low pressure.

▶ **Figure 14** Pressure systems and the position of the jet stream in the Earth's atmosphere.

http://droughtmonitor.unl.edu/ – website of the US drought monitoring service.

Enquiry ❓

How has the Californian drought changed over the period 2012–15?

Use the map archive or the animated maps of the US Drought Monitoring service to investigate how the area affected by the drought has changed over time.

Los Angeles, CALIFORNIA

Mexico City, MEXICO

Key
Air temperature °C @ 850 millibar

25	0	
20	−12.5	
15	−50	
10		

Wind streamlines @ 250 millibar

Polar jet stream

H High pressure

L Low pressure

▲ **Figure 15** The Reluctant Ridge of high pressure in the eastern Pacific in mid-February 2015.

What have been the effects of the Californian drought?

Short-term impacts are easy to see. The amount of discharge in most rivers of California fell to much lower levels than usual. In August 2015, 44 per cent of rivers had flows that were just 10 per cent of their normal flow. In the summer heat, moisture from the soil is evaporated. Plants become withered and dry.

In these conditions a spark can easily trigger a wildfire. If the weather is windy then the fire can spread very quickly, endangering properties and lives. One way that firefighters use to tackle such a problem is to light deliberate fires between the wildfire and any property. The fire burns up any vegetation and is then put out. In this way, the wildfire has no fuel to burn when it arrives.

Farmers in Central Valley lost $810 m during 2015.

Homeowners were told to stop using water to wash down their driveways, or water gardens. Using a hose to wash cars was banned. Californians caught ignoring water restrictions were shamed on Twitter using the hashtag #DroughtShaming.

Most HEP dams stopped producing electricity.

Cracks appeared in buildings and roads due to subsidence. This happened because water was being pumped out of the ground faster than it was being naturally replaced.

California usually produces nearly half of the fruits and vegetables grown in the USA. Shortages meant that prices rose by 6% in the shops. More food was imported.

There was a 36% increase in wildfires. Property was damaged and wildlife killed. 31,000 acres of oak habitat burned.

The state government paid $687m of its savings to compensate farmers and homeowners who lost earnings or property. This money could have been used for other much needed projects.

Salmon and trout died in the San Joaquin River Delta. An increase in river temperature means the water carries less oxygen for fish.

The state lost 17,100 agricultural jobs due to the drought.

▲ **Figure 16** How has the drought affected people and the environment?

Activities

1 Study the data in Figure 18.
   a) Use the data to draw a series of graphs.
   b) Compare the rainfall of 2014 to both the normal rainfall and the 1976 drought.
   c) Identify one strength and one limitation of this evidence and the way you have chosen to represent it.
2 Other than the physical cause of the drought, suggest three other factors that may have led to water shortages.

▲ **Figure 17** A wildfire destroyed several vehicles stuck in a traffic jam on Interstate 15, California, in July 2015. No one was injured.

Rainfall: monthly figures in mm	Jan	Feb	Mar	Apr	May	Jun	Jul	Aug	Sep	Oct	Nov	Dec
Mean rainfall	78	95	45	30	18	3	3	12	8	25	40	105
The 1976 drought	37	42	32	22	0	0	0	4	5	12	19	33
The 2014 drought	25	28	30	2	0	0	1	2	0	9	15	22

▲ **Figure 18** San Francisco, like the rest of California, is experiencing record low rainfall.

What are the long-term impacts?

The long-term impacts of drought could be more serious to the economy and way of life in California. The drought means that groundwater is not recharged by rainfall soaking into the ground. So the water table drops as water is abstracted quicker than it is replaced. In the long term, this is unsustainable for water supplies and the important farming businesses that rely on the abstraction of ground water.

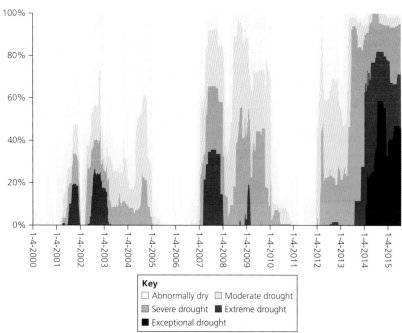

Key
☐ Abnormally dry ☐ Moderate drought
☐ Severe drought ■ Extreme drought
■ Exceptional drought

▲ **Figure 19** The percentage of California experiencing drought conditions (2000–15).

I had to introduce compulsory water restrictions. Every town and city must show how it will reduce water use by 25% compared to 2013 levels. Agricultural users must provide the State with frequent reports about their medium term plans to reduce water consumption. Those who install toilets, domestic washing machines and showers must only use modern, low-water technologies.

Jerry Brown, Governor of California

We have introduced a mixture of voluntary and compulsory water conservation programmes. Watering gardens, cars and driveways is banned. We will offer subsidies to people who want to change their toilets and washing machines for newer models. We have sent out millions of leaflets offering advice on how to conserve water in the home.

Harlan Kelly, General Manager of the San Francisco Water Utility

California needs to reduce the amount of electricity it gets from Hydro Electric Power. Reservoirs must be used for water supply not electricity supply. For the customer this will mean higher prices as we turn to natural gas in the short term. This will certainly mean adding more greenhouse gases into the atmosphere. In the longer term, Californians will need to get more serious about using solar and wind power.

An energy expert

Californians must realise that this problem will not go away. We must pay more for our water and put money into desalination plants that remove salt from sea water. We must encourage farmers to grow crops that are less thirsty, even if the profits are lower and more food is imported. We must hold back some water supplies to protect delicate ecosystems, to allow nature to have a fair chance of survival.

An environmentalist

▲ **Figure 20** The response to the drought.

Activities

3 Study Figure 16.
a) Sort the impacts of the drought into social, economic and environmental effects.
b) Use a diamond ranking technique (see page 83) to rank the impacts of the drought.
c) Choose the three most serious impacts. Explain why you have chosen each one.
4 How should the people of California respond to the drought in the long term? Write a short report highlighting how the house building, farming and energy industries could respond.

Enquiry

How severe was the 2014–15 Californian drought? Study Figure 19. Use evidence from this graph to describe the severity of the 2015 drought. Consider both the length of the drought and the percentage of California that was affected, compared to previous years.

THEME 5

Weather, climate and ecosystems
Chapter 3
UK weather and climate

The temperate maritime climate of the UK

The UK has a temperate climate that is mild, without extremes of temperature. The climate is **maritime** because it is strongly influenced by air masses and ocean currents crossing the Atlantic Ocean. A feature of the climate is its variability throughout the year. The UK has four distinct seasons.

The main factors that affect the UK's climate are:
- latitude
- the track of the jet stream and its effect on the movement of air masses
- the effect of ocean currents
- altitude and aspect.

London	Jan	Feb	Mar	Apr	May	Jun	Jul	Aug	Sep	Oct	Nov	Dec
Temperature °C	6	7	10	13	17	21	23	22	19	14	10	7
Precipitation (mm)	78	59	61	51	55	56	45	51	63	70	75	79

Oban	Jan	Feb	Mar	Apr	May	Jun	Jul	Aug	Sep	Oct	Nov	Dec
Temperature °C	8	8	8	10	13	14	16	16	15	12	10	8
Precipitation (mm)	195	142	155	84	69	83	105	123	174	189	185	197

▲ **Figure 1** Climate data for London in the South East of England and Oban in the North West of Scotland show how the UK's climate varies across the country.

Effects of aspect and altitude

The northern, central and western parts of the UK have upland landscapes. Upland areas are much colder than lowlands. Temperatures decrease by 1°C for every 100 m in height. **Aspect**, or the direction of a slope, is another factor that affects temperatures as it determines the amount of sun received. South-facing slopes tend to be warmer than north-facing slopes.

> **Activities**
>
> 1 Compare the climate of London to that of Oban, making sure that you comment on the seasonality of both graphs.
> 2 a) Make a sketch of Figure 2.
>   b) Complete and add the labels to the correct places on your sketch.

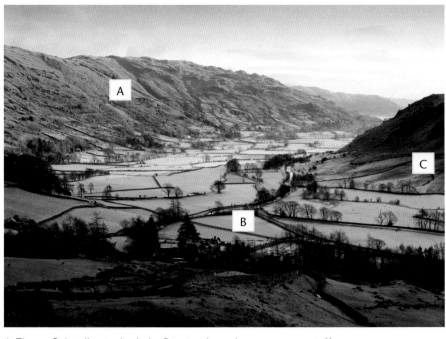

Flat valley floor	... will remain in shadow for most of the day in winter
	... is warmed by early morning sunshine
North-west facing slope	
	... will remain in shadow until the Sun is higher in the sky so frost remains longer in the morning
South-east facing slope	

▲ **Figure 2** A valley in the Lake District shows how aspect can affect temperature.

How does the maritime climate affect the UK?

Oceans contain flowing currents of sea water. These **ocean currents** circulate around the globe. They are able to transfer heat from warm latitudes to cooler ones. The Gulf Stream, and its extension the North Atlantic Drift, is one of these currents. It carries warm water from the Gulf of Mexico across the Atlantic, towards Europe. This warm water transfers heat and moisture to the air above it and influences the climate of the UK. It gives the UK a maritime climate which is warmer and wetter than other places at similar latitudes in continental parts of Europe.

▶ **Figure 3** Comparing temperatures in the maritime climate of the UK to the more continental parts of Europe.

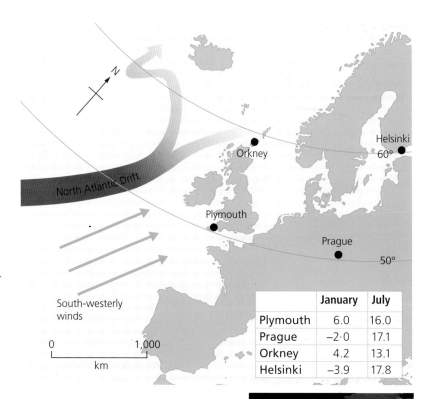

	January	July
Plymouth	6.0	16.0
Prague	−2·0	17.1
Orkney	4.2	13.1
Helsinki	−3.9	17.8

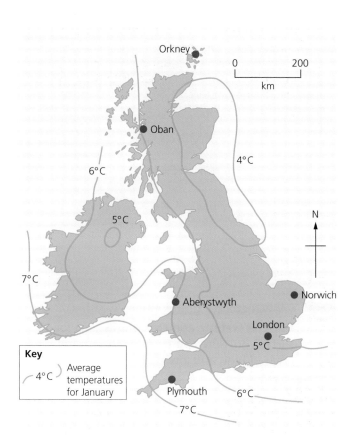

Key

4°C — Average temperatures for January

▲ **Figure 4** Average temperatures for January. Lines of equal temperature are known as isotherms.

▶ **Figure 5** Satellite image of the Gulf Stream. The orange colours show warm water. Cold water is blue. Land is black.

Activities

3 Compare the temperatures that are at the same line of latitude in Figure 3. Explain why this pattern occurs.
4 a) Use Figure 4 to describe the January temperature in:
   i) Aberystwyth
   ii) Norwich
   iii) Orkney.
  b) Which parts of the UK have the lowest January temperatures?
  c) Draw a cross-section to represent the temperature change between Plymouth and Orkney.
5 a) Make a sketch of Figure 5. Label what is happening at A and B.
  b) Suggest how the ocean current at B will affect the climate of Baltimore.

How do air masses affect the UK?

When **air masses** move towards the UK, they bring with them different kinds of weather. Five air masses affect the UK. These are shown in Figure 6. Usually, the UK receives air masses from the west. In the summer, air masses generally come from the south-west. In the winter, air masses generally come from the north-west. The line where these two air masses meet creates a zone of low air pressure. Warmer air from the south-west moves up over colder air to the north. This line is where depressions can form (see page 174). The three other air masses affect the UK less often, but they are responsible for some of the more extreme weather we receive.

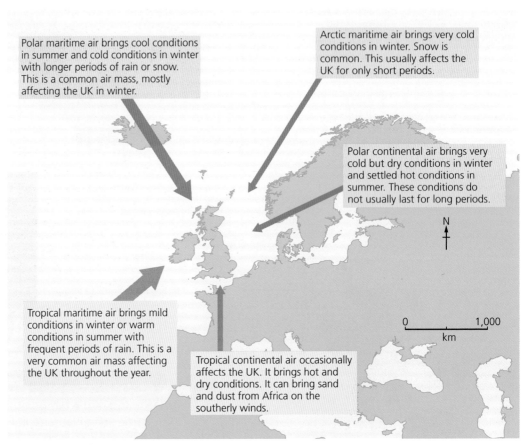

Polar maritime air brings cool conditions in summer and cold conditions in winter with longer periods of rain or snow. This is a common air mass, mostly affecting the UK in winter.

Arctic maritime air brings very cold conditions in winter. Snow is common. This usually affects the UK for only short periods.

Polar continental air brings very cold but dry conditions in winter and settled hot conditions in summer. These conditions do not usually last for long periods.

Tropical maritime air brings mild conditions in winter or warm conditions in summer with frequent periods of rain. This is a very common air mass affecting the UK throughout the year.

Tropical continental air occasionally affects the UK. It brings hot and dry conditions. It can bring sand and dust from Africa on the southerly winds.

▲ **Figure 6** How do air masses affect the UK?

Enquiry ⑦

Can you predict the weather?

Use the Weblink on this page to view the surface pressure chart for the next four days. Use the position of the high and low pressures to predict places across Europe that will have:
- dry, settled weather
- wet weather
- the strongest winds.

 www.metoffice.gov.uk/public/weather
Visit this website and click on the icon for surface pressure charts to see the current areas of high and low pressure across the UK.

How does the jet stream affect the UK's weather?

The jet stream (shown on page 167) is a strong ribbon of wind that circles the globe between 9 and 16 km above the surface of the Earth. It crosses over the UK, taking a sinuous course. It separates the cold polar air masses to the north from the warmer tropical air masses to the south.

When the jet stream takes a northerly track to the west of the UK, it tends to drag high pressure over the UK from the south. Areas of high pressure, also known as **anticyclones**, bring periods of dry, settled weather. The track taken by the jet stream tends to shift slightly over time. But if it stays in the same position for several weeks, then the UK will experience a long spell of similar weather. When high pressure becomes fixed over the UK in winter, the weather is sunny and dry but cold, and especially cold at night. During the summer an anticyclone brings hot dry weather. If the jet stream becomes fixed in this position it can cause problems such as heatwaves or drought. The UK's worst drought in recent years was in 2003 when an anticyclone stayed over Western Europe for several weeks.

Key

1 Track that typically allows high pressure to settle over the UK like in summer 2003

2 Track that will bring unsettled weather conditions

3 Track that will bring a series of depressions across the UK like in winter 2013–14

▲ **Figure 7** Typical paths for the jet stream across the UK.

Activities

1   Use Figures 6 and 7 to explain:
    a) Why the more northerly route (track 1) of the jet stream will bring settled weather.
    b) Why the more southerly route (track 3) of the jet stream will bring unsettled weather.
2   Use Figure 8 and an atlas to describe:
    a) the location of the three zones of high pressure
    b) the cold front.

Weak areas of low pressure are forced to travel to the north of the UK by the blocking anticyclone

Light winds where isobars are far apart

High pressure or anticyclone

Key

Warm front

Cold front

◄ **Figure 8** A weather map showing an anticyclone in August 2003.

The effects of low pressure

Regions of low pressure in the atmosphere are formed when air lifts off the Earth's surface. It is common for several cells of low pressure, also known as **depressions**, to form in the North Atlantic at any one time. They then track eastwards towards Europe bringing changeable weather characterised by wind, cloud and rain. Depressions are more likely to be deeper (have lower pressure) in the winter months. These weather systems can bring damaging gusts of wind and large waves on to the coast, as well as heavy rain leading to floods such as those of winter 2015–16 (see pages 41 to 45). However, low pressure in the summer months is also common: depressions during July 2012 caused flooding across large parts of England.

The winter storms of 2014

Between December 2013 and February 2014 the UK suffered the stormiest period for twenty years. Storms, created by extreme low pressure, battered the North Sea coastline during December 2013 (see pages 130 and 131). The coasts of Devon and Cornwall were badly damaged by a combination of fierce winds and huge waves. Southwesterly winds reached speeds of 146 kmph on the exposed coast of Devon. The storms caused a major incident in Dawlish, Devon, on 5 February 2014 when the sea wall collapsed causing closure of the main London-to-Cornwall rail line. The line was reopened on 4 April 2014 after repairs costing £35 million.

◀ **Figure 9** The weather map for 4 February 2014.

▶ **Figure 10** The coastal rail line at Dawlish was closed on 5 February 2014 after storm damage to the sea wall undermined the railway.

The passage of a depression

Inside the depression there is a battle between huge masses of warmer and colder air. These air masses revolve slowly around each other in an anticlockwise direction (in the northern hemisphere) as the whole system tracks eastward. Huge banks of cloud form along the fronts where cold and warm air meet. Rain fall is heaviest along these fronts.

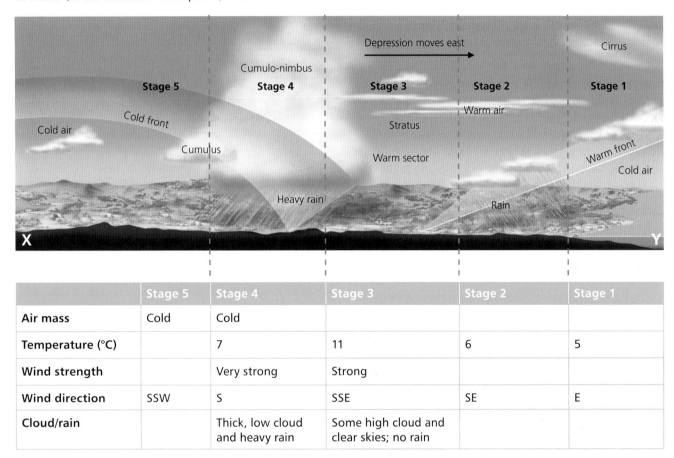

	Stage 5	Stage 4	Stage 3	Stage 2	Stage 1
Air mass	Cold	Cold			
Temperature (°C)		7	11	6	5
Wind strength		Very strong	Strong		
Wind direction	SSW	S	SSE	SE	E
Cloud/rain		Thick, low cloud and heavy rain	Some high cloud and clear skies; no rain		

▲ **Figure 11** Weather that would have been associated with the easterly progress of the depression shown in Figure 9.

Feature	Cyclones or depressions	Anticyclones
Air pressure	low	High, usually above 1,020 millibars (mb)
Air movement	↑	Sinking
Wind strength	high	Light
Wind circulation	anti clock wise	Clockwise
Typical winter weather	windy wet rainy	Cold and dry; clear skies in the daytime; frost at night
Typical summer weather	wet unstable temp.	Sunny and warm

▲ **Figure 12** Comparing cyclones and anticyclones.

Activities

1 Study Figure 9.
   a) Describe the location of the areas of low pressure.
   b) What do the isolines on the area of map to the west of the UK tell you about the strength and direction of the winds?
2 Use evidence from Figure 9 to write a weather forecast for the southern half of the UK on 5 February 2014.
3 Make a copy of the table in Figure 11. Use the evidence in Figure 9 to complete the missing sections.
4 Make a large copy of Figure 12 and use the information on these pages to complete the blank spaces.

Microclimates

The buildings and traffic in a large city influence the local climate, an affect known as an **urban microclimate**. One of the main impacts of a city on the local climate is to create temperatures that are warmer than in the surrounding rural area. This is known as the **urban heat island**. Basically, the city acts rather like a huge storage heater, transferring heat from buildings and cars to the dome of air that covers the city:

- Concrete, brick and tarmac all absorb heat from the Sun during the day. This heat is then radiated into the atmosphere during the evening and at night.
- Buildings that are badly insulated lose heat energy, especially through roofs and windows. Heat is also created by cars and factories, which is lost to the air from exhausts and chimneys.

Parks and green spaces in our cities do not heat up as much as buildings and roads. So, open spaces help to keep our urban areas cool in summer. Vegetation helps to remove dust from the air, such as the particulates emitted by diesel cars, and trees and hedges reduce noise from roads. Parks and gardens soak up rain water and help to prevent the flash floods that might otherwise occur due to all of the impermeable surfaces in our towns and cities.

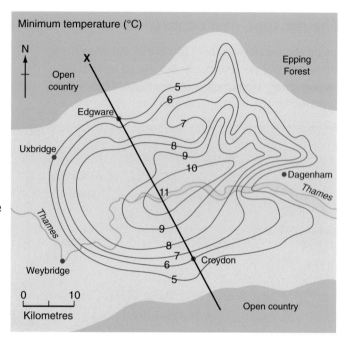

Minimum temperature (°C)

▲ **Figure 13** London's urban heat island.

▲ **Figure 14** Llandaff Fields, a large urban park in Cardiff.

Weather features	Urban microclimate
Sunshine duration	5–15% less
Annual mean temperature	1–2 degrees warmer
Temperatures on sunny days	2–6 degrees higher
Occurrence of frosts	2–3 weeks fewer
Total precipitation	5–30% more
Number of rain days	10% more
Number of days with snow	14% fewer
Cloud cover	5–10% more
Occurrence of fog in winter	100% more
Amount of condensation nuclei	10 times more

▲ **Figure 15** The effects of the urban climate in the UK.

Activities

1 Using Figure 13:
   a) Describe the location of the area of highest temperatures in London.
   b) Describe the distribution of places with lower temperatures.
   c) Suggest reasons for the pattern shown on the map.
2 Make copies of Figures 16 and 17. Sort the labels and add them to appropriate places on your diagrams.
3 Study Figure 15. Outline the advantages and disadvantages of the urban microclimate for the people who live in cities.
4 Give three reasons why planners need to protect urban parks from new homes or other development.

How do cities affect patterns of wind and rainfall?

Tall buildings in a city affect local patterns of wind. In the open countryside farmers plant trees to reduce wind speeds and the damage that wind can do to their crops. The trees act as a barrier, forcing the wind to rise over the treetops and therefore creating a shelter belt on the **leeward side**. Tall buildings in cities have an even greater sheltering effect, so average wind speeds in cities are lower than in the surrounding countryside. However, rows of tall buildings can also funnel the wind into the canyon-like streets between them. As the wind is forced to flow around or over tall buildings, the wind can suddenly gust at speeds that are two to three times the average wind speed. This may cause hazards for pedestrians and, in some extreme weather conditions, has led to the collapse of scaffolding.

During the summer months, the extra heat due to the urban heat island causes air to rise over larger cities. This can lead to convectional rainstorms – usually on hot afternoons. The dust in urban air is another factor that leads to higher amounts of rainfall in urban areas. When water vapour condenses in the air to form water droplets it does so by attaching itself to a dust particle. Urban air has ten times more dust particles in it than in rural air. The dust comes from car exhausts, heating systems in people's homes, industry and building sites.

Wind is funnelled between tall buildings

Gusty winds may be two to three times stronger than average

Prevailing wind

Less wind in leeward side of buildings

Areas with strong winds

▲ **Figure 16** Urban wind patterns.

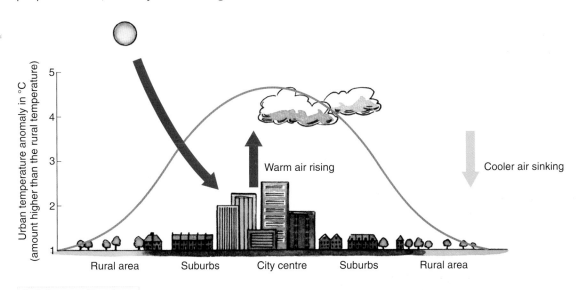

Warm air rising

Cooler air sinking

Rural area   Suburbs   City centre   Suburbs   Rural area

Buildings radiate heat

Condensation

Sun's energy is absorbed by building materials

Cumulus clouds form where rising warm air meets colder air

▲ **Figure 17** Why it rains more often in cities.

How does climate affect the global distribution of biomes?

An **ecosystem** is a community of plants and animals and the environment in which they live. Ecosystems contain both living and non-living parts. The living part includes such things as insects and birds, which depend on each other for food. It also includes plants, which may also depend on insects and birds for pollination and seed dispersal. The non-living part of an ecosystem includes such things as the climate, soils and rocks. This non-living environment provides nutrients, warmth, water and shelter for the living parts of the ecosystem.

Climate is such an important factor in influencing the natural vegetation and wildlife of a region that **biomes** (the largest-scale ecosystems) broadly match the world's climate zones. **Tropical rainforests** grow in a band around the Equator where the Equatorial climate is hot and wet. Treeless **tundra** and forested **taiga** ecosystems exist where winters are cold and summers are short. The effect of latitude on temperature is explained by Figure 1.

Arctic climates and ecosystems

The Arctic region of northern Scandinavia and Iceland has cold winters and short, cool summers. These conditions have a major impact on plant growth. Plants

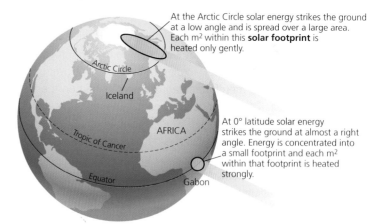

At the Arctic Circle solar energy strikes the ground at a low angle and is spread over a large area. Each m² within this **solar footprint** is heated only gently.

At 0° latitude solar energy strikes the ground at almost a right angle. Energy is concentrated into a small footprint and each m² within that footprint is heated strongly.

▲ **Figure 1** Solar heating of the Earth varies with latitude.

have to survive the long, dark winters when temperatures fall well below freezing and when strong winds or snowfall can damage the branches of trees. In the summer, plants benefit from long hours of daylight but the growing season is very short. Plants therefore grow slowly.

The further north you go in northern Norway and Finland, the smaller the plants become. South of the Arctic Circle, the ecosystem is taiga. This is a forest ecosystem of conifer trees and birches. As you travel north, the trees become shorter and grow further apart. Eventually, a little north of the Arctic Circle, the climate becomes too extreme for trees to grow and the treeless Arctic tundra takes over.

◀ **Figure 2** Short coniferous trees growing in the taiga (or boreal forest) of northern Norway.

Tropical climates and ecosystems

Tropical climates are hot and wet. In the equatorial region of the Amazon Basin (within 5° of the Equator) there is between 1,500 mm and 2,000 mm of rainfall a year. London, by comparison, has an average of 593 mm of rainfall each year. The heat and abundant rainfall allow rapid plant growth and trees can reach a height of 40 m or more. This contrasts greatly with the slow growing plants of the tundra, which never grow more than a few centimetres high.

In tropical regions further from the Equator, temperatures remain high. Rainfall, however, becomes seasonal, with wet and dry seasons. Water shortages during the dry season mean that trees compete for water in the soil. Trees grow further apart and the savanna ecosystem of sparse trees and grasslands develops (see pages 190–1)

▲ **Figure 3** Reindeer grazing on lichen in the tundra region of Arctic Norway.

1. Temperatures are only above 10° C (the temperature at which most plants grow) for two or three months …		… plants grow close to the ground where they are less likely to be damaged.
2. Precipitation in the winter months falls as snow …	… so …	… plants have a short growing season.
3. Rocks weather (break down) slowly in the cold conditions which means soils have few nutrients …		… plants are extremely slow growing.
4. With few trees around there is little shelter from wind …		… plants have small leaves and so don't lose any moisture.

▲ **Figure 4** How the Arctic climate affects plant growth.

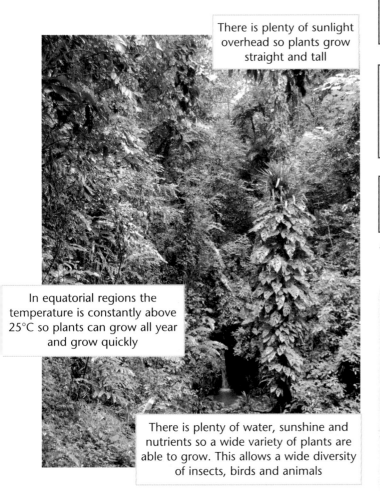

There is plenty of sunlight overhead so plants grow straight and tall

In equatorial regions the temperature is constantly above 25°C so plants can grow all year and grow quickly

There is plenty of water, sunshine and nutrients so a wide variety of plants are able to grow. This allows a wide diversity of insects, birds and animals

▲ **Figure 5** Tropical rainforest plants in Tobago.

Activities

1 Using Figures 2, 3 and 5, describe each ecosystem. Focus on features of the vegetation, such as density, height and variety.
2 Pair up the phrases in Figure 4 to make four sentences that explain the features of Arctic ecosystems.
3 Use Figure 4 and the labels around Figure 5 to explain the differences you noted in your answer to activity 1.
4 Use Figure 1 to help explain the importance of latitude in the development of different biomes.

Nutrient cycles depend on climate

Plants need minerals containing nitrogen and phosphates. These nutrients exist in rocks, water and the atmosphere. The plants take them from the soil and release them back into the soil when the plant dies. This process forms a continuous cycle.

Figure 10 represents nutrient stores and flows in the tropical rainforest ecosystem. The circles represent **nutrient stores**. The size of each circle is in proportion to the amount of nutrients kept in that part of the ecosystem. The arrows represent **nutrient flows** as minerals move from one store to another. The thickness of each arrow is in proportion to the size of the flow, so large flows of nutrients are shown with thick arrows while smaller flows are shown with narrow arrows.

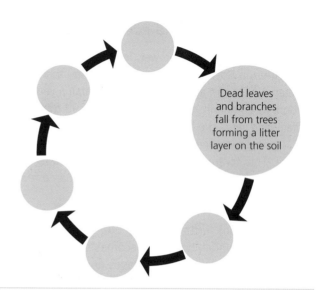

Dead leaves and branches fall from trees forming a litter layer on the soil

Leaf litter breaks down slowly in the cold conditions

Roots are shallow so they can take in nutrients near the surface

Decomposers such as beetles and fungi grow in the litter

Nutrients from leaf litter return to the soil

Plants use nutrients from the soil to help growth

▲ **Figure 7** Nutrient cycles in the taiga.

▲ **Figure 6** Lichens growing on a rotting tree stump in the taiga ecosystem, Norway.

Activities

1   Make a copy of Figure 7 and add the labels to the correct places to make a complete cycle.
2   a) Use Figures 8 and 9 to draw two climate graphs.
    b) Describe three main differences between these two climates.

	Jan	Feb	Mar	Apr	May	Jun	Jul	Aug	Sep	Oct	Nov	Dec
Temperature (°C)	−8.0	−7.5	−4.5	2.5	8.5	14.0	17.0	15.5	10.5	5.5	0	−4.0
Precipitation (mm)	38	30	25	35	42	48	76	75	57	57	49	41

▲ **Figure 8** Climate data for the taiga forest, northern Norway (65° latitude).

	Jan	Feb	Mar	Apr	May	Jun	Jul	Aug	Sep	Oct	Nov	Dec
Temperature (°C)	27.0	26.5	27.5	27.5	26.5	25.0	24.0	25.0	25.5	26.0	26.0	27.5
Precipitation (mm)	249	236	335	340	244	13	3	18	104	345	373	249

▲ **Figure 9** Climate data for the tropical rainforest, Gabon (0° latitude).

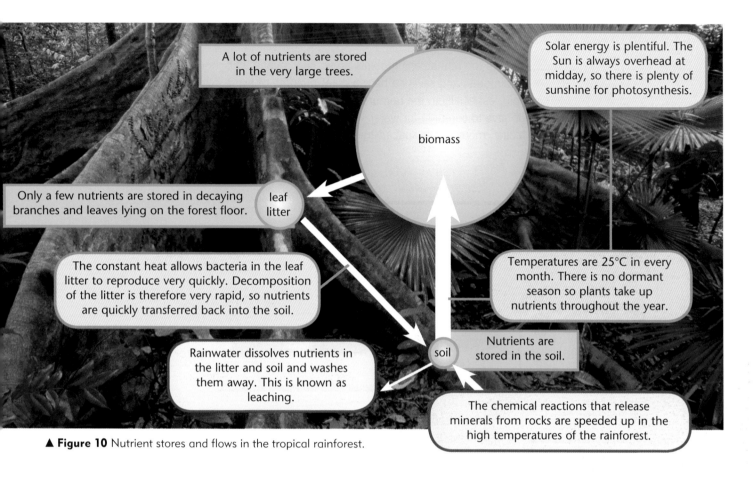

A lot of nutrients are stored in the very large trees.

Solar energy is plentiful. The Sun is always overhead at midday, so there is plenty of sunshine for photosynthesis.

biomass

Only a few nutrients are stored in decaying branches and leaves lying on the forest floor.

leaf litter

The constant heat allows bacteria in the leaf litter to reproduce very quickly. Decomposition of the litter is therefore very rapid, so nutrients are quickly transferred back into the soil.

Temperatures are 25°C in every month. There is no dormant season so plants take up nutrients throughout the year.

Rainwater dissolves nutrients in the litter and soil and washes them away. This is known as leaching.

soil

Nutrients are stored in the soil.

The chemical reactions that release minerals from rocks are speeded up in the high temperatures of the rainforest.

▲ **Figure 10** Nutrient stores and flows in the tropical rainforest.

Activities

3 a) Define what is meant by nutrient stores and nutrient flows.
  b) Describe three places where nutrients are stored in an ecosystem.
4 Study Figure 10.
  a) Describe two ways that nutrients can enter the soil.
  b) Explain why these two nutrient flows are rapid in the rainforest.
  c) Explain why these nutrient flows are likely to be much slower in the taiga.
5 Study Figures 7 and 10. Explain why nutrient cycle diagrams for the taiga would have:
  a) a larger circle for leaf litter than in the rainforest
  b) a thinner arrow for leaching
  c) a thinner arrow showing nutrient flows into the biomass.

Enquiry

How is the climate of the Arctic region affected by latitude? Do temperatures become more extreme as you travel north?

■ Research the climate and record the latitude of each of the following locations:
  a) Reykjavik, Iceland
  b) Oulu, Finland
  c) Murmansk, Russia
  d) Churchill, Canada.
■ Apart from latitude, suggest one other factor that may explain these differences.

Ecosystems as stores

We have seen that the climate affects the rate at which plants grow. This means that tropical ecosystems such as the rainforest and savanna have a great quantity of living things per hectare. Growth is rapid, especially in the rainforest, where the amount of rainfall means that plants do not have to compete for water. Tropical regions that have a long dry season tend to have smaller, more widely spaced trees. These differences are shown in Figure 11.

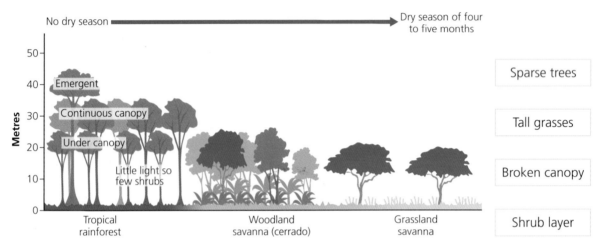

▲ **Figure 11** Typical structures of the tropical rainforest, woodland savanna (known as cerrado in Brazil) and grassland savanna.

Activities

1 a) Make a copy of Figure 11.
   b) Complete your diagram by adding the labels to suitable places.
   c) Describe how the increasing length of the dry season affects the structure of these ecosystems.
2 a) Make a copy of Figure 12.
   b) Add the annotations to appropriate places on your diagram. You can use page 157 to help you.
3 a) Make a copy of Figure 14. Add labels to the correct places to make a complete cycle.
   b) Using evidence in Figures 13, 15 and 16, explain why the tundra provides an important function at a global scale.
4 Using Figure 16:
   a) Calculate the percentage of the global total amount of carbon stored in each ecosystem. Tundra has been done for you.
   b) Represent the percentages using a suitable graphical technique.

Ecosystems store carbon

Ecosystems contain huge amounts of carbon – stored in plants and other organisms. Some is stored above ground in trees, plants, birds, insects and animals. A lot of carbon is also stored in the soil. Some is in living things, such as roots, beetles and earthworms. The rest is stored in dead organic material, such as leaf litter, fallen trees and decaying wood lying in the soil.

Because climate affect rates of plant growth, it also affects how much carbon is stored – and where it is stored. For example, the treeless tundra has a very low amount of carbon stored above ground. However, decomposition is slow because of the cold climate, so this ecosystem stores huge amounts of carbon in the peat-rich soil and in sediment in ponds and wetlands. The tundra is an example of a **carbon sink** (see page 157) where carbon is stored for long periods of time. If the Arctic warms due to climate change there is a concern that some of this carbon will be released into the atmosphere as carbon dioxide (CO_2) and methane (CH_4). This could have an undesirable impact on the greenhouse effect – leading to even more global warming.

Key
▨ Carbon stores
⇒ Flows

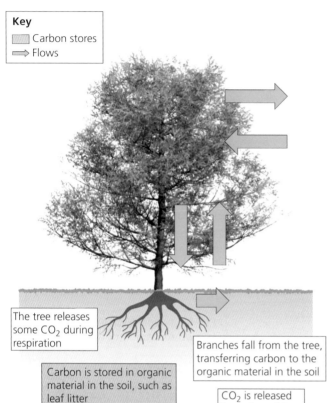

The tree releases some CO_2 during respiration

Carbon is stored in organic material in the soil, such as leaf litter

Carbon is stored in plant tissue

Bacteria and beetles add CO_2 to air in the soil during respiration

Branches fall from the tree, transferring carbon to the organic material in the soil

CO_2 is released from the soil into the atmosphere

During the day the tree absorbs CO_2 during photosynthesis

▲ **Figure 12** A diagram showing carbon stores and flows in a typical ecosystem.

▲ **Figure 13** Tundra ecosystem of an upland area of Arctic Norway; there is little carbon stored above ground but the bogs and peaty soils contain huge stores.

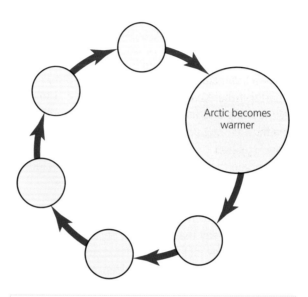

Arctic becomes warmer

Respiration from decomposers releases CO_2 into the soil

Decomposers in the soil become active

The greenhouse effect becomes stronger

CO_2 and CH_4 in the soil is released into the atmosphere

Frozen soil thaws

▲ **Figure 14** The impacts of a warming Arctic on carbon stored in the soil.

Ecosystem	Carbon stored above ground	Carbon stored below ground
Tundra	Less than 1	500+
Taiga	60–100	120–340
Savanna grasslands	2	7–54
Savanna woodlands	30+	7–54
Tropical rainforest	160–200	90–200

▲ **Figure 15** Estimated carbon stores in selected ecosystems (tonnes per hectare).

Ecosystem	Total carbon store	Per cent
Tundra	155.4	7.6
Taiga	384.2	
Temperate forest (e.g. oak)	314.9	
Temperate grasslands	183.7	
Deserts and dry shrublands	178.0	
Savanna grasslands and woodlands	285.3	
Tropical rainforest	547.8	
Global total stored in ecosystems	2,049.3	

▲ **Figure 16** Total amount of carbon stored in each biome (gigatonnes).

Ecosystems provide key services

Sadly logging, oil exploration, intensive farming and over-fishing are all damaging natural ecosystems. But does it really matter if there are fewer forests and less wildlife? After all, farming and fishing provide us with food, jobs and wealth.

Scientists argue that ecosystems should be protected and not just for their scientific value. They argue that ecosystems provide people with a number of essential services which they describe as **key services**. Furthermore, they say that these key services have financial value. They include:

- maintaining a steady supply of clean water to rivers
- preventing soil erosion
- reducing the risk of river floods
- providing natural materials such as timber for building, or plants for medicinal use; 75 per cent of the world's population still rely on plant extracts to provide them with medication
- providing foodstuffs such as honey, fruit and nuts.

▲ **Figure 17** Bees provide a service to humans by pollinating our crops. Beetles also provide a key service. They digest waste materials such as leaf litter and dung.

Provide a safe environment for fish to spawn and juvenile fish to mature, so helping to maintain fish stocks

Tropical rainforests

Provide people with the opportunity to develop recreation or tourism businesses

Coniferous (boreal or taiga) forests

Support thousands of plants and wild animals that contain chemicals that may be useful to agriculture or medicine

Mangrove forests

Inspire a sense of awe and wonder in human beings

Peat bogs/moors

Act as natural coastal defences against storm surges, strong winds and coastal floods

Tropical coral reefs

Soak up rainwater and release it slowly, therefore reducing the risk of flooding downstream

Sand dunes

Act as huge stores of carbon dioxide, so helping to regulate the greenhouse effect

▲ **Figure 18** Key services provided by ecosystems.

Activities

1 Explain what would happen to our food production without bees and beetles.
2 Using Figure 19:
   a) List the places where water is stored in the rainforest.
   b) Explain how water flows from the atmosphere to the forest and back again.
3 a) Describe how tropical rainforests maintain a steady supply of water for local communities.
   b) Describe how damaging the structure of the rainforest could affect local people, and people in the wider region.
4 Discuss the six ecosystems in Figure 18. For each ecosystem identify at least one key service (the yellow boxes) that it provides.

Enquiry

'It is more important to protect the tropical rainforest than the tundra.'

To what extent do you agree with this statement? Use evidence from this page, and your research, to decide which of these two ecosystems has the greatest environmental value. You should consider factors such as biodiversity and carbon stores as part of your argument.

Tropical rainforests regulate water supply

Figure 19 shows how rainforests play an essential role in the regional **water cycle** of tropical areas. The forest acts as a store for water in between rainfall events. After a rainstorm it is thought that about 80 per cent of the rainfall is transferred back to the atmosphere by evaporation and transpiration. This moisture condenses, forming rain clouds for the next rainstorm. So rainforests are a source of moisture for future rainfall events.

At least 200 million people live in the world's tropical rainforests. This includes the tribal groups, or **indigenous peoples**, of the rainforest. Many more people live downstream of the rivers that leave these forests. The forest maintains a constant and even supply of water to these rivers. If the rainforest water cycle were to be broken, then the water supply of many millions of people could be put at risk. The total amount of water flowing in the rivers would be reduced and the supply would become more uneven, with periods of low water supply punctuated by sudden flooding.

Conservationists argue that we need to place a greater value on these key services than on the value of the tropical timber alone. The benefit of a clean and regular water supply can be measured in financial terms. Rebuilding homes after a river flood can also be measured financially. The conservationists argue that these key services are more valuable in the long term than the short-term profits gained from logging.

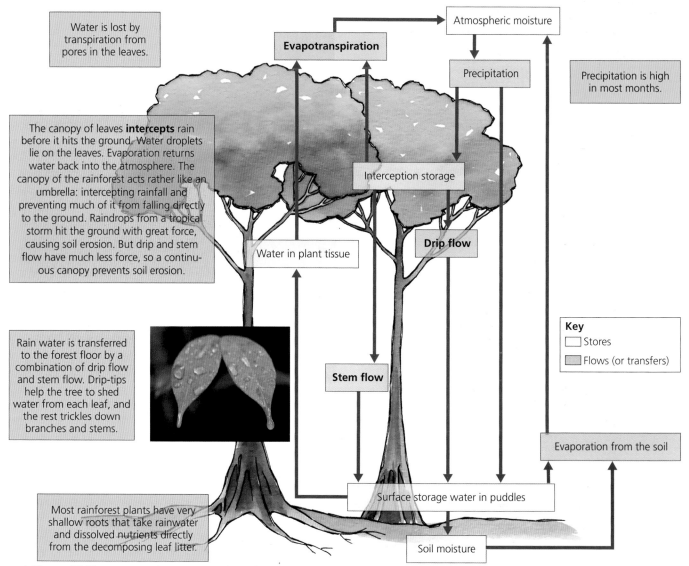

Water is lost by transpiration from pores in the leaves.

Evapotranspiration

Atmospheric moisture

Precipitation

Precipitation is high in most months.

The canopy of leaves **intercepts** rain before it hits the ground. Water droplets lie on the leaves. Evaporation returns water back into the atmosphere. The canopy of the rainforest acts rather like an umbrella: intercepting rainfall and preventing much of it from falling directly to the ground. Raindrops from a tropical storm hit the ground with great force, causing soil erosion. But drip and stem flow have much less force, so a continuous canopy prevents soil erosion.

Interception storage

Water in plant tissue

Drip flow

Rain water is transferred to the forest floor by a combination of drip flow and stem flow. Drip-tips help the tree to shed water from each leaf, and the rest trickles down branches and stems.

Stem flow

Key
☐ Stores
▨ Flows (or transfers)

Evaporation from the soil

Surface storage water in puddles

Most rainforest plants have very shallow roots that take rainwater and dissolved nutrients directly from the decomposing leaf litter.

Soil moisture

▲ **Figure 19** The water cycle in a tropical rainforest.

Managing UK uplands

Most of the UK's ecosystems are heavily modified and managed by people. Forest clearance and farming have changed our natural landscape for hundreds if not thousands of years. Changes have been made to upland landscapes such as these to improve farm productivity. Woodlands have been cleared to make more space for grazing by sheep and cattle. Ditches have been dug across the waterlogged peaty soils and rivers straightened to improve drainage. This allowed different varieties of grass to be sown so that sheep put on weight more quickly. Many of these changes were made to the moorland landscapes of the UK during the nineteenth and mid-twentieth centuries. However, conservationists and planners are now beginning to question the wisdom of these decisions. It is argued that moorland landscapes and their ecosystems absorb and store both water and carbon. The changes that were made in the past have upset these cycles.

The Pumlumon Project

The Pumlumon Project is an attempt to restore upland ecosystems across a huge area of the Cambrian Mountains in Mid Wales. The River Severn has its source here. It is an area used mainly for farming, forestry and tourism. The Pumlumon Project has several different elements – you can read about them using the weblink – including improving carbon storage and storing flood water.

Pumlumon has huge areas of peatland that were drained with ditches in 1950s and 1960s. This peat will have released some of its carbon store as it dried out. The project has identified 1,543 hectares of peat that it wants to restore by blocking the drainage ditches. This will encourage the peat to retain more water. As the water table rises, and organic material in the soil becomes waterlogged, less CO_2 will be released to the atmosphere.

▲ **Figure 20** Impacts of blocking ditches in moorlands.

▲ **Figure 21** Blocking off old drainage ditches has restored this upland bog in the Pumlumon Project.

 www.montwt.co.uk/what-we-do/projects – the website of the Montgomeryshire Wildlife Trust describe the Pumlumon Project in more detail.

Activities

1 Make a copy of Figure 20. Circle the + or – in each box on your flow diagram to indicate increase or decrease.
2 Suggest how the Pumlumon Project might:
   a) benefit people living in towns further downstream on the River Severn
   b) improve the biodiversity of the Cambrian Mountains.

The Belford Catchment Solutions Project

Belford is a small town in Northumberland that has been affected by regular flooding. A partnership project between the Environment Agency, Newcastle University and local landowners has managed the environment to improve water storage in the upland catchment. Wooden structures have been built to slow the flow of water and trap sediment. The project cost £200,000, whereas traditional flood defences would have cost around £2.5 million. The aim has been to create a natural storage area upstream so that water is held back and released slowly at times of flood. The objectives of the Belford Catchment Solutions Project were to intercept, store, slow and filter. Figure 22 shows how they have achieved

Waterlogged fields are no use to farmers. It's difficult for farmers to maintain productivity on waterlogged soil so it makes sense for them to regularly clear out their ditches. However, there is a potential downside to keeping fields well drained. If we increase drainage in fields, it's possible there will be increased and faster transfer of water in the river system with a possible increase in flood risk downstream.

▲ **Figure 24** Professor Alan Jenkins of the Centre for Ecology & Hydrology (CEH) explains why most farmers like to keep their ditches clear.

Placing wooden barriers across steep overland flow routes that feed into the river

Building low wooden structures known as bunds across the stream

Creating ponds on the floodplain that will be flooded at times of peak flow

▲ **Figure 22** Methods used in the Belford Catchment Solutions Project.

Activities

3 Explain why farmers improve the drainage of their land. Make use of Figure 24 to help you.
4 The objectives of the Belford Catchment Solutions Project were to intercept, store, slow and filter. Explain why these objectives help people living downstream.
5 Study the techniques described in Figures 22 and 23. For each technique, describe how it would alter flows and stores of water.

Enquiry

'The management of our moorlands should change. It is more important to use these areas for water and carbon storage than for farming.'

To what extent do you agree with this statement?

Make use evidence from these pages, and from your own research, to justify your decision.

▲ **Figure 23** Wooden barriers have been used to block gulleys in the upland peatlands of Kinder Scout in the Peak District.

Investigating sand dunes

The UK has a number of small-scale ecosystems that you can investigate through fieldwork. You could set up an enquiry to investigate structures or stores and flows in a moorland, woodland or sand dune ecosystem. Data for such an enquiry is usually collected along a transect. A transect is an imaginary straight line drawn across or through a geographical feature. Observations can be taken at regular (systematic), random or stratified intervals along the length of the transect (see page 9 for these sampling strategies).

Step 1: Design your enquiry

A fieldtrip to the sand dunes allows you to see how the plant life and growing conditions vary as you walk through this ecosystem from the strand line to the dune slacks. How quickly do the zones change? What factors cause these changes? Does your sand dune system follow the typical pattern? You could use a hypothesis to organise your enquiry, for example:

The variety of plants increases with distance from the strand line.

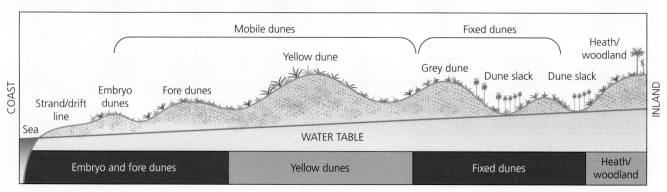

▲ **Figure 25** Cross-section through the zones of a sand dune ecosystem.

▲ **Figure 26** Sea rocket is a pioneer plant. It grows in the embryo dunes. The waxy outer surface of the leaf helps to reduce water loss by evapotranspiration. Shallow roots take nutrients from decaying material on the strand line.

▲ **Figure 27** Marram grass is the main plant of the yellow dunes. Strong leaves bend in the wind without breaking. Long tap roots find water. Burial by sand stimulates new shoots to grow from surface roots.

▲ **Figure 28** Restharrow is a low-growing flowering plant of the yellow dunes. Sticky hairs on leaves reduce water loss by evapotranspiration. Nodules on the long roots are able to take nitrogen from air and turn it into nutrients that are useful for plant growth.

Step 2: Starting and ending your transect

Sand dunes are formed when the wind frequently blows in the same direction. The dunes make ridges that are roughly parallel to the coast and at right angles to the prevailing wind direction. So, your transect should be at right angles to the beach so that it samples each zone within the sand dune system – like in Figure 25. You will need to start on the beach at the strand line. It will end when you have sampled data in each zone. If the dunes are managed you may be asked to use a specific line for your transect.

Collect your data

If your enquiry is about zonation then you will need to record the percentage of plants at each sample point along the transect using a quadrat. You may want to record other variables that could affect the growing conditions in each zone. If so, you could record:
- wind speed
- soil pH
- soil colour (as an indication of the amount of organic material providing nutrients)
- evidence of trampling or management.

| | Distance (m) from embryo dunes | | | | | | | | | | | |
	0	50	100	150	200	250	300	350	400	450	500	550
Sea rocket	20	10	0	0	0	0	0	0	0	0	0	0
Sea spurge	0	10	10	10	10	0	0	10	0	0	0	0
Marram	0	40	60	70	60	70	50	30	30	20	0	0
Restharrow	0	0	0	0	10	10	20	10	0	0	0	0
Fescue	0	0	0	0	0	10	30	50	60	50	30	70
Bramble	0	0	0	0	0	0	0	0	0	0	70	0
Others	0	0	0	0	0	0	0	0	10	30	0	30
Bare sand	80	40	30	20	20	10	0	0	0	0	0	0

▲ **Figure 29** Percentage of each type of vegetation in each quadrat.

Present the data

The percentage of each plant type along the transect is best shown using a **kite diagram** like Figure 30. The axis of this graph represents the length of the transect. The vertical axis is divided by two so that half of the total percentage is displayed on each side of the horizontal axis.

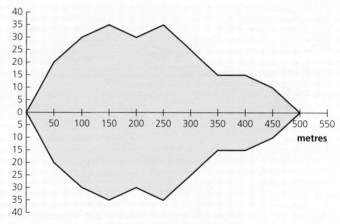

▲ **Figure 30** Kite diagram for marram.

Enquiry ?

How might you design an enquiry to investigate the effects of wind speeds on sand dune zonation? Use Figure 25 when you consider the following points.

- What questions can you pose?
- How should you sample along your transect? Would regular, random or stratified sampling be best? How many sample points should you use? Do you need a control?
- How would you design your data collection sheets?

Activities

1 Study Figures 26, 27 and 28. Describe two adaptations to:
   a) strong winds experienced in the yellow dunes
   b) the lack of nutrients in the sandy soils
2 a) Use the information in Figure 29 to draw a series of kite diagrams.
   b) What conclusions can you reach about?
      i) The plants that commonly grow in each zone.
      ii) How nutrient levels must change as you travel along the transect.

Characteristics of the hot semi-arid grassland biome

The global distribution of the hot semi-arid grassland biome is shown in Figure 32. This biome is a grassland ecosystem. It is sometimes known as savanna grassland and it forms a transition zone between tropical forests and deserts. This biome occurs in regions which have a tropical semi-arid climate. The climate pattern is one of marked wet and dry seasons with the rainfall concentrated in 5–6 months of the year, often in the form of heavy storms and high humidity. This is followed by months of drought with clear skies and fine sunny weather.

	Jan	Feb	Mar	Apr	May	Jun	Jul	Aug	Sep	Oct	Nov	Dec
Average Temp in °C	27	28	27	25	23	23	22	23	25	27	26	26
Precipitation in mm	71	68	151	289	122	27	11	13	12	33	149	106

▲ **Figure 31** Climate data for Arusha, Tanzania.

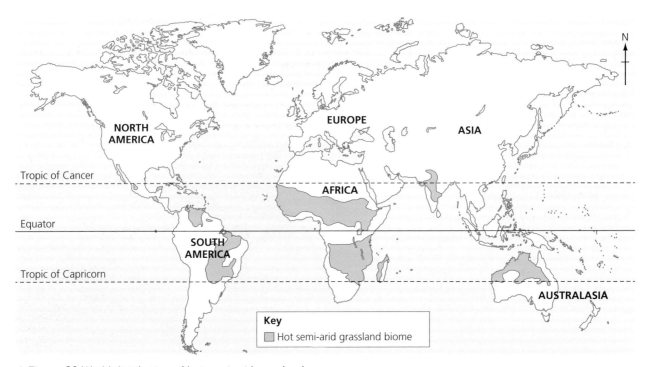

▲ **Figure 32** World distribution of hot semi-arid grassland.

▲ **Figure 33** Semi-arid grassland in Tanzania.

Activities

1   Use Figure 32 to describe the distribution of the semi-arid grassland biome.
2   a)   Use the data in Figure 31 to draw a climate graph for Arusha in Tanzania.
    b)   Add labels to your graph to show the wet season and dry season.
    c)   What is the total annual rainfall in millimetres?
    d)   Describe the annual range of temperature.
    e)   Many people visit Tanzania to go on a safari holiday. What time of year would be the best time to go?

How does vegetation adapt to the hot, dry climate?

In hot semi-arid climates, the soils are porous which means they drain rapidly. The thin humus layer provides nutrients for plants. The typical vegetation is of scattered trees and drought-resistant bushes. The climate is too dry for thick forest to form because trees need a lot of water to grow and survive. Between the widely spaced trees and bushes there are also grasses that grow rapidly to 3–4 m in height in the wet season. In the dry season they turn yellow and die back, leaving the ground vulnerable to soil erosion. The baobab and acacia are examples of xerophytic (drought-resistant) trees found in this biome – this means they can survive long periods with very little rainfall during the dry season of the year. The baobab and acacia are adapted to survive drought in a number of ways – these are shown in Figure 34.

▶ **Figure 34** Adaptations of plants to the climate of the semi-arid grassland.

ACACIA TREE

Broad flat canopy reduces water loss. It provides shade for animals.

Thorns on branches deter animals from eating them.

Long tap roots reach ground water deep underground.

Small leaves with waxy skins reduce the amount of water lost through transpiration.

Grows up to 20 m in height and 2 m in diameter with whitish bark.

BAOBAB TREE

Grows over 30 m in height and 7 m in diameter. Can live for thousands of years.

Lots of shallow roots spread out from the tree. They collect water as soon as it rains.

Thick bark is fire-resistant.

Few leaves reduce water lost by transpiration.

Large barrel-like trunk stores up to 500 litres of water.

Activity

3 Study Figures 33 and 34.
   a) Describe the vegetation shown in each photograph.
   b) At what time of year do you think each photograph was taken? Give reasons for your answer.
   c) Draw a table like the one below. Use the information in Figure 34 to describe how these plants have adapted to the climate conditions.

.	High rates of transpiration	Long periods of drought and high temperatures	Animals such as zebra eat the leaves
Acacia tree			
Baobab tree			

Enquiry ?

Australia has a large area of hot semi-arid grassland. Research the climate and ecosystems of East Kimberley, Australia. Hall's Creek is one of the only large towns in this region.

How do the climate and ecosystem of East Kimberley compare to the hot semi-arid grasslands of Africa that are introduced on these pages? What are the main similarities and differences?

How do ecosystem processes operate within hot semi-arid grasslands?

Within the hot semi-arid grassland ecosystem there are two main processes. These are the movement of energy (energy flows) and the recycling of nutrients.

Energy flows

The main source of energy for all living things is sunlight. This is absorbed by **producers** such as plants. They convert the light energy from the Sun into chemical energy by the process of photosynthesis. This energy is passed on to animals when they eat the plants. These animals are called herbivores or **primary consumers**. In turn, these are eaten by other animals called carnivores or **secondary consumers**. This is called a food chain. Energy flows up the food chain.

However, most producers and consumers are part of many different food chains. A food web shows the flow of energy through the whole ecosystem. A food web has many interconnecting food chains.

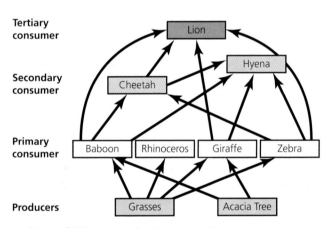

▲ **Figure 35** Food web for the semi-arid grassland ecosystem in Africa.

Nutrient cycles in the hot semi-arid grassland ecosystem

As well as energy, plants need essential chemical elements and compounds such as iron, phosphate and nitrogen. These nutrients are recycled through the ecosystem between the soil, biomass and leaf litter. When plants and animals die, they decompose and the nutrients are released and returned to the soil. This process is called the nutrient cycle.

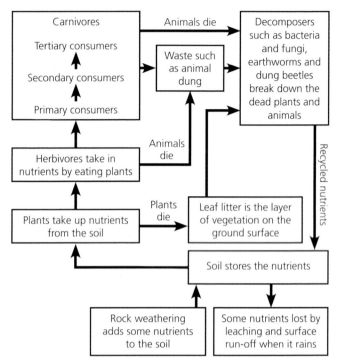

▲ **Figure 36** How nutrients are recycled in the semi-arid grassland ecosystem.

Activities

1   a) Draw a food chain by putting the following into the correct sequence.
       lion   grass   energy from the Sun   zebra
    b) Explain the difference between a food chain and a food web.
    c) Draw a table like the one below and add examples from the hot semi-arid grassland food web in Figure 35.

Biotic (living) part of the ecosystem	Examples
Producer	
Primary consumer	
Secondary consumer	
Tertiary consumer	

    d) Explain why the hyena is both a secondary and tertiary consumer.
    e) What would be the effect on the hot semi-arid grassland ecosystem if most of the lions were killed by people?
2   Study Figure 36.
    a) Explain why nutrients are important to this ecosystem.
    b) What role do decomposers play in the nutrient cycle?

Why is the biodiversity of Africa's grasslands under threat?

Hot semi-arid grasslands are under threat from both human activity and natural processes. During the dry season, fires are caused both by lightning strikes and by local farmers burning the grass to encourage new growth when the rains arrive. Grass can survive these fires, but young trees are destroyed.

This ecosystem contains a huge variety of plants, insects, birds, reptiles and mammals. This **biodiversity** – or range of living things – makes the grasslands of Africa a popular tourist destination. People come to see endangered species such as elephant, cheetah, lion and rhino. The safari industry is very important to the economy of countries like Kenya and Tanzania but it is difficult to create a sustainable balance between allowing visitor access to the natural scenery and wildlife, while protecting and conserving it. One of the greatest threats is hunting and poaching which has led to the illegal killing of over 40,000 animals each year in Kenya's Serengeti National Park. There were once over 100,000 black rhinos in Africa, now there are less than 2,700. They are killed for their horns which are used in traditional Asian medicines and sell for over five times the price of gold. Over 100,000 elephants were killed between 2013 and 2015 for the ivory in their tusks.

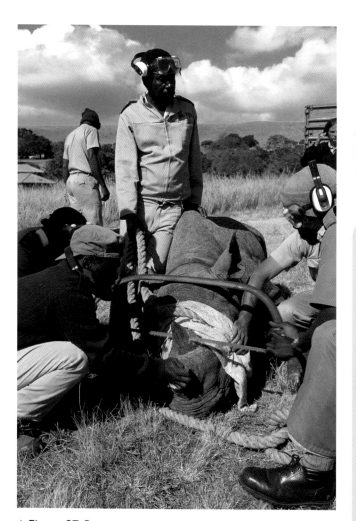

▲ **Figure 37** Conservationists remove the horn from a black rhino to discourage poachers from killing the rhino for its horn.

Biodiversity

Biodiversity is a measure of the richness of wildlife – the variety of plants, insects, birds and other animals that live in any ecosystem. For example, one hectare of tropical rainforest supports a greater variety of wildlife than the same area of hot desert. Some plants and animals are only found in certain places. These are **endemic** species. Places with a high biodiversity, which also have a variety of endemic plants or animals, are especially worthy of conservation.

Enquiry

Poaching of wild animals is a serious problem in many parts of Africa. Rhino and elephant are key targets for poachers in the hot semi-arid grassland environments of Africa. Debate the following enquiry questions. You may want to do some research first.

- Why should we conserve elephant and rhino?
- How do these animals benefit the environment and people?
- What is the best way to protect these animals? Which of the following options might work best?
  i) Dehorning the wild rhino
  ii) Moving (translocating) wild rhino and elephant to National Parks
  iii) Lifting the trade ban and exporting 'farmed' rhino horn and elephant ivory that has been reared sustainably.

THEME 5
Weather, climate and ecosystems
Chapter 5
Ecosystems and people

How is the marine environment used for energy production?

With 1,200 km of coastline, Wales has huge potential to generate renewable energy using wind, wave and tidal technologies. The Gwynt y Môr offshore wind farm opened in June 2015. It is the second largest wind farm in the world and consists of 160 tubines. Gwynt y Môr is located off the coast alongside the smaller Rhyl Flats and North Hoyle wind farms. Another very large offshore development in the Bristol Channel, near the island of Lundy, has been shelved for the moment. Gwynt y Môr took twelve years to complete. It was opposed by many who were worried about the visual impact and its effect on tourism.

Pembrokeshire probably provides the greatest potential for wave energy in Wales. Swansea-based Marine Power Systems has developed a technology called WaveSub. The device is to be tested in the water at Milford Haven for between six and twelve months. If tests are successful they will build a full-scale version (between 35 and 40 m long) which will have an output of 1.5 MW.

Technology	Target capacity (GW)	Target date(s)
Onshore wind	2.0	2015–17
Offshore wind	6.0	2015–16
Biomass	1.0	2020
Tidal range	8.5	2022
Tidal stream/wave	4.0	2025

▲ **Figure 1** Renewable energy potential for Wales (1 gigawatt equals 1,000 megawatts).

Tidal energy

The Skerries are a group of small rocky islands lying close to the northwest coast of Anglesey. The area between the Skerries and Carmel Head has strong tidal currents and will be the site of Wales' first commercial tidal energy farm – the Skerries Tidal Stream Array. The scheme will generate electricity for up to 10,000 homes in Anglesey. It should deliver other benefits to the local community also, such as long-term jobs in maintenance and environmental monitoring.

▲ **Figure 3** Coastal areas with greatest potential for tidal and wave power and the location of the Gwynt y Môr offshore wind farm.

◄ **Figure 2** The Gwynt y Môr offshore wind farm near Llandudno.

The building of a tidal lagoon in Swansea Bay has also been given the go-ahead by the UK Government, and work could start in 2016. The tidal lagoon on the eastern side of Swansea Bay, between the docks and the new university campus, will use the flow and ebb of the tide to generate electricity. A 9.5 km long sea wall would be built between 5 m and 20 m in height. It would house sixteen underwater turbines. Enough electricity could be produced for 155,000 homes for 120 years. Figure 4 shows the possible size of the proposed lagoon.

Key
▬▬ Possible extent of lagoon

0 ⌐ 1
km

▲ **Figure 4** The possible extent of the Swansea Bay Tidal Lagoon.

Activities

1 What is the difference between renewable and non-renewable types of energy? Give examples of each.
2 Discuss the arguments for and against building more offshore wind farms.
3 Use Figure 3 to describe the distribution of those areas in Wales with high potential for developing marine energy.
4 Use Figure 5 to identify the arguments for and against building a tidal lagoon at Swansea.

Enquiry

Should the Swansea Bay Tidal Lagoon be built?

Prepare a speech so that the issue can be debated in class. Make sure that you consider:
■ the environmental, social and economic issues
■ the arguments for and against.

Welsh Assembly Government spokesperson

We need more clean and home-grown energy which reduces our imports of fossil fuels. Wales is well-placed to develop marine energy and the Swansea Bay Tidal Lagoon project could create thousands of jobs in construction and maintenance.

Swansea councillor

The project is hugely encouraging for Swansea as it will boost leisure and tourism in an area which has already seen much regeneration.

Friends of the Earth Cymru

Instead of relying on climate-changing fossil fuels, it could help us build a clean and safer energy future and improve our energy mix. However, there are environmental concerns about the impact on migratory fish as the lagoon would be between the Tawe and Neath estuaries. There are also worries regarding silting and sand dredging.

Spokesperson for the nuclear energy sector

The estimated cost of the project has almost doubled to £1 billion. A government subsidy for the power generated – a strike price – has to be agreed. The company is asking for a higher subsidy than solar or nuclear power. The energy output would be a third of an average-sized power station.

▲ **Figure 5** Opinions about Swansea Bay Tidal Lagoon.

How and why do we use tropical ecosystems?

The Amazon rainforest is the largest remaining rainforest in the world. It is a vast lowland rainforest covering much of the drainage basin of the River Amazon and its tributaries. On the southern edge of the Amazon rainforest is the cerrado – another huge forest that grows in a region that has a tropical wet and dry climate.

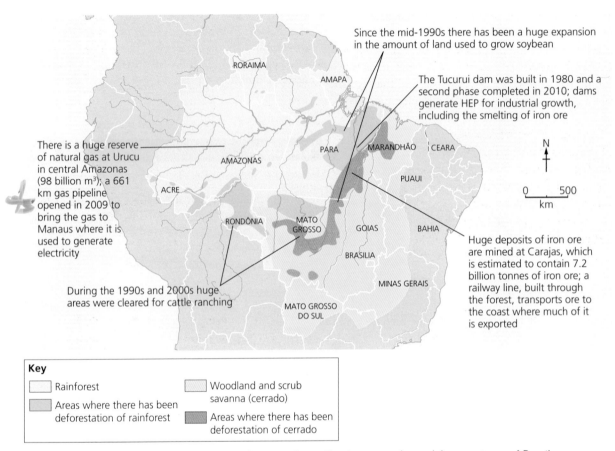

Since the mid-1990s there has been a huge expansion in the amount of land used to grow soybean

The Tucurui dam was built in 1980 and a second phase completed in 2010; dams generate HEP for industrial growth, including the smelting of iron ore

There is a huge reserve of natural gas at Urucu in central Amazonas (98 billion m³); a 661 km gas pipeline opened in 2009 to bring the gas to Manaus where it is used to generate electricity

Huge deposits of iron ore are mined at Carajas, which is estimated to contain 7.2 billion tonnes of iron ore; a railway line, built through the forest, transports ore to the coast where much of it is exported

During the 1990s and 2000s huge areas were cleared for cattle ranching

Key

- ☐ Rainforest
- ☐ Areas where there has been deforestation of rainforest
- ☒ Woodland and scrub savanna (cerrado)
- ■ Areas where there has been deforestation of cerrado

▲ **Figure 6** Deforestation of the tropical rainforest and woodland savanna (cerrado) ecosystems of Brazil.

State	2007	2008	2009	2010	2011	2012	2013
Mato Grosso	8,951	12,987	8,486	2,502	11,632	3,273	2,121
Para	3,899	8,264	1,559	3,499	6,283	1,359	1,511

▲ **Figure 7** Deforestation of tropical rainforest (hectares per year) in the states of Mato Grosso and Para.

Activities

1 a) Describe the distribution of areas where there has been most deforestation.

   b) Use map evidence to explain why so much forest has been destroyed.

2 a) Use Figure 7 to draw a line graph showing deforestation rates in Mato Grosso and Para.

   b) Describe the trend shown by your graph.

   c) Brazil's government has been trying to protect the Amazon rainforest since 2009. How successful do they seem to have been?

Why has soybean farming expanded so rapidly?

Agribusiness exported US$99 billion of agricultural products from Brazil in 2014 including meat, soybean and maize. The agricultural sector is a huge boost to the country's growing economy. It is creating jobs, wealth for agricultural businesses, and tax revenue for the government. The government needs this money to repay debts and to invest in welfare services, such as education and health.

Soybean, or soya, is a very useful product. It is high in protein so can be used as a meat substitute in vegetarian cooking. It is also used widely in agriculture as a source of protein in the feed given to pigs and chickens. Soybean can also be crushed to extract oil that is used in the manufacture of cooking oils.

Soybean will not grow in the hottest regions of the tropical rainforest ecosystem, but varieties have been created that will grow in the transition zone between the rainforest and savanna woodland (cerrado). Huge plantations now produce soybeans, which are exported to Europe and China. The rich biodiversity of the rainforest has been replaced by a single plant or **monoculture**. This change in habitat greatly reduces the variety of insects, birds and mammals that can continue to live here. The growth of soybean plantations has, therefore, been opposed by environmental pressure groups.

Year	Metric tonnes (million)
2000	39.0
2001	43.5
2002	52.0
2003	51.0
2004	53.0
2005	57.0
2006	59.0
2007	61.0
2008	57.8
2009	69.0
2010	75.3
2011	66.5
2012	82.0
2013	86.7
2014	94.5

▲ **Figure 8** Production of soybean in Brazil.

Country	Metric tonnes (million)
USA	108.0
Brazil	94.5
Argentina	56.0
China	12.4
India	10.5
Paraguay	8.5
Canada	6.1
Other	19.4
Total	315.4

▲ **Figure 9** Global production of soybean, 2014.

Source	Metric tonnes (million)
Soybeans	197.1
Rapeseed	39.8
Sunflower	15.9
Cottonseed	15.5
Palm kernel	7.7
Peanut	6.7
Fish	4.7
Copra	1.6
Total	288.9

Figure 10 World protein meal consumption, 2014.

Source	Metric tonnes (million)
Palm	60.7
Soybean	46.8
Rapeseed	27.0
Sunflower	15.2
Palm kernel	6.9
Cottonseed	5.1
Peanut	5.5
Coconut oil	3.5
Olive	2.6
Total	173.3

Figure 11 World vegetable oil consumption, 2014.

Activities

3 Suggest why biodiversity is lower on soybean plantations than in rainforest or cerrado. Use pages 182–4 to help you.
4 Explain why the growth of agribusiness has benefitted the economy of Brazil. Use evidence from Figures 8 to 11 to support your statement.

Enquiry ?

'Consumers in Europe need Brazil's soybean plantations.'

■ Discuss this statement. Do consumers have any options?
■ Suggest whether European consumers should be concerned about the production of soybean used in products that they buy in the supermarket. Use evidence from this page, and your own research, to support your argument.

How do human activities change processes in the tropical rainforest ecosystem?

Study Figure 12. It shows the continuous **canopy** of the rainforest which acts rather like a giant umbrella. Raindrops from a tropical storm can hit the ground with great force, causing soil erosion. By intercepting rainfall, the canopy prevents much of it from falling directly to the ground. Water then drips from the leaves with much less force.

In Figures 13 and 16 the canopy has been removed. Where the canopy has been removed by human activities, such as logging or forest clearance for palm oil plantations or other agriculture, there is an increased risk of soil erosion. The soil is washed into local rivers where it reduces the capacity of the river channel. This can lead to flooding problems.

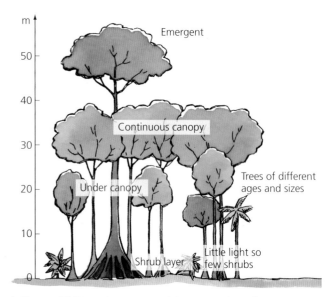

▲ **Figure 12** Typical structure of the tropical rainforest.

The forest in the foreground was burnt a few months ago. The stumps and roots of larger trees have helped to retain soil. What was once the forest floor (and therefore starved of direct sunlight) is now open to sunlight and weeds have quickly colonised. Seeds from trees in the background could blow into this area and the forest could regrow in around 40 years (creating what is known as a secondary rainforest).

This fragment of forest is now an ecological island, and animals here are separated from animals in other remnants of the forest. This forest has probably been selectively felled: trees such as teak and mahogany have already been cut for their timber. The use of heavy machinery in such a confined space will have damaged many other trees and shrubs. This process opens up holes in the canopy. It also deprives insects of a food source (some of which only feed on selected trees) so begins to damage the food chain.

The forest here has been clear felled and recently burnt. The entire structure of canopy, under-canopy and shrub layer has been destroyed. The soils are vulnerable to erosion, especially on this slope. Obviously, since the canopy has been removed, the nutrient cycle has been broken.

▲ **Figure 13** Tropical rainforest cleared in Madagascar.

Forest type	Location of study	Percentage intercepted and evaporated from canopy
Sitka spruce (conifer)	Scotland	28
Douglas fir (conifer)	Oregon, USA	19
Beech (deciduous)	England	15
Tropical rainforest	Indonesia	21
Tropical rainforest	Dominica	27
Tropical rainforest	Malaysia	27

▲ **Figure 14** Interception and evaporation of water from different forest canopies.

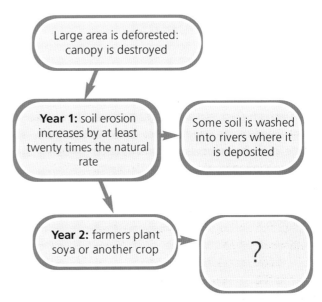

Large area is deforested: canopy is destroyed

Year 1: soil erosion increases by at least twenty times the natural rate

Some soil is washed into rivers where it is deposited

Year 2: farmers plant soya or another crop

?

▲ **Figure 15** The consequences of deforestation.

A

B

C

▲ **Figure 16** Logging next to a river in Borneo.

Activities

1 Explain how the canopy of the rainforest reduces the risk of soil erosion.
2 Study Figure 14.
   a) Choose a suitable method to create a graph to represent this data.
   b) Calculate the mean interception rates for
      i) coniferous forest
      ii) deciduous forest
      iii) tropical rainforest.
   c) Suggest why the deciduous forest has significantly lower figures.

Enquiry

How does human activity affect water stores and flows in the tropical rainforest?

■ Using Figure 15 as a starting point, create a flowchart or spider diagram to explain the links between deforestation, soil erosion, silt deposition in rivers, and river floods.
■ Write suitable annotations to fill the boxes on Figure 16.

Sustainable rainforest management in Central America

Deforestation causes fragmentation of the forest and this is a major problem for wildlife. As clearings get bigger the wildlife is restricted to isolated fragments of forest that are separated by farmland. You can see this in Figure 13 on page 198. The animals become trapped in islands of forest surrounded by an ocean of farmland.

The governments of Central America (also known as Mesoamerica) are co-operating with each other in an ambitious conservation project. They want to create a continuous **wildlife corridor** through the length of Central America. These corridors are created by planting strips of forest to connect the remaining fragments of forest together. Creating wildlife corridors allows animals to move freely from one area of forest to another without coming into conflict with people. It means that animals can find new sources of food. It also allows them to find mates in other forest areas, so helping to maintain healthy genetic diversity. The project is called the Mesoamerican Biological Corridor (known by its Spanish initials, CBM) and involves all seven governments of Central America, plus Mexico.

Country	1996	2000	2010
Belize	18.0	35.2	36.5
Costa Rica	20.7	23.9	26.9
El Salvador	0.4	0.1	6.8
Guatemala	28.4	29.5	30.9
Honduras	15.0	21.0	21.1
Mexico	4.1	7.7	12.9
Nicaragua	29.3	30.5	30.8
Panama	17.7	19.0	20.6

▲ **Figure 18** Protected areas in Central America and Mexico as a percentage of total land area.

Activities

1 Using Figure 17:
   a) Describe the location of Tikal National Park.
   b) Describe how the pattern of conservation areas in Honduras will change if new wildlife corridors are created.
2 Working in pairs, draw a spider diagram to show how fragmentation of the rainforest affects wildlife. Consider the likely impacts of fragmentation on:
   - food chains
   - success of mating
   - predator–prey relationships
   - pollination and seed dispersal.
3 Explain how the new wildlife corridors will help to conserve wildlife.

Creating conservation zones and buffer zones – how do they work?

It is difficult to conserve tropical rainforests and prevent damage, even if the forest is protected by National Park status. In reality, many protected forests suffer from some illegal logging, clearance of farmland or poaching of wild animals. Forests are often large and remote, so it is difficult for forest rangers to catch poachers or loggers or prevent clearance by burning. Besides, many of the people doing the damage are very poor. They have few other options for making a living and are tempted by opportunities for poaching or farming. Sustainable development of a forest should take into account the needs of local communities, who could make a living by using the forests' resources. At the same time, the overall biodiversity of the forest needs to be conserved for future generations of local people.

▲ **Figure 17** Protected areas, including forest reserves, in Central America and Mexico, and the proposed wildlife corridors.

▲ **Figure 19** The motmot lives in the rainforests of Central America; it eats insects, small lizards and forest fruit. Bird-watching holidays bring valuable income to local communities.

One way to achieve this balance between the needs of local people and the desire to conserve the forest is to create **buffer zones**. These are areas in which some human use of the forest is permitted. A buffer zone surrounds and helps to protect the central conservation area, which will hopefully remain unspoilt and unaffected by human activities. Local people are encouraged to use the buffer zone sustainably – to understand what can be done without doing lasting damage to the forest. For example, by planting food, fruit and nut crops among the trees people can create a diverse environment for insects and birds, and protect the soil from erosion. This type of farming is known as **agro-forestry**. Ecotourism is another permitted activity – with local people becoming guides. Hunting may also be permitted in the buffer zone – as long as animals are only killed for meat when the populations are high and can easily recover. Meanwhile, few if any activities are permitted in the central conservation zone, except perhaps scientific study.

The use of buffer zones may be a more realistic approach to forest management than banning all use of the forest entirely. If managed well, they involve local communities in decision making. They also help people to make a living and educate them about the value of conservation. However, buffer zones may also encourage migration – people see economic opportunities in agro-forestry or ecotourism and move into the buffer zone, putting pressure on local resources such as food, water and firewood.

The Talamanca Highlands buffer zone

◄ **Figure 20** The location of the Talamanca Highlands.

The Talamanca Highlands are a mountainous area of Costa Rica and Panama. The region contains large areas of unspoilt tropical rainforest that are conserved as a World Heritage Site. The diversity of plants and birds is nationally and globally important. Rainfall in the mountains feeds into rivers that supply fresh drinking water for communities in lowland Costa Rica. In order to protect the central conservation zone, a buffer zone has been created.

The buffer zone has not prevented damage to the environment, however. Land has been cleared for smallholdings, banana plantations and cattle ranching, which has led to soil erosion. The rivers have washed the sediment out to sea where it has damaged coral reefs. There are now plans for HEP dams and roads that could cause further damage to the rivers and forests of the buffer zone.

Activities

4 Describe the location of the Talamanca Highlands.
5 Describe the benefits of creating buffer zones for:
   a) wildlife
   b) local communities.
6 Do you think buffer zones are a sustainable strategy for a tropical rainforest? Explain your answer.

Enquiry

How good is Costa Rica's record on conservation compared with that of its neighbours?

- Study Figure 18. Calculate the average amount of land that is protected in Central America and Mexico.
- Present the data in graphical form – include a bar for the mean.
- What conclusions can you reach?

How does human activity affect the savanna grassland?

Desertification occurs in regions of savanna grassland. The trees are scattered. They do not form a continuous canopy like that of a tropical rainforest. However, the trees, shrubs and grasses all protect the soil from erosion. In regions where the trees and shrubs have been cut down or burnt, the process of desertification has been rapid. Therefore, it seems that the process of desertification is caused, at least in part, by poor management of the land:

- Vegetation is an important regulator of the water cycle. In more heavily forested areas, as much as 80 per cent of rainfall is recycled back into the atmosphere by a combination of evaporation and transpiration from the leaves. Slash and burn of savanna trees and bushes to make space for farming significantly reduces evapo-transpiration and so eventually leads to reduced rainfall totals. This in turn leads to a reduction in water for people, who rely on rivers for water supply.
- The removal of vegetation means that leaf litter can no longer fall into the soil. The nutrient cycle is broken and shrubs no longer replace nutrients or help to maintain a healthy soil structure by adding organic material to the soil.
- The destruction of the tree canopy exposes the soil to rain splash erosion. During heavy rainfall the water flows over the surface of the ground in sheets, eroding all the organic material from the upper layers of the soil. On steeper slopes the power of the water picks up and carries soil particles and smaller rocks. It uses these to erode downwards into the soil in a process known as gulley erosion.

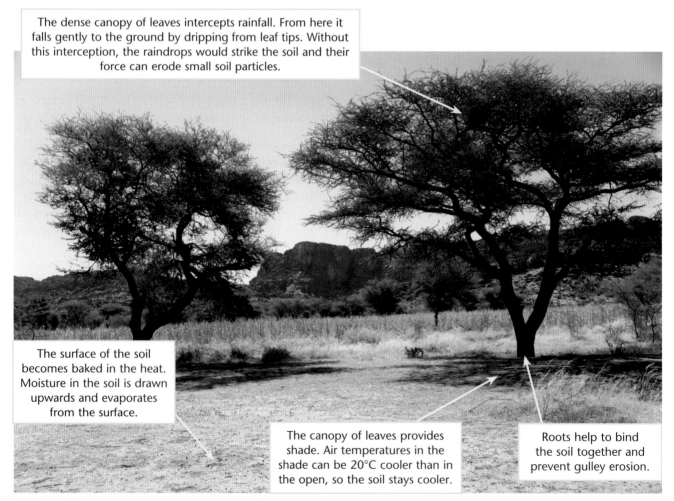

The dense canopy of leaves intercepts rainfall. From here it falls gently to the ground by dripping from leaf tips. Without this interception, the raindrops would strike the soil and their force can erode small soil particles.

The surface of the soil becomes baked in the heat. Moisture in the soil is drawn upwards and evaporates from the surface.

The canopy of leaves provides shade. Air temperatures in the shade can be 20°C cooler than in the open, so the soil stays cooler.

Roots help to bind the soil together and prevent gulley erosion.

▲ **Figure 21** Interactions between vegetation, soils and climate.

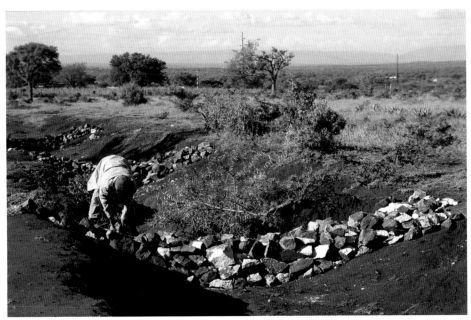

▲ **Figure 22** Gulley erosion is a common problem in areas suffering from desertification. This farmer is placing large stones across the width of the gulley.

Farmers allow their goats to overgraze shrubs, and vegetation is killed

Annual rainfall totals are gradually falling

Trees and shrubs are burnt to clear land for farming or urbanisation

Trees are cut down for firewood for cooking

The rain in the wet season is unpredictable and can be very heavy, causing soil erosion

Commercial farms use the land so intensively that the soil is quickly worn out

Less vegetation means less water is returned to the atmosphere by evapotranspiration

▲ **Figure 23** Physical and human factors that may cause desertification.

Activities

1　Sort the causes of desertification listed in Figure 23 into physical and human factors.
2　Study Figures 21 and 22. Use the information to write an explanation of what will happen if…

Farmers allow goats to overgraze	Effect on vegetation	
	Effect on soils	
	Effect on climate	

3　Explain why the farmer is placing rocks across the gulley in Figure 22.
4　a)　Use page 37, and the Glossary, to make sure you understand the following key terms:
　　　　infiltration
　　　　interception
　　　　overland flow
　　　　evaporation of soil moisture
　　　　transpiration
　　　　gulley erosion

　　b)　Predict whether each of the processes in question 4a will increase or decrease during desertification.
　　c)　Write a short news report about the issue of desertification. Make sure you use each of the key terms from question 4a in your report.

How has food production affected the savanna?

Farming in the savanna grasslands of Africa is a mixture of arable (crop-growing) and pastoral farming (animal grazing). Farmers keep goats and cattle for both their milk and meat. Crops are grown using a traditional bush fallow system. Scrub vegetation is removed by slashing and burning. Crops such as maize, root crops and vegetables are grown for between one and three years. The land is then abandoned for between eight and fifteen years. This is known as the **fallow period**. During this fallow period, the natural shrubs grow back. Leaves from the shrubs decompose in the soil, replacing organic fibre and nutrients that have been taken out by farming. This system is sustainable as long as the fallow period remains long enough. However, in some villages the fallow period is now only two to three years. This does not give the soil enough time to recover. It loses its organic content and its structure becomes dusty. This means that the soil is at risk of erosion from both wind and rainfall.

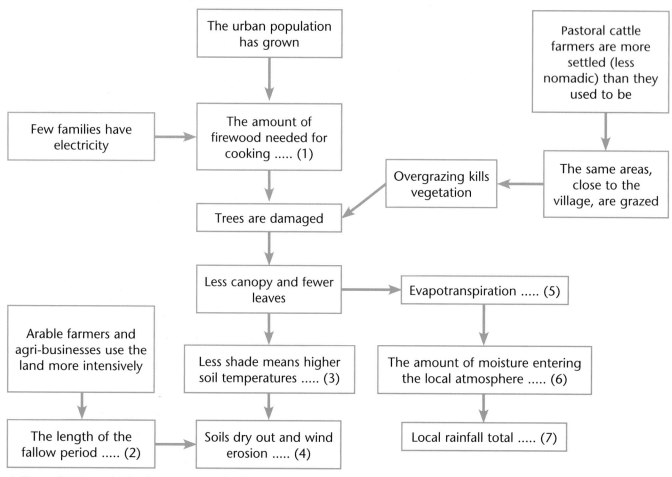

▲ **Figure 24** How poor land management leads to desertification.

Activities

1 Copy and complete the following description of the bush fallow system:
   Natural vegetation is cleared using slash and .... techniques. Crops are grown for one to .... years. The land is then allowed to rest for at least .... years in between crops. This is known as the .... period. During this time .... are returned to the soil.

2 Explain why:
   a) the traditional bush fallow system is sustainable
   b) reducing the length of the fallow period has degraded the soil.

3 Make a copy of Figure 24. Complete the boxes numbered 1–7 by adding the word *decreases* or *increases*.

Can drought resistant crops help solve the problem?

Ghana is a tropical country in West Africa. Northern Ghana has a hot semi-arid climate with a dry season that can last up to eight months of the year. Trees are used for firewood and shrubs are over-grazed so soil erosion has become a serious issue in the Northern, Upper West and Upper East regions. Farmers are also concerned about the impacts of climate change. Rainfall patterns seem to be increasingly unpredictable. Crop failures and the death of livestock lead to economic losses for farmers, food shortages and higher food prices. According to UNICEF, one in five children in Ghana is stunted because they are suffering from chronic malnutrition. In the Northern region it is thought that 37 per cent of children are stunted due to malnourishment.

Drought-resistant crops may help this region produce food even when rains are poor. These are crops that can grow well even if rainfall totals are low. Crops like chickpea, pigeonpea, groundnut, millet and sorghum can all grow in hot semi-arid regions and are all suitable for growing on smallholdings. The Ghanaian government is encouraging farmers to use four new varieties of maize that have been developed with the help of the Nippon Foundation which is a non-government organisation (NGO). Local farmers, however, have complained that the new seeds are more expensive than the usual varieties that they grow.

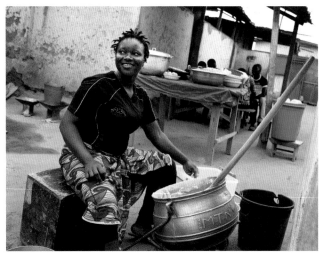

▲ **Figure 26** Clementia Talata cooking banku, a staple made from maize, at a local 'chop bar' (simple restaurant) using water from a Safe Water Network distribution point.

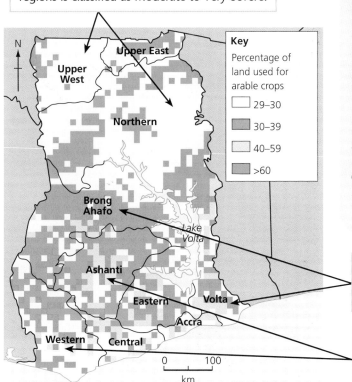

Natural vegetation is savanna grassland. The risk of soil erosion in the Northern and Upper West regions is classified as Moderate to Very Severe.

Key

Percentage of land used for arable crops

- 29–30
- 30–39
- 40–59
- >60

Natural vegetation is savanna woodland. The risk of soil erosion in Brong Ahafo and Volta is classified as Slight to Moderate.

Natural vegetation is tropical rainforest. The risk of soil erosion in Ashanti and Western regions is classified as Moderate to Severe.

▲ **Figure 25** Arable farming and the risk of soil erosion.

Activities

4   Use Figure 25.
   a) Estimate the amount of the Upper West and Upper East regions that is used for arable farming.
   b) Compare the arable farming in Ashanti to the Northern region.
   c) Suggest why the risk of soil erosion is highest in regions that have:
      i)   high rainfall totals, like Ashanti
      ii) a long dry season, like Upper West.
5   Describe one benefit and one disadvantage of growing drought-resistant crops in Ghana.
6   Explain the links between climate change, desertification and poverty (including health issues such as malnutrition).

How can intensive farming affect water cycles and climates?

Lake Chad is in the **Sahel** region of Africa. In the last 50 years, Lake Chad has shrunk dramatically. The reasons are complex. They include overgrazing and deforestation in the lake's **drainage basin**, which have resulted in a drier climate. However, a more significant reason may be the over-abstraction of water from the rivers that supply Lake Chad. Since 1970 a large number of dams have been built in both the Komodougou-Yobe river basin and Chari-Logone river basin. Some water is abstracted for domestic supply in cities such as Kano. The rest is used for intensive farming in irrigation projects that grow crops such as onions, tomatoes, chilli peppers and rice. It is thought that only five to ten per cent of the water in the Chari-Logone river now flows into Lake Chad. The rest evaporates or is abstracted and used. Twenty dams have been built in northeastern Nigeria since the construction of the Tiga Dam in 1974. This leaves only about two per cent of the water in the Komodougou-Yobe river basin to flow into Lake Chad.

▲ **Figure 27** The drainage basin of Lake Chad is shown by the pale green area.

Country	Total area (km²)	Area within the basin (km²)
Nigeria	923,770	179,282
Niger	1,267,000	691,473
Algeria	2,381,740	93,451
Sudan	2,505,810	101,048
Central Africa	622,980	219,410
Chad	1,284,000	1,046,196
Cameroon	475,440	50,775
Total area of Lake Chad basin		2,381,635

▲ **Figure 28** The drainage basin of Lake Chad.

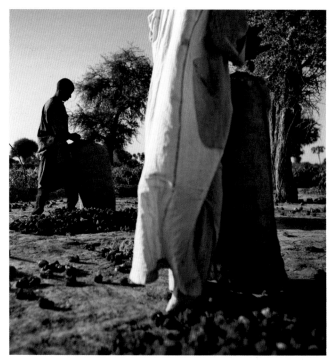

▲ **Figure 29** People harvest chilli peppers on a farm that is irrigated with water from the River Yobe in northern Nigeria; chilli peppers are an essential part of Nigerian cooking and fetch a good price, but have a very high water footprint.

Activities

1 Study Figure 27.
   a) Describe the location of Kano.
   b) Describe the drainage pattern within the Lake Chad drainage basin.
   c) Use your understanding of tropical climates to explain why Lake Chad has this drainage pattern.
2 Study Figure 28.
   a) How could this information be adapted to make it easier to use?
   b) What percentage of Nigeria is within the Lake Chad drainage basin?

How has the shrinking lake affected people and the environment?

This is a very poor part of Africa. There are 40 million people living in the drainage basin of Lake Chad and 60 per cent of them live on less than $2 a day. Over-abstraction means that:

- Some people rely on the lake for their water supply; this is not safe for human health and is a source of cholera and polio.
- Soils have suffered from salinisation. This process occurs when too much water is used to irrigate crops. Water evaporating from the soil leaves behind harmful minerals.
- The wetland ecosystems surrounding the lake have dried out. Wetland bird populations and fish stocks have declined. Less lake fish has meant declining incomes for fishermen.
- Poverty has increased, leading to increased migration to cities such as Kano. Increased poverty has also led to a rise in support for extremist groups such as Boko Haram.

Can Lake Chad be saved?

Thirty years ago an ambitious plan was announced to save Lake Chad. It was proposed that the Transaqua Project would transfer water from the Democratic Republic of Congo (DRC). A 2,400 km canal would transfer 100 billion m³ of water every year from the River Congo to the River Chari. Few people have taken the project seriously until now. The governments of India, China and Brazil see this project as an opportunity to invest in Africa – a continent that is rich in resources that would help support their rapidly growing NIC economies. This infrastructure project would provide water for agriculture, industry and electricity production. It would create job opportunities and water security. This peace-through-development approach to tackling poverty may also reduce extremism and violence in the region.

▲ **Figure 30** The shrinking of Lake Chad.

Activities

3 Use Figure 30 to describe the changes in the shape and size of Lake Chad between:
   a) 1963 and 2007
   b) 1987 and 1997.
   c) Suggest reasons why Lake Chad has reduced in size so erratically.

4 Outline the impacts of over-abstraction on the people, economy and environment of the region.

The Great Green Wall of Africa

The Great Green Wall (GGW) is one example of an initiative where countries are working in partnership with one another to try to tackle an environmental issue. Eleven countries signed an agreement in 2010 to begin planting this 'wall'. The plan is to plant a 15 km-wide strip of land with trees and shrubs across the width of Africa. It is hoped that this wall of vegetation will help prevent further soil erosion from the Sahel and improve incomes.

The plan is to encourage local communities to plant a mixture of native trees. These will include fruit and nut trees. Small fields between the trees can be planted with food and cash crops – a type of farming called agro-forestry because it combines farming and forestry.

▲ **Figure 31** Fields of millet growing between native shrubs and trees in Zinder, Niger.

▲ **Figure 32** The proposed location of the Great Green Wall.

Activities

1 Describe the environment in Figures 31 and 34.
2 Use Figure 32.
   a) Describe the location of the Great Green Wall.
   b) What is its approximate length?

Reduce soil erosion during the rainy season	Diversify farm incomes by growing fruit trees
Improve soil fertility by using leaves as a mulch	Increase the ability of communities to cope with climate change
Increase the amount of fodder (plant food) for livestock	Trees will provide shade for crops and increase their yield
Reduce the amount of time women spend collecting firewood	Grow medicinal plants
Increase biodiversity	

▲ **Figure 33** Benefits of the Great Green Wall.

How successful is the GGW?

Huge progress has been made by Niger. But Niger had a head start. It began its tree-planting programme 25 years before the 2010 international agreement was signed. Five million hectares of land in the Zinder region of Niger have been planted with trees since the mid-1980s. Senegal has also made good progress. Eleven million trees have been planted across 27,000 hectares of land. The Senegal Government wants local communities to develop ecotourism in the newly planted areas to take advantage of the larger number of bird species that live in these new forests.

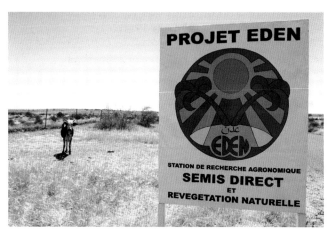

▲ **Figure 34** The Project Eden Research station in Niger. Project Eden is a Swedish NGO. It funds research into plants that will grow in semi-desert conditions without the use of fertilisers or irrigation.

Enquiry ❓

How do changes in climate over time affect spatial patterns (i.e. change over a map) in the environment?

Figure 35 uses isohyets to show spatial patterns of rainfall. Every place along an isohyet has an equal amount of rainfall over the year.

- Use the isohyets on Figure 35 to explain the change in ecosystems as you travel south to north through Niger.
- Use evidence from Figure 35 to explain why relatively small changes in rainfall can have significant impacts on people and the environment.

Activities

3 a) Discuss the benefits of the Great Green Wall shown in Figure 33.
   b) Classify each benefit as economic, social or environmental. Do any of the benefits fit into more than one category? Explain why.
   c) Make a copy of the diamond nine ranking diagram (page 83) and place each of the benefits into your diagram.
   d) Explain why you have chosen your top three benefits.
4 Suggest why some people may be suspicious of top-down development.

The Food and Agriculture Organization (FAO) of the United Nations claims that tree planting in these two countries has been a success:

- crop yields have increased
- livestock is better fed
- the trees are providing medicines and firewood.

Progress has been slow in the other nine countries who signed the agreement. This may be because some local communities do not feel as though they have been involved in the decision-making process and they feel suspicious. This is an example of a 'top-down development' and some communities are disappointed because they have not been consulted. They cannot imagine how their own community might benefit.

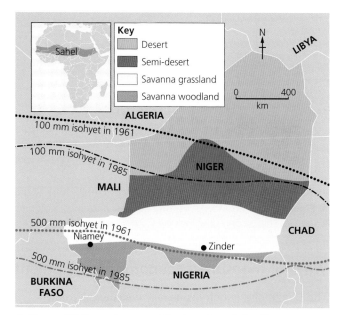

▲ **Figure 35** Ecosystems and the location of the Great Green Wall in Niger.

Where is the development gap?

Figure 1 shows the economic gap that exists between the wealthiest and poorest countries of the world today. This gap was first identified in a report written in 1980 by a German politician, Willy Brandt. His report drew a line, shown as the Brandt Line on Figure 1, separating richer countries from poorer ones.

- The line showed that most wealthy countries were in the northern hemisphere, so these became known as the 'global north'. The line loops around Australia and New Zealand in the southern hemisphere so that they could be included in the 'north'.
- Poorer countries became known as the 'global south' because many were in the southern hemisphere.

The line dividing these groups became known as the 'North–South divide'. Other people call it the 'development gap'. Nearly 40 years later, what, if any, progress has been made in closing the gap?

Activities

1 Study Figure 1. Describe the distribution of:
   a) high income countries (HICs).
   b) low income countries (LICs).
2 Identify any countries that do not fit the Brandt 'development gap' from 1980.

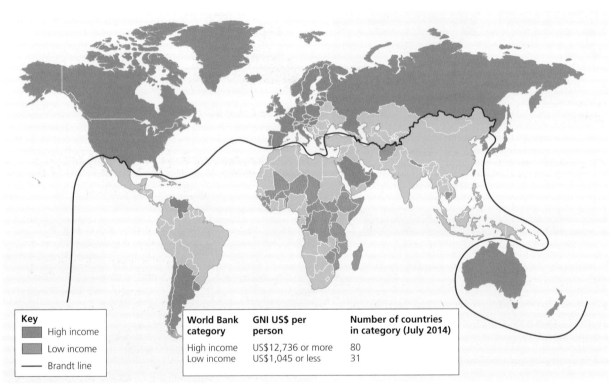

Key

▮	High income
▮	Low income
—	Brandt line

World Bank category	GNI US$ per person	Number of countries in category (July 2014)
High income	US$12,736 or more	80
Low income	US$1,045 or less	31

▲ **Figure 1** The world's richest and poorest countries; colours on this map indicate GNI per capita for High Income Countries (HICs) and Low Income Countries (LICs).

Ways of measuring economic development

The wealth of a country is usually measured by how much its economy earns each year. This is measured in a variety of ways, but the most common are:

- gross domestic product (GDP), which is the total value of the economy each year

- **gross national income (GNI) per person**, which is a little like the average wage
- poverty line – this measures the percentage of the population who earn less than a certain amount per day; the World Bank set this figure at US$1.90 in 2015.

These ways of measuring wealth have limitations. For example, GNI is an average for the whole country. The GNI in Malawi is around US$225, but some people in Malawi earn much more than this while others earn less. Also, comparing GNI for different countries can be a bit misleading. Food is cheaper in Malawi than in many countries, so US$225 will buy more there than in, for example, the UK. To take account of this, the World Bank changes its data to **Purchasing Power Parity (PPP)**. This converts GNI into a figure that describes what that money will buy in local prices. For Malawi, the GNI per capita figure in PPP in 2014 was US$780, over three times more than GNI, because prices there are three times cheaper.

Rich and poor?

In 2016 Oxfam published a report on global inequality. In this report they point out that the richest 62 people in the world own the same amount of wealth as the poorest 3.5 billion people (which is 50 per cent of the world's population). This is a shocking fact. It reminds us that wealth is still very unevenly distributed. However, unlike the Brandt Line, which drew our attention to the gap between rich and poor *countries*, this report highlights the gap between rich and poor *people*.

Using GNI to measure development

The GNI per person of a country is calculated as follows:

1 Add up the value of goods and services produced by people living in that country and by people overseas who are still citizens of that country. For example, the total earnings for Malawi in 2014 were US$4.26 billion.

2 Divide this figure by the number of citizens of that country. For example, the total number of citizens in Malawi in 2014 was 16.8 million. By dividing Malawi's earnings by its population we can see that the average per capita GNI was about US$225.

▲ **Figure 2** How do you see the world?

The gap between richest and poorest is widening

Oxfam is calling for governments to take urgent action to tackle the inequality crisis. It says there is a widening pay gap in most countries between the poorest and highest earners. Oxfam is urging world leaders to take three forms of action:

1 Crack down on large companies that avoid paying tax.

2 Increase investment in public services such as health care and education.

3 Boost the income of the lowest paid workers in society – especially women.

Oxfam points out that low pay particularly affects women, who make up the majority of low-paid workers around the world. Those on low wages do not seem to be benefitting from national economic growth. By contrast, people who are already wealthy benefit most from banking and tax systems that reward further investment.

▲ **Figure 3** An article based on Oxfam's 2016 report.

Activities

3 Describe two different limitations of using GNI as a measure of economic development.

4 Study the cartoon in Figure 2.
   a) Describe the two characters – what each is doing and how each is dressed?
   b) Suggest who the two characters represent, and why they have been represented in this way.

Enquiry

What should be done to tackle the gap between rich and poor?

The Oxfam's 2016 report suggests that there are three forms of action that would help reduce the gap between rich and poor.

■ Describe how each action would help.
■ Which of these three would you prioritise and why?

A continuum of economic development

It is very simplistic to divide the world into rich and poor as is shown in Figure 1 on page 210. In reality, every country fits somewhere along a line, or continuum, between very poor countries such as Malawi and super-rich ones such as the UK. If we put the world's countries into rank order, by GNI, it is possible to see this continuum. The World Bank does this ranking exercise, and then divides the world's 215 countries into four categories using GNI per capita:

- High Income Countries (HICs) have a GNI greater than US$12,736
- Upper Middle Income Countries have a GNI between US$4,126 and US$12,735
- Lower Middle Income Countries have a GNI between US$1,026 and US$4,125
- Low Income Countries (LICs) have a GNI less than US$1,025.

Figure 4 shows the distribution of Middle Income Countries. This large group, which the World Bank divides into two, includes **newly industrialised countries (NICs)** such as Brazil, India, Mexico and China.

Activities

1 Use Figure 4 to:
  a) describe the distribution of the world's Upper Middle Income Countries
  b) describe the distribution of the world's Lower Middle Income Countries.
2 Identify examples of:
  a) Upper Middle Income Countries that are south of the Brandt Line
  b) Lower Middle Income Countries that are north of the Brandt Line.
  c) What does this tell you about how patterns of inequality have changed since 1980?
3 Study Figures 6 and 8.
  a) Classify each country in 2015 by its World Bank category.
  b) Choose a suitable technique to represent the data.
  c) How much progress has each country made in closing the development gap?
  d) What conclusion can you make about the progress of these two groups of countries in closing the development gap?

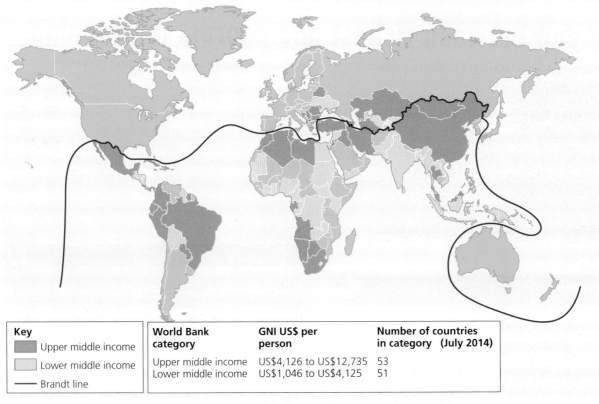

Key	World Bank category	GNI US$ per person	Number of countries in category (July 2014)
▨ Upper middle income			
▦ Lower middle income	Upper middle income	US$4,126 to US$12,735	53
— Brandt line	Lower middle income	US$1,046 to US$4,125	51

▲ **Figure 4** The world's Upper Middle and Lower Middle Income Countries; colours on this map indicate GNI per capita.

Is the development gap closing?

Figure 1 on page 210 shows the distribution of HICs and LICs. They clearly lie on either side of the Brandt Line – does this mean nothing has changed in nearly 40 years? Figure 4 shows a more complex pattern. NICs such as India have experienced rapid economic growth since 1980. Investment in education has created a skilled workforce. This has encouraged investment by foreign-owned **multinational companies (MNCs)**, creating jobs in the manufacturing industry. India's manufacturing sector now employs 22 per cent of the total workforce. Chemicals, electronics and engineering are all growth industries that employ millions of highly skilled and well-paid workers. The development of global cities in India, such as Mumbai (see pages 90–7) has connected India to the global economy – encouraging further investment. Foreign MNCs such as Siemens, IKEA, Samsung and Suzuki have all recently invested in factories in India. Indian-owned MNCs, such as Tata, are now investing Indian money in other countries – including the UK. Modern India has a complex economy – it earns foreign income by exporting a wide range of goods and providing a range of services.

However, other countries have made much less economic progress. Malawi, an LIC in southern Africa, is one example. Malawi is a **landlocked** country – without a coastline it has been unable to develop a port and its global connections with the world economy are much fewer than those of India. Malawi's economy depends on the export of a very small range of farm products including tobacco, tea, cotton and sugar. Unprocessed farm products like these have a low value compared to the processed products that Malawi imports, such as oil and farm machinery.

▲ **Figure 7** A tea picker working in Malawi.

	1985	1990	1995	2000	2005	2010	2015
Gambia	310	320	740	670	410	580	387
Kenya	310	380	270	420	530	1,000	1,410
Mali	150	270	250	230	400	610	691
Malawi	160	180	160	160	220	350	225

▲ **Figure 8** GNI for selected sub-Saharan African countries.

▲ **Figure 5** Wealth and poverty in India.

	1985	1990	1995	2000	2005	2010	2015
China	290	330	540	930	1,750	4,300	8,081
India	300	390	380	450	730	1,260	1,611
Indonesia	520	610	990	560	1,220	2,530	3,523
Mexico	2,130	2,750	4,570	5,750	7,720	8,720	9,951

▲ **Figure 6** GNI for selected newly industrialised countries (NICs).

Activity

4 Use the information on this page to suggest why Malawi has failed to make as much economic progress as India.

Enquiry

How should we tackle the development gap in the twenty-first century?

Discuss whether it would be better for world leaders to focus on inequality between different countries (like the Brandt Report) or between rich and poor people (like the Oxfam report). Justify your decision.

213

What is globalisation?

Economic development is now closely linked to the process of **globalisation**. Globalisation means the free flow of goods, people, ideas and money. Together, these are making a complex global web of interdependence, linking people and places in distant continents. Few people in the world are now untouched by it. But what impacts does globalisation have on trade, culture, companies and communications?

Example: Local people demonstrating about the falling water levels in their wells after this soft-drinks company opened a bottling plant in Kerala, India.

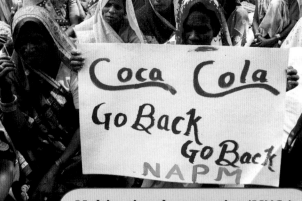

Example: Avocados grown in Mexico will be flown to a UK supermarket. This improves customer choice but food air miles have an impact on carbon emissions.

Multinational companies (MNCs): Large companies open branches in several different countries throughout the world.

Communication: The growth of fibre and satellite communication technology has increased global connections via smart phones, the internet and satellite television.

The factors that drive globalisation

Trade: Improved technology and cheap aviation fuel mean that fresh food can be flown from distant places to our supermarkets.

Culture: Western styles of music, TV and film are released throughout the world at the same time.

Example: Films made in Hollywood, USA, advertised in an Asian street. But will local styles of music and entertainment survive?

▲ **Figure 9** The impacts of globalisation.

Activities

1 In pairs, study the four impacts of globalisation in Figure 9. Draw a spider diagram with four arms – labelled Trade, Culture, Multinational companies (MNCs), and Communications. For each 'arm', write in one colour pen the advantages that globalisation brings. In a second colour pen, write the disadvantages. Use examples where you can (e.g. of products, or films and music).

2 Based on your spider diagram, write about 200 words on whether you believe globalisation brings more advantages or disadvantages.

3 Based on the data and images on pages 214–15, create a display to show the growth of the economies of Newly Industrialising Countries, and their influence. Include details about:
   a) their largest companies
   b) movement of their populations across the world
   c) the ways in which new technologies have helped this growth
   d) the ways in which they now influence global culture.

How do newly industrialised countries benefit from globalisation?

Newly industrialised countries (NICs) such as India and China have benefited from globalisation with rapid economic growth. In the 1990s, they offered cheap labour so their manufacturing industries boomed. Their economies have benefited from changes in technology (e.g. container shipping) and from investment of capital by their governments and by multinational companies (MNCs). Now they are becoming centres of the world's largest companies – just look at how rapidly the growth of companies in Asia now puts them in the Forbes 'rich list' of the top 2,000 companies.

Flows of people: Indian migrants work in many parts of the world, earning money which is often sent home to the family in India. In 2013, 734,000 people who were born in India lived and worked in the UK.

Flows of ideas and culture: The Hindi movie industry based in Mumbai (known as Bollywood) produced over 1,000 films in 2013. These films are extremely popular in South Asia and, with the growth of satellite TV, are easily accessible in other parts of the world.

Rank	Country of birth of resident UK population (2013)	Population (1,000s)
1	India	734
2	Poland	679
3	Pakistan	502
4	Republic of Ireland	376
5	Germany	297
6	South Africa	221
7	Bangladesh	217
8	United States of America	199
9	China	191
10	Nigeria	181

Forbes Top 2000 Companies List			
Rank in 2015	Rank in 2008	Country	Number of companies
1	1	United States	579
2	4	China (with Hong Kong)	232
3	2	Japan	218
4	3	United Kingdom	94
5	8	South Korea	66
6	5	France	61
7	10	India	56
8	6	Canada	52
9	-	Taiwan	47
10	7	Germany	45

	Mobile subscriptions (millions)	Mobile subscriptions (% population)	3G/4G subscriptions (% population)
World	6587.4	93	27
China	1246.3	92	33
India	772.6	62	3
United States	345.2	110	92
Indonesia	285.0	115	18
Brazil	272.6	137	55
Russia	237.1	165	29
Japan	137.1	108	85
Nigeria	128.6	76	8
Vietnam	127.7	144	20
Pakistan	126.1	70	-
Bangladesh	116.0	75	22
Germany	113.6	139	56
Philippines	109.5	113	17
Mexico	102.7	95	16

Foreign investments: Indian companies, such as Tata, are very successful in the world economy. In 2015, India's companies had taken it from 10th to 7th in the Forbes Top 2,000 companies.

Improved communication technologies: India and China dominate the global communications market with over 2 billion customers. India produces thousands of IT and software graduates from its universities each year.

▲ **Figure 10** Examples of the growth of NICs and their influence in the global economy.

215

Globalisation: Nike are just doing it

Every year, the Forbes Directory researches and puts a value on every major company in the world. It publishes a Top 100 called 'The World's Most Valuable Brands', which tries to put a value on brand names. It also groups them by category, such as technology or clothing. In 2015, the most valuable clothing company in the world was Nike. Forbes valued its 'brand', that is to say the value of the name if it were to be sold, at US$26 billion. Most people immediately associate the 'swoosh' logo as Nike, and their 'Just do it' slogan is also an asset. Nike's global sales in 2014 were US$28 billion, that's bigger than the gross national income (GNI) of some countries! US$9 out of every US$10 the company earned came from merchandise with Nike logos.

Nike is a multinational company (MNC) because it operates and sells in over 140 countries around the world. 41 of these countries manufacture Nike products, as Figure 11 shows. In 2014, it employed 48,000 people directly worldwide. It provided jobs for 20 times this number in factories which are under contract to make Nike products. This process is known as **outsourcing**, where companies work for Nike for a period of time under a signed contract. It gives Nike one big advantage – that it can negotiate on price. In 2012, China was Nike's biggest source of outsourced workers. By 2015 China had lost its place to Vietnam, because China's currency has increased in value, which made its products more expensive.

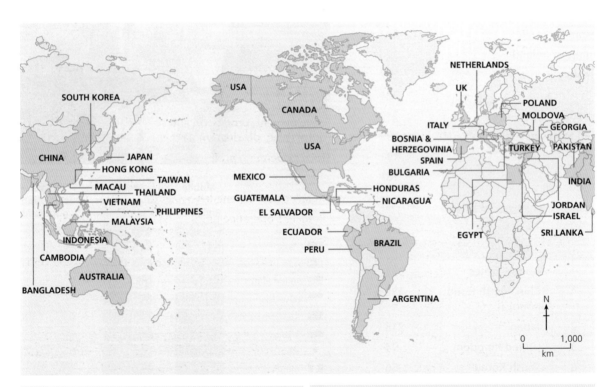

Japan: 1960s A factory making training shoes opened in Japan because labour was so cheap at the time. It was probably one of the world's first outsourced factories.

Taiwan and South Korea: 1970s Nike opened up its manufacturing here, using local companies who were contracted to make sportswear.

China: 1980s Nike began production here, taking advantage of cheaper labour in China as labour in South Korea and Japan became more expensive.

Thailand and Indonesia: late 1980s South Korean-owned companies making Nike products moved their manufacturing into Thailand and Indonesia in search of cheaper labour.

Vietnam: 2010s Now that China's currency is worth more, it is cheaper to make many items in Vietnam, so Vietnam has become the largest producer. Companies working for Nike in Vietnam employed over 140,000 more people between 2012 and 2015. China lost 43,000 jobs in the same period.

USA: today The location of Nike Head Office: Nike World Campus in Beaverton, Oregon. All research and development, and new product design is done in the USA.

▲ **Figure 11** World map showing the countries in which Nike manufactures its products.

Although small amounts of Nike clothing are made in the USA and Europe, almost all factories are located in Asia (Figure 12). Most factories employ a majority of women because pay is rarely equal for women compared to men. In Vietnam, the largest producer, many workers are migrants from rural areas. Workers live in hostels owned by the factory.

Manufacturing country	Manufacturing workers 2015	Workers + or -
1 Vietnam	341,204	Up 143,000
2 China	228,732	Down 43,000
3 Indonesia	186,425	Up 60,000
4 Sri Lanka	33,587	Up 13,000
5 Thailand	31,770	Down 20,000
6 India	28,165	Down 4,000
7 Honduras	26,090	Up 16,000
8 Brazil	20,935	No data
9 Bangladesh	15,090	No data
10 Pakistan	14,899	Up 4,400
Global total	1,016,657	

▲ **Figure 12** Nike's ten largest manufacturing countries by number of employees.

Activities

1 a) Represent the information in Figure 12 using a suitable map or graph.
   b) What are the strengths and limitations of your chosen technique?
2 Suggest why Nike contracts companies to do its work instead of opening its own factories.
3 Explain the risks for Nike manufacturing overseas.
4 Why do many countries such as Vietnam want to attract MNCs such as Nike?
5 a) Using Figure 13, calculate the percentage of a US$65 pair of trainers that goes to
   i) the country of manufacture
   ii) the USA
   iii) the retailer.
   b) Calculate the percentage of US$65 that consists of profit.

Nike and outsourcing

The company we know as Nike began in 1964 when Phillip Knight, a former athlete, began manufacturing training shoes in Japan, because of its cheap labour, and importing them to the USA. But all management operations and decisions – from design to finance and marketing – operate from the USA. The jobs in Nike's Asian and Central American companies are low-paid and unskilled. You can calculate from Figure 13 just how much of a US$65 pair of trainers goes to the manufacturing country, and how much goes to the headquarters in the USA.

	Cost
Production labour	$2.50
Materials	$9.00
Factory costs	$3.25
Supplier's operating profit	$1.00
Shipping costs	$0.50
Cost to Nike	$16.25
Nike costs (Research and development, promotion and advertising, distribution, admin.)	$10.00
Nike's operating profit	$6.25
Cost to retailer	$32.50
Retailer's costs (rent, labour, etc.)	$22.50
Retailer's operating profit	$10.00
Cost to consumer	$65.00

▲ **Figure 13** Where the money goes: breakdown of a US$65 pair of Nike training shoes.

Enquiry

What are the common features of MNCs?

Compare Nike with a company of your choosing, such as Apple, L'Oréal or Coca-Cola. For your chosen company, research:

■ where it manufactures in different parts of the world
■ their methods of outsourcing
■ who they use as outsourced workers
■ the benefits and problems that each company gets from outsourcing.

What are the benefits and problems brought by MNCs?

The benefits for companies who outsource their manufacturing overseas are clear. If labour costs are low, then a product can be made more cheaply and the price of the product falls. American, European and Asian consumers gain through cheaper goods. Job done.

But what about the countries, like Vietnam, in which MNCs such as Nike operate? Do they gain as well? These are the **host countries** in which MNCs invest. In theory, host countries should gain, as after all, factories bring jobs. In theory, investment brings even more jobs. People move closer to a factory, which is usually in a city, to work. In turn, this means a demand for housing, which in turn leads to shops and services to cater for the working population. These have to be built, which creates a huge increase in employment in the building industry. New networks develop for transport services and energy and water supplies known as **infrastructure**. The process creates an upward spiral known as the **multiplier effect**.

So is there a downside to MNC investment?

Many NICs have few workers' rights (e.g. maximum working hours) and no minimum wage. The governments of these countries think a minimum wage might put companies off from investing there. Thailand introduced a minimum wage of US$10 a day in 2013. Within two years, Nike had cut the number of jobs there by a third. As wages increase in one country, an MNC might decide to move production to another country where wages are lower. Wage levels in 2015 were as low as US$1 a day in Indonesia.

An MNC such as Nike opens a new branch

Jobs are created directly within the firm

Local firms that supply the MNC with parts or services such as cleaning, maintenance or catering have more work. They take on extra staff

Local families have larger incomes. They have more spare cash

Workers can afford to take out larger loans so they might buy new cars or extend their homes

More money is spent in local shops, pubs and restaurants

Local shops, pubs, etc. have more business. They may have to take on extra staff

As businesses expand they pay more tax in the form of business rates and income

Local government has more money to spend on improving roads, reclaiming derelict land and marketing the region

The image of the region is improved and the other new businesses may be attracted to locate there

▲ **Figure 14** The multiplier effect – how investment brings growth that builds on itself.

Activities

1 Copy and complete the following table to show the advantages and disadvantages brought by MNCs such as Nike for:
   a) the host countries
   b) the MNC.

	Advantages	Disadvantages
For the host country (e.g. Vietnam)		
For the MNC (e.g. Nike)		

2 Explain why, in spite of disadvantages, an NIC might decide to attract investment from MNCs such as Nike.

3 In pairs, decide whether you think Nike should have invested in Vietnam in 1995. Explain your reasons.

Nike in Vietnam

Nike began producing sportswear in Vietnam in 1995. Vietnam was one of the world's poorest countries. But its people had a reputation for hard work from other companies who had already invested there. Costs were much lower:

- There were no trade unions, or strikes for higher pay, so wages were low.
- The Communist government was keen to develop exports.

Getting to know Vietnam

Vietnam has become one of South East Asia's most rapidly industrialising and growing countries. It has a Communist government which is keen to raise the standard of living through the growth of manufacturing and services. The government began to open up opportunities for investment by overseas companies in the mid-1990s. It began by welcoming travel companies and overseas tourists. More recently a programme of industrialisation has rapidly increased Vietnam's GNI and other economic indicators (shown in Figure 15).

	Vietnam 2000	Vietnam 2014
GNI per person (in US$) PPP	2,070	5,350
Where GNI comes from (%)	Agriculture: 26 Industry: 33 Services: 41	Agriculture: 22 Industry: 40.3 Services: 37.7
Percentage of people by occupation	Agriculture: 67 Industry and Services: 33	Agriculture: 48 Industry: 22.4 Services: 29.6
Value of exports (US$)	11.5 billion	147 billion
Export goods (in rank order	Crude oil, seafood, rice, coffee, rubber, tea, garments, shoes	Clothing, shoes, electronics, seafood, crude oil, wooden products, machinery, rice

▲ **Figure 15** Comparing the economy of Vietnam in 2000 and 2014.

Enquiry ?

What should Nike do? Write a letter to the chief executive of Nike to show how you feel about reports of abuses in NICs such as Vietnam or Indonesia.

Nike became Vietnam's largest foreign employer with ten factories employing 40,000 people. In 2015, it employed 300,000 people. But Nike made mistakes in the late 1990s:

- All its sub-contracted companies in Vietnam were South Korean and Taiwanese, so all profits went overseas, instead of Vietnam.
- Factories gained reputations for sweatshop conditions. There were stories of abuse of workers.

The Vietnamese Government attacked Nike for its practices. Nike found itself in the newspapers every day. Some stories were later found to be false, but by then the stories had reached overseas. The harm was done. Nike told the Vietnamese Government that if attacks continued, it would leave. The criticism stopped.

Many pressure groups have tried to persuade Nike to improve workers' conditions. Many consumer groups want to see fair treatment for workers overseas. Pressure from groups such as the 'Boycott Nike' campaign in the early twenty-first century also came from US Congress. Nike now argues they have improved factory conditions, working hours and wages. Their workers live in hostels which are high quality, and there are agreements to restrict working hours. Nike now publishes data about all of its suppliers on its website, nikebiz.com.

▼ **Figure 16** Photo showing protestors in the USA against Nike.

Why have NICs emerged so quickly?

If you're wearing anything from a supermarket budget range of clothing, it's worth looking at the label to see where it has come from. Almost all budget items have been made in factories in Bangladesh. Bangladesh is a typical example of an NIC. Its economy doubled in size during the decade up to 2014, making it one of the fastest-growing economies in the world.

Figure 17 shows countries that are usually classified as NICs. Four of the world's five most populated countries are in the list (China, India, Indonesia and Brazil). Between them, they have nearly 40 per cent of the world's population. This means they have huge numbers of workers. They also have huge numbers of increasingly wealthy consumers, which means they are important markets for products as GNI increases.

Every NIC wants investment from industry because manufacturing creates jobs and increases GNI. In 2014, the Bangladesh clothing industry employed 5.5 million people and earned over US$28 billion in GNI for Bangladesh. The attractions for companies are twofold:

- NIC government policies have encouraged overseas MNCs to invest in factories. This is called **foreign direct investment**. In Bangladesh, most investment has been in the clothing industry. To help companies, Bangladesh has created export processing zones. These mean their exports to the EU or USA are duty-free, which reduces their price.
- Large supplies of cheap labour. In 2015, average wages in Bangladesh were 95 per cent lower than those in the EU and the USA.

Country	GDP per capita (PPP) 2014 in US$	GDP growth rate during 2014 (%)
Bangladesh	3,340	4.8
Brazil	15,900	0.1
China	13,130	7.4
India	5,760	7.4
Indonesia	10,250	4.8
Malaysia	23,850	6.0
Mexico	16,710	2.4
Philippines	8,300	6.0
Thailand	13,950	2.4
Turkey	19,040	2.9
Vietnam	5,350	5.4

▲ **Figure 17** Economic data for countries classified as NICs.

Social impacts

Increased GNI leads to improvements in education and health, and therefore life expectancy. Together, these form the basis of the HDI figures which have improved, some hugely, between 2000 and 2014, as you can see in Figure 18.

Country	HDI 2000	HDI 2014	Percentage improvement
Bangladesh	0.453	0.558	23.2
Brazil	0.682	0.744	9.1
China	0.591	0.719	21.7
India	0.483	0.586	21.3
Indonesia	0.609	0.684	12.3
Malaysia	0.717	0.773	7.8
Mexico	0.699	0.756	8.2
Philippines	0.619	0.660	6.6
Thailand	0.649	0.722	11.2
Turkey	0.653	0.759	16.2
Vietnam	0.563	0.638	13.3

▲ **Figure 18** Improvements in HDI 2000–14 for the world's NICs.

Enquiry

Should consumers in the UK buy clothing that has been made in Bangladesh?

- Survey your year group with three questions about their attitudes towards buying low-cost clothing (for example, their attitudes towards sweatshops and child labour).
- Collate the results and present them in a short report.
- Explain the possible reasons why people still buy clothing produced in such conditions.

Activities

1 Describe three features of NICs listed in Figure 17.
2 Explain why low wages and sweatshops make buying low-cost brands of clothing controversial.

Economic impacts

Employment in Bangladeshi clothing factories is controversial. People in the UK ask whether it is right that clothing should be produced in this way. The main arguments are these:

- Poverty is common in Bangladesh, so there is no shortage of people willing to work long hours for a low wage. Are factories taking advantage?
- Although conditions have improved, there are many sweatshops deliberately employing women, who can be paid less.
- Bangladeshi laws mean that children can work in factories from the age of 14.
- Many workers begin work at 7 a.m. and finish 12 hours later – six days a week, Factory workers say that the usual minimum wage is £25 a month. Sewing-machine operators earn £40 a month, about 15p an hour. But a living wage in Bangladesh should be £160 a month!

'This trade has provided employment to over 3 million impoverished Bangladeshis, the vast majority of them women, and transformed the economic and social landscape of the country. Since 1971, the poverty rate has plummeted from 80 per cent to less than 30 per cent, GNI growth has averaged 5–6 per cent for over 20 years, and the garment industry has had a lot to do with it.'

▲ **Figure 19** The view of the textile industry from Bangladeshi journalist Zafar Sobhan.

Activities

3 Suggest why Figures 19 and 20 take different views of the clothing industry in Bangladesh.

4 Make a large copy of the table below. Using Figures 18, 19, 20 and 21, explain the economic, social and environmental impacts of rapid industrial growth in NICs.

	Advantages	Disadvantages
Environmental		
Economic		
Social		

▶ **Figure 21** Sewers working in a factory in Bangladesh that makes items for Ikea.

Environmental impacts

One of the reasons that many companies are attracted to NICs is that they have far more relaxed environmental and planning laws. In the EU, pollution laws are very strict. By locating in countries such as Bangladesh, companies can often reduce costs by not having to comply with strict pollution or building regulations. As a result, factories working in the textile industry may discharge waste water into open drains and ditches. You can tell which colours are trendy in the fashion design studios of Europe simply by looking at the waste water in the ditch! The impacts of poor construction can be very serious. In 2013 the Rana Plaza building in Bangladesh collapsed, killing 1,100 people – mainly young women who were working in a clothing factory.

'**The collapse of the Rana Plaza building is, to date, the deadliest disaster in the history of the garment industry worldwide.**

Some 3,639 workers toiled in five factories housed in the Rana Plaza building producing clothing for US, Canadian and European clothing labels and retailers.

Eighty per cent of the workers were young women, 18, 19, 20 years of age. Their standard shift was 13 to 14 and a half hours, from 8:00 a.m. to 9:00 or 10:30 p.m., toiling 90 to 100 hours a week with just two days off a month. Young 'helpers' earned 12 cents an hour, while 'junior operators' took home 22 cents an hour, $10.56 a week, and senior sewers received 24 cents an hour and $12.48 a week.'

▲ **Figure 20** Report from the Institute for Global Labour and Human Rights on conditions in the Rana Plaza building.

Tata, an Indian MNC

The Tata Group is an Indian MNC. Its headquarters are in Mumbai. In 2013–14, Tata earned US$103 billion from its 100 companies. Those earnings mean that:

- Tata is the world's 60th largest company (four places below Tesco).
- If it were a country, Tata would be the world's 61st largest economy!

Of Tata's earnings, 67 per cent came from outside India. Its companies employ 580,000 people worldwide. It owns subsidiary companies, including steel makers, car manufacturers, chemicals, energy and hotels. In the UK, Tata owns 38 companies, employing 50,000 people. Its UK subsidiaries include:

- Jaguar Land Rover
- Tetley Tea
- Tata chemicals, which is based in Nantwich, Cheshire.

How do MNCs grow?

Every MNC started small and grew. This happened through:

- Sales growth – e.g. Apple, whose product range has moved from desktop computers to a range of electronic products.
- Mergers, by consolidation (merging with companies making similar products, to give more market share) or creating a conglomerate (building a range of different products as a safety net in case one fails).

Getting to know India

India has the world's second largest population, after China. Its population of 1.27 billion people is 17.5 per cent of the global total. Its economy grew by 7 per cent per year on average from 1997, and had quadrupled in size by 2015! India is now one of four NICs that have real global economic power – Brazil, Russia, India and China are known as the **BRICs**.

One reason for India's growth is its willingness to develop a globalised economy, combining a huge population and economy with the world's major MNCs. Its economy has grown because of globalisation – global flows of people, ideas and investment have helped India.

	India, 2000	India, 2014
GNI per person (in US$) PPP	2,000	5,760
Where GNI comes from (%	Agriculture: 25 Industry: 30 Services: 45	Agriculture: 17.9 Industry: 24.2 Services: 57.9
Percentage of people by occupation	Agriculture: 67 Industry: 18 Services: 15	Agriculture: 49 Industry: 20 Services: 31
Value of exports (US$	36.3 billion	342.5 billion
Export goods (in rank order	Clothing, precious stones, engineering goods, chemicals, leather goods	Petroleum products, precious stones, vehicles, machinery, iron and steel, chemicals, pharmaceutical products, rice, clothing

▲ **Figure 22** India's economy in 2000 and 2014.

◄ **Figure 23** The Tata steel works at Port Talbot, South Wales. There has been a steel plant here since 1902. In 2015, Port Talbot and its sister plant at Llanwern employed 5,000 people.

Tata Steel and the global steel industry

Tata Steel is the steel-making subsidiary of Tata Group. Tata Steel employs over 80,000 people making steel in countries all over the world including India, China, Thailand and Australia. In 2006 Tata bought Corus – a large steel-making company with plants in the UK and Holland. Buying European factories meant that Tata could sell steel more easily to buyers in Europe. Tata's steel is used in the car industry as well as in construction of steel-framed buildings and rail tracks. Since 2006 Tata has spent £3 billion improving steel making in Europe.

In the winter of 2015–16 steel makers in the UK reached a crisis point. Cheap steel, imported from China, was being sold for less money than it cost to make it in Europe. China is able to make steel cheaply because it has lower labour costs than Europe. Another reason is the cost of energy. Steel making uses huge amounts of energy and the Chinese government keeps the cost of energy low to protect its steel industry. The EU could protect its own steel industries (including Tata) from these cheap imports by placing a tariff, or tax, on Chinese steel. In 2016 the EU tariff on Chinese steel is just 16 per cent whereas the USA charges a 236 per cent **tariff** on Chinese steel. You can read more about tariffs on page 225.

Steel makers in the UK struggled to sell their steel. SSI, a Korean MNC, was forced to close its steel plant at Redcar, in Teesside, with the loss of 2,200 jobs. Tata claimed that its UK steel plants were losing £1 million every day. At first, Tata announced that it would lay off some of its 15,000 UK workforce. Then, in March 2016, Tata decided to sell the UK part of its steel-making business. If no one could be found to buy the business, it was feared that parts of South Wales and Yorkshire would go into a spiral of economic decline – the opposite of the multiplier effect that is shown in Figure 14 on page 218.

> If Tata closes its steel making in the UK and a buyer cannot be found, 15,000 British workers will lose their jobs. It's not just the people employed directly by Tata – another 25,000 people work in jobs that supply Tata with parts and services. All of these jobs are at risk.

Institute for Public Policy Research

> China makes more steel than it needs and it is dumping its own unwanted steel on the European market. The EU could make this steel more expensive for European buyers but the EU's tariff of 16 per cent is too low. We have been arguing that it should be increased to protect our own steel makers but the UK government has opposed this plan.

Spokesperson for the European Steel Association

> The UK government has created this problem by refusing to agree to an increase in the EU tariff on cheap Chinese steel. They are too concerned about keeping on good terms with China in the hope that China will import more British-made products in the future.

Stephen Kinnock, MP in South Wales

> The cost of energy is between 20 and 40 per cent of all of our steel-making costs. If the government agreed to subsidise our energy costs we would be able to make a cheaper product and sales would increase.

Spokesperson for the UK steel industry

▲ **Figure 24** Viewpoints on the global steel crisis.

Activities

1 Give one reason why Tata bought Corus in 2006.
2 Explain why Chinese steel is cheaper than European steel.
3 Give one advantage and one disadvantage of globalisation for the UK steel industry.
4 Study Figure 14 on page 218. Draw another flow diagram to show how the region around Port Talbot, South Wales, could be affected if the steel industry closes.

Enquiry

What might happen to the UK steel industry?

- Use evidence from Figure 24 and your own research to suggest what would happen to the UK steel industry if:
  a) EU tariffs on Chinese steel were increased
  b) the UK Government subsidised energy costs for the UK steel industry.
- What do you think the UK Government could have done, if anything? Justify your choice.

How far has trade hindered economic progress in LICs?

The theory says that trade is good for all. If no country can produce everything it needs, then trade makes sure everyone has all they want. Speaking in the 1960s, Martin Luther King (seen in Figure 25) reminded us that countries rely on each other for goods and services.

Since he spoke, larger, faster and more fuel-efficient aircraft and container ships move goods around the world. Globalisation brings everything from strawberries in December to the latest smart phones from China. Increasingly, countries rely on goods traded with others. Trade is made easier where partnerships have been agreed between countries. These trading partnerships are known as **trade blocs**. The European Union (EU), G20 and APEC are all examples.

> Before you finish eating breakfast this morning, you've depended on more than half the world.

Shop in any UK supermarket and you can buy ingredients for hot drinks: tea, coffee, or chocolate! Each is likely to have come from Malawi (tea and coffee) or Ghana (cocoa beans, the basis of all chocolate). Goods from overseas are known as **imports**. For both Malawi and Ghana, the European Union (EU) is its biggest customer.

Figure 26 shows that the trade of each country is different to that of the UK:
- UK earnings (US$834 billion) are 50 times those of Ghana (US$16 billion), and 640 times those of Malawi (US$1.3 billion).
- Ghana and Malawi's largest exports are either foods or minerals. These haven't been processed, like tea (leaves) or cocoa beans, so they are known as **raw materials**.
- More than half of their imports are **manufactured goods**.
- The UK, by comparison, exports a huge range of manufactured goods. Manufactured goods are worth more: a wooden chair is worth more than a piece of wood.
- The UK is also a global banking centre, so financial services earn over a third of its exports, e.g. interest charged on loans, and shares sold overseas.

◄ **Figure 25** Martin Luther King, the American civil rights leader.

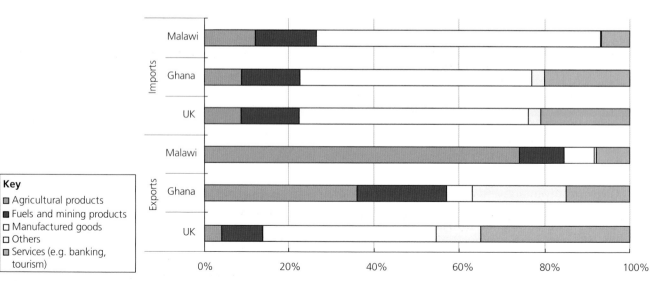

Key
- Agricultural products
- Fuels and mining products
- Manufactured goods
- Others
- Services (e.g. banking, tourism)

▲ **Figure 26** Comparing trade data for Ghana and the UK in 2013.

Free trade

Developing countries rely on trade to increase their GNI. Since the 1980s, the world has moved towards **free trade**, that is, trade without limits, duties or controls. Each country within a trade bloc has a free trade agreement with other countries in the bloc, or is working towards a free trade agreement. Countries can export as many goods as they wish. This is good for producers who export goods and services. The disadvantage of free trade is that a country can find itself swamped by cheap imports from other countries, with job losses in its own producing industries.

To avoid this, some countries protect themselves from cheap imports in one of three ways:

- Placing **quotas** that restrict the amount of imports each year.
- Placing an **import duty** or tariff on imports. This is a tax on imports to make them more expensive.
- Paying a **subsidy** to businesses so that their own goods can be sold at a lower price.

Free – but fair? Fair trade and Ghana

Ghana joined the World Trade Organization (WTO) in 1995. The WTO exists to promote free trade between its members. Until it joined, Ghana's government had paid farmers a subsidy to encourage them to grow food for Ghana's cities.

It sounds fine. But WTO rules are that farmers cannot be subsidised, even though the USA and EU (who are members of WTO) pay subsidies to their own farmers. These subsidies make American and European food cheaper. Farmers in Ghana suffer because of imports of subsidised EU food.

- Ghana's tomato farmers find it hard to sell their produce, because imported EU tomatoes are cheaper, and factories canning Ghanaian tomatoes have closed.
- Ghana's rice growers have been affected by cheap imported rice from the USA.

▲ **Figure 27** Most Ghanian farmers sell at street markets. Farmers find it difficult to compete with the low prices of these imported tomatoes.

Enquiry

Are subsidies fair? Write a 300-word letter to the WTO, arguing why either **a)** subsidies to EU and US farmers should be allowed to continue, or **b)** subsidies should be abolished.

Activities

1 In pairs, research the internet to find out where breakfast items come from, e.g. cereal, orange juice, tea, coffee.
2 Using Figure 26, compare Malawi's and Ghana's trade with that of the UK as follows: **a)** export value, **b)** import value, **c)** type of goods exported, and **d)** type of goods imported.
3 Using the data in Figure 26, identify three priorities that would improve trade for Ghana and Malawi.
4 Explain the advantages and disadvantages of farm subsidies for:
  a) consumers in Europe
  b) tomato growers in Ghana.

How does trade help to create global inequality?

Farming in sub-Saharan Africa tends to be of two types:

- Small, **subsistence** plots, where farmers trade very little and consume most of what they produce. Almost 90 per cent of Ghana's cocoa is grown on smallholdings. These are small farms of under three hectares. About 2.5 million smallholders in Ghana grow cocoa as their main crop.
- Plantations in which single crops are grown are known as a monoculture (the production of a single item). In Malawi, almost all tea is grown on large plantations.

Each country exports most of its coffee or tea to earn foreign currency.

Most tea and cocoa beans are exported to the EU, as Figure 29 shows. The main importing countries are the Netherlands, Germany, Belgium and France. The beans are ground into cocoa powder in these countries. Some of this powder is then re-exported to other EU countries where the chocolate is made. The main producers of chocolate are in Belgium, Germany, Ireland, the UK and Austria. Ninety per cent of Malawi's tea is sold either to the UK or to South Africa.

What decides the price of commodities?

Tea and coffee are examples of raw products known as commodities. Commodity prices depend on global supply and demand. Traders buy tea and cocoa beans on the London Stock Exchange. If prices of cocoa beans from Ghana are too high, dealers shop around and buy from whichever country is cheapest. The pressure on prices is downwards. The same is true for tea.

Figure 28 also shows how production of cocoa beans varies from year to year. Production depends on weather conditions, pests and diseases. In 2010 production was lower in all countries. In that year, global prices rose because supply was short. When demand is high, the price for cocoa beans is high. Figure 30 summarises how price can be decided by supply and demand.

Producing country	1,000s of tonnes 2010	1,000s of tonnes 2012
Cote d'Ivoire	1,610	1,650
Indonesia	574	936
Ghana	490	879
Nigeria	212	383
Brazil	180	253
Cameroon	129	256
Ecuador	94	133
Mexico	37	83
Total (all eight countries)	3,326	4,573

▲ **Figure 28** The world's top producers of cocoa beans (1,000s of tonnes).

▲ **Figure 29** Typical flow of exports of cocoa from Ghana.

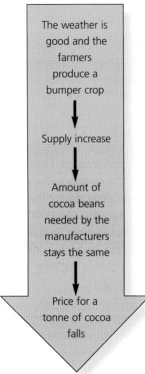

The weather is good and the farmers produce a bumper crop

↓

Supply increase

↓

Amount of cocoa beans needed by the manufacturers stays the same

↓

Price for a tonne of cocoa falls

▲ **Figure 30** Supply and demand.

▶ **Figure 31** How a) cocoa and b) tea vary in price on global markets.

Activities

1 Use Figure 28.
   a) Choose a suitable technique to illustrate the data.
   b) Compare the amount of cocoa grown in Ghana with that grown in other countries.
   c) If the EU imports more tea or cocoa from other producers, what would happen to the price of tea or cocoa in Malawi and Ghana?

2 Study Figure 30. Make a similar flow chart which starts with the following statement: 'A disease in many cocoa or tea plantations means that the harvest is poor.'

3 a) Using Figure 31, compare the cocoa price with that of tea on the global markets between 2014–15.
   b) Identify the highest and lowest prices of i) cocoa and ii) tea.
   c) Explain the problems faced by farmers with such variable prices.

4 Look at Figure 32. Suggest what will happen to the price of tea and cocoa on the world market based on each of these future scenarios.

▲ **Figure 32** A futures wheel for cocoa and tea.

Key drivers of the globalised tourist industry

The global tourist industry employs one in eleven of all worldwide jobs and generates income equivalent to six per cent of world exports. The process of globalisation (discussed on pages 214–5) has made it easier for more people to travel abroad. The key drivers have been:

- changes in technology – especially in transport and mobile technologies
- growing levels of wealth – allowing more people to pay for more frequent holidays
- the globalisation of multinational companies and the ways in which MNCs package our holidays.

International tourist arrivals (millions)			
	1995	2014	2030
Africa	18.7	55.7	134
Middle East	12.7	51.0	149
Americas and the Caribbean	109.1	181.0	248
Asia and the Pacific	82.1	263.3	535
Europe	304.7	581.8	744
Total	527.3	1,132.8	1,810

▲ **Figure 33** The growth of the global tourist industry – the number of tourists in 1995 and 2014 and the predicted number in 2030.

The modern age of **mass tourism** began in the 1960s. MNCs began putting together packages of flights and accommodation to make holidays more affordable. The first mass tourist holidays were offered in new resorts in the Mediterranean region, such as Benidorm in Spain. Since the 1960s, transport technologies have improved and aeroplanes have become faster, larger and more efficient. As air travel became more affordable it allowed the growth of **long-haul** flights and the development of mass tourism in the Caribbean and Kenya during the 1970s and 1980s, and then in Asia during the 1990s. The development of this type of mass tourism is due to the growth of large MNCs, for example Singapore Airlines (a Singapore-based MNC) and hotel chains such as Marriott International (a US-based MNC).

Another factor that is having an impact on the tourist industry is the rapid growth in mobile communication technologies, such as tablets and smart phones. These devices allow travellers to be independent. Instead of relying on a holiday company to provide information and support while they are away, travellers can use mobile technologies to access information, timetables, translation services, maps and online banking. These technologies make **independent travel** easier by reducing the tourists' reliance on MNCs to arrange their holidays for them.

▲ **Figure 34** Changes in flight time between London and Australia.

Activities

1. Use Figure 34 to describe and explain how the time it takes to get to Australia has changed.
2. Identify the economic, social and technological factors that have allowed the global growth of the tourist industry.

A more recent trend in mass tourism has been the development of cruise holidays. Like earlier forms of package holiday, cruises provide the customer with the convenience of packaging a flight with accommodation and meals. It has been made possible by the growth of a few large MNCs, such as US-based Royal Caribbean Cruises.

9 million passengers took cruises in 1999

25 million cruise passengers are predicted in 2019

6,000 passengers on an average Caribbean cruise ship

70 per cent of cruise destinations are in biodiversity hotspots

£40 the average amount of money spent by a passenger each day in local businesses when they leave the ship

0.43 kg of CO_2 per passenger per mile is estimated to be emitted by cruise ships: that's 0.17 kg more than aircraft on a long-haul flight

3.5 kg of rubbish per day is estimated to be made by each cruise ship passenger, compared to an average of 0.8 kg per person in the Caribbean

▲ **Figure 35** Cruise ships in numbers.

The growth of demand for tourism in NICs

As wages rise in newly industrialised countries (NICs), so the demand for tourism is growing. Countries such as India, China and Nigeria all have a large, emerging middle class. These are well-paid, professional men and women who have enough money to buy luxury consumer items including holidays. About 100 million tourists travelled abroad from China in 2014. Affluence in China is growing so quickly that this figure is expected to grow to 234 million by 2020. Chinese tourists are estimated to have spent US$229 billion on foreign holidays in 2015. By comparison, UK tourists spent about US$60 billion. Many Chinese tourists travel within Asia, but the UK's tourist attractions, including cities like London and Oxford, are keen to attract more Chinese tourists.

▲ **Figure 36** A large cruise ship moored in the Caribbean Island of Saint Lucia; around 21 million tourists took cruise holidays in the Caribbean in 2014.

Leakage

Most tourists still book their holiday through an agent and purchase a package that includes flights, hotels and meals. In such packages, it is estimated that between 40 per cent and 80 per cent of the money spent by the tourist goes to the MNCs that own the airline or hotel chain. Most of these have their head offices in Europe or North America – not the country in which the tourist is taking their holiday. This loss of income is known as leakage.

Activities

3 Explain why cruise tourism may not benefit the local economy as much as independent travel.
4 Study Figure 33.
   a) Calculate the number of tourists arriving in Europe in 1995.
   b) What was this as a percentage of all tourists?
   c) Compare the growth in tourist arrivals in Asia with the growth of tourist arrivals in Europe.
   d) Give one technological and one economic reason to explain why tourism in Asia is expanding so rapidly.

Enquiry

'Cruise tourism is bad for the economy and bad for the environment.'

To what extent do you agree with this statement?

229

How important is tourism to Mexico's economy?

Mexico is an NIC. It has a large and complex economy with exports in a wide variety of manufactured goods. Around 19 million foreign tourists visit Mexico each year, making it the world's ninth most popular holiday destination. About 3.6 million Mexicans work directly in travel and tourism, and this is expected to rise to 4.8 million by 2025. The growth of tourism creates jobs in construction and leads to improved infrastructure, such as airports and ports. The industry itself creates **direct employment** in travel (for example in airports and on aircraft) and in hotels and restaurants. It also creates **indirect employment** – these are existing jobs that benefit because of the arrival of tourists. For example, demand for food in hotels supports jobs in agriculture and fishing.

Activities

1 Working with a partner, make a list of the kinds of jobs that are created by tourism:
   a) directly
   b) indirectly.
2 Describe the location of Mexico's tourist resorts/ regions of:
   a) Cancun
   b) Acapulco
   c) Baja California.
3 a) Describe how the data in Figure 39 could be represented on a map.
   b) What would be the strengths and limitations of using this technique?

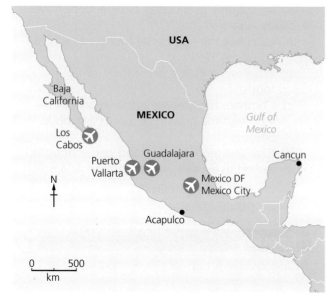

◀ **Figure 37** A street vendor selling fruit, Cancun. One example of how tourism can boost employment indirectly.

▲ **Figure 38** The location of Mexico's busiest international airports and the mass tourist resorts at Cancun and Acapulco.

Figure 39 American tourist arrivals to Mexico by airport, January to March 2014.

Airport	American arrivals
Cancun	791,066
Los Cabos	303,252
Mexico DF	240,742
Puerto Vallarta	225,791
Guadalajara	133,832
Others	278,709

The growth of mass tourism in Cancun, Mexico

In the 1970s Cancun was a tiny fishing village. Cancun is now the largest mass-tourist resort in the Caribbean. Cancun's hotel zone has over 150 hotels with a total of 35,000 rooms. This is expected to grow to 46,000 by 2030. Three million visitors to Cancun add US$4.36 billion to Mexico's economy each year.

Cancun's hotel zone is separate from the local community. It was planned like this as a **tourist enclave**. While the tourists stay in air-conditioned comfort in the hotel zone, the hotel workers live in the separate city of Cancun. Local people aren't even allowed on the beaches. The beaches are owned by the state but access is controlled by the hotels. They keep locals away to prevent tourists from being hassled by vendors who try to sell food, drinks or their services as guides.

Enclave tourism

Hotels often sell 'all-inclusive' packages. This means that tourists pay one price and get all their food, drink and entertainment from the hotel. Cruise ships offer the same kind of deal. In either case, their customers have no real need to leave the hotel or cruise ship. A consequence of enclave tourism is that tourists do not visit or spend money in locally owned bars or restaurants. If they did, less money spent by tourists would leak away from the local economy.

Activity

4 Study Figure 40.
   a) Suggest a new caption for this cartoon.
   b) Justify the view that enclaves are bad for both tourists and local people.
   c) Suggest why the Mexican government developed Cancun as an enclave.

"Dear George, here we are in the middle of things having a great time. We feel we're really getting to know this exotic country . . ."

▲ **Figure 40** Enclave tourism.

Has tourism been good or bad for Cancun?

Tourism creates direct employment for 52,000 people in Cancun and as many as 175,000 jobs indirectly. However, many workers in the large hotels are only offered short, temporary contracts. This means that workers can be laid off at the end of a one- or three-month contract if the seasonal pattern of visitors means there is insufficient work.

▲ **Figure 41** Flooded streets in the city of Cancun during tropical storm Sonia, 2013.

> I work long hours but only earn about US$5 a day. I can't afford a decent home. I live in a rented shack. It costs US$80 a month. I share the outside toilet with neighbours and the tin roof leaks when it rains heavily. The tourists have everything they need, but we have no space or leisure facilities. We're not even allowed on the beach!

Hotel worker

> Many people who work in the hotels of Cancun are migrants from other parts of Mexico. They suffer because they are separated from their families and original communities. Most of them are badly paid and rely on tips to make up their wages. Many work long hours and have stressful working conditions. Some suffer from alcohol or drug abuse.

Social worker

> We use security guards to keep locals off the beach. The problem is that some 'beach boys' hassle the tourists. They try to sell fast food or souvenirs. Sometimes there have been problems with drug dealers or even muggings.

Hotel manager

▲ **Figure 42** Views on the development of tourism in Cancun.

Activities

1 a) Draw a graph to represent the data in Figure 43.
   b) Using Figure 41, and your understanding of other global cities, suggest the problems that such rapid urban growth may cause in Cancun.
2 Discuss the points of view in Figure 42.
   a) Identify three different issues created by tourism in Cancun.
   b) What are the main causes of these issues?
   c) Suggest possible solutions to one of these issues.
3 Summarise what you consider to be the advantages and disadvantages of mass tourism for the local people and economy of Cancun.

Year	Cancun	Acapulco
1970	0	178
1980	34	304
1990	192	658
2000	438	794
2010	680	864
2020	993	944
2030	1,161	1,075

▲ **Figure 43** Population of Cancun and Acapulco (1,000s).

The impacts of tourism on Cancun's environment

Cancun is built on a long thin barrier of sand – the Cancun–Nizuc barrier. The **lagoon** behind this barrier was largely filled with mangrove forest. Offshore is another important habitat – a tropical coral reef. Scientists are concerned that all three parts of this environment have been damaged by the growth of tourism:

- Sewage from the resort has caused the spread of disease in the coral reef.
- Sand was taken from the beach during the 1970s and 1980s to be used in the construction of the hotels.
- Mangrove trees have been cleared away and the lagoon has become polluted.
- Plants that naturally grow along the top of the beach, which help to hold the sand together, have been stripped away. This makes the beaches more attractive to tourists but it means that sand is more easily eroded during storms.
- The high-rise hotels are too heavy for the soft sediments beneath them. Some hotels have had structural problems due to subsidence.

Coral reefs, beaches and mangroves all act as natural buffer zones during a tropical storm. Scientists believe that damage to these environments has left Cancun at greater risk to natural disasters. Cancun has been hit by several storms. The worst was Hurricane Wilma (2005), which caused US$19 million damage to Cancun's hotel zone. Wilma eroded all of the sand from the 20 m wide beach. The beach was replenished in 2016 at a cost of US$19 million.

Activities

4 Describe three ways that the development of Cancun has damaged the environment.
5 a) Make a sketch of Figure 44.
  b) Label the tombolo (the thin spit of sand), the beach and the lagoon.
  c) Add an annotation to explain why the hotel zone is at risk of tropical storms.

Enquiry

'The resort of Cancun has no long-term future.'

Make use of evidence from these pages to decide whether or not you agree with this statement. Explain your decision carefully.

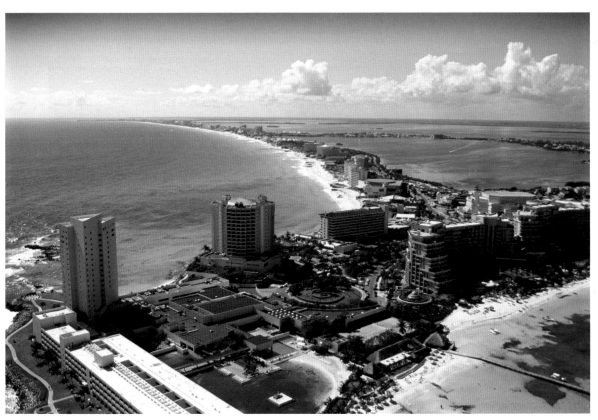

▲ **Figure 44** Cancun's hotel zone.

Tourism in the Gambia

The Gambia is a low income country (LIC) in West Africa. Poverty, poor health care and education place this small country among the poorest 25 in the world. The UN estimates that 40 per cent of the population live in poverty.

About 75 per cent of the population are employed in agriculture, although farm products only contribute about 20 per cent of Gambia's wealth. Peanuts are the main export and tourism is Gambia's second highest earner. The Gambia has few natural resources and only a very limited manufacturing sector. So, with golden beaches and a warm climate, Gambia has become dependent on tourism. Tourism contributes about 40 per cent of all national wealth. It is estimated that between 20,000 and 35,000 people are employed directly in tourism. At least another 35,000 are employed indirectly. The Gambia relies on the money it earns from tourism to import basic food stuffs such as rice.

The first tour operator began flying tourists to the Gambia, from Sweden, in 1965. Today, most tourists come from the UK, Germany, Belgium, the Netherlands, Denmark, Sweden and Norway. The Gambia is only six hours flight time from most European cities. It is in the same time zone as London, so tourists don't get jet-lagged.

Dependency

The economies of most small island developing states (SIDS) rely heavily on tourism. Many of these small countries have few exports, so money earned by tourism represents more than 30 per cent of their total exports. By comparison, the average amount of money earned by tourism for the world is just over five per cent. The Maldives, Seychelles and Jamaica are particularly dependent. Some LICs, such as the Gambia, also rely very heavily on tourism compared with other ways of earning foreign income. Dependency on tourism is risky for an economy. A natural disaster such as a cyclone, earthquake or tsunami can severely reduce visitor numbers. Political instability, conflict, disease and economic recession can also affect visitor numbers.

Enquiry

How dependent is the economy of the small island developing states (SIDS) on tourism?

- Research the location of the SIDS.
- Choose one SID to research further. How many tourists visit? What are the positive and negative impacts of tourism here?

▲ **Figure 45** Informal work is common in the Gambia; here, a vendor tries to sell souvenirs to tourists.

Is tourism good for the Gambia?

Gambia has a seasonal climate with a rainy season during the summer months. Tourism is also seasonal, with most European tourists visiting during the winter from October to March. This means that many tourist workers are under-employed or unemployed for several months of the year and they consequently rely on other, informal work. Figures for unemployment and informal employment are unreliable, but both are very high.

The Gambia cannot rely on earning the same income from tourism each year. Tourists want to feel safe and secure when they are on holiday. They are fearful of problems such as disease, terrorism and political unrest. If a destination seems to be unsafe, it is very simple to book a flight to another destination. In recent years some tourists have been put off visiting the Gambia by the country's political unrest. The country's leader has been very outspoken on some topics, including the rights of gay and lesbian people. His views have triggered protests that have been reported in European news broadcasts. In 2014, parts of West Africa were affected by Ebola (see pages 282–3). There were no cases in Gambia but tourist numbers were exceptionally low in 2014.

Year	Tourists
2000	79,000
2001	57,000
2002	81,000
2003	89,000
2004	90,000
2005	108,000
2006	125,000
2007	143,000
2008	147,000
2009	142,000
2010	91,000
2011	106,000
2012	157,000
2013	171,000
2014	70,000 (estimate)

▲ **Figure 47** Annual visitor numbers to the Gambia.

Activities

1. a) Use an atlas to find the location of the Gambia.
   b) Draw a sketch map and label it to show why it is popular with tourists from Europe.
2. a) Explain why the tourist industry in Gambia is seasonal.
   b) What problems does this create?
3. a) Compare tourism in the Gambia and Cancun. Include facts and figures.
   b) Explain why the Gambia is more heavily dependent on tourism than Mexico.
   c) Explain why this is a problem for:
      i) the Gambian government
      ii) ordinary people in the Gambia.
4. a) Choose a suitable technique to represent the data in Figure 47.
   b) Describe the trend shown on your graph.
   c) Explain why visitor numbers fell so sharply in 2014.
   d) Give one other reason why visitors from Europe may stop visiting the Gambia.

Hotel owner in the Gambia

Our hotel is usually 80–95 per cent full during the winter months. But during the winter of 2014 it was only 30 per cent full. I think it will take at least three years for our business to recover.

Tourist from the UK

I think tourists are frightened to come here. They know that Ebola has affected West Africa, but they don't realise that West Africa is twelve times the size of the UK and only some parts are have been affected.

Hotel cleaner

Things are much worse when we have a bad tourist season. Obviously there is less work, so I have less money to buy food. The price of rice and oil, which I use for cooking, also goes up!

▲ **Figure 46** Views on the Gambia's 2014 tourist season.

How should we respond to inequality?

The United Nations (UN) is an international organisation supported by 192 different countries. One of the UN's aims is to encourage and assist human development. In 2015 the UN set seventeen Sustainable Development Goals to be achieved by 2030. These build on the work of the **Millennium Development Goals (MDGs)**, which ran from 2000–15. Each of the goals, described in Figure 48, are divided into specific targets – 169 of them in all.

Sustainable Development Goals

Goal 1: End poverty in all its forms everywhere.

Goal 2: End hunger, achieve food security and improved nutrition, and promote sustainable agriculture.

Goal 3: Ensure healthy lives and promote well-being for all at all ages.

Goal 4: Ensure inclusive and equitable quality education and promote lifelong learning opportunities for all.

Goal 5: Achieve gender equality and empower all women and girls.

Goal 6: Ensure availability and sustainable management of water and sanitation for all.

Goal 7: Ensure access to affordable, reliable, sustainable and modern energy for all.

Goal 8: Promote sustained, inclusive and sustainable economic growth, full and productive employment and decent work for all.

Goal 9: Build resilient infrastructure, promote inclusive and sustainable industrialisation, and foster innovation.

Goal 10: Reduce inequality within and among countries.

Goal 11: Make cities and human settlements inclusive, safe, resilient and sustainable.

Goal 12: Ensure sustainable consumption and production patterns.

Goal 13: Take urgent action to combat climate change and its impacts.

Goal 14: Conserve and sustainably use the oceans, seas and marine resources for sustainable development.

Goal 15: Protect, restore and promote sustainable use of terrestrial ecosystems, sustainably manage forests, combat desertification, and halt and reverse land degradation and halt biodiversity loss.

Goal 16: Promote peaceful and inclusive societies for sustainable development, provide access to justice for all and build effective, accountable and inclusive institutions at all levels.

Goal 17: Strengthen the means of implementation and revitalise the Global Partnership for Sustainable Development.

▲ **Figure 48** The seventeen Sustainable Development Goals.

Goal 1: End poverty in all its forms everywhere

- There has been a significant decline in extreme poverty. In 1990, nearly 50 per cent of the population of developing countries earned less than US$1.25 a day. By 2015, the percentage living in extreme poverty (less than US$1.90 a day) had fallen to fourteen per cent.
- In 1991, only eighteen per cent of the workforce of developing countries earned more than US$4 a day. These were the emerging middle classes. In 2015, 50 per cent of the workforce was in this category.
- In 1991, 23 per cent of the population of developing countries were malnourished. By 2016 this had fallen to thirteen per cent.
- By the end of 2014, conflicts had forced nearly 60 million people to abandon their homes.

▲ **Figure 49** How much progress have we made to eradicate poverty and hunger since 2000?

Enquiry

If you could only achieve five of the seventeen Sustainable Development Goals, which ones would you make the highest priority? Justify your choice.

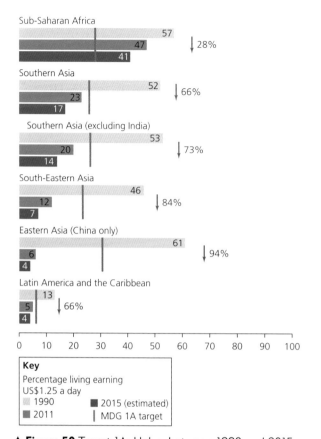

▲ **Figure 50** Target 1A: Halve, between 1990 and 2015, extreme poverty (the proportion of people whose income is less than US$1.25 a day).

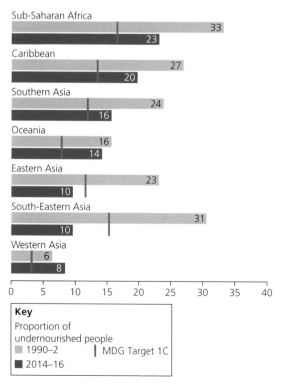

▲ **Figure 51** Target 1C: Halve, between 1990 and 2015, the proportion of people who suffer from hunger.

How can we achieve these goals?

The Sustainable Development Goals apply to all countries, but ending extreme poverty in countries such as Malawi will require **development aid** from governments and the voluntary sector in wealthier countries. There are two main types of development aid. These are described in the panels below. Another approach would be to make trade fairer so that workers get decent wages. Examples of aid and fair trade are given on pages 238–41.

Bilateral aid

Bilateral aid is when help is given directly from the government of one country to another. The Australian government, for example, gives about A$42 million of bilateral aid to the Pacific island of Vanuatu each year. This money is spent on a wide range of development projects, for example, to reduce malaria or improve rural roads. Australia gives about A$1,500 million in bilateral aid each year.

Multilateral aid

Multilateral aid is when money is given by a large number of different governments to a large organisation such as the UN, the World Bank or UNICEF (the world's largest charity for children). The organisation then uses the money to fund development projects. Australia gives about A$3,500 million in multilateral aid each year.

Activities

1 Study the list of Sustainable Development Goals in Figure 48. Sort each of the goals into one of three categories:
   ■ economic
   ■ social
   ■ environmental.
2 a) Represent the information in Figure 49 using suitable graphs, images or pictograms.
   b) Suggest how conflict can lead to poverty.
3 Study Figures 50 and 51. Use evidence from these graphs to identify:
   a) regions that more than achieved both targets
   b) regions that failed to meet either target
   c) regions that are wealthier but where hunger is still an issue.
4 How successful do you think the world has been in achieving Goal 1? Evaluate the evidence from this page.

Investigating long-term aid

Why give aid? Who gives it and what is it for? We are all familiar with the TV appeals after there has been a natural disaster such as a major earthquake. Such aid is known as **emergency aid**. However, most aid is, in fact, planned over long periods of time to tackle poverty and improve health and education. This type of aid is known as long-term or development aid. One example can be seen in Malawi, an LIC in southern Africa.

Getting to know Malawi

Malawi was one of sub-Saharan Africa's poorest countries in the 1970s, and it remains so. Although keen to develop manufacturing and services, there are several barriers:

- It is landlocked (it has no coast) which raises the costs of transporting goods to the coast for export.
- It exports little compared to other countries.
- It has suffered major impacts from deaths caused by HIV/AIDS.

	Malawi 2000	Malawi 2014
GNI per person (in US$) PPP	490	780
Population living below poverty line (%)	54	53
Where GNI comes from (%)	Agriculture: 37 Industry: 29 Services: 34	Agriculture: 30.1 Industry: 18.5 Services: 51.3
Percentage of people by occupation	Agriculture: 86 Industry and services: 14	Agriculture: 90 Industry and services: 10
Value of exports (US$	0.5 billion	1.3 billion
Export goods (in rank order)	Tobacco, tea, sugar, cotton, coffee, peanuts, wood products	Tobacco (53%), tea, sugar, cotton, coffee, peanuts, wood products, clothing

▲ **Figure 52** Comparing the economy of Malawi in 2000 and 2014.

Activity

1 Use data in Figure 52 to provide evidence that Malawi is an LIC.

Providing development aid to Malawi

Middle Shire is a district in southern Malawi named after a local river, the Shire. The river is vital to this part of Malawi, because it provides most of Malawi's hydro-electric power (HEP). It's an agricultural region. Most families are subsistence farmers, growing crops such as maize or cassava. Others work on large sugar cane and cotton plantations.

▲ **Figure 53** Map showing the location of the COVAMS project in Middle Shire.

But Middle Shire has a problem. It is affected by **soil erosion** during the intense rainy season each year. Between 1990 and 2005, Malawi lost 13 per cent of its forest due to land clearance for farming. Two pressures have caused this:

- A rapidly rising population. The population of Middle Shire has doubled since 1980, so farmers have cut down forest to grow more food.
- Tobacco, Malawi's most valuable export, has suffered falling prices because of global over-production and falling consumption in HICs of the world. So, if farmers are to earn the same income, they must grow more tobacco.

▲ **Figure 54** An agricultural training scheme in Malawi.

COVAMS – saving the soil

A project in Middle Shire aims to save soils and re-plant trees. It's known as Community Vitalization and Afforestation in Middle Shire (COVAMS), a ten-year aid project funded by the Japanese government. It is designed to build **capacity**, which means it aims to allow Malawi to increase food and jobs. The project uses several methods to prevent soil erosion:

- Explain to communities what causes soil erosion.
- Build rock, wood and bamboo barriers across streams to prevent soil loss during rainy seasons.
- Train villagers how to conserve soil and plant trees.
- Train farmers to plough around hillsides, following the contours rather than ploughing up and down the hills, which increases surface run-off.
- Build terraces into hillsides to reduce surface run-off.
- Supply fast-growing tree species from local nurseries to speed up **reafforestation**.

This approach uses **intermediate technology**, teaching local people skills in using local materials to provide low-cost solutions to problems. It has had three impacts:

- By 2011, 75 per cent of households in Middle Shire had taken part.
- Crop yields improved dramatically.
- With less soil erosion, water quality improved in the dams, so Malawi produces more HEP.

Why do countries give aid?

Malawi benefits from aid, especially long-term projects such as COVAMS. But Japan also benefits for the following reasons:

- **Diplomacy and good relations.** Aid improves relations between countries, and enables the Japanese to influence politicians in southern Africa.
- **Tactics.** Japan is keen to become a member of the UN Security Council, and needs the support of African countries.
- **Economics.** Sub-Saharan Africa countries have averaged 5 per cent annual economic growth during the 21st century. Japan sees opportunities to sell more Japanese products in Malawi if it invests in Malawi.

Enquiry

Analyse the impacts of COVAMS. Create a table to show the economic, social and environmental impacts of COVAMS on Middle Shire.

Activities

2 In pairs, design a flow diagram to show causes, processes and effects of soil erosion.
3 Explain why it is important to train Malawian farmers about how to prevent soil erosion.
4 Write a five-minute script for local radio in Middle Shire to tell people about the COVAMS project.

Is fair trade the way forward?

One of the ways in which Low Income Countries (LICs) can increase wealth is by developing manufacturing industries to process their raw materials. Why doesn't Ghana develop its own cocoa processing or make chocolate?

There would be a number of processes: making cocoa powder or butter, and then adding ingredients to make chocolate. Each stage would add value, boosting the economy. Each would create jobs, and chocolate would earn more money for Ghana than raw cocoa beans.

▲ **Figure 55** Thornton's chocolate – made in Britain using raw cocoa products.

The trade barrier

In fact, chocolate is made in Europe, the world's biggest market for chocolate. The manufacturers import cocoa beans or partly processed cocoa powder. It's cheaper that way because of import tariffs – or duties charged on imports. Import on cocoa beans in the EU are lower than those on processed cocoa. In 2015, the EU charged a 7.7 per cent tariff on cocoa powder imports and between 8 per cent and 18 per cent on chocolates, but zero per cent on raw cocoa beans. This is a process known as 'tariff escalation': the duty gets higher the more the item is processed. By the time VAT (value-added tax) is added to the finished product, a £1 bar of chocolate may be £1.25 instead. It would make Ghanaian chocolate expensive, and people would buy cheaper products instead. Similarly, Japan and the USA have no duty on unprocessed cocoa beans but charge large tariffs on imported chocolate of up to 65 per cent.

So Ghana has little option but to export cocoa beans, and loses the opportunity to develop its own manufacturing economy.

Where does fair trade fit in?

The idea that trade should be 'fair' is not new. The Fairtrade Foundation was established in 1992 to issue the Fairtrade Mark to products meeting particular international standards. These standards, and the Fairtrade Mark, guarantee a better deal for farmers and workers in developing countries to improve their standard of living.

It works like this:
- Farmers receive a payment that is agreed and stable – not like the variable prices on pages 226–7.
- Communities also receive an additional payment called a Fairtrade Premium to be used for local projects.
- One of Fairtrade's aims is to develop a long-term partnership with farmers, so they can plan, knowing how much they will earn.

It's not just about cocoa, Fairtrade deals with a range of foods, including bananas, coffee, tea, sugar, and flowers.

The Kuapa Kokoo co-operative of cocoa farmers

Kuapa Kokoo is a co-operative of cocoa farmers in Ghana. It sells part of its cocoa bean crop to Divine Chocolate Ltd in the UK who make Fairtrade chocolate products such as Divine and Dubble. The main benefits of this are:
- Farmers receive US$2,000 per tonne for their cocoa, or about 10 per cent more than the usual price on the world market.
- Farmers receive training to help them deal with pests or diseases, such as black pod, that affect the cocoa crop.
- Members of the co-operative can borrow small amounts of money from a **micro-credit** bank to invest in improving their farms.

- Farmers elect a trusted member of the village to weigh and record their cocoa beans. This makes trading more official and people more accountable, and raises the status of women who have been elected.
- Kuapa Kokoo are shareholders in Divine Chocolate Ltd. Profits from the sale of chocolate are invested in projects in Ghana.

The co-operative also receives an extra Premium of US$200 per tonne that is then used to fund community projects such as the well in Figure 56. Other projects include village schools, corn mills, and toilet construction.

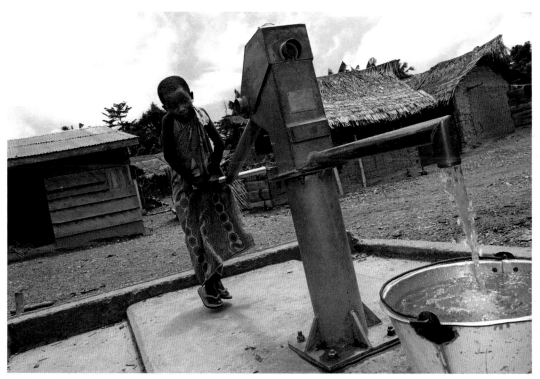

▲ **Figure 56** The Premium is used by the producers for community projects such as this village well.

Activities

1 Use the terms 'add value', 'processing', 'tariffs', 'manufacture' to explain why the EU, and not Ghana, makes chocolate.
2 Explain three differences that belonging to a Fairtrade organisation can bring farmers.
3 Draw and complete a table to show the economic, social and environmental impacts of Fairtrade on communities in Ghana.
4 In pairs, discuss whether 'all trade should be fair trade'. Feed back your ideas to the class. Make sure you justify your decision.

Enquiry

Are Fairtrade products more expensive? Use two UK supermarket websites to research whether Fairtrade bananas, coffee, tea and chocolate are more expensive than non-Fairtrade products.

THEME
6
Development and resource issues
Chapter 2
Water resources and their management

How much water do we use?

Everyone needs water. It is essential for healthy life. We also use vast quantities of water to grow food and in many industrial processes. However, the total amount of water used varies greatly from one country to another. For example, the average American family uses 1,300 litres of water a day, whereas the average African family uses only 22 litres of water a day. Generally, much more water is used per person in the richer nations of the world than in the poorest. This may be because:

- Water **abstraction** is expensive – it requires huge investments to build dams and water-transfer schemes.
- Wealthier people tend to use more water in non-essential ways, such as watering gardens, washing cars or filling swimming pools.

However, the global pattern of water use is not quite as simple as that. Some countries have higher rainfall totals than others and many countries have major rivers which bring water into their territory. These countries have the opportunity to use a lot of water for agriculture. Pakistan is an example. Rivers that are fed by snow melt in the Himalayan Mountains flow into Pakistan. This water is taken, or abstracted, and used to irrigate crops. So, even though Pakistan is a Middle Income Country it uses a lot more water per person than the UK which has a much higher **gross national income (GNI)**.

Country	Annual water use by agriculture (km³/year)	Annual water use per capita (m³/inhab/year)	GNI per capita, PPP (current international $)*
Cambodia	2.05	158.9	2,260
Egypt	59	1,000	6,160
Ghana	0.65	49.63	1,820
India	688	615.4	3,620
Malawi	1.17	98.95	870
Niger	0.66	69.28	720
Nigeria	7.05	89.07	2,300
Pakistan	172.4	1,024	2,880
UK	0.99	171.8	35,940
USA	192.4	1,575	48,890

▲ **Figure 1** How much water is used by selected countries.

Activities

1 a) Working with a partner, make a list of all the ways that you use water every day.
   b) How many of these uses are essential and how many could you live without?
2 a) Use data in Figure 1 to represent the per capita water use in the UK and the two poorest nations in the table.
   b) Suggest five reasons why families in richer countries like the UK use more water than families in the world's poorest countries.

▲ **Figure 2** An extravagant use of water? A desert golf course in USA.

Some groups of people have very poor access to water. Many people in rural regions of sub-Saharan Africa have to collect water and carry it some distance from their home. Collecting water is time-consuming and heavy

▲ **Figure 3** Street vendor selling water in Nigeria.

– BUT WHAT WILL WOMEN DO IF THEY DON'T HAVE TO CARRY WATER FOUR HOURS A DAY?

▲ **Figure 4** African women of the Sahel (see page 284) spend a lot of time doing work that does not contribute directly to family or state income.

work. In Africa, 90 per cent of the work of collecting water and firewood is done by women and children. A piped supply to the home would not only be safer, it would save time. A study in Tanzania showed that reducing the distance to a source of water from 30 to 15 minutes increased girls' attendance at school by 12 per cent. Having piped water also gives families privacy and dignity. Imagine how unhappy children must feel if they have nowhere private to wash.

In sub-Saharan Africa, people living in urban areas are twice as likely to have access to safe, piped water as people living in rural areas. However, even within urban areas, there are massive differences between the way that rich and poor have access to water. In the informal settlements of Africa's cities, many people do not have access to piped water and cannot afford to drill a borehole. They are forced to buy water from street vendors like in Figure 3. As a result, people who live in the shanty towns of some African cities can pay up to 50 times the amount for water as people living in European cities.

Long working days are the norm for women in the Sahel. Women work up to a total of 16 hours per day in the growing season, of which about half is spent on agricultural work. Time allocation studies from Burkina Faso and Mali show women working one to three hours a day more than men. In rural areas, the lack of basic services such as reliable water supplies, health centres, stores (shops) and transport adds considerably to the time women must also spend on household chores. Shortage of time constrains women's attendance at activities to benefit them, the time and attention they can pay to productive activities, and visits to health facilities.

▲ **Figure 5** Extract from a World Bank report.

Enquiry

How close is the connection between a nation's wealth and its water use?

- Study Figure 1. Suggest a hypothesis that links wealth and water use.
- Draw a scattergraph to investigate the possible relationship between these sets of data.
- What conclusions can you draw?
- How could you improve this enquiry?

Activity

3 Study Figures 4 and 5.
   a) Give three reasons why women in Sahel countries such as Mali have such long working days.
   b) Suggest a number of ways in which the lives of rural African women and children would be improved if they had access to a clean and safe water supply close to their home.
   c) Suggest how women in Mali might use four extra hours a day.

What is your water footprint?

Every day each of us drinks between 2 and 4 litres of water a day. You use a lot more water through washing, bathing and flushing the toilet. For example, you will use about 95 litres in a five-minute shower. However, even this is only a small fraction of the total amount of water you will use in a day. Our food and clothing contain **embedded** water. This is water that has been used to grow our food and make our clothes. Each of us uses 2,000–5,000 litres of embedded water every day. So, as **consumers** we each have a **water footprint** – the impact of our water use on the planet. Our water footprint is a measure of our individual water use and our impact on this vital resource.

Other footprints	Litres
T-shirt and pair of jeans	10,000
Pizza	1,260
100 g chocolate	1,700
A dozen bananas	1,920
1kg beef	13,500

▼ **Figure 6** Water footprints for selected items.

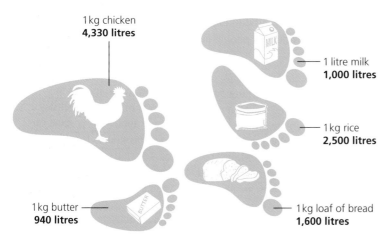

1kg chicken
4,330 litres

1 litre milk
1,000 litres

1kg rice
2,500 litres

1kg butter
940 litres

1kg loaf of bread
1,600 litres

Activities

1 Present the data for other footprints in Figure 6 as five pictograms. Try to make your pictograms roughly proportional so that larger water footprints are shown using larger pictures.
2 Explain why drip irrigation is more suitable for farming in hot semi-arid climates than other forms of irrigation.

Water is not delivered to where plants are not growing.

Small pipes deliver drips of water to the roots of each individual plant.

Some water will evaporate from the damp soil.

◄ **Figure 7** Drip irrigation reduces the amount of water lost by evaporation. The system was invented in Israel where water supply is an issue.

Water for food

Globally we use about 70 per cent of our water to grow food, 20 per cent to supply industry and just 10 per cent to give us a safe domestic water supply. There are 7 billion people in the world today and the world's population is expected to rise to 9 billion by 2050. To feed these extra people, and overcome poverty and malnutrition, we need to produce 60 per cent more food by 2050.

This won't be a problem in regions which have an equatorial climate where high quantities of rainfall provide water for farming without the need for irrigation. However, in regions where rainfall totals are low, water is withdrawn or abstracted from the ground or reservoirs so that it can be used to irrigate crops. In these regions farmers will need to adopt techniques that use less water to produce more food. Figure 7 shows one example of these techniques.

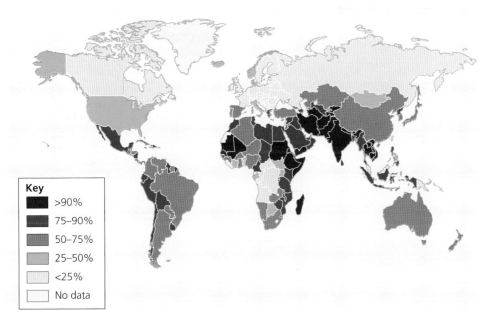

▲ **Figure 8** The percentage of water withdrawn for use by agriculture.

Activities

3 Use the data in Figure 9 to compare global water use in 2000 and 2050.

4 Study Figure 8.
   a) Describe the location and distribution of countries that use more than 90 per cent of water withdrawals for agriculture.
   b) Suggest one way that this style of map could be improved to make it more effective.

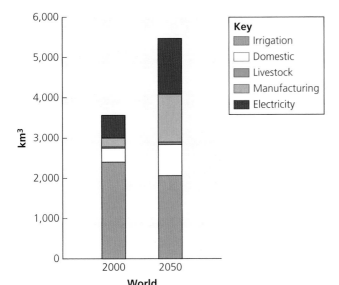

▲ **Figure 9** Global water demand in 2000 and 2050.

	Agriculture	Industry	Domestic
Cambodia	94.0	1.5	4.5
Egypt	86.4	5.9	7.8
Ghana	66.4	9.7	23.9
India	90.4	2.2	7.4
Malawi	85.9	3.5	10.6
Pakistan	94.0	0.8	5.3
UK	9.2	32.4	58.5
USA	40.2	46.1	13.7

▲ **Figure 10** The percentage of water, withdrawn for each sector, in selected countries.

Maintaining water security

We have seen that we need fresh water to provide drinking water, grow food and supply industry. Without enough fresh water our health and the development of our economies could suffer. So, **water security**, which means making sure that sufficient fresh water supplies are always available, is essential for any country. Water security means that:

- people have enough safe and affordable water to stay healthy
- there is sufficient water for agriculture, industry and energy
- ecosystems that supply our water, such as wetlands, are conserved
- people are protected from water-related hazards such as drought.

Some parts of the world suffer from a lack of water, or water insecurity. This may be because of drought or because insufficient money has been invested in water resources. One way to solve the problem is to transfer water from places that have too much to places that have too little. This is a more common solution than you might think. Rivers transfer water long distances, often from one country to another. Indeed, it is estimated that 90 per cent of the world's population live in countries that take water from shared river basins.

Investigating water supply in South Africa

Around 91 per cent of South Africa's population has access to fresh piped water. That means that about 4 million South African's do not. Many of these live in rural places. In urban areas, the theft of water is becoming a serious issue. People make illegal connections to water supplies because they cannot afford a legal connection. So, improving water security is a high priority for the South African government.

Rainfall is not distributed evenly over South Africa. Moist air comes in from the Indian Ocean forming rain clouds over the highlands of eastern South Africa and the landlocked country of Lesotho. This means that Lesotho and eastern parts of South Africa receive a lot more rain than western parts of South Africa (see Figure 11). Parts of Lesotho receive 1,200 mm of rain a year (similar to mid Wales). This is good for Lesotho because it can sell its excess water to South Africa where the population is higher but rainfall is lower. Water is transferred from reservoirs in Lesotho, via pipelines and then the River Vaal into Johannesburg in Guateng.

Key
- Neighbouring countries

Mean annual rainfall (mm)
- 0–334
- 335–668
- 669–1,000
- 1,001–1,337
- 1,338–2,340

The most densely populated part of South Africa. Total annual rainfall here is similar to Birmingham. However, Birmingham gets its water from mid Wales, where rainfall is roughly twice as much.

Rainfall is a little less than in London, but much more seasonal.

Annual rainfall here is less than half that received in the Cambridge region which is the driest part of England.

▲ **Figure 11** Average annual rainfall in South Africa.

	Jan	Feb	Mar	Apr	May	Jun	Jul	Aug	Sep	Oct	Nov	Dec	Total
Western Cape	8	4	11	24	40	41	47	45	24	12	12	10	278
Gauteng	125	90	91	54	13	9	4	6	27	72	117	105	713

▲ **Figure 12** Rainfall (mm) for selected regions of South Africa.

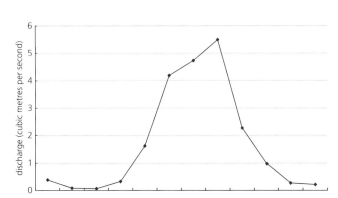

▲ **Figure 13** Hydrograph for the River Dorling, Western Cape Province, South Africa. The catchment area of the River Dorling before this station is 6,900 km².

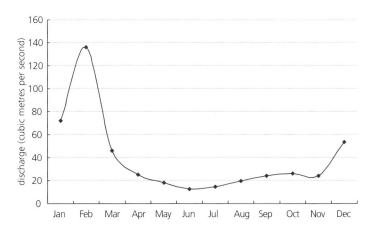

▲ **Figure 14** Hydrograph for the River Vaal, Gauteng Province, South Africa. The catchment area of the River Vaal before this station is 38,560 km².

▲ **Figure 15** Relief rainfall patterns in South Africa and Lesotho.

Activities

1 Use Figure 11 to describe the distribution of rainfall in South Africa.
2 Explain why Lesotho is able to sell water to South Africa and why South Africa wants to buy it.
3 a) Use Figure 12 to draw a pair of rainfall graphs.
   b) Compare your rainfall graphs with Figures 13 and 14.
   c) At which times of year do these two regions face possible water shortages?
4 Use Figure 15 to explain why Lesotho has so much more rainfall than Free State in South Africa. Describe what is happening at each point (1–6) on the diagram.

Investigating a major water-transfer scheme

The Lesotho Highlands Water Project (LHWP) is an example of a large-scale water-transfer scheme. Dams collect water in the mountainous areas of Lesotho to supply water to areas of water deficit in the neighbouring country of South Africa. It is the largest water-transfer scheme in Africa, diverting 40 per cent of the water in the Senqu river basin in Lesotho to the Vaal river system in the Orange Free State of South Africa via 200 km of tunnel systems. The River Vaal then carries the water into Gauteng Province.

The first phase of the project, started in 1984, is complete. Two dams, the Katse and the Mohale, have been built. The LHWP transfers 24.6 m³ of water per second to South Africa. A second phase of construction has just begun with the building of the Polihali Dam. This development will deliver an extra 45.5 m³ per second of water to South Africa. The new dam will also generate 1,000 MW of electricity for Lesotho. Phase two will cost $1 billion and be completed by 2020. There are plans for two more dams to be built in later phases of the LHWP.

Key

⌐→ Pipe transferring water into the River Vaal catchment

▬ Land over 3,000m   ▬ Land over 2,000m

▶ **Figure 16** A map of the Lesotho Highlands Water Project water management and transfer scheme.

Year	Urban areas			Rural areas		
	Improved supplies			Improved supplies		
	Piped in home (%)	Other improved (%)	Unimproved (%)	Piped in home (%)	Other improved (%)	Unimproved (%)
1990	85.9	12.2	1.9	24.0	42.3	33.7
2000	87.5	11.0	1.5	27.9	42.7	29.4
2010	90.3	8.9	0.8	34.5	43.3	22.2
2015	91.7	7.9	0.4	37.7	43.7	18.6

▲ **Figure 17** Improved and unimproved water supplies in urban and rural areas of South Africa.

Year	Urban areas			Rural areas		
	Improved supplies			Improved supplies		
	Piped in home (%)	Other improved (%)	Unimproved (%)	Piped in home (%)	Other improved (%)	Unimproved (%)
1990	26.3	66.3	7.4	2.3	72.6	25.1
2000	39.4	53.7	6.8	2.9	72.6	24.5
2010	61.3	32.8	5.9	3.9	72.5	23.5
2015	70.0	24.5	5.4	4.3	72.6	23.0

▲ **Figure 18** Improved and unimproved water supplies in urban and rural areas of Lesotho.

What are the advantages and disadvantages of the LHWP?

Lesotho is one of the world's poorest countries. It has few natural resources so selling water to South Africa provides 75 per cent of Lesotho's income. However, many people in Lesotho do not have access to improved water sources. A new dam, the Metlong Dam is being constructed to supply lowland areas of Lesotho with water. The project is costing US$31.80 million – money that Lesotho has borrowed and will have to pay back. The dam is finished and the pipes and tunnels to transfer the water should be completed by 2020. Until then, many people in rural areas of Lesotho will spend many hours fetching and carrying water.

▼ **Figure 19** Impacts of the LHWP.

Roads have been constructed in the highlands to gain access to the dam sites.	Phase two dams will generate 1,000 megawatts of electricity for Lesotho.
Farmland is flooded to create the reservoirs. About 20,000 people were displaced when the Katse Dam was built.	Phase one created around 20,000 jobs. Many workers moved to shanty towns on the construction sites. Alcoholism and HIV/AIDs became significant problems in the shanty towns.
Compensation is paid to families who lose land during construction of the dams. Many families have complained that the compensation is too little and too late.	

▲ **Figure 20** A family in Lesotho collecting water.

Activities

1 Summarise the aims of the Lesotho Highlands Water Project.
2 Use the text on these pages to complete a copy of the following table. You should find more to write in some boxes than in others.

Country	Short-term advantages (+) and disadvantages (–) of LHWP	Long-term advantages (+) and disadvantages (–) of LHWP
Lesotho	+	+
	–	–
South Africa	+	+
	–	–

3 Summarise what each of the following groups of people might think about the LHWP:
   a) a farmer in the Lesotho Highlands
   b) a government minister in Lesotho
   c) residents in Johannesburg, South Africa.

Enquiry

How much progress have Lesotho and South Africa made in providing improved water supplies?

Use the evidence in Figures 17 and 18 to:

a) Compare progress in urban and rural areas.
b) Compare progress in South Africa and Lesotho.
c) What conclusions can you draw about the benefits of the LHWP?

Are there alternative ways to manage South Africa's water?

South Africa has 539 large dams, which is almost half of all the dams in Africa. But despite this, there are still a large number of South Africans without access to clean drinking water. Many of these people live in rural, remote parts of South Africa; they are too isolated to become part of the big projects such as the LHWP and they are too poor to drill boreholes to tap into groundwater supplies. Instead they have to rely on cheap, small-scale methods of **rainwater harvesting**.

Sustainable water management on a small farm

Ma Tshepo Khumbane is a South African farmer who teaches rainwater harvesting techniques. Her management strategies (shown in Figure 21) are affordable and practical for families, no matter how small the farm is or how little money they have. They use ways that are cheap, practical and easy to maintain using appropriate technology. They are commonly used in rural areas of Limpopo that do not have piped water. They are designed to:

- collect and use rainwater, for example, by collecting water from the roof of the farm
- maintain soil moisture by encouraging as much infiltration as possible. In this way groundwater stores are recharged.

Rainwater harvesting techniques and soil moisture conservation are examples of sustainable water development. They benefit people now without doing any lasting damage to the environment or using up valuable resources. These methods of water management are not usually big enough to have negative impacts on the surrounding drainage basin – unlike the big dam building schemes used by governments.

▲ **Figure 21** Rainwater harvesting techniques used by Ma Tshepo Khumbane.

Activities

1 Choose five techniques shown in Figure 21. For each technique explain how it either collects rainwater or recharges groundwater.
2 Explain why the type of management shown in Figure 21 is sustainable.

Enquiry ?

Should South Africa invest in big schemes like LHWP or small-scale sustainable water management schemes?

- Contrast the impacts of this type of water management with the building of large dam and water-transfer schemes like the LHWP.
- Which would you prioritise? Explain your answer.

Could South Africa harvest water from fog?

Fog has been 'harvested' to provide clean drinking water to isolated rural communities since 1987 when a scheme was set up in Chungungo, Chile. Since then, similar systems have been used successfully in Peru, Ecuador, Tenerife, Ethiopia and South Africa. It is another form of appropriate technology because it is relatively cheap to install and maintain. To collect water from fog, a simple system of fine-mesh nylon nets are suspended vertically between tall poles. The fog condenses on the net and drips into a gutter below. It then passes through sand before being piped to where it is needed.

Fog harvesting works best in upland regions (at least 400 m above sea level) that experience moist air being blown from the coast. As the air rises it condenses to form fog. So would fog harvesting work in Limpopo in South Africa? Most of Limpopo is over 1,000 m above sea level. Moist air from the Indian Ocean is blown inland by prevailing easterly winds. The first fog harvesting scheme was built at Tshanowa Primary School in Limpopo. All 130 school children used to bring bottled water to school every day. Now they drink pure water collected from fog.

It is not foggy every day.
The nets and poles are relatively cheap to buy.
Repairs are essential. Nets are easily torn in the wind.
Repairs are easy to make and require little training.
Ground water is contaminated.
Fog harvesting technology does not need any electrical energy.
Many rural areas do not have a piped supply from a reservoir.
Some of the foggiest sites are some distance from rural communities.

▲ **Figure 23** Advantages and disadvantages of fog harvesting in Limpopo.

▲ **Figure 22** Fog collectors in Tenerife. The nets, which look like giant volley ball nets, trap moisture as it condenses from the air.

Activity

3 a) Use Figure 23 to sort the advantages and disadvantages of fog harvesting.
   b) Based on the evidence in Figure 23, explain why fog harvesting may be considered to be an appropriate technology for a poor rural community.

Enquiry

Research the fog harvesting systems in Chungungo and Tshanowa by typing the names into an internet search engine. To what extent has each scheme been a success?

http://www.weathersa.co.za
This is the website of the South African weather service. Click on the Limpopo link to find out how foggy it will be in the next five days. Or, scroll to the bottom of the home page to find recent rainfall maps.

Over-abstraction of groundwater

Some layers of porous rock, known as **aquifers**, store huge quantities of water under the ground. Water from rain and melting snow percolates down into the ground where it is stored in these aquifers – this process is known as **recharge**. To use this water, all we have to do is dig or drill into the ground and the water can be abstracted. The abstraction of water from the ground is a major source of water supply in India. In fact, groundwater provides 65 per cent of all water used in agriculture and 85 per cent of the domestic supply. But in some areas, **over-abstraction** is taking place. This is when water is taken from the ground faster than it can be recharged by natural processes. In many places the water table is 4 m lower than it was in 2002. There are concerns that, as demand for water in India continues to increase, water shortages will become more common.

	Jan	Feb	Mar	Apr	May	Jun	Jul	Aug	Sep	Oct	Nov	Dec
Temperature (°C)	19	20	24	27.5	30	31	30	29.5	28	27.5	24	20
Rainfall (mm)	13	10	7	3	3	18	81	40	13	3	3	7

▲ **Figure 24** Climate data for West Gujarat.

Groundwater Level
(meters below ground level)

- High (<1.5)
- Medium to High (1.5–5.9)
- Medium (5.9–10.3)
- Low to Medium (10.3–14.6)
- Low (>14.6)
- No Data

▲ **Figure 25** Groundwater level, India.

I own three and a half hectares of farmland and two hectares have been submerged. The compensation given to us is not enough. Unless they visit this place, and listen to our complaint, how can government officials understand our plight? We depend on our land for our livelihood and we will die with our land!

Local farmer

The farmers have received compensation. The water will not enter their homes – just flood a few fields. The extra water in the Omkareshwar Dam is needed by other farmers. It will provide water for 60,000 hectares of farmland.

Government official

▲ **Figure 26** Points of view on the raising of the Omkareshwar Dam.

Activities

1 a) Use Figure 24 to draw a climate graph for West Gujarat.
   b) Describe the annual rainfall pattern.
   c) Explain why farmers in West Gujarat need to abstract groundwater.
2 In which parts of India is the level of groundwater lowest? Use Figure 25 to help your answer.

www.indiawatertool.in – an interactive map that allows you to investigate India's water issues.

Why is so much water abstracted?

There are a number of reasons for India's reliance on groundwater. There are physical and human factors:

1 India has a seasonal rainfall pattern. States in the northwest, such as Gujarat, have a long dry season. Surface stores such as lakes and rivers can be dry for long periods of time.

2 Surface stores are often polluted by human waste. Groundwater is considered to be cleaner – although groundwater can be also be polluted, especially by pesticides used on farms and shrimp farms.

3 Urban water supplies are poor. Many people buy water from water vendors at very high prices. Drilling a well is seen by many as a cheaper source in the long term.

4 The Indian government has encouraged farmers to grow more food to feed the growing population. This 'green revolution' has used crops that tend to need more water than traditional crops.

5 Cheap electricity has encouraged farmers to drill very deep wells and install pumps to extract water. The water table falls and the wells of neighbouring farms dry out, so they too have to drill deeper.

6 India's monsoon rainfall (see pages 162–3) is unpredictable. In seasons with lower than average rainfall (like 2012) the aquifers are not fully recharged.

Who should solve this problem?

India has over 3,200 major and medium-sized dams, which provide water for farms and industry. The Indian government could borrow money to build even more dams as the demand for clean water increases. This type of project is known as **top-down development** – where big decisions are made by public officials and business leaders. However, dam construction has sometimes been very unpopular in India. Farmers often complain that they are not offered enough compensation for their land when it is flooded. Figure 27 shows farmers protesting about the Omkareshwar Dam. This height of this dam was increased by 91 m, flooding an extra 1,100 hectares of farmland.

An alternative approach would be for farmers to work together on water conservation techniques – like those in South Africa shown on page 250. One successful approach is for groups of farmers to build low stone and earth check dams. These create small pools of water for a few months after the rainy season. The water soaks into the ground and naturally recharges the aquifers. This type of **self-help** scheme doesn't need powerful decision makers or lots of money like a top-down development project. It comes from grassroots level – sometimes called a bottom-up approach to development.

◄ **Figure 27** Farmers stand in waist-height water to protest about the raising of the Omkareshwar Dam in 2015.

Enquiry ❓

Who should solve India's water shortage?

Should India use top-down development solutions or self-help schemes to solve the over-abstraction problem? Justify your decision.

Activities

3 Why is so much groundwater abstracted in India? Give two physical and three economic reasons.

4 Explain why the Indian Government will find it difficult to solve the problem of over abstraction.

THEME
6

Development and resource issues
Chapter 3
Regional economic development

Inequality in India

India is a newly industrialised country (NIC). Public investment in education, followed by investment in manufacturing and service industries have created well-paid jobs and personal wealth for many. The economy has grown and India is beginning to close the development gap (see pages 212–3). However, India still has millions of low-paid workers. It is estimated that 51 per cent of India's workforce is self-employed.

Many of these are farm labourers who are unemployed for long periods of the farming year. Many others work irregular hours and earn very low incomes in the **informal sector** of the economy. These jobs include selling food on street markets or collecting and recycling rubbish (see page 95). Consequently, there is huge inequality between the richest and poorest members of Indian society.

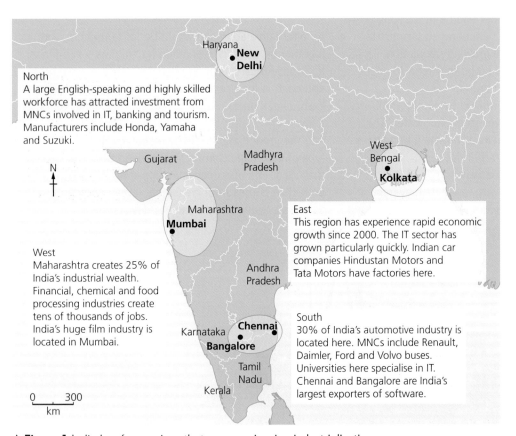

Haryana
New Delhi

North
A large English-speaking and highly skilled workforce has attracted investment from MNCs involved in IT, banking and tourism. Manufacturers include Honda, Yamaha and Suzuki.

N

Gujarat

Madhyra Pradesh

West Bengal
Kolkata

Maharashtra
Mumbai

East
This region has experience rapid economic growth since 2000. The IT sector has grown particularly quickly. Indian car companies Hindustan Motors and Tata Motors have factories here.

West
Maharashtra creates 25% of India's industrial wealth. Financial, chemical and food processing industries create tens of thousands of jobs. India's huge film industry is located in Mumbai.

Andhra Pradesh

Karnataka **Chennai**
Bangalore

South
30% of India's automotive industry is located here. MNCs include Renault, Daimler, Ford and Volvo buses. Universities here specialise in IT. Chennai and Bangalore are India's largest exporters of software.

Tamil Nadu

Kerala

0   300
     km

▲ **Figure 1** India has four regions that are experiencing industrialisation.

Regional patterns of inequality

Each state in India is responsible for providing health and education services. This helps to explain some of the differences in inequality between India's states. In Kerala, for example, the state government has always been generous in funding public education and health care. Life expectancy is high and the birth rate is low. Almost 92 per cent of the population can read and write. By comparison, Bihar's state government has only recently begun to invest effectively in public health

and education services. It is India's poorest state – average incomes are four times lower than in Kerala or Maharashtra. Almost 58 per cent of the population are below the age of 25 and only 47 per cent can read and write. It is also extremely rural, with 85 per cent of the population living in rural areas with few opportunities for better-paid work in manufacturing or service industries.

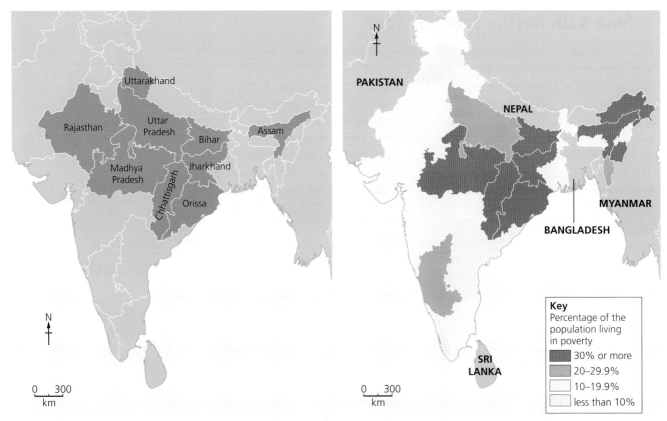

▲ **Figure 2** These nine states have 50 per cent of India's population but 71 per cent of infant deaths (before the age of one), 72 per cent of child deaths (before the age of five) and 62 per cent of maternal deaths.

▲ **Figure 3** Percentage of the population of India living in poverty, 2013.

	1974	1984	1994	2004	2013
Bihar	62	62	55	41	34
Kerala	60	40	25	15	7
Maharashtra	53	43	37	31	17

▲ **Figure 4** Percentage of the population living in poverty in three selected states.

Activities

1 Draw a labelled sketch to show the location of the four main economic growth areas in India.
2 Compare Figure 1 with Figure 2. What conclusion can you reach?
3 Suggest how each of the following may be a cause of poverty in India:
   a) Reliance on farming jobs in rural areas like Bihar
   b) Lack of formal jobs in cities like Mumbai
4 Study Figure 3.
   a) Describe the distribution of states that have the lowest levels of poverty.
   b) How well does this pattern match Figure 1? Are there any differences? If so, how can they be explained?
5 a) Choose a suitable technique to represent the data in Figure 4.
   b) Compare the trends shown in each state.
   c) Suggest why Maharashtra still has higher levels of poverty than Kerala, despite having more industrial development.

Is there a UK North–South divide?

In the UK the term 'North–South divide' refers to the perceived economic and social differences between southern England and the rest of the UK. The divide is usually shown as a diagonal line across England from the Severn Estuary to the Humber Estuary. In general, a higher standard of living is enjoyed by people who live in London and southern England compared to those in the rest of the UK. People here can expect to have higher average incomes, slightly longer life expectancy, and fewer long-term health problems. For example, of the ten local authorities where male life expectancy is below 75 years, seven are in Scotland and the remaining three are in the North West region of England. Almost every local authority where male life expectancy is over 81 years is in the south of England.

▲ **Figure 6** The UK's North South divide.

Key

Earnings per week (£s)

390 469 522 588   694   921

| Local authority | Earnings per week (£) | |
	Men	Women
Aberdeen	657	411
South Tyneside	480	324
Hull	470	299
Liverpool	478	369
Solihull	575	328
Gwynedd	367	300
Powys	426	296
Cardiff	479	344
Cornwall	402	266
Bristol	533	370
Mid Devon	468	254
North Norfolk	436	221
Winchester	575	363
Thanet	404	273
Hounslow	681	464
Westminster	706	565
City of London	1,045	780
North		
South		

▲ **Figure 7** Average weekly earnings, 2015.

▲ **Figure 5** Average earnings per week in England, Wales and Scotland, 2015; the map is distorted to show the number of jobs available in each area.

 www.neighbourhood.statistics.gov.uk/ HTMLDocs/dvc126/ – Figure 5 is a screenshot taken from this interactive map; the data in Figure 7 was extracted from the map.

Enquiry ?

To what extent does the evidence in Figure 7 reveal a gap in earnings between the north and south of the UK?

You might want to consider whether the pay gap between men and women or between urban and rural areas is greater than the North–South divide.

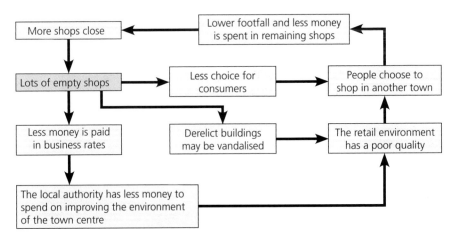

▲ **Figure 8** The impact of empty shops on the high street.

Activities

1 a) Use Figure 5 to describe the average wage and the relative number of jobs in:
      i)   London
      ii) Birmingham
      iii) the North East region.
   b) To what extent does this map confirm that there is a north–south divide?

2 a) Put the earnings of men in Figure 7 in rank order.
   b) What is the median wage?
   c) How many of the local authorities that have higher than median wages are in the south?

3 Using Figure 9, describe the distribution of towns that have:
   a) high vacancy rates
   b) low vacancy rates.
   To what extent is it true that there is a North–South divide in the high street?

4 What are the impacts of high vacancy rates on our town centres? Study Figure 8 and divide the impacts into the following categories:
   a) social
   b) economic
   c) environmental.

5 a) Explain why a few empty shops can lead to other shops closing.
   b) Suggest three ways that local authorities might try to solve the problem of shop vacancies.

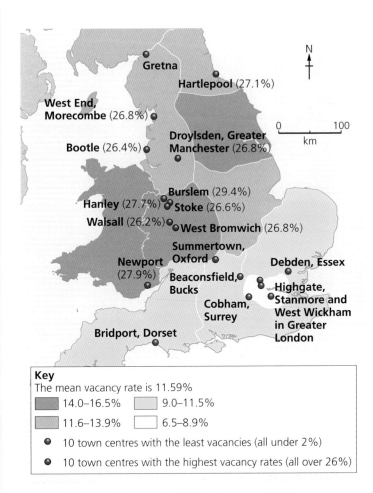

▲ **Figure 9** Empty shops in the UK's high streets, 2015; vacancy rates with the highest and lowest percentages of empty shops.

Factors that influence economic growth and decline

The UK's northern cities were the traditional centres of UK manufacturing industry. But, as it became cheaper to import electrical goods, textiles and steel from abroad, these industries declined. Highly skilled and relatively well-paid jobs have been lost. Unemployment is still a problem in some of these regions of the UK. Where jobs have been created, in retailing for example, the jobs are less highly skilled and less well paid.

In contrast, the zone stretching along the M4/M11 corridor between Bristol, London and Cambridge, has attracted modern high-tech manufacturing industries and jobs in service industries such as finance. These businesses are located close to a skilled workforce and with great transport links to their market.

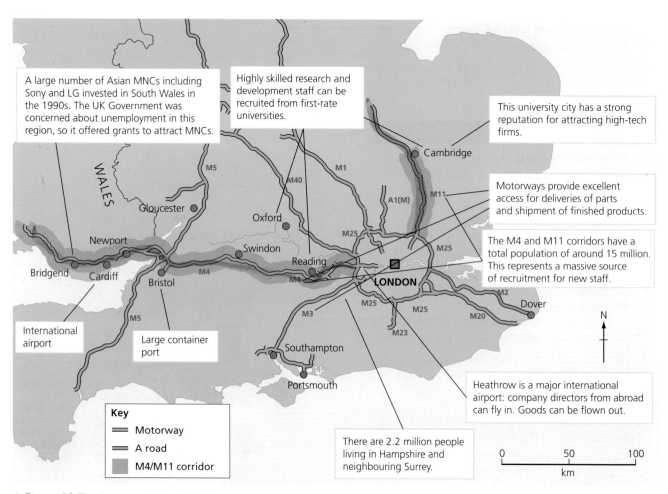

A large number of Asian MNCs including Sony and LG invested in South Wales in the 1990s. The UK Government was concerned about unemployment in this region, so it offered grants to attract MNCs.

Highly skilled research and development staff can be recruited from first-rate universities.

This university city has a strong reputation for attracting high-tech firms.

Motorways provide excellent access for deliveries of parts and shipment of finished products.

The M4 and M11 corridors have a total population of around 15 million. This represents a massive source of recruitment for new staff.

International airport

Large container port

Heathrow is a major international airport: company directors from abroad can fly in. Goods can be flown out.

There are 2.2 million people living in Hampshire and neighbouring Surrey.

Key
— Motorway
— A road
▮ M4/M11 corridor

▲ **Figure 10** The location of the M4/M11 corridor, shown in lilac.

Activities

1 Study Figure 10.
   a) Identify five specific reasons why MNCs might wish to locate in the M4/M11 corridor.
   b) Describe the location of Newport.
   c) Suggest why businesses might be more attracted to locations to the east of the M4/M11 corridor rather than the west.
2 Give two reasons why Chinese steel is cheaper than UK steel.

3 Study Figure 11.
   a) Give four-figure grid references for the two grid squares that contain the steel works.
   b) Compare the relief of the area to the south and north of the railway line.
   c) Use map evidence to suggest three reasons why the steel works were located here.

When regions decline

In the winter of 2015-16 steel manufacturers reached a crisis point. Tata, the Indian owned multinational company (MNC), announced that it would have to lay off workers. 900 jobs were lost at Scunthorpe in North East England, 750 at Port Talbot and another 250 at Llanwern, both in South Wales. SSI, a Korean MNC was also forced to close its steel plant at Redcar, in Teesside, with the loss of 2,200 jobs. All of these job losses were in regions already affected by low pay and higher than average levels of unemployment. The job losses were blamed on cheap steel, imported from China, which was being sold in Europe for less money than it cost to make it in the UK. China is able to make steel more cheaply than in Europe. China has lower labour costs and the Chinese government keeps the cost of energy low.

GEOGRAPHICAL SKILLS

Locating places on an OS map

The vertical lines on an OS map are eastings. The horizontal ones are northings. Each grid square is known by the intersection in its lower left corner. When you locate a place on an OS map you must give the easting first, then the northing.

▲ **Figure 11** The location of the Llanwern Steelworks, owned by Tata, near Newport; scale 1 : 50,000.

How can regional inequalities in the UK be reduced?

One way to tackle the lack of jobs in the UK's regions is through investment in major infrastructure projects, such as road and rail schemes. Better transport links should attract new investment from business and create economic multiplier effects in the region (see pages 218–9).

The main transport route that runs through southeast Wales is the M4 motorway, which connects this region to London. However, between Newport and Cardiff the motorway narrows to two lanes as it crosses the River Usk and through the Brynglas Tunnels. This causes congestion and traffic hold ups, especially at peak times. In 2014 the Welsh government confirmed its intention to build a £1 billion relief road: a 23 km, three-lane motorway will be built around Newport to bypass the congested section of the M4.

This is the largest capital investment programme ever announced by the Welsh government. Construction could start in early 2018 with the motorway being opened to the public in the autumn of 2021. Figure 12 shows the proposed route.

Key

—— Black Route (the proposed route of the new road)

▨ Land identified by Newport council for the creation of new employment

▨ Urban area of Newport

—— Newport southern distributor road

—— Steelworks access road

-•- Existing railway

▢ Sites of special scientific interest (SSSI)

▨ River Usk SAC and SSSI

▲ **Figure 12** The proposed M4 relief road.

Activities

1 Describe the route of the proposed M4 relief road.
2 Use evidence from Figure 12 to suggest:
   a) one major cost of taking this route
   b) one environmental disadvantage of this route.

3 Use evidence from Figure 11 on page 259 and Figure 13 to suggest why this route is better than one to the north of the railway line.
4 Create a flow diagram to suggest the likely positive multiplier effects for southeast Wales if this road is built.

▲ **Figure 13** Llanwern Steelworks: the camera is pointing east; the new road will be built to the south of the steelworks.

Spokesperson for British Associated Ports

These plans will jeopardise future investment in Newport. I don't think it is a good idea to put the route through the centre of Wales' most important general cargo port.

Director, Friends of the Earth Cymru

The decision will see the motorway plough through a part of one of Wales' most protected and environmentally sensitive landscapes – the Caldicot and Wentloog Levels. This hugely expensive transport route is the worst possible choice.

Spokesperson for Confederation of British Industry (CBI) Wales

The M4 around Newport is simply not fit for the twenty-first century. It is already congested and predicted to get worse. We need a transport system that will ease congestion and improve our economic competitiveness as well as providing jobs and growth.

Spokesperson for Sustrans Cymru

We should be investing in clean forms of public transport – like the electrification of the main railway line between London and Swansea. Electric trains are cheaper to operate than diesels. They require less maintenance and have lower energy costs. They are also lighter and do less damage to the tracks.

Spokesperson for Newport Council

Newport needs investment and jobs. The town is the third most deprived place in the whole of Wales. The construction of the relief road would create better access to land to the southwest and east of the steelworks – land that we have set aside for future development for industrial estates.

Enquiry ❓

Should the Newport Relief Road be built?

Imagine that you live in this part of Wales. Write a letter to the Welsh Government expressing your views on this matter. Weigh up the pros and cons before making your final decision.

▲ **Figure 14** Conflicting opinions about the M4 relief road.

What is meant by social development?

Development means 'change'. Wealth is one way to measure development, and we examined this in Theme 6 Chapter 1. However, measuring the state of the economy is not the only way to find out whether society is changing for the better. Figure 1 lists a range of ways in which development could be defined.

Development is ...

- reducing levels of poverty
- increasing levels of wealth
- bringing benefits to all, not just to the wealthiest in a society
- reducing the gap between richest and poorest
- creating equal status and rights for men and women
- creating justice, freedom of speech and the right to vote (democracy) for everyone
- making everyone safe from conflict or terrorism
- making sure that everyone has their basic needs of food, water and shelter
- making sure every child has the right to a good standard of education and actually gets it.

▲ **Figure 1** Different ways of seeing development.

▲ **Figure 2** Development is …

▲ **Figure 3** Development is …

Activities

1 Work in pairs to discuss Figure 1.
   a) What are the advantages and disadvantages of each of these statements?
   b) Choose the five statements that you think are the best definitions of development. Join with another pair and justify your choice.
2 Working on your own, explain which aspects of human development are illustrated by Figures 2 and 3. Complete the caption for each figure.
3 Describe the pattern shown on:
   a) Figure 4
   b) Figure 5.
4 Which of these two maps is more useful to a geographer who is studying patterns of education across South Africa? Explain your answer.

Enquiry ?

How much regional inequality is there in South Africa?

Use the weblink to investigate access to clean water supply across South Africa. Remember that water is needed for good health. How similar or different are Figures 4 and 5 to the maps for water? What conclusions can you reach about regional inequality?

How do we measure social development?

There are many ways to measure social development. Many measures relate to health and education, and most can be easily quantified. This is useful because numbers allow us to identify the size of the social development gap. For example, one simple measure is the percentage of adults who had no formal education as a child. In an HIC like the UK this number will be close to zero. But in South Africa, an NIC, this figure was 8.7 per cent at the last census (2011).

We can also use numbers to measure progress. In South Africa, progress in education is good: the percentage of the population aged twenty years and older who had no schooling decreased from 19.1 per cent in 1996 to 8.7 per cent in 2011. However, figures like this can be misleading. There are wide variations in education across South Africa, as shown in Figures 4 and 5.

GEOGRAPHICAL SKILLS

Using choropleth maps

A **choropleth** is a coloured or shaded map. Darker colours or darker shading represent higher values on the map. Choropleth maps are useful for showing patterns. You don't need to know pin-point locations for your data. A choropleth may be drawn when you have data for each area or district on a map. There are two factors to consider when you draw a choropleth:

1 How many colours or shades should you use? Too many colours and patterns will be difficult to see. However, if you have too few then any small differences between areas will be lost.
2 If the data is available for different-sized areas, which data set should you choose? This issue is illustrated by Figures 4 and 5.

Key

No schooling, age 20+ (percentage)

20 or higher	5–10
15–20	5 or less
10–15	

▲ **Figure 4** Percentage of adults who had no schooling using data from each state of South Africa.

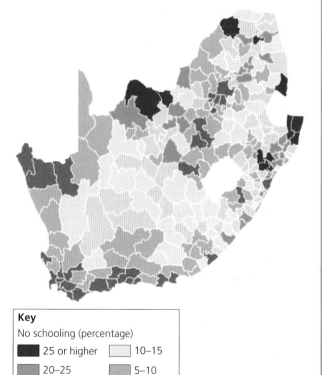

Key

No schooling (percentage)

25 or higher	10–15
20–25	5–10
15–20	5 or less

▲ **Figure 5** Percentage of adults who had no schooling using data from each municipality of South Africa.

  http://tellmaps.com/mapsalive – this website uses a geographical information system (GIS) to display an online atlas of South Africa.

Using health data as a measure of development

Health data is often used to describe a country's level of development. Two commonly used measures are:

- **Infant mortality rate (IMR)** – the number of children who die before the age of one for every thousand that are born.
- **Average life expectancy** – the average age to which people can expect to live.

A number of factors contribute to improved life expectancy and lower IMR. Increased government spending on health care, better access to clean water and improved sanitation (sewage disposal) will all have a beneficial impact on health data. That's why this data is a useful indication of development.

Just as it would be simplistic to assume that there is a gap between rich and poor countries (pages 210–13), so it would be too simple to divide the world into healthy and unhealthy countries. There is, in fact, a continuum of social development from countries like Sierra Leone (which has an IMR of 87) to Sweden (which has an IMR of 2). Furthermore, Figures 6 and 7 indicate that there has been much progress, since the Brandt Report in 1980, to close the development gap.

	1985	1990	1995	2000	2005	2010	2015
Gambia	91	80	71	63	57	52	48
Kenya	63	66	72	67	54	42	36
Mali	144	131	125	116	97	83	75
Malawi	147	143	122	104	71	58	43

▲ **Figure 6** Infant mortality rate (IMR) for selected sub-Saharan African countries.

	1985	1990	1995	2000	2005	2010	2015
Bangladesh	118	100	81	64	51	39	31
India	101	88	78	66	56	46	38
Pakistan	115	106	97	88	80	74	66
Sri Lanka	25	18	17	14	12	9	8

▲ **Figure 7** Infant mortality rate (IMR) for selected countries in South Asia.

	High life expectancy and low IMR might indicate that …	Low life expectancy and high IMR might indicate that …
Government spending on hospitals and clinic	A wealthy government has prioritised health spending so …	
Diet		
Access to safe drinking water		
State of sanitation	Most people have clean water piped to their homes so …	Many people live in shanty housing or rural homes that have no sewerage system so …
Standards of personal and social education		

▲ **Figure 8** What health data may be telling us about a country's development.

Activities

1 Study Figures 6 and 7.
   a) Classify each country by its World Bank category (see pages 210–13).
   b) Choose a suitable technique to represent the data.
   c) What conclusion can you make about the progress of these two groups of countries in closing the development gap?

2 Make a copy of Figure 8.
   a) Complete the three statements by adding elaboration at the end of the sentence.
   b) Complete the blank spaces in the table.

Changes to average life expectancy

Since 1980, life expectancy has increased in almost every country of the world, as shown in Figure 9. The map represents countries according to what has happened to their life expectancy since 1980. The greater the increase in life expectancy, the bigger the country appears:

- Countries with large populations and the biggest improvements to life expectancy are the largest on this map.
- Countries with an already large life expectancy appear smaller, because they have less room for improvement.

Some of the biggest improvements have been in poorer countries. For example, in Cambodia, average life expectancy has increased from 54 years (in 1980) to 68 (in 2015).

Population and health

In most wealthy countries primary health care is generally very good and people have long life expectancy. However, as a country's population ages, the causes of death also change:

- Deaths in countries with low life expectancy tend to be caused by infectious disease (e.g. HIV/AIDS, malaria), and conditions caused by dirty water (e.g. diarrhoea, which particularly affects children). These deaths are reducing quickly, as global organisations such as UNICEF vaccinate against infectious disease, and as campaigns to get rid of malaria have some success.

- Deaths in wealthier countries with the longest life expectancy are most commonly caused by diet and lifestyle. The main causes of death are heart disease (deaths from which could be reduced by improved diet and exercise), cancer (caused by smoking and poor diet) which together account for over 80 per cent of deaths.

▲ **Figure 9** Increase in global life expectancy, 1980–2013.

Activities

3 Study Figure 9. Describe the distribution of countries which have most improved life expectancy.

4 Suggest reasons why life expectancy has increased in some countries more than others.

5 a) Explain why not all people in wealthy countries have healthy diets.

b) Explain what effect these diets might have on health data.

Enquiry

How and why does health vary across the globe?
- Research the phrase 'main causes of death in the world's poorest and wealthiest countries'.
- Choose one major cause of death that is preventable and explain how the number of deaths could be reduced.

Human Development Index

Economic development usually brings social change. So, as GNI per capita increases, a number of social indicators tend to change as well.

- There is more money to spend on health, for example, fighting disease or spending on doctors and hospitals. As health improves, so death rates fall, as do infant and maternal mortality rates. Overall, life expectancy increases.
- As more money is spent on education, more children spend longer in school and so literacy rates increase.

The UN uses the **Human Development Index (HDI)** as a way of showing a country's level of development. HDI is calculated using an average of four development indicators:

- education – average length of schooling in years
- education – literacy (as a percentage of the adult population)
- GNI per capita (PPP) in US$
- life expectancy in years.

The HDI gives a single figure per country, between 0 and 1. The closer the figure is to 1, the better.

The advantage of using HDI rather than just GNI is that it identifies those countries which have not used their wealth to benefit people's health or education. For example, in Figure 10, Nigeria has a relatively high GNI but a low HDI. Nigeria is an oil-rich country but most of its wealth goes to a few wealthy families and multinational companies. In the case of Nigeria, increased wealth seems to make little difference to the majority of the people.

Country	GNI in US$ (PPP)	Life expectancy	Infant mortality rate	Maternal mortality rate	HDI
Bangladesh	3,340	71	33	170	0.558
India	5,760	66	41	190	0.586
Nepal	2,420	68	32	190	0.540
Pakistan	5,100	67	69	170	0.537
Sri Lanka	10,270	46	8	29	0.750
Ghana	3,960	61	52	380	0.573
Malawi	780	55	44	510	0.414
Mozambique	1,170	50	62	480	0.393
Nigeria	5,680	52	74	560	0.504
Sierra Leone	1,830	74	107	1,100	0.374
Tanzania	2,530	60	36	410	0.488
Uganda	1,690	59	44	360	0.484
Zambia	3,860	58	56	280	0.561

Selected South Asian countries

Selected sub-Saharan African countries

▲ **Figure 10** Table of GNI and social development indicators for selected countries in South Asia and sub-Saharan Africa.

Life expectancy: the average number of years a person can expect to live when they are born.

Infant mortality rate: the number of children per thousand live births who die before their first birthday.

Maternal mortality rate: the number of mothers per 100,000 who die in childbirth.

Activities

1 Explain why geographers shouldn't rely only on HDI when investigating patterns of development.
2 Using data from Figure 10, draw a scattergraph to investigate the relationship between GNI and life expectancy. Add a line of best fit and describe what your graph is telling you.

GEOGRAPHICAL SKILLS

Testing relationships between sets of data

Is economic development related to improved health care and education? It is possible to answer this question by analysing data, using graphs. Before starting, it helps to make a prediction, or hypothesis, for example 'countries with lowest GNI have low HDI indicators'. Testing this hypothesis needs two sets of data that are related – known as bivariate data. In this case, the data are GNI per capita (PPP) and HDI. Find these columns of data in Figure 10. These data are known as variables. To test their relationship, you should draw a scattergraph. Follow these steps:

1 Draw the graph axis. The scale on the vertical axis should be for the data that you are trying to find out about – in this case, HDI. We want to know whether HDI is affected by GNI. HDI is what we call the dependent variable.

2 The independent variable is GNI – we want to test to see whether it affects HDI. This goes along the horizontal axis.

3 Label the axes 'HDI' (vertical) and 'GNI' (horizontal).

4 Plot the points for each country. These are called 'scatter points', and the graph is therefore called a scattergraph.

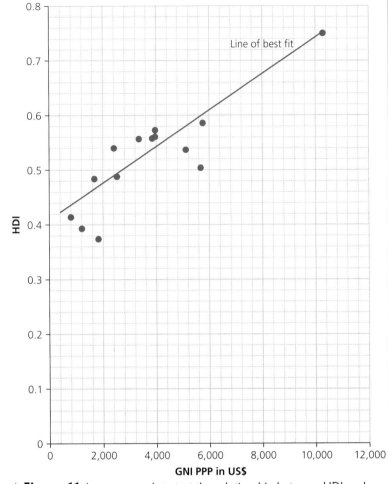

▲ **Figure 11** A scattergraph to test the relationship between HDI and GNI using data from Figure 10.

5 Your points should look like the one in Figure 11. There is a pattern to the plotted data – a line has been plotted to help you to identify this. This is known as a line of best fit. It does not join up points, but simply follows their general trend. There should be the same number of points on each side of the line of best fit.

6 In this case, the best fit line shows that as one indicator increases – (GNI) so does the other (HDI). The hypothesis has been proved correct!

Enquiry

What should Nigeria do to reduce inequality?

- In pairs, devise hypotheses to test the relationship between any two other pairs of data shown in Figure 10.
- Draw a scattergraph with a best fit line to investigate this relationship.
- Describe what your graph is telling you.

- Explain how well the hypothesis that you devised has worked out.
- Based on what you have found out, write a 400-word report to the Nigerian government about why you think more money should be invested in health and education, and what benefits the government would get in return.

The challenge of child labour

The International Labour Organisation (ILO) estimates that 168 million children (aged five to seventeen) worldwide are child labourers. The good news is that this figure is down from 246 million in 2000. However, child labour is a problem that needs to be tackled – children have a right to an education and countries need an educated workforce for their economy to grow.

Child labourers are children of poor families who cannot afford to send some or all of their children to school. School is free in the UK, but this is not the case in all countries. School fees or the cost of exercise books may be too great for the poorest families. Children are expected to help support the family by earning some money. Many work on farms. Others work in factories, for example, making carpets or clothing. Other children work in the informal sector – jobs such as collecting and recycling rubbish, street vending or cleaning shoes. Some child labourers work in hazardous jobs that may lead to damaging effects on the child's safety or health. The ILO describes a very wide range of hazardous jobs, including working underground or in quarries and working with dangerous machinery or manual work with heavy materials. Hazardous work also includes child soldiers and those who work in the sex industry.

More boys than girls are involved in child labour. However, daughters are sometimes kept off school to help look after younger brothers and sisters or do household chores, such as fetching water or firewood. So, the number of girls who do child labour is probably underestimated, because those doing household chores are not included in official figures.

◄ **Figure 1** Kavita, who is twelve years old, works along with her family at a brick kiln on the outskirts of Jammu, India.

◄ **Figure 2** Child labour and children working in hazardous jobs by region, 2015.

Region	Child labour		Hazardous work	
	(millions)	%	(millions)	%
Asia and the Pacific	77.7	9.3	33.9	4.1
Latin America and the Caribbean	12.5	8.8	9.6	6.8
Sub-Saharan Africa	59.0	21.4	28.8	10.4
Middle East and North Africa	9.2	8.4	5.2	4.7

How should we tackle child labour?

The ILO works at an international scale to end child labour. They collect data so that targets can be set and progress can be monitored – like that shown in Figure 4. They cannot pass new laws banning child labour – this is the responsibility of individual governments – but they can advise governments on policies that work based on their experience of working with countries in which child labour is falling. The ILO recommends that governments look at two main areas:

- Improving access to education, so that all children are in school.
- Improving social security systems, so that the poorest and most disadvantaged members of society can rely on the state to give them support rather than relying solely on their children.

Official figures show that India has about 5 million child labourers, although the actual number could be much higher. About 60 per cent of these children do not attend school at all. Some children have to work to help pay off a family debt – it is a modern form of slavery. India is making slow progress at reducing child labour. For example, in rural parts of Tamil Nadu and Madhya Pradesh, trade unions are working with local leaders and employers to create child-labour-free villages.

168 million children in child labour. This is roughly equal to the entire population of the UK, Germany and Spain!

99.8 million boys involved in child labour

68.2 girls involved in child labour

98 million child labourers work in farming

85 million children work in hazardous jobs

▲ **Figure 3** Child labour in numbers, 2015.

Activities

1 Explain why some poor parents do not send all of their children to primary school.
2 Study Figure 2. Which region has:
   a) the largest number of children in child labour and hazardous work?
   b) the largest percentage of children in child labour and hazardous work?
3 Use evidence from Figures 2 and 3 to create a poster that presents information about child labour in graphical form.
4 Describe the trends shown in Figure 4.
5 Explain why the ILO cannot prevent child labour in India.

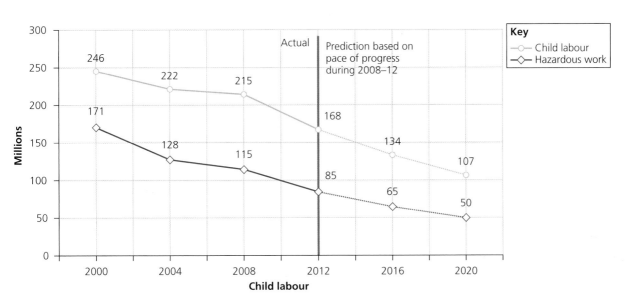

▲ **Figure 4** Actual and predicted trends in child labour.

Why is it particularly important to improve education for girls?

Millennium Development Goal 2 was a target set by the UN to halve the number of children missing from primary school by 2015. Globally the number fell from 104 million (1990) to 57 million (2015). Of these, 33 million are girls. In countries such as India, where more women than men are uneducated, there are serious consequences, for example:

- the child of an uneducated mother is twice as likely to die before the age of one as a child whose mother had a full education
- women who are well educated tend to marry later and have smaller families
- education (especially at secondary and university level) empowers women, i.e. it gives them a higher status and better chances in life.

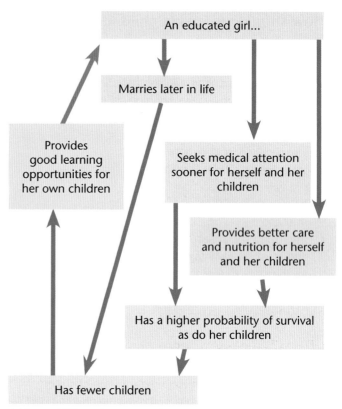

▲ **Figure 5** The advantages of improving education for girls.

Breaking free from child labour

Until a year ago, eight-year-old Laxmina was too busy working to even think of going to school. She earned about 30 rupees (less than a dollar) a day in return for delivering milk to nearby villages more prosperous than her own.

But all that has changed now. Laxmina has been attending an alternative learning centre (ALC), along with 40 other children in Uttar Pradesh. It is one among many such centres set up four years ago with UNICEF support to help educate children who have never been to school.

Over twenty per cent of India's working children are from Uttar Pradesh. Most of them work at odd jobs, in factories and in the carpet industry, for meagre wages. But their labour plays a key role in supplementing their families' meagre income. One of the main reasons for the high prevalence of child labour in these areas is the burden of debt, which forces families to send their children to work.

UNICEF addresses the issue of child labour through a combination of approaches. These include changing attitudes of parents, forming self-help groups, improving the quality of mainstream education, providing

transitional schools to return children to learning levels appropriate to their age.

Education plays a crucial role in eliminating child labour. UNICEF's approach therefore focuses on motivating communities to send girls and boys (who have never been to school or who have dropped out) to ALCs.

The centres have been set up mostly in areas that do not have a school within a 1.5 km radius. Each ALC has around 40 students. The aim is to help children complete primary education – which normally takes five years – within three years. At the end of this period, the children are integrated into formal school.

The initiative, funded by IKEA (with about US$500,000), through UNICEF's German National Committee has covered around 650 villages in two districts of Uttar Pradesh. There are currently around 200 ALCs. These provide an education for more than 7,000 children, of whom 55 per cent are girls.

▲ **Figure 6** Text extract from UNICEF India website. It is estimated that 23 per cent of children in Uttar Pradesh are involved in child labour; about 70 per cent of the population can read and write, and 57 per cent of women are literate.

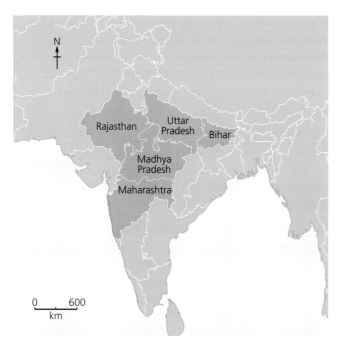

▲ **Figure 7** Child labour in India is highest in the five states of Bihar, Uttar Pradesh, Rajasthan, Madhya Pradesh and Maharashtra.

	Poverty (%)	Sex ratio	Female literacy (%)
Andhra Pradesh	9.20	993	59.1
Arunachal Pradesh	34.67	938	57.7
Assam	31.98	958	66.3
Bihar	33.74	918	51.5
Chhattisgarh	39.93	991	60.2
Goa	5.09	973	84.7
Gujarat	16.63	919	69.7
Haryana	11.16	879	65.9
Himachal Pradesh	8.06	972	75.9
Jammu and Kashmir	10.35	889	56.4
Jharkhand	36.96	948	55.4
Karnataka	20.91	973	68.1
Kerala	7.05	1,084	92.1
Madhya Pradesh	31.65	931	59.2
Maharashtra	17.35	929	75.9
Manipur	36.89	985	70.3
Meghalaya	11.87	989	72.9
Mizoram	20.40	976	89.3
Nagaland	18.88	931	76.1
Orissa	32.59	979	64.0
Punjab	8.26	895	70.7
Rajasthan	14.71	928	52.1
Sikkim	8.19	890	75.6
Tamil Nadu	11.28	996	73.4
Tripura	14.05	960	82.7
Uttar Pradesh	29.43	912	57.2
Uttarakhand	11.26	963	70.0
West Bengal	19.98	950	70.5

▲ **Figure 8** Selected data for Indian states; sex ratio is the number of women for every 1,000 men in the population; where men and women have equal health opportunities, this figure is close to 1,000.

Activities

1 Study Figure 6.
   a) Describe how this project is helping to reduce child labour.
   b) Suggest the strengths and limitations of this project.
2 Use Figure 5 to extend the explanation of each of the following statements.
   An educated mother…
   ▪ spots the early signs of ill health in her child so …
   ▪ understands the importance of a balanced diet so …
   ▪ recognises the importance of a full education for her daughter so …
3 Use the data in Figure 8 to investigate the relationship between poverty and female literacy.
   a) Create a hypothesis.
   b) Draw a scattergraph to investigate your hypothesis (see page 267).
   c) What conclusions can you reach?

Enquiry

How closely are education and health issues linked?

Use the data in Figure 8 to investigate the relationship between female literacy and sex ratio in Indian states. If there is a relationship, how can you explain it?

The challenge of international refugee movements

Most people become migrants because they believe that their move will end in a better job and quality of life. Such migrants are usually called **economic migrants**. They expect that their move will result in better pay, and better training and career opportunities. These benefits are described as **pull factors**.

However, the decision to migrate is also influenced by **push factors** – problems that are pushing people away from their existing homes. Push factors include:

- unemployment or underemployment and poverty
- natural hazards, political change, persecution or conflict.

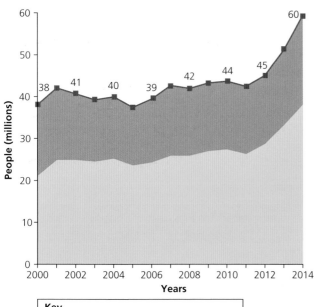

▲ **Figure 9** The number of people forced to move due to conflict (millions).

Country	Refugees (millions)
Syria	3.9
Afghanistan	2.6
Somalia	1.1

▲ **Figure 10** The three main sources of refugees, 2014.

In some cases, the push factors are extreme. Migrants move because they are in danger, perhaps because of conflict. The main reason they move is because of this danger rather than the pull factor of a better job elsewhere. These migrants are known as **refugees** or **asylum seekers**.

The majority of the world's refugees are cared for by countries in the developing world. The top five host nations for refugees are Turkey, Pakistan, Lebanon, Iran and Ethiopia. However, the UK media tends to focus on refugees who enter Europe.

The movement of refugees into and across Europe is not a new thing. During the Second World War, huge numbers of refugees moved across Europe because of the fighting. Since 2000, there has been an increasing number of refugees trying to enter Europe because of persecution, conflict or terrorism. Many are from countries in Africa, the Middle East and Asia. The conflicts in Iraq/Syria, Afghanistan and Somalia have created especially large numbers of migrants – some of whom are trying to enter Europe.

43,000 people were forced to leave their homes each day

51 per cent of the world's refugees are children

86 per cent of the world's refugees are cared for by developing countries–not HICs

If refugees were a country, it would be the **24th** largest country in the world

0.6 per cent of the world's refugees are cared for by the UK

▲ **Figure 11** Refugees in numbers, 2014.

Activities

1 Study Figure 9.
   a) Describe the overall trend in displaced persons.
   b) What percentage of displaced persons were international refugees and asylum seekers in 2014?
2 a) Use a world map to show the location of:
      i) the three countries that are main sources of refugees
      ii) the five main hosts of refugees.
   b) What conclusions can you reach?
3 Describe an effective way that each number in Figure 11 could be represented in a form that would grab attention.

The refugee crisis in Lebanon

Lebanon is a small country of 4.5 million people in the Middle East. A civil war has been fought in the neighbouring country of Syria since 2011. In 2015 there were at least 1.1 million Syrian refugees, who had fled the war, living in Lebanon. Living conditions for the refugees are harsh. Some live in refugee camps – tent cities – while others are squatters, living in overcrowded buildings in Lebanon's cities.

Lebanon is a relatively poor country: GNI per person is US$9,500, and there is not enough work for the local population and the refugees. It is estimated that the refugee crisis costs Lebanon US$4.5 billion each year. Access to clean water and proper sanitation are major concerns. Lebanon has a dry, Mediterranean-style climate and clean water is scarce. Over half of refugees consider that local water supplies are unsafe.

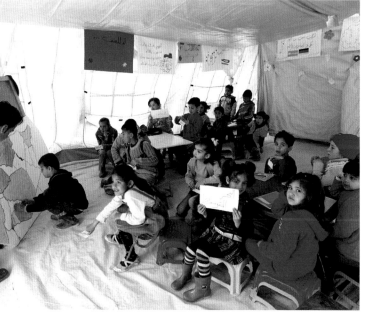

▲ **Figure 12** Syrian refugee children attending a class in a UNICEF school in Lebanon, 2015.

> We are not living – we are surviving. I live in an overcrowded tenement block with hundreds of other refugees. I have no privacy. My husband made the dangerous journey by boat to Europe. He is now in Germany. One day, perhaps, we will join him.

Syrian refugee mother of three children

> I no longer go to school. I do odd jobs here to try to support my family. I want to save US$1,000 – that's how much the people smugglers charge to get you into Europe by boat. I know that it's dangerous and that people drown, but there is no future here.

Refugee boy, aged 15

▲ **Figure 14** The views of a Syrian refugee and her son.

▲ **Figure 13** The location of Syria and Lebanon.

Activities

4 Describe the location of Lebanon.
5 What is the ratio of refugees to local population in Lebanon?
6 a) Describe the school conditions in Figure 12.
   b) Describe one strength and one limitation of this UNICEF project.

Enquiry

What challenges face Lebanon and the Syrian refugees living there?

Use evidence from this page, and your own research, to sort the challenges facing refugees in Lebanon under these headings: economic, social and environmental.

Refugee movements into Europe

The Schengen Agreement (1995) enables the easy movement of people between most EU states. Passports do not usually have to be shown when people travel from one country to another within the **Schengen Zone**. However, Europe's leaders want to control the movement of people from non-EU countries – including refugees and economic migrants from African and Asian countries. So migration into Europe is controlled carefully. This has led to some migrants trying to enter Europe illegally, avoiding the border control agencies.

Most illegal migrants from Africa or Asia try to enter Europe by making a sea crossing across the Mediterranean into one of the countries in southern Europe. They usually pay people smugglers large amounts of money to transport them across on small, overcrowded fishing boats or inflatables. Many of these boats are not seaworthy and have no navigation equipment. The immigrants have no food and little water onboard, and the boats rarely have life rafts. In doing so, the migrants are put in great danger and many have drowned during attempted crossings.

◀ **Figure 15** Migration routes into and across Europe.

Key
- EU Schengen states
- Non Schengen EU states
- Non-EU Schengen states
- Migrant flow

 http://data.unhcr.org/mediterranean/regional.php – data about refugee movements across the Mediterranean from the UN Refugee Agency.

Enquiry ?

How big was the Syrian refugee crisis in 2015 and 2016?

Use the weblink to the UNHCR to research the crisis. Use evidence from this and other sites to find out how many refugees were on the move, and where they settled.

Crossing Europe

When illegal migrants manage to enter Europe, their problems do not necessarily end. Many want to travel across Europe to join family or friends who moved earlier. For example, some Iraqi refugees try to reach the UK as they have relatives already living here. But not every country in Europe is a member of the Schengen Zone. This creates blockages, where migrants are held at borders, unable to move. One such blockage is at the Jungle – a squatter settlement in Calais, France. Here, migrants and refugees wait for an opportunity to be smuggled on to a lorry that is crossing into the UK.

Tackling the refugee crisis

There are different national approaches to refugee movements within Europe. Some countries, including Germany and Sweden, have welcomed refugees and try to integrate them into society. They see the refugees as victims who need help – 54 per cent of refugees to Europe in 2015 were women and children. They also believe that refugees will help their economies – many Syrian refugees are highly educated.

Other countries, like Austria, have tried to limit the number of refugees entering the country to just 80 per day. They claim that, for security reasons, it would be difficult to take more.

It has also been necessary to get international agreement between several European countries during the crisis. Italian and Greek coastguards have worked extremely hard to save migrants who are in danger in the Mediterranean. The UK navy has also been involved. One solution to the crisis may be to seize and destroy the boats used by people smugglers.

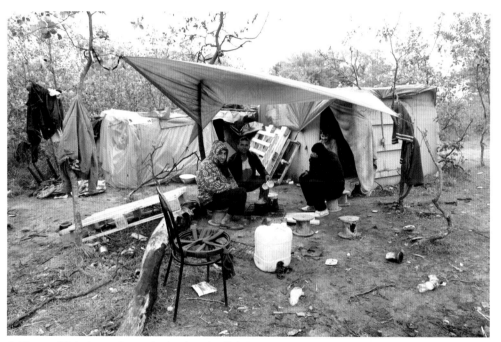

▲ **Figure 16** A shanty home in the Jungle, Calais.

Activities

1 Explain why the Schengen Zone has made the movement of refugees across most of Europe easier.
2 Study Figure 15.
   a) Describe two different routes used by illegal migrants and refugees entering Europe.
   b) Explain why routes into southern Europe are dangerous.
   c) Explain why many migrants take the longer route through Bulgaria.
   d) Explain why refugees in Greece found it difficult to get to Germany when Austria restricted entry at its border.

3 Use evidence from Figure 16 to suggest how living in the Jungle may affect quality of life for migrants.
4 Describe the potential opportunities and challenges created when refugees from Syria settle in European countries.
5 Explain why international agreements are necessary to help tackle the issue of refugee movement into and across Europe.

Health issues in sub-Saharan Africa

Sub-Saharan Africa remains the world's poorest region. Huge advances have been made in improving health care across this region during the period of the Millennium Development Goals (1990 to 2015) as you can see in Figure 17. However, sub-Saharan Africa still has the highest infant mortality rates in the world. A key population issue for Africa is to reduce infant mortality and improve primary health care. How can this be done?

Investigating the impact of malaria

Malaria is spread by mosquitoes carrying a parasite that infects a person when bitten. It is an entirely preventable disease. Malaria is a health threat in tropical regions of the world. Around 40 per cent of the world's population live in areas where malaria is endemic (i.e., malaria is constantly present) but 80 per cent of deaths occur in just fifteen countries, and most of these are in sub-Saharan Africa. About 65 per cent of deaths occur in children under five.

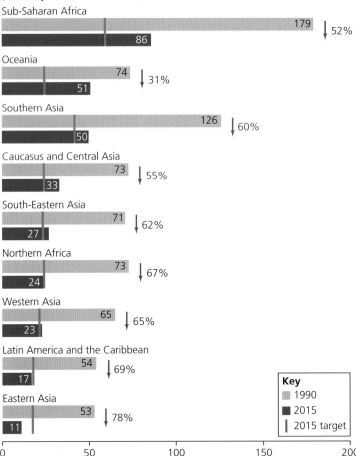

Under-five mortality rate, 1990 and 2015 (deaths per 1,000 live births)

Sub-Saharan Africa — 1990: 179, 2015: 86, ↓52%
Oceania — 1990: 74, 2015: 51, ↓31%
Southern Asia — 1990: 126, 2015: 50, ↓60%
Caucasus and Central Asia — 1990: 73, 2015: 33, ↓55%
South-Eastern Asia — 1990: 71, 2015: 27, ↓62%
Northern Africa — 1990: 73, 2015: 24, ↓67%
Western Asia — 1990: 65, 2015: 23, ↓65%
Latin America and the Caribbean — 1990: 54, 2015: 17, ↓69%
Eastern Asia — 1990: 53, 2015: 11, ↓78%

Key
- 1990
- 2015
- 2015 target

▲ **Figure 17** An evaluation of Millennium Development Goal 4: Reduce by two-thirds, between 1990 and 2015, the under-five mortality rate.

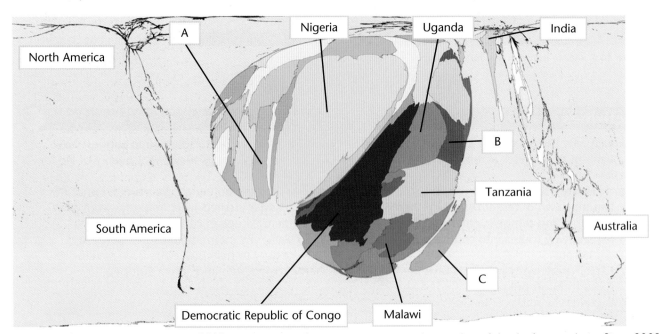

▲ **Figure 18** Deaths from malaria in 2002; countries are shown in proportion to the number of deaths from malaria. Since 2002 the number of deaths globally has fallen by 60 per cent; however, the global pattern remains unchanged, with most cases still in sub-Saharan Africa.

Malaria in Malawi

Malaria is one of Malawi's most serious health problems. In Malawi, the risk from malaria varies across the country and also throughout the year. The shores of Lake Malawi provide ideal breeding conditions for mosquitoes, with warm temperatures and stagnant water. The highland areas are generally cooler and drier. Here, malaria is seasonal with cases reaching a peak during the rainy season when ditches and puddles quickly form and attract mosquitoes. Around 83 per cent of Malawi's population live in rural areas. Deaths from malaria are significantly higher in rural areas, such as Nkhata Bay, than they are in the cities of Blantyre and Lilongwe. Houses in rural areas are often constructed of mud bricks with thatched roofs. These homes offer little protection from mosquitoes.

Key
- Malaria under 5 years – new
- Malaria 5 years and older – new

◀ **Figure 19** New malaria cases by month in Malawi.

	Nkhata Bay		
	Mean min. temperature (°C)	Mean max. temperature (°C)	Average precipitation (mm)
Jan	21	30	232
Feb	21	30	237
Mar	21	30	260
Apr	19	29	322
May	17	28	97
Jun	14	27	71
Jul	13	26	47
Aug	14	29	9
Sep	15	30	2
Oct	17	34	11
Nov	20	34	90
Dec	21	32	181

▲ **Figure 20** Climate for Nkhata Bay, 2004–13 averages.

Activities

1 Use Figure 18 and an atlas to find out:
   a) which tropical region has very few cases of malaria
   b) the names of countries A, B and C
   c) which region of the world, after sub-Saharan Africa, has the next largest number of cases of malaria.
2 Study Figure 19. Describe the annual pattern of new malaria cases for children under five. Refer to figures in your answer.
3 Use Figure 20.
   a) Draw climate graphs for Nkhata Bay.
   b) Describe the annual pattern of rainfall.
4 Using evidence from Figures 19 and 20, explain why new cases of malaria are more common at certain times of the year.

Enquiry

How successful was sub-Saharan Africa at meeting Millennium Development Goal 4?

Use evidence from Figure 17 to compare health improvements in sub-Saharan Africa with other regions.

Are some people at more risk from malaria than others?

The health risks of malaria vary widely for different groups of people. Not everyone who catches malaria will die. In fact, over time, continued infection from mosquito bites will lead to a person becoming immune. Prevalence rates in Malawi show that 60 per cent of babies and children under three years old had malaria compared with only 12 per cent for adult men. As children and adults age, they develop resistance to the disease and the number of deaths go down.

Some people are at greater risk of death from malaria than others. The groups at higher risk are children and pregnant women, especially those in their first pregnancy. Around 40 per cent of child deaths are from malaria. People with poor immune systems are also at high risk. It is estimated that 10 per cent of Malawi's population is living with the HIV virus (see page 281), which destroys a person's immune system. They are unable to fend off diseases and the death rate from malaria is higher than for people without HIV.

Pregnancy also leads to a slight decline in immune levels. This results in slightly more pregnant women dying from the disease than non-pregnant women.

Key
- less than 10
- 10–25
- 25–50
- 50–100
- 100–200
- 200–400
- 400–800
- 800–1,600
- 1,600–3,200
- more than 3,200

▲ **Figure 21** Population densities in Malawi; rural areas generally have lower population densities than urban areas.

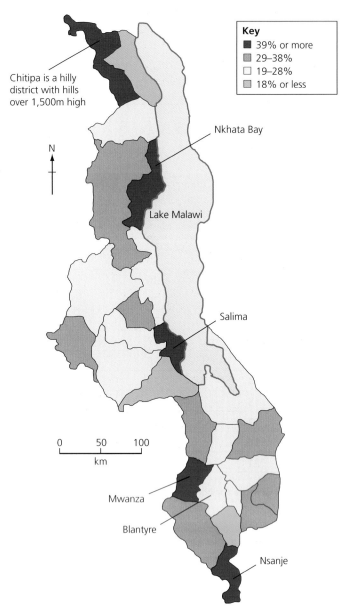

Key
- 39% or more
- 29–38%
- 19–28%
- 18% or less

Chitipa is a hilly district with hills over 1,500m high

Nkhata Bay

Salima

Mwanza

Blantyre

Nsanje

▲ **Figure 22** Distribution of malaria in Malawi.

Combatting malaria

A number of strategies have been implemented in Malawi to combat the disease. One strategy has been to encourage people to use insecticide-treated bed nets (ITNs). This is a very effective way of reducing incidents of malaria and is relatively cheap. Each bed net only costs only £3. However, many people in rural Malawi are unable to afford this. In the last fifteen years, the Ministry of Health, and charities such as Nothing but Nets, have distributed bed nets across Malawi. In 1997 only eight per cent of homes in Malawi had bed nets. By 2004 the average was 50 per cent. By 2015, 80 per cent of households have an ITN. However, this doesn't mean that there are enough bed nets to protect everyone in those households. Only 33 per cent of households have one net for every two people. It's important to protect the people who are most vulnerable. The good news is that 66 per cent of children under five and 60 per cent of pregnant women sleep under an ITN.

Another strategy is the use of insecticides. Insecticides are sprayed in areas where mosquitoes are likely to come into contact with humans. The problem is that mosquitoes have developed resistance to some insecticides and they aren't as effective as they could be. Similarly, the mosquito parasite has become resistant to drugs. New drugs need to be developed urgently. Once a person starts to show signs of malaria, they need to take anti-malarial drugs as soon as possible to stand a better chance of fighting the disease. Unfortunately, not everyone in Malawi is able to access drugs when they need them. This is often because people in rural areas have to travel a long way to reach a doctor. Also, because the early symptoms of malaria are similar to many other conditions, people often don't realise until it's too late. Malaria has the biggest impact on poor people, as they cannot afford to buy nets and get the treatment they need. It can be a vicious circle: people are prevented from getting out of poverty because of the burden malaria has on their lives.

▲ **Figure 23** Deaths due to malaria can be prevented using insecticide-treated bed nets (ITNs).

Activities

1 a) Identify which three groups of people are most at risk from malaria.
  b) Explain why some people are more at risk than others.
2 a) Use Figure 22 to describe the distribution of malaria in Malawi.
  b) Use evidence from pages 277–9 to suggest different reasons for the high rates of malaria in two of the named regions on in Figure 22.
  c) Compare Figures 21 and 22. Use these maps to provide evidence that malaria is more common in rural areas.
3 Work in pairs. Discuss each of the following and then summarise your conclusions in two spider diagrams.
  a) Does malaria cause poverty or is it a result of poverty?
  b) Which groups should be targeted for ITNs?
4 Evaluate the success of the use of ITNs in Malawi. What can they achieve? What else needs to be done?

The challenges created by HIV

Sub-Saharan Africa is the region of the world that has been hardest hit by HIV, an incurable disease that attacks the immune system and which eventually leads to AIDS. HIV is a major cause of poverty in many communities. HIV most commonly infects people of working age. Deaths among the workforce not only cause distress for families but also reduce the earning power of the family.

Rates of infection from HIV reached a peak in the late 1990s. Since then, in most countries of sub-Saharan Africa, the percentage of adults who are living with the virus has levelled out or fallen. This is because fewer people are becoming infected because of the success of education programmes. In Uganda, for example, HIV infection rates fell when the government introduced a programme of training for health care workers and education and counselling for the public.

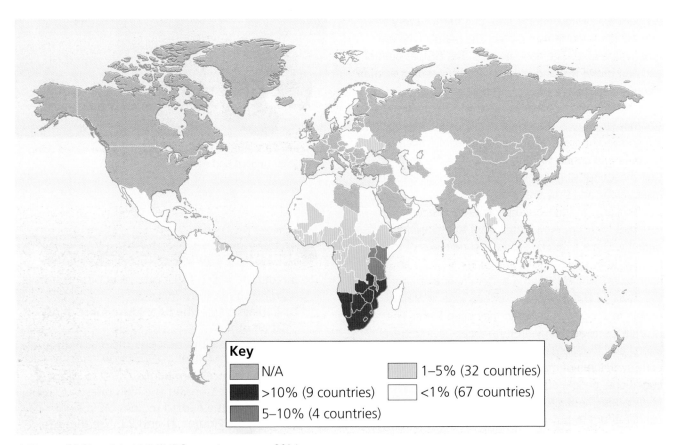

Key

N/A

\>10% (9 countries)

5–10% (4 countries)

1–5% (32 countries)

<1% (67 countries)

▲ **Figure 24** The global HIV/AIDS prevalence rate, 2014.

Activities

1 Use Figure 24 to:
   a) describe the global distribution of people with HIV/AIDS.
   b) describe how prevalence rates vary across Africa.
2 Explain the links between HIV and poverty. Use Figure 26 to help you.
3 Explain why improving education may help reduce the prevalence of HIV.

HIV in Malawi

Malawi has one of the highest numbers of people infected by HIV anywhere in the world. It is estimated that 1.1 million people in Malawi are living with HIV. Deaths from AIDS and malaria help to explain why the average life expectancy in Malawi is just 54 years.

Huge efforts have been made by the government of Malawi and non-government organisations (NGOs) to combat the HIV epidemic. The number of new infections each year has fallen from 98,000 in 2005 to 34,000 in 2013. The number of children affected by HIV has fallen by 67 per cent in the same period.

Rates of HIV vary greatly across Malawi. Rates in southern regions are around 14.5 per cent, whereas the average is around ten per cent for the whole of Malawi. Rates are higher in urban areas than rural areas: 17.4 per cent compared to 9 per cent.

Young adult contracts HIV and eventually becomes too ill to work.

↓

Income is lost and family become poor.

↓

Family no longer pay income tax, so government receives less revenue which it would spend on health and education.

The economy has one less worker. The AIDS sufferer may have been a doctor, nurse or teacher. All sectors of the economy lose productivity.

Children of AIDS sufferer have to give up school. They become carers and main earners in the household.

▲ **Figure 26** The social and economic consequences of HIV.

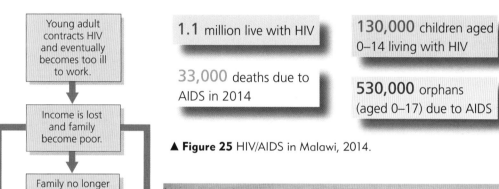

1.1 million live with HIV

130,000 children aged 0–14 living with HIV

33,000 deaths due to AIDS in 2014

530,000 orphans (aged 0–17) due to AIDS

▲ **Figure 25** HIV/AIDS in Malawi, 2014.

▲ **Figure 27** A poster in the West African country of the Gambia.

The Ebola outbreak 2014–15

The villages of coastal West Africa rarely make the news in the UK. However, in March 2014, some of the world's poorest LICs, Guinea, Sierra Leone, and Liberia, shown in Figure 28, were under the media spotlight. The reason was Ebola, one of the world's deadliest diseases. A lethal strain of Ebola had appeared in these countries. First discovered in 1976, this was the most serious outbreak to date.

▲ **Figure 28** Map showing deaths from Ebola in West Africa.

What is Ebola?

Ebola is a virus (the same sort of illness as flu and a common cold, but much more serious). It spreads by direct contact, including water molecules from someone sneezing. Because of this, it poses a danger to health workers as well as patients.

Ebola's symptoms are like flu, but rapidly become more serious. Symptoms begin between 2 and 21 days after infection. It begins with a fever and headache, joint and muscle pain, sore throat, and muscle weakness. Diarrhoea, vomiting, a rash, stomach pain and reduced kidney and liver function follow. The patient bleeds internally, and from the ears, eyes, nose or mouth. Ebola is fatal in about 40 per cent of cases, though that is falling. The earlier that treatment is given, the better the chances of survival. During 2015, treatment became possible and death rates fell.

Poverty and vulnerability

Before the outbreak, over half of Liberia's population lived below the **poverty line**. Ebola made this worse.

Activities

1 Use Figure 28 to describe the location and distribution of the largest number of deaths during the Ebola outbreak.
2 Using data in Figure 29, explain how poverty and vulnerability are connected.
3 Using the Ebola Factfile, calculate the percentage of:
   a) those infected who died
   b) deaths in each country affected.

Country	GNI per capita (US$ PPP)	HDI score (and ranking out of 187)	Doctors per 1,000 people	Infant mortality
Guinea	1,140	0.392 (179th)	0.1	53.4
Sierra Leone	1,830	0.374 (183rd)	0.02	71.7
Liberia	820	0.412 (175th)	0.01	67.5
UK	38,370	0.892 (14th)	2.8	4.4

▲ **Figure 29** Poverty indicators for the three most-affected countries.

This part of West Africa contains some of the world's poorest countries, as Figure 29 shows. Poverty makes people **vulnerable**:
• They are less well fed or able to resist disease.
• Living conditions, e.g. lack of sanitation, make the spread of disease likely.
• They are likely to carry on working because they cannot afford not to, and so treatment often comes too late.
• They have no savings, and cannot afford private medical care.

Many people lost friends and relatives, as well as jobs, savings (after paying for health care) and a season planting crops. Oxfam found that incomes of three-quarters of the population fell, and 60 per cent said they hadn't had enough food in the past week. To cope, many had to borrow money, reduce meals each day, or miss meals to allow children to eat.

Oxfam's response to the Ebola outbreak

Oxfam raised money to fight the outbreak, together with the Red Cross and the French charity Médecins Sans Frontières. They organised emergency fundraising campaigns, and during 2014–15 spent £28 million in the countries affected.

In total, Oxfam helped 3.2 million people. They had two main roles:
- Supporting medical care with water, sanitation and cleaning equipment.
- Working with communities to raise awareness of the disease and help with treatment, safe burials and tracing contacts.

▲ **Figure 30** An ambulance driver in protective clothing is disinfected with chlorine after returning from transporting an Ebola victim to a treatment centre in Freetown, Sierra Leone (2014).

Medical care

Health care helped doctors in diagnosing, isolating and treating those affected. Oxfam provided funding for:
- Building medical facilities and equipping them, e.g. facemasks, boots, gloves and soap.
- Providing infrastructure for dozens of health centres in Sierra Leone and Liberia, e.g. water tanks and pipes.
- Building community hand-washing stations.
- Providing teams to carry out contact tracing.
- Safe burial of the dead, providing kits containing e.g. masks, overalls, boots, gloves, body bags.

Working with communities

In Liberia, Oxfam:
- provided financial support to 15,000 families
- built and repaired toilets and water points in 400 schools
- trained teachers and students in good hygiene to improve community health and reduce the risk of future outbreaks.

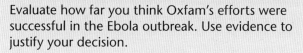

Enquiry

Evaluate how far you think Oxfam's efforts were successful in the Ebola outbreak. Use evidence to justify your decision.

Factfile: Ebola 2014 to 2015

Total number of cases: 27,741

Deaths: 11,284

Death toll by country:

- Liberia: 4,808
- Sierra Leone: 3,949
- Guinea: 2,512
- Nigeria: 8
- Mali: 6
- USA: 1

In 2014, there was a separate outbreak of Ebola in the Democratic Republic of Congo, killing 43 people. However, this was a different strain, and not linked to the outbreak in West Africa. In July 2015, a new vaccine against Ebola was announced.

Activities

4 a) Create a table to show the economic, social and environmental impacts of Ebola.
   b) Decide which impacts were greatest and explain why.
5 Using Figure 30, explain why treating Ebola is more expensive than many other diseases.
6 Design a poster to assist Oxfam's campaign to either
   a) make people more aware of Ebola and its symptoms, or
   b) improve public hygiene to prevent further spread of Ebola.

The link between health and water security

It is estimated that around 2.2 million people die each year as a result of infections of the gut caused by drinking or bathing in unsafe water. Many of these are children.

Clean water is essential to social and economic development. Safe water is needed to maintain water supplies, provide hygiene, grow food and supply industrial processes. Without sufficient safe water, infant mortality and maternal mortality rates increase. Having **water security** is an important aim for a country. It means having enough water to keep the population healthy and fed, and for the economy to develop sustainably – without damaging the prospects for future generations.

Water supply and polio in sub-Saharan Africa

The northeastern part of Nigeria is in the Sahel region of Africa. This region suffers from water insecurity. There are a number of reasons for this problem:

- The region has a hot, semi-arid climate with a long dry season.
- The rainy season is unreliable; in many years since 1965 there has been below-average rainfall.
- The Nigerian government has failed to provide enough piped water supply or sanitation to fast-growing cities, such as Kano.
- Poverty and drought have led to political instability and the rise of an extreme Islamist group called Boko Haram.

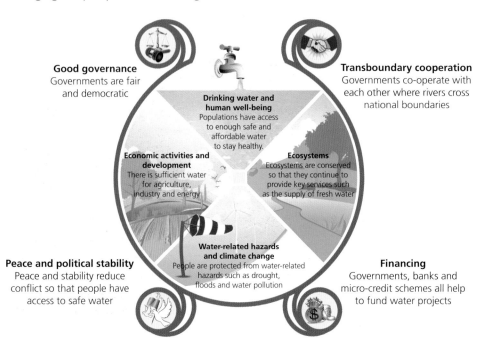

Good governance
Governments are fair and democratic

Drinking water and human well-being
Populations have access to enough safe and affordable water to stay healthy.

Transboundary cooperation
Governments co-operate with each other where rivers cross national boundaries

Ecosystems
Ecosystems are conserved so that they continue to provide key services such as the supply of fresh water

Economic activities and development
There is sufficient water for agriculture, industry and energy

Water-related hazards and climate change
People are protected from water-related hazards such as drought, floods and water pollution

Peace and political stability
Peace and stability reduce conflict so that people have access to safe water

Financing
Governments, banks and micro-credit schemes all help to fund water projects

◀ **Figure 31** UN definition of water security (2013). The central part of the diagram describes the features of water security. The outer part of the diagram describes how water security can be achieved.

Activities

1 Study Figure 31. List the benefits of water security for people, the economy and environment. Record your answer in a Venn diagram.
2 Study the information about water insecurity in Kano State and Kano City.
   a) Make a list of the physical and human causes.
   b) Suggest at least four reasons why Kano is at huge risk of water insecurity.

   c) Use this example to explain why water security can only be achieved if political leaders work hard.
3 a) Use Figure 34 to draw a line graph showing population growth of Kano City.
   b) Describe the trend of your graph.
   c) Outline two main reasons for this trend.
4 a) Use Figure 32 to draw a line graph of polio cases in Nigeria.
   b) Explain the factors that have influenced the shape of this graph.

Water insecurity and health in Kano

Kano is Nigeria's third-largest city. Its population continues to grow quickly, partly because of rural to urban migration from the surrounding rural areas where low rainfall and poverty are push factors. Kano's water supply comes from the Tiga Dam (completed in 1974) and the Challawa Gorge Dam (completed in 1992). The Tiga Dam also supplies water to the Kano River Irrigation Project, which uses water to grow food for Kano. However, Kano has no sewerage system or sewage treatment plants. People living in high-density shanty towns in the city use pit latrines. Poor sanitation means that people are at risk of diseases such as cholera and polio. Polio attacks the nervous system and can cripple its victims. But polio can be eradicated by immunising young children.

Between 2003 and 2004, local Muslim leaders and the state government of Kano decided to oppose any future vaccination of children in Kano State. The state government now supports the vaccination programme, but some people have remained violently opposed to it. In February 2013, extremists opened fire on two polio clinics in Kano, killing nine health workers. The state government and UNICEF have led a huge programme to educate local people about the benefits of the polio vaccine. It is now hoped that polio can be eradicated from Nigeria by 2018.

Year	Cases of polio reported
2001	56
2002	202
2003	355
2004	782
2005	830
2006	1,122
2007	285
2008	798
2009	388
2010	21
2011	62
2012	122
2013	53
2014	6

▲ **Figure 32** Polio cases in Nigeria.

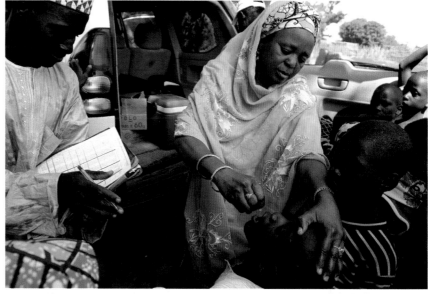

▲ **Figure 33** Immunisation campaign worker Hassan Makama keeps count while Riskat Giwa, UNICEF officer of social mobilisation, vaccinates children against polio in Kano, Nigeria.

1970	1975	1980	1985	1990	1995	2000	2005	2010	2015	2020	2025	2030
0.54	0.86	1.36	1.86	2.06	2.34	2.60	2.90	3.22	3.59	4.17	5.11	6.20

▲ **Figure 34** Population of Kano (millions).

Enquiry

Can polio be eradicated?

■ Research the countries in which polio was endemic in 2000 and again in 2015. What is happening to the disease and what seems likely to happen in the future?
■ Focus on the problem of polio in Afghanistan and Pakistan. Can polio be eradicated in these countries? Justify your decision.

What links the UK consumer to the global environment?

Food miles are a measure of the distance your weekly shopping has travelled before it arrives on your plate. Food grown in the UK is transported further now than it ever was 50 years ago. That is because of the growth of large supermarket chains and their complex distribution systems (see Figure 1). Food and other agricultural products now make up almost a third of goods carried on our roads – with lorries using diesel and emitting CO_2, a greenhouse gas.

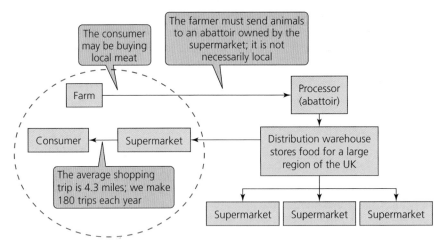

▲ **Figure 1** Food miles are increased by complex supply chains; you may be eating meat reared on a local farm, but it may still have travelled many food miles.

Much of our food is grown abroad and then imported into the UK, so the food miles for these products are even higher. We import half of our vegetables (most come from the EU) and 95 per cent of our fruit. Meats such as beef (from South America), lamb (from New Zealand) and chicken (from the EU) can be frozen and transported to the UK by container boat. Energy costs, and carbon emissions, for transporting this meat will be higher than buying locally produced meat.

Carbon emissions are even higher if goods are transported by air. Products such as soft fruit (for example raspberries and strawberries) and flowers need to be transported quickly by air to keep them fresh. Many can be grown in the UK, but only for a few months each year. They are imported from tropical countries (such as Kenya) or southern hemisphere countries (such as South Africa) so we can have them out of season.

Type of transport	Grams per tonne/km
Large container ships (over 35,000 tonnes)	3.0
Container ships (10,000–35,000 tonnes)	7.9
Trucks/lorries	80.0
Air freight	435.0

▲ **Figure 2** Carbon emissions from different types of transport.

Imports from	Volume (millions tonnes)
Turkey	0.4
Chile	0.45
Brazil	0.5
South Africa	1.1
Colombia	1.2
Ecuador	1.5
Costa Rica	1.8

▲ **Figure 3** Imports of fresh fruit to the EU in 2014.

Enquiry

Should we only eat locally grown food that is in season?

Research the UK's fruit imports.

- Using Figure 3 to help you, which fruits do we import and from which countries?
- Can we reduce our demand for imported fruit? Which fruits are grown in the UK?
- Design a survey to investigate attitudes to this issue. What questions will you ask? What would be a representative sample for your survey?

So, should I eat locally produced food?

You would imagine that buying locally grown food is good – especially if you buy from an independent shop that does not have complex supply chains like those shown in Figure 1. You are supporting local farmers and the food miles should be shorter. However, some argue that the concept of food miles simplifies a complex subject and we should not ignore food grown abroad, like the Kenyan beans in Figure 4. The production of food uses all sorts of resources, including fertiliser, pesticides and water. Fertilisers and pesticides need to be manufactured, which uses energy, then supplied by lorry to retailers and to the farmer, using diesel, then applied to the fields with a tractor, using more diesel. Each of these processes emits greenhouse gases and has an impact on the environment. This way of thinking about products is called **life cycle analysis**. It is a more sophisticated way of thinking about the impacts of consumerism than food miles.

▲ **Figure 4** Should we buy these green beans that have been flown from Kenya?

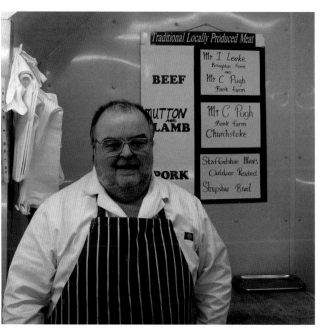

▲ **Figure 5** Mr Pugh, the family-run butcher's shop, in Bishop's Castle; Mr Pugh buys all of his meat from farms less than 10 km from the shop; it is slaughtered in Leintwardine, 22 km from the shop.

Beans (in Kenya) are grown using manual labour – nothing is mechanised. They don't use tractors, they use cow muck as fertiliser; and they have low-tech irrigation systems in Kenya. They also provide employment to many people in the developing world. So you have to weigh that against the air miles used to get them to the supermarket.

▲ **Figure 6** Professor Gareth Edwards-Jones of Bangor University, an expert on African agriculture, talking about green beans grown in Kenya, quoted in 'How the myth of food miles hurts the planet' by Robin McKie and Caroline Davies, *Guardian*, 23 March 2008. Courtesy of Guardian News & Media Ltd.

Activities

1 Use Figure 1 to explain why meat bought from a supermarket is likely to have more food miles than meat bought from a local butcher.
2 Represent the data in Figure 2 using a suitable technique.
3 Study Figure 3.
   a) Which of these countries are:
      i) in the EU
      ii) tropical?
   b) Choose a suitable technique to represent this data.
4 Describe the strengths and limitations of the food miles concept.
5 Create a table that outlines the arguments for and against buying fruit and vegetables from abroad.

Consumerism and waste

We all consume stuff – food, water, clothes, electronics and energy. We don't often think about where it came from or its impacts on our environment when we finish with it – but we should. The population of Earth today uses resources equal to 1.6 planets. We call this our **ecological footprint**. As the population grows, and our desire for more consumer goods grows too, our footprint grows. By the 2030s the UN estimates we will need two Earths to support us. Increasing consumer demand can be linked to the destruction of rainforests (see pages 294–5) and the collapse of fish stocks (see pages 290–1), as well as increased greenhouse gas emissions.

Country	Footprint per capita (GHA)	HDI
Australia	8.3	0.935
Germany	4.4	0.916
USA	6.8	0.915
UK	4.2	0.907
UAE	8.1	0.835
Mexico	2.4	0.756
Brazil	2.9	0.755
China	2.5	0.727
Indonesia	1.3	0.684
South Africa	2.5	0.666
Vietnam	1.4	0.666
India	0.9	0.609
Ghana	1.7	0.579
Bangladesh	0.7	0.570
Malawi	0.7	0.445
Gambia	1.1	0.441

▲ **Figure 7** Ecological footprint compared to Human Development Index (HDI) for selected countries.

Ecological footprint

Ecological footprint is a measure of the impact each of us has on the environment. It considers the amount of land we need, each year, to provide the food, water, energy and services each of us needs – including the amount of space and resources needed to get rid of our waste. Ecological footprint is measured in global hectares per person (GHA). We have enough on Earth for 2.1 GHA each. If we use more than that each year, our lifestyle is unsustainable because we are consuming resources faster than they can be replaced.

Consumer societies create huge quantities of waste – households throw away food and packaging every week. In the past, most of this was collected and burnt or dumped in a landfill site. However, we create so much waste that we are running out of space to dump it. Besides, useful materials such as card, paper, plastics, metals and glass can be recycled. This reduces demand for new resources and, in some cases, it's cheaper to recycle than create packaging from scratch. Aluminium drinks cans are a good example – it takes much less electricity to recycle a drinks can than to smelt aluminium from its ore.

Recycle by processing materials so they can be used again

Refuse or rethink – change your habits

Reduce your consumption

Repair or repurpose by finding a new way to use an old object

Reuse items instead of throwing them away

▲ **Figure 8** Ways to reduce our ecological footprint.

1 Study Figure 7.
   a) Design a hypothesis linking ecological footprint and HDI and make a prediction.
   b) Draw a scattergraph to test your hypothesis. Think carefully about which is the dependent variable (which should be plotted on the vertical axis). See page 267.
   c) What conclusions can you draw about the links between consumerism and development? Make sure you explain the reasons for the links.
2 Discuss the five Rs in Figure 8.
   a) Make a list of at least ten items around your home. Give an example of how each could be treated using the ideas in Figure 8.
   b) What should we do about waste? Is one of the five Rs better than the others? Explain your answer.

What happens to our e-waste?

What happens to your old phone, computer or tablet when you have finished with it? We describe this as **e-waste**. These items contain various metals, including copper (covered in plastic) and small amounts of gold (in computer chips), indium and palladium. Recycling these materials reduces the need to extract more raw materials from the Earth – so reducing our ecological footprint. However, they also contain some hazardous materials, such as mercury, lead and flame-retardant chemicals. They need to be recycled carefully or these materials can pollute the environment and threaten human health.

The UN estimates that 50 million tonnes of e-waste is created each year. Much comes from the rapidly growing economies of NICs such as India and China, as well as from European countries and other HICs. Environmental campaigners are concerned that some e-waste generated in Europe is exported to countries such as India, China, Ghana and Nigeria where recycling costs are much lower. This results in places like Agbogbloshie, a huge e-waste recycling dump in Accra, Ghana. It is estimated that between 50,000 and 80,000 people live and work in the informal settlement that has grown up next to the dump. Computers, monitors and phones are broken down and burnt – melting the plastics and exposing the metals for recycling. Smoke from the fires fills the air and is a health hazard. Tar from the molten plastics pollutes the stream that runs alongside the dump.

▲ **Figure 10** Young men dismantle computer servers at Agbogbloshie; the work is informal and unregulated so there are no health and safety rules.

Activities

3 Describe the pattern shown in Figure 9. Consider whether each source and destination country is an HIC, NIC or LIC.

4 Describe the social and environmental consequences of e-waste recycling in informal settlements such as Agbogbloshie in Ghana.

Key	
▓	Known source
▒	Known destination
☐	Suspected destination

▲ **Figure 9** Known and suspected movements of e-waste. The export of some e-waste is banned; however, used e-goods are sometimes labelled as being in working order when they are shipped, even though they are actually waste. It is, therefore, difficult to track the movement of all e-waste products that are dumped abroad

Are there enough fish in the North Sea?

'Fish and chips' is a popular UK take-away food. Traditionally, the fish was cod or haddock caught in the North Sea – an example of a marine ecosystem. But in recent years, cod has been replaced with other fish such as coley or pollock as cod has been in short supply. Why has this happened?

Over-fishing is not sustainable because, when too many young fish are caught, there are not enough fish left in the sea to breed and replace the fish stocks. This is shown in Figures 12 and 14. It can take up to four years for cod to become mature enough to breed, so fish stocks have to be managed to give them a chance to survive. It is illegal in the UK to land a cod fish that is less than 35 cm long. These fish have not yet bred and if caught they must be thrown back into the sea.

How can cod be protected?

The EU manages the fish stocks around Europe, including the North Sea, by imposing quotas. This is where a limit is put on the number of fish that can be caught by member states in certain sea areas. They also limit the number of days in a month when the fishermen can go out to fish. The quota system has angered UK fishermen. They have argued that the restrictions have been too severe. Quotas mean they catch less fish so they earn less money and some fishermen have gone out of business. There was also criticism of how quotas were allocated to different member states of the EU. Catching too many or small fish leads to hefty fines, so fish are sometimes thrown back into the sea, dead or alive. A minimum net size should mean that small fish can swim back out of the net and escape.

▲ **Figure 11** Cod for sale at the market in Peterhead, Scotland. Peterhead is the UK's largest fishing port.

Activity

1 a) Describe the overall trend of Figure 12.
  b) Suggest how changes to the catch affected people working in the North Sea fishing industry.
  c) What proportion of the cod catch was discarded (thrown back) in 2008?

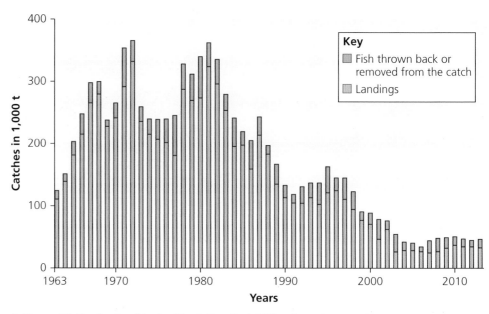

Key
■ Fish thrown back or removed from the catch
■ Landings

▲ **Figure 12** Catch of cod in the North Sea (in 1,000s of metric tonnes).

Has the cod been saved?

Figures released in September 2015 show that stocks of North Sea cod are beginning to increase (see Figure 14). Preventing over-fishing has allowed the cod to breed and increase in number. The fishing industry is now much smaller than it was in the 1990s, with fewer smaller family businesses still working. So is it okay for **consumers** to eat cod again? Scientists warn that the cod is not yet out of danger.

> Quotas don't go far enough. We need to stop fishing over-exploited stocks altogether for one year. Then stocks would be restored to a fully sustainable level in four years.
>
> **Scientist**

> We need to look at how we catch the fish. Trawlers use dragnets and catch more fish but damage the sea bed. Gillnets are vertical nets which catch less fish with less waste. We need to fish responsibly.
>
> **Environmental campaigner**

> We need to protect our fishing industry. If we set quotas as low as the scientists would like, our fishing industry would collapse. We have set quotas low enough to conserve fish stocks but high enough to keep people in jobs.
>
> **Government minister**

> I like cod, but we have a responsibility to conserve the world's resources. If I have to buy other sustainable types of fish for a while, so be it.
>
> **Consumer**

> This town relies on the fishing industry. People work on the boats, in the fish market and in the boat repair yard. When the government limits the amount of fish we can catch then the whole town suffers.
>
> **Fish and chip shop owner in Peterhead**

▲ **Figure 13** Views of fishing.

Activities

2. a) Compare the trend of Figure 14 to Figure 12.
   b) At what date might scientists have asked for fishing quotas to be introduced?
   c) Explain why fishermen and scientists might disagree about the meaning of the final three years of this trend line.

3. Discuss the views shown in Figure 13. Give one reason why it is important to:
   a) protect the ecosystem of the North Sea
   b) protect jobs in the fishing industry.

4. Suggest two different ways that UK consumers could help conserve the North Sea ecosystem and support the fishing industry.

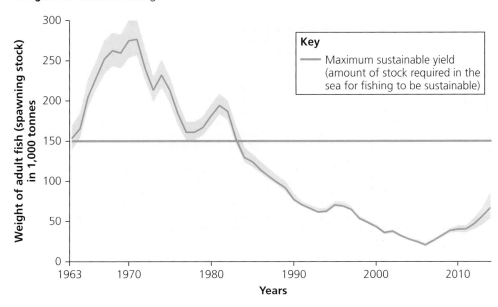

◀ **Figure 14** The weight of adult cod (spawning stock) in the North Sea.

Is shrimp farming sustainable?

Mangrove forests grow on tropical coastlines. The trees of the mangrove tolerate flooding by both fresh and salt water, so this is both a forest and a wetland, and it supports a very wide range of fish, insects and animals.

Mangroves help to absorb wave energy during storms so they help to protect coastal communities. Despite this, big business regards mangroves as useless wasteland. Trees are cut down and the swampy land redeveloped for tourism or **aquaculture**. Over 25 million hectares of mangrove forest are estimated to have been destroyed in the last 100 years. The fastest rates of destruction have been in Asia during the late 20th century. Globally, around 150,000 hectares of mangrove are destroyed every year, which is equal to about 1 per cent of the global total. Only 6.9 per cent of mangrove forests are protected. One of the most common reasons for the destruction of mangroves has been the rapid growth of shrimp (or prawn) farming. Mangroves are cleared away to make space for artificial ponds. These ponds are flooded with salt water and used to rear the shrimp.

Shrimp is low in fat and high in protein. Most consumers are in Europe, North America and Japan. Around 55 per cent of all shrimp we eat is farmed. The rest is caught from our oceans, largely from tropical waters such as the Bay of Bengal where large trawlers catch wild shrimp in nets. Over-fishing wild shrimp damages the food web of the marine ecosystem. A smaller quantity is caught in cold waters such as in the North Atlantic around the coast of Iceland.

Most shrimp aquaculture is in China, Thailand, Indonesia, Brazil, Ecuador and Bangladesh. Shrimp farming is carried out by both big business and many small farmers. Some argue that shrimp farming has helped poor farmers to diversify their income and reduce poverty. The global shrimp industry is thought to be worth US$12–15 billion.

Shrimp aquaculture is an **intensive** form of farming. It takes between three and six months to rear shrimp so farmers produce two to three crops a year. The shrimp are treated with pesticides and antibiotics. Organic waste, chemicals and antibiotics escape from the ponds polluting fresh groundwater supplies that local communities use for drinking.

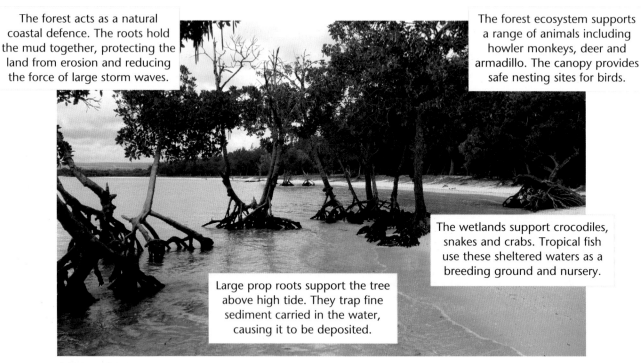

The forest acts as a natural coastal defence. The roots hold the mud together, protecting the land from erosion and reducing the force of large storm waves.

The forest ecosystem supports a range of animals including howler monkeys, deer and armadillo. The canopy provides safe nesting sites for birds.

The wetlands support crocodiles, snakes and crabs. Tropical fish use these sheltered waters as a breeding ground and nursery.

Large prop roots support the tree above high tide. They trap fine sediment carried in the water, causing it to be deposited.

▲ **Figure 15** Why mangroves are important ecosystems.

Activities

1 Describe how mangrove forests provide benefits for wildlife and people.
2 Do you think shrimp farming is a sustainable use of this ecosystem? Explain your point of view.

Activities

3 a) Use a suitable technique to represent the data in Figure 12.
   b) Describe the trends shown by your graph.
   c) What percentage of shrimp production came from aquaculture in:
      i) 2008
      ii) 2014?
4 Study the points of view in Figure 18.
   a) What are the long-term benefits of shrimp farming and who gets these benefits?
   b) What problems does shrimp farming create for:
      i) people
      ii) the environment?
   c) Discuss what consumers in the UK can do to help ensure that ecosystems (either mangroves or other ecosystems) are used sustainably.

▲ **Figure 16** A shrimp farm in Bangladesh.

Shrimp production (1,000s of metric tonnes)							
	2008	2009	2010	2011	2012	2013	2014
Wild	3,217	3,269	3,263	3,442	3,568	3,541	3,591
Aquaculture	3,400	3,532	3,629	4,046	4,168	4,320	4,581

▲ **Figure 17** Global shrimp production (2008–14) in 1,000s of metric tonnes.

Local people lose out because they can no longer use the timber or other resources available in the mangrove forest. Local fishermen have noticed a fall in the number of fish they catch. This may be because the mangroves are a nursery ground for young fish. Shrimp farming releases a lot of fertilisers and other chemicals into the environment. Fresh-water wells are polluted by these chemicals. These are problems that are likely to affect coastal communities for many years after the farms have been abandoned.

A local fisherman

People make quick profits from shrimp farming. However, after a few years ponds are abandoned because of disease and pollution. In Asia there are approximately 250,000 hectares of abandoned, polluted ponds where healthy forests once grew. This boom–bust cycle is about to be repeated in Latin America, Africa and the Pacific where shrimp farming is growing in popularity.

Economics expert

Enquiry

'Mangroves are a swampy wasteland. There is nothing wrong in clearing them away if it means jobs are created and poverty reduced.'
To what extent do you agree with this statement? Justify your point of view.

The biggest consumers of shrimp are the USA, Canada, Japan and Europe. Perhaps consumers will be able to influence what happens to mangroves if we demand to know more about how our food is produced. Then we might decide to only buy shrimps or other fish that have been farmed sustainably.

Consumer in the UK

▲ **Figure 18** Views on whether the use of mangroves for shrimp farming is sustainable.

How are tropical rainforests used for food production?

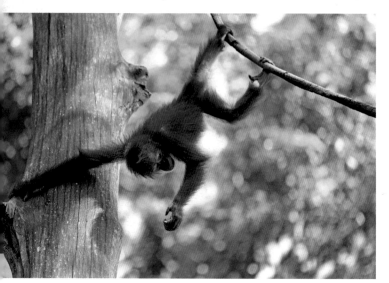

▲ **Figure 19** The Borneo orang-utan.

Global resources

Malaysia and Indonesia are newly industrialised countries (NICs). Their economies have grown as they have traded their natural resources and developed manufacturing industries. They have cashed in on the global demand for produce such as timber, fuel and food. Borneo's rainforests provide much needed timber, but at what cost? In 1985, 73.3 per cent of Borneo was covered in forest. By 2005, only 50.4 per cent was left. Many areas of rainforest have been cleared, destroying the homes of indigenous people, and the habitat of animals such as the orang-utan.

As the rainforest is cleared, it is replaced with crops such as oil palm. Global production of palm oil doubled between 1997 and 2008. Palm oil is a healthier alternative for other fats used in food and cooking. The desire to find greener fuels has led to oil palm being grown to produce biofuel. Oil palm plantations are a form of **monoculture** with a much lower biodiversity than the rainforest they replace.

Percentage	Use
71	Foods, e.g. margarine and processed foods such as cake, biscuits, chocolate
24	Consumer products, e.g. cosmetics and detergents
5	Fuel

▲ **Figure 21** How palm oil is used.

Borneo is an island in South East Asia, divided between Malaysia, Brunei and Indonesia. It has 1 per cent of the world's land area but 6 per cent of the world's species of wildlife. This makes Borneo an important **biodiversity hotspot**. The rainforest is thought to be 140 million years old and contains many thousands of species of plants and animals, some of which are now endangered, like the Borneo orang-utan.

▲ **Figure 20** The island of Borneo and the 'Heart of Borneo'.

Activity

1 a) Represent the data in Figure 21.
   b) Explain why palm oil production creates benefits for Malaysia and Indonesia.
   c) Outline the environmental and social problems created by palm oil production.

Enquiry

How much palm oil is in your home?

■ Design a survey that could be used to investigate the food ingredients and cleaning products that are commonly used in the UK that contain palm oil.
■ As part of your design, consider how you might question people about:
   a) their awareness of the issue
   b) their willingness to change their consumer behaviour.

Is palm oil good for Borneo?

Palm oil has higher yields and lower production costs than other oilseed crops, such as soybean and sunflower. It requires less fertiliser and pesticides and can be grown on small farms as well as large plantations.

Country	Metric tonnes
Colombia	1,100,000
Indonesia	35,000,000
Malaysia	21,000,000
Nigeria	970,000
Thailand	2,200,000
Others	4,895,000

▲ **Figure 22** Estimated world palm oil production 2015–16 (values in metric tonnes).

What about the rainforest?

Clearing the land and putting in infrastructure, such as roads and electricity supply, provides jobs and incomes, but often these go to migrant workers, and not the local communities. Many indigenous people, who rely on the rainforest for their food and homes, have been displaced. Animals can become isolated living in the fragments of habitat that are still intact between the oil palm plantations. The rapid decline in areas of the rainforest, especially through illegal logging, is a threat to many species of plants and animals. The loss of the rainforest can even change local weather patterns.

In 2007, the three countries of Malaysia, Brunei and Indonesia, along with NGO support, declared to conserve and manage the forest resources that are still largely undamaged in the central part of Borneo. This is the 'Heart of Borneo' and you can see the location of this forest in Figure 20. NGOs such as WWF and Greenpeace have campaigned to raise public awareness of the deforestation. They have encouraged multinational companies to support sustainable use of land for palm oil production. In 2015, 18 per cent of palm oil was produced using sustainable methods. In 2015, Colgate-Palmolive and Procter & Gamble both pledged to responsibly source **primary commodities** such as palm oil that are used in their products.

▲ **Figure 23** Plantations of oil palms. Sabah, Borneo Island, Malaysia.

▲ **Figure 24** Greenpeace Protect Paradise campaign.

Activities

2 Use Figure 22 to calculate the percentage of global palm oil production in:
   a) Malaysia
   b) Indonesia.
3 a) Use an atlas to locate the countries listed in Figure 22. Describe their distribution.
   b) Explain why most palm oil production is located in these countries.
4 a) Suggest why the oil palm plantations are not a suitable habitat for orang-utans.
   b) Suggest why tropical monocultures have much lower biodiversity than tropical rainforests.

How might climate change affect people and environments?

So far we have seen how our consumerism affects specific environments, such as the mangrove forests of South Asia. However, our ecological footprint also has a global impact: the emission of greenhouse gases. These gases cause climate change, a process we examined on pages 156–7. A warmer atmosphere is a more unstable one, meaning that wild weather events will become more common. A warmer atmosphere will mean that the air masses over oceans will have greater moisture content. For the UK, this is likely to mean milder and wetter weather with more frequent storms. Many scientists interviewed by the media during the winter storms of 2015–16 (pages 41–5) argued that the extreme rainfall was consistent with predictions of climate change. The 'Foresight Report' considered how climate change and growing populations might affect the UK by the year 2080. The main findings were:

- The number of people at high risk of flooding could rise from 1.5 million to 3.5 million.
- The economic cost of flood damage will rise. At the moment flooding costs the UK £1 billion a year. By 2080 it could cost as much as £27 billion.
- Towns and cities will be at risk of flash floods even if they are not built near a river. Drains that are supposed to carry rainwater away will not be able to cope with sudden downpours of rain. This kind of flooding could affect as many as 710,000 people.

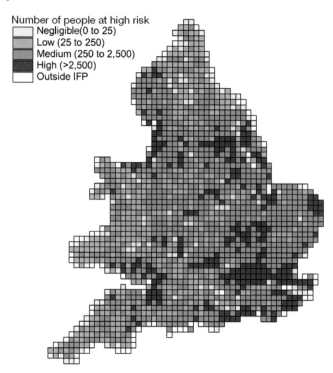

Number of people at high risk
- Negligible(0 to 25)
- Low (25 to 250)
- Medium (250 to 2,500)
- High (>2,500)
- Outside IFP

▲ **Figure 25** The number of people at risk of river and coastal floods in 2080, assuming that carbon dioxide emissions remain high.

Category 5: Over 250 kph. Complete failure of some smaller buildings. Failure of the roofs of large industrial buildings. Extensive coastal flooding damages the ground floor of many buildings.

Category 4: 211–250 kph. Complete destruction of the roofs of smaller buildings and more extensive damage to the walls. All signs and trees are blown down. Flooding of coastal areas 3 to 5 hours before the arrival of the storm may cut off escape routes.

Category 3: 178–210 kph. Severe damage to the roofs of small buildings. Some structural damage to walls. Mobile homes destroyed. Poorly constructed road signs destroyed. Large trees blown down.

Key
Predictions for 2080
◆ Number of hurricanes with extra levels of CO_2
◇ Number of hurricanes with today's level of CO_2

Lower air pressure and stronger winds

▲ **Figure 26** The National Oceanic and Atmospheric Administration (NOAA) has used computer models to predict the frequency and intensity of hurricanes (cyclones) in 2080.

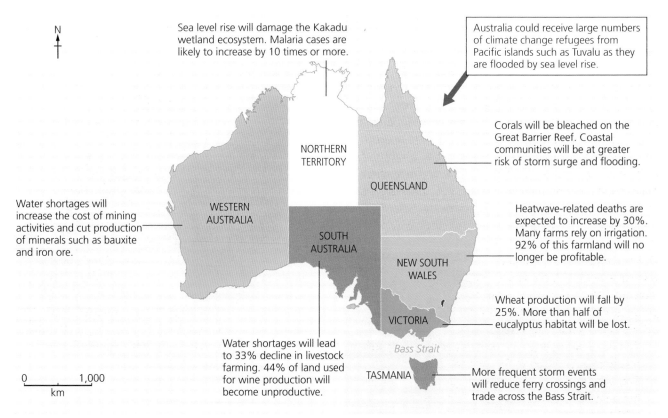

Sea level rise will damage the Kakadu wetland ecosystem. Malaria cases are likely to increase by 10 times or more.

Australia could receive large numbers of climate change refugees from Pacific islands such as Tuvalu as they are flooded by sea level rise.

Corals will be bleached on the Great Barrier Reef. Coastal communities will be at greater risk of storm surge and flooding.

Water shortages will increase the cost of mining activities and cut production of minerals such as bauxite and iron ore.

Heatwave-related deaths are expected to increase by 30%. Many farms rely on irrigation. 92% of this farmland will no longer be profitable.

Wheat production will fall by 25%. More than half of eucalyptus habitat will be lost.

Water shortages will lead to 33% decline in livestock farming. 44% of land used for wine production will become unproductive.

More frequent storm events will reduce ferry crossings and trade across the Bass Strait.

▲ **Figure 27** The predicted impacts of climate change on Australian states by 2100.

Australia is a vast country and the impacts of climate change are likely to be varied. The Australian Bureau of Meteorology warn that wild weather will be more common, with longer and more severe droughts affecting central and southern regions. Frequent tropical storms and stronger cyclones (see pages 163–5) could affect Australia's northern coastlines. Climate change means that areas of extremely low pressure will develop more frequently, as shown in Figure 26. Australia's famous Great Barrier Reef, on the tropical Queensland coast could be affected by bleaching – a process described on page 298.

Activities

1 Use Figure 25 to describe the distribution of areas where there are high numbers of people at risk of flooding.
2 Describe how climate change will have negative impacts for people, the economy and environment of the UK. Use evidence from pages 41–5 to help you.
3 Study Figure 26. Describe how the frequency and magnitude of hurricanes (cyclones) is expected to change.
4 Study Figure 27. Select three impacts and explain how climate change may cause these issues.

Enquiry

How serious is the threat of climate change in Australia?

- Select five impacts of climate change in Australia and place them in rank order. The top-ranked one should be the most problematic/serious impact.
- Justify your ranking.
- Suggest who should be responsible for trying to fix the most serious of these problems.

How will climate change affect tropical coastlines?

Reefs provide **key services** to coastal communities. They reduce wave energy by up to 97 per cent, which reduces coastal erosion and damage to coastal settlements. This is especially important during tropical storms or cyclones. Coral reefs contain a huge biodiversity. They provide a habitat for fish to spawn and a nursery environment for juvenile fish where they are relatively safe from predators. As such, reefs are a major source of commercial fish species. They are also a popular tourist attraction. Australia's Great Barrier Reef attracts over 2 million visitors each year.

Coral reefs are highly complex structures that are vulnerable to the effects of warmer air and ocean surface temperatures. The main effects are:
- **Coral bleaching** caused by higher than normal sea temperatures. This results in the **zooxanthellae** leaving the coral tissue, turning them white. Bleached corals are unhealthy and vulnerable to diseases such as blackband and white plague. Climate change is causing bleaching to occur more often and the reefs take longer to recover.
- Much of the carbon dioxide entering our atmosphere is dissolved in the oceans and, as this increases, the pH of the water becomes more acidic. **Ocean acidification** means corals are not able to absorb as much calcium carbonate so the reef becomes unhealthy and may dissolve.
- Rising sea levels caused by melting ice and thermal expansion of the ocean can make the water too deep for corals to receive adequate sunlight.
- More frequent tropical storms may damage already fragile coral reefs.

◄ **Figure 28** The bright colours of coral come from the zooxanthellae, which also provide them with nutrients and energy.

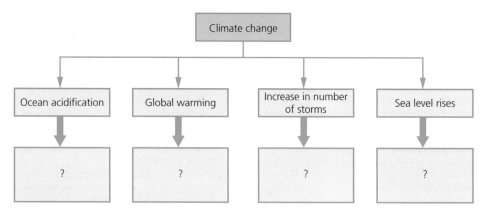

◄ **Figure 29** Impact of climate change on coral reefs.

Higher sea temperatures cause coral bleaching which weakens the structure

Deeper water leads to reduced amounts of sunlight and poorer water quality

Acidified water has lower pH levels which means less calcium carbonate is absorbed so coral skeletons dissolve faster

Delicate reef structures are damaged by heavy rain and run-off from the land

Activities

1 Describe three key services provided by coral reefs.
2 Make a copy of Figure 29. Add the labels (right) in their correct places to complete the diagram, summarising the effects of climate change on coral reefs.

How can we respond to climate change?

Since 1990 representatives of governments from around the world have met periodically to discuss the issue of climate change. The Kyoto Protocol (1997) is an international agreement that commits countries to targets to reduce greenhouse gas emissions. The latest version is the Paris Agreement (2015). The outcome of the Paris Agreement was a long-term aim to keep global warming to well below 2°C compared to pre-industrial levels.

However, the Paris Agreement recognises that countries can make cuts to emissions at different rates, depending on their level of economic development. Wealthy countries, such as Australia and the UK, should be able to make cuts by investing in new and renewable technologies. Some of these are described on pages 300–1. NICs such as India and China, however, have recently invested in coal-fired power stations. Even so, some parts of their populations do not have access to a reliable electricity supply. These countries want to continue to make economic progress. Doing so will mean further greenhouse gas emissions.

▲ **Figure 31** Patterns of solar energy across Europe and Africa (kilowatts/m²/year).

Activities

3 Use Figure 31 to describe the distribution of countries that have:
   a) between 1,100 and 1,400 kilowatts/m²/year
   b) more than 2,200 kilowatts/m²/year.

4 Using Figure 30, suggest the advantages and disadvantages of solar farms for the UK's economy and environment.

Enquiry

'European countries should adopt new technologies while NICs continue to emit greenhouse gases.'

To what extent do you agree with this statement? You should suggest:

■ a range of different new technologies that could be used in Europe
■ the reasons for and against allowing NICs to continue to emit greenhouse gases.

▲ **Figure 30** Solar farms in England, like this one, generate electricity using PV cells.

How can individuals and government reduce the risk of climate change?

The UK Government has an international role in combatting climate change. It is a signatory of the Doha Amendment and the Paris Agreement (2015). The outcome of the Paris Agreement was a long-term aim to keep global warming to well below 2°C compared to pre-industrial levels. The UK Government also works at a national scale. It provides targets for local government and works with industry to reduce greenhouse gas emissions by:

- investing in low-carbon energy sources;
- improving fuel standards in cars;
- increasing energy efficiency in new buildings.

Councils must publish a policy statement on climate change by law.

Figure 32 describes some of the ways in which Bristol City Council is trying to meet its own climate change targets.

Activity

1   Study Figure 32.
   a) Explain why ideas 5 and 7 will help Bristol meet its climate change target.
   b) Make a diamond nine diagram (like the one on page 83) and place the strategies from Figure 32 in the diagram, putting those that you think are essential at the top of the diagram.
   c) Justify your choice of the top three strategies.

	What will it do?	Why it helps
1	Warmer homes. £105 million will be spent fitting external wall insulation to homes (including blocks of flats).	£3.5 million could be saved each year on heating bills. Possible 5 per cent reduction in the amount of gas used. 17,900 tonnes of CO_2 saved each year.
2	Install district heating (or heat networks). These will duct spare heat between the university, the hospital and buildings in the city centre.	Heating buildings and hot water use are two of the main reasons for CO_2 emissions in large cities. District heating uses energy efficient boilers.
3	Lead by example. Improve the energy efficiency of council offices, the museum, library and two schools.	£500,000 energy saving and 2,000 tonnes of CO_2 saved each year.
4	High energy performance. Install efficient boilers in all new council buildings, including schools, care homes and council housing.	It is cheaper in the long term to install energy efficient technologies when buildings are new rather than trying to modify older buildings.
5	Solar photovoltaic programme. Two solar farms were constructed in 2014 at a cost of £35.9 million.	
6	Metro-bus scheme. Build 6 km of new roads, 18 km of new bus lanes and purchase 50 new hybrid vehicles.	Shift passengers from car to bus to reduce congestion and CO_2 emissions from commuter traffic.
7	Sustainable transport. Invest in 10 km of cycle lanes and promote cycling and walking for people aged 8–80.	
8	Land use planning. Locating new homes to reduce the need for commuting and allow the use of district heating.	Future proof new housing developments by making them sustainable.
9	Improve mass transit. Spend £90 million improving suburban train services.	Improve air quality and transport safety. Reduce congestion and CO_2 emissions.

▲ **Figure 32** How Bristol City Council hopes to meet its targets to reduce CO_2 emissions.

Collecting qualitative data

Some geographical data is easily quantified – meaning that it is easy to measure and record an actual number. Examples include pedestrian counts or the number of vacant shops in a high street. Other useful data is difficult to quantify: other people's opinions, for example, on their views about leading a low-carbon lifestyle. This is **qualitative data** and it can be collected in a number of ways:

- in a lengthy interview
- using a questionnaire
- with a quick survey such as a Likert scale.

If you are designing a questionnaire it is a good idea to have examples of both closed and open questions. Closed questions have set answers which you can tick.

For example: How do you get to school?

Walk [ ]   Cycle [ ]   Bus [ ]   Car [ ]

An open question is where people can give their own unstructured answer, e.g. How do you think the school could reduce its GHG emissions?

A **Likert scale** is where people are asked to use a scale when responding to a question.

Only offshore wind farms should be developed in future			
1	2	3	4
Agree	Slightly agree	Slightly disagree	Disagree

▲ **Figure 33** An example of a Likert scale.

Question, with responses measured on a Likert scale of 1–10 (1 = not at all seriously and 10 = very seriously)	Mean score
How seriously do you regard the threat of climate change?	7.5
How effective do you think that individuals can be in reducing the threat of climate change?	4.5

▲ **Figure 34** An example of a climate change enquiry.

A group of geography students were interested in investigating how people of different ages are responding to climate change. They set an enquiry question:

Are younger people more willing to change their lifestyles than older people?

As part of their enquiry, they used a Likert Survey with 100 people. They also asked the respondents to tick up to five things that they already do (as individuals) to help reduce the threat of climate change. The results are shown below.

Possible actions that individuals can take	Number of responses
Use low-energy bulbs	82
Choose energy-efficient goods	57
Improve insulation for the home	53
Recycle all plastics, glass, etc.	89
Lower the thermostat settings for heating	23
Walk or cycle to avoid using the car	2
Use public transport	17
Buy locally produced food	11

▲ **Figure 35** Possible actions that individuals can take.

Activities

2. Show one way you would represent each of the data sets from the survey. Justify your choice.
3. What conclusions can you draw from the responses given?
4. Suggest two other questions you could ask to investigate individual attitudes to climate change.
5. Explain why data representation and data analysis are easier if closed rather than open questions are asked in questionnaires.
6. Suggest an open question that you might ask. Explain why this open question would reveal useful information about how individuals feel about climate change.

Can the tourist industry reduce its impact on the environment?

In 2012 the number of tourists passed the 1 billion mark for the first time in history. We saw in Theme 6 that tourism can have huge impacts on the economies of many developing countries. Tourism can have negative, as well as positive, impacts on the people and communities who are visited, however. Travel emits greenhouse gases and tourism generates waste products as well as increasing demands on resources such as water, food and energy. So, how can these negative impacts of tourism be reduced?

Ideally, tourism should be sustainable, meaning that it should have long-lasting benefits. However, for tourism to be developed sustainably it needs to satisfy several conflicting needs. These are summarised in Figure 1.

Local people need to benefit. This may take the form of new jobs and better pay. Where poverty is widespread it should also provide better basic services such as clean water, sewage treatment systems and schools for local people.

The environment (including wildlife/ ecosystems) should not be damaged so much by the growth of tourism that it cannot recover.

The growth of tourism should not create problems for future generations of local people. For example, if the development of tourism uses more clean water than can be replaced by natural processes then tourism is unsustainable.

The growth of tourism should not create so many problems that tourists soon stop coming (because the environment has been spoilt).

▲ **Figure 1** The conflicting demands of sustainable tourism.

Ecotourism

Ecotourism is tourism that has very low environmental impacts. Ecotourism supports the conservation of habitats and wildlife. In some cases this means that money generated by tourism helps to fund conservation projects. In other cases, the tourists are volunteers who become involved in conservation while they are on holiday – sometimes known as voluntourism.

Ethical tourism and responsible travel

Ethical tourism and responsible travel are concepts used to describe sustainable forms of tourism. **Ethical tourism** means that the needs of local people are considered. It means that local beliefs, traditions and customs are respected and conserved. Ethical tourism also aims to reduce the negative impacts of the industry on the environment. **Responsible travel** has a similar meaning. Local families benefit economically from jobs and services that are created by ethical tourism and responsible travel.

▼ **Figure 2** Tourism can have several negative impacts on the environment.

Activities

1 Outline at least three different environmental impacts of tourism. Use Figure 2 to help you.
2 Use Figure 4 to describe the distribution of conservation areas in Limpopo.
3 Explain what it is meant by the phrase 'diversify the rural economy'.

Wildlife tourism in Limpopo, South Africa

Limpopo Province, South Africa, has a semi-arid climate and largely unspoilt savanna ecosystem that is a major tourist attraction. Farming, ecotourism and game reserves are the largest employers in Limpopo. However, most jobs in these industries are low skilled and poorly paid. Unemployment is high – as much as 37 per cent in some rural areas. The climate makes farming difficult and incomes are low. There is an urgent need to **diversify** the rural economy: this means creating a variety of new jobs that are not necessarily connected to farming. One option is the creation of jobs in ecotourism.

District in Limpopo	Population	Population with piped water (%)	Households with electricity (%)
Mutale	91,870	27	8
Lephalale	115,767	67	70

▲ **Figure 3** Percentage of the population who have access to piped water and electricity in selected rural districts of Limpopo.

▲ **Figure 4** Conservation areas in Limpopo.

South African and foreign tourists already visit a number of sites in Limpopo, most notably the Kruger National Park in the east of the province. The Waterberg Biosphere Reserve in Lephalale is another popular destination. The reserve contains 75 mammal species (including the big five: lion, leopard, rhino, buffalo and elephant) and 300 species of bird. About 80,000 people live in the reserve. Tourists visiting Waterberg create jobs in a variety of ways. They pay to stay with local families or in luxury lodges that employ cleaners, cooks and bar staff. Local people are also employed to act as tour guides and wardens in the reserve.

Game ranching is one way that wealthy land owners are creating new incomes and managing wildlife. It involves the capture of wild animals, such as the buffalo in Figure 5, and transferring these animals to wildlife reserves as breeding stock where they can be protected from illegal poaching. In this way the population of these wild animals has gradually been rising.

A limited amount of hunting by tourists is then allowed. The main income comes from tourists who pay large sums of money to shoot antelope, buffalo and other wild animals. The meat is sold in South Africa, generating more income. This money is then used to pay for conservation projects such as breeding programmes, habitat conservation and anti-poaching patrols.

▲ **Figure 5** A darted buffalo is lifted on to a truck on a private farm near Lephalale; after medical checks it will be sold to a breeder.

Activities

4 Calculate the actual number of people in Mutale and Lephalale who do not have access to piped water and electricity.
5 Explain how a new ecotourism project in Mutale or Lephalale could:
   a) improve standards of living for local people
   b) conserve wildlife.

Enquiry

'All hunting in South Africa should be banned.'

To what extent do you agree with this statement?

- Discuss whether hunting by tourists can be considered to be a form of ethical tourism.
- Outline the arguments for and against the controlled hunting of wild animals in South Africa as part of an ecotourism project.

The impact of tourism on water supply

Tourism places a high demand on local water resources. Water is needed for food preparation, cleaning hotels, laundry of sheets and towels, and keeping hotel gardens watered and swimming pools full. A lot of water is also used to keep golf courses green – an especially big problem in hot, dry climates such as those of Mediterranean holiday destinations.

Data on water consumption by the tourist industry is not collected at a national scale, so those who research this issue need to base their work on estimates. A recent study by the Travel Foundation concluded that tourism uses more water than local residents – their findings are summarised in Figure 7.

Is preventing the development of golf courses the answer?

Saint Lucia is a Caribbean island that depends heavily on mass tourism for income. It is estimated that a huge 33 per cent of its fresh water supplies are used by the tourist industry and a further 6 per cent are used to irrigate golf courses to keep them green.

Region	Amount of water used by tourists compared to local residents (%)
Mediterranean	150–200
Caribbean (except Jamaica)	150–200
Jamaica	400–1,000
North Africa (e.g. Tunisia)	400–1,000
Kenya	1,800–2,000
Sri Lanka	1,800–2,000

▲ **Figure 7** Water consumption by tourists compared to local residents; 200 per cent means that tourists use twice as much water as locals.

▲ **Figure 8** A cruise ship moored in Castries.

▲ **Figure 6** Location of Le Paradis and the location of other golf courses in Saint Lucia.

Activities

1. a) Explain why the tourist industry uses more water than local residents.
    b) Suggest two ways that the tourist industry could reduce its water use.
2. a) Represent the data in Figure 7 using a suitable graph or pictogram.
    b) Suggest why water consumption is so much higher in some tourist destinations.
3. Use Figure 6 to describe the:
    a) distribution of golf courses in Saint Lucia
    b) location of Le Paradis resort and golf club
4. Outline at least two ways in which the development of Le Paradis may not have been sustainable. Use Figure 1 on page 302 to help you.
5. Explain the limitations of cruise tourism for the economy of Saint Lucia (see pages 229 and 231 to help you).
6. Describe the benefits of saving the remaining mangrove in Praslin Bay (use Figure 15 on page 292 to help you).

The Atlantic coast of Saint Lucia is largely undeveloped for tourism. Developers bought 200 hectares of land in Praslin Bay to build a luxury resort and golf course called Le Paradis. Local campaigners protested about the destruction of mangrove forest and dry tropical rainforest but the development began. It was scheduled to be completed in 2007 but the developers ran out of money and the project has never been completed – the empty shells of the resort are still unfinished in 2016.

▲ **Figure 9** The remaining area of mangrove forest in Praslin Bay. Most mangrove was destroyed when the resort was built; the remaining area is under threat if the development is completed.

▲ **Figure 10** The abandoned Le Paradis complex in 2010.

Saint Lucia government spokesperson

We want the owner of the site to drop their asking price so that another developer can buy the project and complete it. The project includes a hotel, marina for small yachts and a luxury golf course. Completing the project will create much-needed jobs in the east of the island.

Local resident and forest worker

The planned golf course would destroy a dry tropical woodland habitat that is home to rare endemic birds of the thrush family. I work for the forest authorities and as an ecotourism guide in my spare time. If the golf course goes ahead Saint Lucia's biodiversity will be damaged further and I may get less work.

Local resident

I do not want the golf course to be completed. A few hundred families live in Praslin Bay. Our water comes from the stream and boreholes. The water table drops in the summer months and I am worried that our borehole will run dry if water is used to irrigate the golf course.

▲ **Figure 11** Conflicting attitudes towards the development of Le Paradis resort.

Enquiry

Do you think that Le Paradis resort and golf course should be completed? Justify your decision.

Sustainable management of the Great Barrier Reef Marine Park

The Great Barrier Reef Marine Park in northern Australia was established in 1975. It was the first coral reef ecosystem to be given UNESCO World Heritage Status in 1981. It is now considered to be one of the best managed marine ecosystems in the world. As well as being important for its biodiversity, protection is given to more than 70 Aboriginal and other groups whose traditions and culture are under threat from development. The area also has many places of historical significance including lighthouses and shipwrecks. The Marine Park attracts over 2 million tourists a year as well as 5 million recreational users.

▲ **Figure 12** The location of the Great Barrier Reef Marine Park.

Zone	What is and isn't allowed
Preservation	No one can enter without written permission.
Marine National Park	Fishing and oyster collecting are not allowed. Boating, swimming, snorkelling and sailing are allowed.
Scientific research	For scientific study. Members of the public are usually not allowed.
Buffer	Some fishing is allowed. The public are allowed to enjoy the natural environment in this zone.
Conservation park	Only a limited amount of fishing is allowed.
Habitat protection	Sensitive and vulnerable habitats are protected from damaging activities.
General use	Trawling is not allowed. Crabbing, boating, diving, photography, line fishing and trawling are all allowed.

▲ **Figure 13** Zones of the Great Barrier Reef Marine Park to the east of Gladstone.

How is the park managed?

The Great Barrier Reef Marine Park has been divided into different **management zones**. A zoning plan identifies which activities are permitted in each zone. The aim is to separate uses of the ecosystem that might conflict with each other. The level of protection increases from General Use Zone up to the most restrictive Preservation Zone. At honeypots like Cairns and the Whitsunday Islands, there are special management plans. Boat length and visitor group size are restricted to prevent overcrowding of these vulnerable locations. There is also a joint programme of education and enforcement with the Queensland Parks and Wildlife Service. Every five years the Great Barrier Reef Outlook Report is published and from this, a detailed management plan is produced. Reef 2050 is the latest long-term sustainability plan.

▲ **Figure 14** The dugong, a large marine mammal sometimes known as the sea cow.

Is zoning effective?

Zoning the reef protects the unique marine animals, plants and habitats, as well as threatened species like the green turtle and dugong. Industries that rely on the reef, such as fishing and tourism, can continue. This provides social and economic benefits to local communities and the national economy. Wider benefits include opportunities for recreational, cultural, educational and scientific research into coral reef ecosystems. Research from the latest report has shown that fish numbers and average size are increasing. Coral trout is now 50 per cent more abundant. Bigger fish mean more eggs, and increasing numbers in closed areas mean the fish population can spill into other zones.

▲ **Figure 15** The green turtle is threatened by habitat loss, the wildlife trade, fishing for its meat and accidental drowning in fishing nets.

Activities

1 Why do you think the Great Barrier Reef Marine Park was given World Heritage Status?
2 Explain why it needs to be managed.
3 a) Describe how the Marine Park zoning system works.
   b) Explain why the system is an example of sustainable management.
4 Describe the advantages and disadvantages of the zoning system for each of the following groups of people:
   a) fishermen
   b) research scientists
   c) divers and tourists.

Enquiry

Do you think that such a zoning system would work in a National Park in England and Wales such as Snowdonia or the Norfolk Broads?

Weigh up the benefits and problems of such a system. Support your answer by referring to a particular National Park in the UK.

Why should we restore ecosystems?

China has 53 million hectares of wetland. Wetland ecosystems are sometimes described as the kidneys of the Earth because they store and filter water. In this way they protect people from floods and help to sustain a clean supply of drinking water. But wetlands in China are vulnerable to damage by farming and urban growth. A survey in 2014 showed that 60 per cent of China's wetlands were in very poor or relatively poor condition. We saw on pages 186–7 how and why wetland and moorland ecosystems in the UK are now being restored. Similar projects are happening in other parts of the world, including in Heilongjiang Province in China. Here, a mixture of wetland restoration, tree planting and ecotourism projects has helped to improve biodiversity and increase local incomes.

53 per cent of the 8 million population are farmers.

10,090 hectares of trees have been planted.

6 bird reserves have been created.

39,769 hectares of woodland is managed.

3,441 hectares of farmland have been converted back to wetland.

▲ **Figure 18** Sanjiang Plain restoration project in numbers.

▲ **Figure 16** Tourists taking a boat trip on the Ussuri River in the Sanjiang wetlands.

▲ **Figure 17** The location of the Sanjiang wetlands.

The Sanjiang Plain, in Heilongjiang, is a huge wetland ecosystem of natural marshes, water meadows and forests. These habitats flood seasonally. They naturally support a wide biodiversity, especially of ducks and geese. Years of digging ditches and straightening rivers had destroyed 4.32 million hectares of wetlands – 80 per cent of this ecosystem's original extent.

Activities

1 Use Figure 17 to describe the location of Heilongjiang Province.
2 Describe the features that make the landscape of Figure 16 distinctive.

In 2005 a ten-year project began to restore the wetlands, increase biodiversity and increase local incomes through tourism. The project, which cost in excess of US$30 million, focused on the restoration of six large wetland bird reserves. Field ditches were blocked so that the water table would rise – recreating ponds and water meadows. Thousands of hectares of trees were planted around the edge of the reserves. This meant that there was less land available for farming, so the project has supported farmers to diversify into ecotourism. Some farmers now keep bees and sell the honey to tourists. Others are involved as guides for tourists on bird-watching holidays. Greenhouses were built so that farmers can earn more money from much smaller amounts of land, releasing land for conservation. Farmers involved in conservation can now earn up to 40 times more than before.

The project has run campaigns to raise public awareness of the value of conservation. Wetland conservation has been introduced to the curriculum in local schools. The reserves are monitored by patrols and CCTV cameras to try to prevent illegal farming, fishing and hunting.

Impacts of the Sanjiang wetlands project

Li Yuanwen was anxious and unhappy when local government authorities told him to quit farming a piece of land in the Zhenbaodao reserve in Heilongjiang Province in the northeast of the People's Republic of China (PRC).

For twelve years, he had been earning $3,300 to $6,500 a year growing corn, soybean and rice on a twenty-hectare plot he had developed on vacant land, even though it was in one of 24 officially designated nature reserves on the vast alluvial Sanjiang floodplain.

His fears proved to be unfounded. Yuanwen now works as a salaried custodian of a new ecotourism area in the Zhenbaodao reserve where visitors come to fish, boat, hike, camp and watch birds. His income, further increased by eco-friendly beekeeping and the sale of honey and mushrooms to tourists, is far greater than in his best years of farming.

Zhiang Liang had been growing corn on ten hectares of altered nature reserve for six years when his plot was incorporated into the restoration project. He now produces tomatoes in three greenhouses that occupy no more than 1,050 m^2 of space – less than one per cent of what he cultivated before – but his income has risen from $4,410 to $6,860 a year.

Official monitoring of birds in the six nature reserves has shown an increase in their numbers from 510,559 in 2008 to 683,612 in 2011. In the Qixinghe reserve, scientist Cui Shoubin, who has been tracking the egret population, has seen it rise from 600 in 2011 to more than 1,000 in 2014.

Shoubin is delighted that the nature reserves are being visited by more tourists and scientists. 'I'm convinced that what we're finding out in wetland management and the work we're doing on the habitats of rare migratory birds is important not just for the Sanjiang Plain and the PRC but for the whole world.'

▲ **Figure 19** Text extract from a Chinese website describing the Sanjiang wetlands project.

Activities

3   Explain why it was necessary to:
  a) diversify jobs so that incomes could be increased
  b) involve local communities in campaigns and education programmes.
4   Describe the main advantages of the Sanjiang Project for:
  a) local environments and wildlife
  b) local communities.
5   Suggest how the project may help:
  a) communities living downstream (pages 186–7 may help you)
  b) the global environment.

 www.wwt.org.uk – the website of the Wildfowl and Wetland Trust in the UK.

Enquiry

Who should conserve habitats in the UK?

- Use the weblink to the Wildfowl and Wetland Trust and follow links to the London Wetland Centre. This wetland habitat has been restored.
- How is the centre used for conservation and tourism?
- Who is responsible?

Abrasion – Erosion, or wearing away, of the landscape caused by friction. Abrasion occurs when rivers or waves are carrying sand or pebbles. The water uses these materials to do the work of erosion.

Abstraction – When water is taken from a river, reservoir or underground source to be used it is abstracted.

Aerosol – Tiny particles of dust, volcanic ash and gas in the atmosphere that can reflect the Sun's energy back into space.

Afforestation – The planting of forests.

Ageing population – A country which has a high proportion of people aged over 65 is said to have an ageing population.

Agribusinesses – Farming that is organised by large businesses – often by multinational companies.

Agro-forestry – A type of farming in which a mixture of crop, shrubs, fruit trees and nut trees are grown.

Air mass – A large parcel of air in the atmosphere. All parts of the air mass have similar temperature and moisture content at ground level.

Annual regime – The way in which a river's discharge varies throughout the year.

Anomalies – Evidence that does not fit the general trend.

Anticyclone – A high pressure system in the atmosphere associated with dry, settled periods of weather.

Aquaculture – The commercial farming of fish and shellfish.

Aquifers – Rocks in the ground that are capable of holding large quantities of water.

Aseismic – A description of buildings that are designed to withstand the shaking during an earthquake.

Ash cloud – Powdered rock fragments thrown from a volcano during an explosive eruption.

Aspect – The direction in which a slope or other feature faces.

Asylum seekers – People who move from one country to another because they are in danger or because they are persecuted because of their religion or political views.

Attrition – A type of erosion where rocks smash against each other making them smaller and more rounded.

Average life expectancy – The average age someone can expect to live to. Average life expectancy is usually calculated separately for men and women.

Backwash – The flow of water back into the sea after a wave has broken on a beach.

Bi-lateral aid – Financial support, or the gift of food, clothing or other emergency support, that is given directly from the government of one country to another.

Biodiversity – The variety of living things.

Biodiversity hotspot – A region with a particularly great variety of organisms. Central America (or Meso-America) is one such hotspot.

Biomes – Very large ecosystems e.g. tropical rainforests or deserts.

Birth rate – The number of children born in one year for every 1,000 people in a country's population.

Bivariate data – Two sets of numbers that are linked by some kind of relationship.

Braided – A river pattern made when a shallow river has deposited gravel islands so that the river is split into several smaller channels. From above the river looks a little like platted (or braided) hair.

Break in slope – A line on a slope where the gradient changes.

BRICs – Brazil, Russia, India, China, Mexico. Large and growing economies that contribute to global patterns of trade and interdependence.

Brownfield site – A development site where older buildings are demolished or renovated before a new development takes place.

Buffer zone – Part of a conservation area in which some activities, such as farming and tourism, may be allowed.

Built environments – Places which are dominated by human structures rather than natural landscapes. Towns and cities are examples of built environments.

Caldera – A huge hollow in the earth's surface caused by the collapse of a volcano after a massive eruption.

Canopy – The upper layer of a forest. The canopy receives most sunlight so contains many leaves, flowers and fruit.

Capacity – The ability of a group of people to withstand a problem such as a natural disaster. Capacity is the opposite of **vulnerability**.

Carbon sinks – Places where carbon is stored over very long periods of time, for example in fossil fuels.

Carrying capacity – The ability of a landscape or ecosystem to absorb the activity of people without any lasting damage. Some ecosystems have larger carrying capacities than others.

Central Business District (CBD) – The area of a town or city in which most shops and offices are clustered together.

Chawl – The name for a type of flat or tenement building found in many Indian cities.

Choropleth – A type of map that uses different colours or shades to represent data shown in areas of the map.

Cinder cone – A volcanic hill that is conical in shape. A cinder cone is formed by the eruption of red hot lava that is thrown from the vent. The globs of lava are full of gas bubbles. They solidify to form pebble-sized fragments of rock that have the texture of honeycomb.

Commuting – The regular (daily or weekly) movement of workers from their home in one place to their work in a different place.

Constructive plate margin – A boundary between two plates of the Earth's crust which are moving away from one another. The term **divergence zone** has the same meaning. See **destructive plate margin** for the opposite type of plate boundary.

Consumers – A name used to describe people in wealthy economies who buy and use food, resources, energy and other stuff.

Control – A sample or experiment to set the standard with which other samples can be compared.

Convection – A process by which hot liquids or gases rise and then spread apart before cooling and sinking. Convection occurs in the atmosphere and also in the mantle where it may be one process that helps to drive plate movement.

Coral bleaching – A process which results in zooxanthellae being forced out of the tissue of corals, turning the colourful corals white. The process occurs when the temperature of sea water increases.

Coriolis Effect – The way in which the rotation of the Earth deflects the movement of objects such as airplanes or hurricanes.

Corrosion – The wearing away of the landscape by chemical processes such as solution.

Counter-urbanisation – The movement of people and businesses from large cities to smaller towns and rural areas.

Cumecs – An abbreviation of cubic metres per second – which is a measure of the **discharge** of a river.

Cyclone – A low pressure system in the atmosphere associated with unsettled weather, wind and rain.

Dependency – When a country relies too heavily on one way of earning foreign income. For example, some Caribbean countries rely too much on money from tourism.

Dependent variable – A set of data whose values depend on another set of data which is the independent variable. The relationship may be tested in a **scattergraph**.

Depopulation – The net loss of people from an area due to outward migration and low birth rates.

Deposition – The laying down of material in the landscape. Deposition occurs when the force that was carrying the sediment is reduced.

Depression (weather) – A weather system associated with low air pressure. Depressions bring changeable weather that includes rain and windy conditions.

Deprivation – To lack features, such as employment or basic services, which are usually regarded as necessary for a reasonable standard of living.

Destructive plate margin – A boundary between two plates of the Earth's crust which are moving towards one another. See **constructive plate margin** for the opposite type of boundary.

Development aid – Help which is given to tackle poverty and improve quality of life over the long term to improve education or health care.

Direct employment – Jobs that are created within a business. For example, direct employment is created for baggage handlers if a new airport is constructed. See **indirect employment**.

Discharge – The amount of water flowing through a river channel or out of an aquifer. Discharge is measured in cubic metres per second (cumecs).

Divergence zones – A boundary between two plates of the Earth's crust which are moving away from one another. The term **constructive plate margin** has the same meaning.

Diversify – Where a much wider variety of new business opportunities and jobs are created in a region.

Drainage basin – The area a river collects its water from. This is also called a catchment area.

Drought – A long period of time with little precipitation.

Drought-resistant – Plants that are able to survive periods with below average rainfall.

Ecological footprint – The amount of land that is needed to support a person's lifestyle.

Economic migrants – People who move to another country in search of work. Economic migrants are sometimes encouraged to move by the host country in which case they are known as guest workers.

Ecosystem – A community of plants and animals and the environment in which they live. Ecosystems include both living parts (e.g. plants) and non-living parts (e.g. air and water).

Ecotourism – Small scale tourist projects that create money for conservation as well as creating local jobs.

Embedded – The amount of water or energy that is required to make a product.

Emergency aid – Help that is given urgently after a natural disaster or a conflict to protect the lives of the survivors.

Emerging middle class – The growing number of people in developing countries who are well educated and reasonably well paid.

Empower – To create opportunities for a disadvantaged group in society so that they have the ability to help themselves.

Endemic – An endemic disease is one that is often found amongst people in a particular place. An endemic species (of plant or animal) is one that is found in a certain place.

Enivronmental refugees – People who have to flee their homes because of a natural disaster such as coastal floods, drought or climate change.

Epicentre – The place on the surface of the Earth that experiences ground shaking from an earthquake first. The epicentre is directly above the focus.

Escarpment – A long, steep-sided slope. The term is often shortened to scarp. **Rift valleys** usually have steep escarpments on either side.

Ethical tourism – Tourism that benefits local people and which respects their culture, environment, beliefs and traditions.

E-waste – Electronic waste products such as computers and mobile phones.

Fallow period – A term used in agriculture to describe the period of time during which a piece of land is allowed to rest between crops.

Fertility rate – The average number of children born to each woman in a country. If the fertility rate is greater than two, the population will grow.

Fetch – The distance over which wind has blown to create waves on the sea. The greater the fetch, the larger the waves.

Flash floods – Flooding caused by a sudden downpour of rain. The rain falls so quickly it cannot soak into the ground.

Floodplain – The flat area beside a river channel that is covered in water during a flood event.

Focus – The underground point from which energy spreads during an earthquake.

Fold mountains – Large mountain ranges that have been formed by folding as two tectonic plates collide into one another.

Food miles – How far the food has been transported to get from producer to consumer.

Foreign direct investment – An investment of money by a company in a development, such as a new factory, located in another country.

Formal occupations – Jobs that receive a regular wage and which are recognised and controlled by the state.

Fractures – Cracks in the Earth's crust or in rocks at the surface that are often formed by plate movement or volcanic activity.

Free trade – When countries trade without any limits to the amount of goods that can be exported and imported

Garden cities – New, planned urban areas (towns) that have village-like communities and plenty of space for private gardens and public open space.

Geochemical (monitoring) – Scientific research into the Earth's chemistry by measuring gases that escape from the ground. This research may be used to check volcanic activity before and during an eruption.

Geomagnetic (monitoring) – Scientific research into the Earth's magnetic field. This research may be used to check volcanic activity before and during an eruption.

Geyser – A geothermal feature of volcanic landscapes in which groundwater, heated by hot rocks, is ejected from the ground.

Glacials – Cold periods in Earth's history when glaciers have advanced and ice sheets increased in size.

Global cities – Cities that are well connected by the process of globalisation. For example, global cities are usually important transport hubs with major airports and ports. They often have headquarters for **multinational companies**.

Globalisation – Flows of people, ideas, money and goods are making an increasingly complex global web that links people and places from distant continents together.

Gorge – A steep-sided, narrow valley. Gorges are often found below a waterfall.

Graben – A valley with a wide, flat bottom that has been formed by downward faulting. The term **rift valley** has the same meaning.

Green belt – A government policy used to prevent the spread of cities into the countryside. It is very difficult to get planning permission for new homes in a green belt.

Greenfield site – A plot of land that has not been used before for building.

Greenhouse gases (GGs) – Gases such as carbon dioxide and methane that are able to trap heat in the atmosphere.

Gross national income (GNI) per person – The average income in a country. It is also known as gross national product (GNP) per person.

Groundwater (store) – Water in the ground below the water table.

Groundwater flow – The flow of water through rocks.

Gulleys – Narrow, V-shaped channels cut by running water on steep slopes.

Hard engineering – Artificial structures such as sea walls or concrete river embankments.

Hazard map – A type of plan or map that shows the extent of a hazard such as flood risk or danger of volcanic eruption.

Hazard mapping – Plotting the predicted levels of risk of a natural hazard, such as a volcanic eruption, on to a map.

Hierarchy – The rank order of places, from hamlets to towns to cities.

Highly skilled – Workers who have high levels of qualification or technical ability and training. See **unskilled workers**.

Honey pot site – A place of special interest that attracts many tourists and is often congested at peak times.

Host countries – Countries that receive investment from multinational companies.

Human Development Index (HDI) – A measure of development that takes into account a country's level of education, its wealth and average life expectancy.

Hydraulic action – Erosion caused when water and air are forced into gaps in rock or soil.

Hydrograph – A line graph that shows either the discharge or height of a river over time.

Hypothesis – An idea or theory that can be investigated.

Identity – The features (e.g. social, cultural or landscape) that give each place its distinctive character.

Impermeable – Soil or rock which does not allow water to pass through it, such as clay.

Import duty – A tax placed on goods brought into a country to make them more expensive.

Imports – The purchase of goods from another country.

Independent travel – When tourists make their own holiday arrangements rather than buying a package holiday from a travel agent.

Independent variable – A set of data whose values stand alone and are not altered by other sets of data. See **dependent variable**.

Indigenous peoples – Tribal groups who are native to a particular place.

Indirect employment – Jobs that come as a result of the investment by a business but not within the business itself. For example, indirect employment is created for existing taxi drivers if a new airport is constructed.

Infant mortality rate (IMR) – The number of children who die before the age of one for every 1,000 that are born.

Infiltration – The movement of rain water or snow melt into the soil.

Informal sector (informal jobs) – The sector of the economy that includes many types of irregular jobs as well as types of work such as household chores, child care, and studying.

Infrastructure – The basic structures and services needed by any society such as water supplies, sewage systems, roads or bridges.

Inner-urban – The inner-most parts of a town or city. Inner-urban places are surrounded by the suburbs.

Intensive – Farming that needs the input of a lot of labour and food stuffs, pesticides or fertilisers.

Inter-glacials – Warmer periods in Earth's history when glaciers have retreated and ice sheets have decreased in size.

Interlocking spurs – A feature of V-shaped valleys where the river meanders from side to side so that the hillsides interlock rather like the teeth of a zip.

Intermediate technology – Technology that is appropriate for use in a developing country because it does not need expensive parts or high-tech repairs.

Intertidal zone – The part of the shoreline that is between high tide and low tide.

Intertropical convergence zone (ITCZ) – A broad band of atmosphere that circles the tropical latitudes. The ITCZ is characterised by low pressure, cloud and heavy rain.

Jet stream – A strong wind that circulates around the Earth.

Key services – The way in which ecosystems provide benefits for people. For example, mangrove forests act as coastal buffers, soaking up wave energy during a storm and reducing the risk of erosion and flooding.

Kite diagram – A special type of graph, in the shape of a kite, which is typically used to show changes in vegetation.

Knowledge economy – Jobs that require high levels of education or training.

Lag time – The time delay between a rain event and the maximum (peak) discharge.

Lagoon – A shallow pond of salt water

Lahar – An Indonesian word that describes a flood of water and volcanic ash or a mudslide down the slope of a volcano. Lahars are caused when rainwater mixes with loose volcanic ash. Lahars are very dangerous hazards.

Landlocked – A country that has no coastline and, therefore, has no sea ports. Many of the world's poorest countries are landlocked.

Landslide – The sudden collapse of a hillside under its own weight. Landslides are sometimes triggered by an earthquake or by erosion at the foot of the slope.

Lateral erosion – The process by which a river can cut sideways into its own river bank.

Lava field – A very large, rather flat landform that is created when a large lava flow solidifies. Lava fields are usually formed by the eruption of lava from a shield volcano or a fissure eruption.

Lava flows – Features formed as molten rock (lava) runs away from a volcanic vent. Lava flows often form large flat features known as **lava fields**.

Lava tube – A natural tunnel through solidified volcanic rocks that is formed when hot lava flows just below the surface of the ground.

Leakage – When money, spent by tourists, benefits companies in other countries rather than people working in the country that the tourists are visiting.

Leeward side – The side of a hill or mountain that is sheltered from the wind.

Life cycle analysis – A way of trying to determine the full impact of every stage of the manufacture and delivery of consumer goods.

Likert Scale – A type of survey. Those who answer the survey respond by agreeing or disagreeing with the statements, or by giving a score (e.g. out of 10).

Line of best fit – A line that represents the trend through the points plotted on a scattergraph.

Load – The sediment carried by a river.

Long-haul (flights) – Flights to distant places. Long-haul flights from the UK go to locations outside of Europe.

Longshore drift – A process by which beach material is moved along the coast.

Low Elevation Coastal Zone (LECZ) – Flat, low-lying land close to the sea that could be at risk of coastal flooding or sea level rise.

Magma – Molten, or semi-molten, rock that is stored beneath the Earth's surface in, for example, a **magma chamber** beneath a volcano.

Magma chamber – A hollow or cavern beneath a volcano that contains hot, molten rock.

Magnitude – A description of the strength and scale of natural hazards such as a volcanic eruptions, tsunami or earthquakes.

Managed realignment – A strategy that is used to manage some coastal environments. Managed realignment means that defences are breached and the coastline is allowed to retreat inland.

Management zones – Within an area of conservation, such as a National Park, different activities will be permitted within area or zone.

Mangrove forests – A type of tropical forest that grows in coastal regions.

Mantle – A zone of hot rocks that lies beneath the solid rocks of the Earth's crust.

Manufactured goods – Items that have been made in a workshop or factory.

Maritime (climate) – The climatic condition of land close to sea. The sea moderates temperatures meaning that there are only small variations in temperature.

Mass movement – When soil, rocks and stones slip, slide or slump down a slope. Some mass movement is very slow, for example, soil creep. Other mass movements are very rapid, for example, a rock fall.

Mass tourism – When very large numbers of tourists, who have bought a package holiday, visit a large resort.

Mass transit – A type of transport system that is able to move large numbers of people through a city, for example, an underground rail system.

Mean – The average value which is calculated by adding all of the values together and dividing by the number of values.

Meander – A river landform. A sweeping curve or bend in the river's course.

Mega-cities – Urban areas (cities) that have a population greater than 10 million people.

Micro-credit – Where small loans are given to businessmen and women who are too poor to qualify for traditional bank loans.

Mid-ocean ridge – Long chains of mountains that run down the centre of several oceans, including down the middle of the Atlantic Ocean. The ocean ridges are formed by plate movement.

Millennium Development Goal (MDG) – Millennium Development Goals. These are targets set by the United Nations to try to encourage and measure improvements to human development.

Moment magnitude scale (M_w) – A measure of the strength of an earthquake.

Monoculture – A type of agriculture (farming) in which only one crop is grown over very large areas of land.

Monsoon – A climate type experienced in South Asia in which a seasonal pattern of wind brings a distinct wet season.

Multilateral aid – Financial support that is given by a large number of different governments to a large organisation like the United Nations or the World Bank. This organisation then uses the aid to support countries that are in need of support.

Multinational companies (MNCs) – Large businesses such as Sony, Microsoft and McDonalds, who have branches in several countries. Multinational companies are also known as transnational companies.

Multiplier effect – An upward spiral of the economy and its benefits on employment. Positive multipliers are often triggered by a large investment, for example, the opening of a new factory.

Natural increase – A population increase which is due to their being more births than deaths.

Net immigration – When more people move into the region than leave it.

Newly industrialised country (NIC) – Newly industrialised countries such as India, Thailand or Indonesia have a large percentage of the workforce working in the secondary (manufacturing) sector.

NIMBYism – Not In My Back Yard. People who object to a development because they live close by are said to be NIMBYs.

Nutrient flows – The movement of minerals from one store to another.

Nutrient stores – A part of an ecosystem in which nutrients are kept.

Ocean acidification – A process by which the pH level of sea water decreases, making the water more acidic. Acidification is caused when extra CO_2 is absorbed into the sea.

Ocean currents – Predictable flows of water through the seas and oceans. Some currents are flows of relatively warm water, like the Gulf Stream. Other currents are relatively cold, like the Labrador.

Oceanic trenches – Long, deep gorges in the sea bed that occur around the edges of some oceans including the Pacific Ocean. The ocean trenches are formed by plate movement.

Offshore bar – A feature on the sea bed formed by the deposition of sand.

Outsourcing – To get a product or service from a supplier that is outside the company.

Over-abstraction – When water is abstracted at a faster rate than it is recharged, leading to a store of water decreasing in size.

Overland flow – The flow of water across the ground surface.

Pavement dwellers – People who live in make-shift homes on the footpaths of some developing cities, especially in Indian cities.

Peak discharge – The maximum amount of water in a river during a flood.

Permeability – The ability of a rock to allow water to pass through it.

Permeable – A rock which allows water to pass through it, such as limestone.

Place – A geographical concept used to describe what makes somewhere special, unique or distinct.

Plates – Rigid sections of crust. The plates lie on top of the mantle. They are able to move relative to each other. The movement is slow, but the force generated by their movement creates earthquakes and volcanic hazards.

Plunge pool – The pool of water found at the base of a waterfall. Plunge pools are erosional features created by abrasion and hydraulic action of the plunging water.

Point bar – A river beach formed of sand and gravel that is deposited on the inside bends of a meander.

Population density – The number of people living in a set area of land (e.g. in one square kilometre or one hectare).

Porosity – The ability of a rock to store water in tiny air spaces (pores).

Porous – A rock which has many tiny gaps within it (pores) that allow it to store water, such as chalk and sandstone.

Postglacial rebound – An adjustment in the level of the Earth's crust. The crust was depressed by the mass of ice lying on it during glacial periods of the ice age. Since the end of the last glacial period the crust has been slowly rising back to its original level.

Poverty line – People who live below this amount of income are said to live in poverty.

Primary commodities – Raw materials which have not been processed. Coal, minerals and unprocessed food stuffs are all examples.

Primary consumers – Animals that eat vegetation (**producers**) in the food chain. These animals may be eaten by **secondary consumers**.

Producers – Plants that are able to create starch from the sun's energy. Producers are at the bottom of the food chain.

Pull factors – Reasons that attract migrants to move to a new home.

Purchasing Power Parity (PPP) – A way of comparing the average wealth of a country by taking the cost of living in those countries into account.

Push factors – Reasons that force people to move away from their existing home.

Pyroclastic flows – A mixture of hot gas, ash and fragments of volcanic rock that fall, in a tumbling motion, down the slopes of a volcano during some explosive eruptions.

Quadrat – A piece of equipment used in fieldwork. Quadrats are square frames that come in several different sizes that are used during sampling.

Qualitative data – Information that is not numerical.

Quantitative data – Information that can be measured and recorded as numbers.

Quotas – Restrictions on the amount of particular goods that can be imported each year.

Rainwater harvesting – The collection and storage of rain water, for example from the roof of a house.

Raw materials – Materials such as timber, stone or crude oil that have not been processed or refined.

Re-afforestation – The planting of large areas with trees.

Recharge – Water that enters an aquifer and refills a groundwater store.

Refugees – People who are in danger and who leave their homes for their own safety. Refugees may move because of a natural disaster such as a volcanic eruption or because of conflict.

Responsible travel – Tourism that benefits local people and respects their culture, environment, beliefs and traditions. This term has the same meaning as **ethical tourism**.

Retreat – The gradual backward movement of a landform due to the process of erosion. The coastline retreats due to the erosion of a cliff and a waterfall retreats towards the source of a river as it is eroded.

Re-urbanisation – The recent trend for the population of city centres to grow.

Rift valley – A steep-sided valley formed by the pulling apart (or rifting) of the Earth's crust during plate movement.

Rock fall – The sudden collapse of rocks from a cliff or steep slope.

Rural to urban migration – The movement of people from the countryside to towns and cities.

Sahel – The semi-arid region of North Africa to the south of the Sahara desert. Sahel means 'shore' in Arabic.

Scale – A geographical concept used to describe the size or area covered by a feature. Scale varies from small (or local) through to regional, national and global.

Scattergraph – A type of diagram that can be used to test whether or not there is a relationship between two sets of data. See **dependent variable** and **independent variable**.

Schengen Zone – The area within the EU in which border control has been abandoned allowing people to cross from one country to another without showing a passport.

Scoria – Small fragments of volcanic rock that are ejected during an eruption. Scoria is full of bubble-like holes.

Sea arches – Natural arch-shaped features in cliffs on the coastline that are formed by the erosion of a cave in a headland.

Secondary consumers – Animals that are higher up the food chain and that eat **primary consumers**.

Seismometers – Scientific instruments used to measure the strength and frequency of earth shaking or earthquakes.

Self-help – Improvement projects carried out by ordinary people rather than by businesses or governments. Compare this to **top-down development**.

Shield volcano – A large volcano that has gentle slopes. Some of the volcanoes in Iceland and Hawaii have this shape.

Shoreline Management Plan – The plan that details how a local authority will manage each stretch of coastline in the UK in the future.

Slab pull – A process by which the sinking of the crust at a destructive plate margin pulls the oceanic plate away from the constructive plate margin.

Slip-off slope – The gentle slope on a river beach (or **point bar**) that is formed by deposition of sediment on the inside bends of a meander.

Slumping – The gradual collapse of a hillside under its own weight. Slumping sometimes occurs where an **unconsolidated** rock glides over an impermeable rock type such as clay.

Soft engineering – Alternative method of reducing floods by planting trees or allowing areas to flood naturally.

Soil erosion – The loss of soil due to either wind or heavy rain. Gulley erosion is a major cause of soil erosion in countries that have a seasonal wet and dry climate.

Spatial – Patterns or geographical features that vary over two dimensions so that they can be shown on a map.

Sphere of influence – The area over which a geographical feature or event is able to create an impact. These impacts may be good or bad.

Spit – A coastal landform formed by the deposition of sediment in a low mound where the coastline changes direction, for example, at the mouth of a river.

Squatter homes (slums) – Homes where the householders have no legal rights to the land, i.e. they do not have legal housing tenure. Informal settlements are commonly known as shanty towns or squatter homes. They are referred to as slums in India.

Stacks – Natural features of an eroded cliff landscape. Stacks are formed by the collapse of a sea arch.

Standard of living – The level of wealth and comfort experienced by any group of people or individual.

Storm beach – A steeply sloping beach. Strong waves throw pebbles into a steep ridge at the top of the beach during a storm.

Storm surge – The rise in sea level that can cause coastal flooding during a storm or hurricane. The surge is due to a combination of two things. First, the low air pressure means that sea level can rise. Second, the strong winds can force a bulge of water on to the shoreline.

Stratovolcano – A large, steep-sided volcano formed from layers of solidified lava and ash that have been built up by many different eruptions.

Subduction – The process where one plate is destroyed as it is slowly pulled underneath another plate.

Subjective – Evidence that is personal and which varies depending on someone's point of view.

Subsidy – A payment that a country makes to its own farmers and businesses so that their goods can be sold at a lower price to consumers.

Subsistence – A type of economic activity where very little money is used. In subsistence farming the farmer only produces enough food to feed the family. There is very little surplus that can be sold for cash.

Suburban – The outer area of towns and cities. Suburban areas are usually less densely built-up than inner-urban areas.

Surface stores – Places where water is found on the surface such as lakes and rivers.

Sustainable community – A community which is designed to have minimum impact on the environment. Such communities may make use of energy efficiency, renewable technologies and local services in order to reduce transport costs.

Swash – The flow of water up the beach as a wave breaks on the shore.

Taiga – Natural forest ecosystems found in the cold climates of Northern Europe and America.

Tariffs – A type of tax that may be charged on goods as they enter a country.

Telework – To work from home using technologies such as phones and the internet to communicate with a central workplace or office.

Throughflow – The downhill flow of water through soil.

Tiltmeter – A scientific instrument that is used to measure tilting of the ground. Tiltmeters can be used to measure small changes in ground shape that occur when the magma chamber beneath a volcano is filling with molten rock.

Top-down development – When decisions about development are made by governments or officials rather than by ordinary people. Compare this to **self-help** schemes.

Tor – A natural pile of stones found on top of a low hill.

Tourist enclave – A tourist resort that is separated from local communities. Some tourist developments are designed so that tourists are discouraged from leaving the hotel or resort. In this way, the tourist spends more money with the company, and very little with local businesses.

Trade blocs – Trading partnerships between different countries. The European Union is one example.

Transect – A line along which data is collected. Transects usually cut across different geographical features.

Transport – The movement of material through the landscape.

Tributary – A smaller river which flows into a larger river channel.

Tropical rainforest – Large forest ecosystems (or biomes) that exist in the hot, wet climate found on either side of the Equator.

Tsunami – A series of large and powerful waves on the surface of a lake or the ocean. A tsunami may be caused when water is displaced by the movement of the ocean floor/lake bed during an earthquake.

Tundra – An ecosystem largely found in the Arctic region. The tundra is treeless because the growing season is short and the average monthly temperature is below 10°C.

Unconsolidated – A rock that is only loosely compacted and that is not properly glued together. Deposits left by melting of ice at the end of the last age are largely unconsolidated.

Unskilled workers – Workers who have low levels of qualification or little technical ability and training. See **highly skilled**.

Unstable – Warm air that is rising may be described as unstable. Unstable air causes clouds to build up and form rain.

Upland – A landscape that is hilly or mountainous. Upland landscapes contain large areas of open space with few field boundaries.

Urban heat island – When a city has temperatures that are warmer than in the surrounding rural area.

Urban microclimate – The small scale, local climate of a large city which is influenced by its buildings and traffic.

Urbanisation – The physical and human growth of towns and cities.

Urban–rural continuum – The range of human environments one can experience from the very densely built-up parts of our largest cities to the most remote, sparsely populated rural communities.

U-shaped valleys – Valleys that have steep slopes and a flat valley floor. U-shaped valleys are erosional features created by the movement of a glacier.

Variables – Sets of data. See **dependent variable** and **independent variable**.

Vertical erosion – When the force of water, that is wearing away the landscape, is concentrated downwards. Vertical erosion is common in steeply flowing streams and also in gulley erosion.

Viscosity – A measure of the stickiness of lava. Viscosity depends on factors such as the temperature of the lava and its chemical composition.

Volcanic Explosivity Index (VEI) – A measure of the size of a volcanic eruption that is based on the amount of ash ejected and the height of the ash cloud.

Volcanic hotspot – An area of the Earth's crust in which volcanic activity is concentrated. Some hotspots are on plate margins (such as Iceland) and other hotspots are in the middle of plates (such as Hawaaii).

Vulnerable – To be exposed to a risk such as a natural disaster. Some groups of people in society are more vulnerable to risk than others. Vulnerability can be overcome by building **capacity**.

Water cycle – The continuous flow of water between the earth's surface and the atmosphere – also called the hydrological cycle.

Water footprint – The amount of water used to make an item of food or make a product such as an item of clothing.

Water security – When a society has enough water to ensure that everyone has clean water, sanitation and good health and the economy has enough water to grow food and make things.

Waterfalls – A land form created when a river plunges over a vertical or near vertical surface

Wave-cut notch – A slot with overhanging rocks that has been cut into the bottom of a cliff by wave action.

Wave-cut platform – A coastal landform made of rocky shelf in front of a cliff. The wave-cut platform is caused by erosion and left by the retreat of the cliff.

Wholesale clearance – The demolition of a large quantity of old unfit housing and the redevelopment of new, better homes.

Wildlife corridor – Strips of habitat that allow wild animals to migrate from one ecosystem to another, for example hedgerows.

Zooxanthellae – Algae that live symbiotically within the cells of other organisms. This relationship creates the coral polyps that we see in coral reefs.

INDEX

319

PHOTO ACKNOWLEDGEMENTS

The publishers would like to thank the following for permission to reproduce copyright material:

p.3 *t* © Janet Baxter Photography; **p.5** © Jeff Morgan 13/Alamy Stock Photo; **p.6** © Realimage/Alamy Stock Photo; **p.18** © David Waters/Alamy Stock Photo; **p.19** © robertharding/Alamy Stock Photo; **p.22** © B&JPhotos/Alamy Stock Photo; **p.25** © Billy Stock/Alamy Stock Photo; **p.28** *t* © Ashley Cooper/Alamy Stock Photo; *m* © Anthony Collins/Alamy Stock Photo; **p.31** © PHILIP SMITH/Alamy Stock Photo; p.32 © Peter Barritt/Alamy Stock Photo; **p.33** *t and m* © Glyn Owen; *b* © Tony Boydon/Alamy Stock Photo; **p.35** © robertharding/Alamy Stock Photo; **p.43** © Ashley Cooper pics/Alamy Stock Photo; **p.44** © Andrew Calverley/Alamy Stock Photo; **p.45** © Cumbria Crack; **p.47** © SWNS/Alamy Stock Photo; **p.48** *m* © Paul Glendell/Alamy Stock Photo; *b* © JMF News/Alamy Stock Photo; **p.50** *t* © Richard Stanton/UPPA/Photoshot; **p.60** © Foster + Partners; **p.64** *bl and br* © Glyn Owen; **p.68** © Sport In Pictures/Alamy Stock Photo; **p.69** © Commission Air/Alamy Stock Photo; **p.71** © Peter Macdiarmid/Getty Images News/Getty Images; **p.72** © Raf Makda/View Pictures/Rex Features; **p.76** © Andy Leeder; **p.77** © Andy Leeder; **p.79** © Dead Shot Keen/Alamy Stock Photo; **p.86** © UMA Press, Inc./Alamy Stock Photo; **p.88** *t* © Robert Gray/Alamy Stock Photo; *bl* © vdbvsl/Alamy Stock Photo; *br* © Jeffrey Blackler/Alamy Stock Photo; **p.90** © dbimages/Alamy Stock Photo; **p.91** © Dinodia Photos/Alamy Stock Photo; **p.94** © Punit Paranjpe/AFP/Getty Images; **p.95** © roger parkes/Alamy Stock Photo; **p.96** *t* © ZUMA Press, Inc./Alamy Stock Photo; *b* © galit seligmann/Alamy Stock Photo; **p.97** © Saifee Burhani Upliftment Trust; p.106 © Efrain Padro/Alamy Stock Photo; **p.109** © Warren Kovach/Alamy Stock Photo; **p.110** *t* © Martin Hertel/360cities.net via Getty Images; *b* © frans lemmens/Alamy Stock Photo; **p.113** © Manuel Ribeiro/Alamy Stock Photo; **p.117** © epa european pressphoto agency b.v./Alamy Stock Photo; **p.118** © Stocktrek Images, Inc./Alamy Stock Photo; **p.121** © Lianne Milton – Panos; **p.122** © CLARA PRIMA/AFP/Getty Images; **p.123** © Andrea Fitrianto (http://creativecommons.org/licenses/by-nc-sa/3.0/); **p.125** © ephotocorp/Alamy Stock Photo; **p.127** © ABARI; **p.128** © NICOLAS ASFOURI/AFP/Getty Images; **p.129** © Philip Game/Alamy Stock Photo; **p.130** © nobleIMAGES/Alamy Stock Photo; **p.134** © Environment Agency; **p.142** © robertharding/Alamy Stock Photo; **p.146** © Stephen Pond/Stringer; **p.147** © Mark Richardson/Alamy Stock Photo; **p.149** © Irene Abdou/Alamy Stock Photo; **p.151** © Chris Wood/Alamy Stock Photo; **p.152** *bl* © Richard Smith/Alamy Stock Photo; *r* © Cartoonstock; **p.155** Chichester Canal © Joseph Mallord William Turner via Getty images; **p.156** © US Marines Photo/Alamy Stock Photo; **p.158** © Arctic Images/Alamy Stock Photo; **p.162** © Xinhua/Alamy Stock Photo; **p.165** © epa european pressphoto agency b.v./Alamy Stock Photo; **p.168** © Press Association Images; **p.170** © Ashley Cooper/Alamy Stock Photo; **p.174** © Toby Melville/Thomson Reuters; **p.179** *b* © FLPA/Tui De Roy/Minden Pictures; **p.181** © FLPA/Tui De Roy/Minden Pictures; **p.184** *l* © Brad Simmons/Beateworks/Corbis; *r* © Ben Cranke/The Image Bank/Getty Images; **p.185** © Gerry Ellis/Minden Pictures/FLPA; **p.186** *t and b* © Montgomeryshire Wildlife Trust; **p.187** © M Williams/Alamy Stock Photo; **p.190** © Val Davis; **p.191** © Val Davis; **p.193** © Images of Africa Photobank/Alamy Stock Photo; **p.194** © Ken Edwards/Alamy Stock Photo; **p.198** © Photoshot License Ltd/Alamy Stock Photo; **p.199** © blickwinkel/Alamy Stock Photo; **p.202** © Ian Nellist/Alamy Stock Photo; **p.203** © Neil Cooper/Alamy Stock Photo; **p.205** © Nyani Quarmyne/Panos Pictures; **p.206** © Jacob Silberberg/Panos Pictures; **p.208** © Prisma Bildagentur AG/Alamy Stock Photo; **p.209** © Ullstein Bild/Getty Images; **p.211** © Colm Regan, Man eating the world that someone else is holding, cartoon, Thin Black Lines: Political Cartoons & Development Education (Teachers in Development Education 1988); **p.213** *l* © david pearson/Alamy Stock Photo; *r* © Ariadne Van Zandbergen/Alamy Stock Photo; **p.214** *tl* © Danita Delimont/Alamy Stock Photo; *tr* © Getty Images/Raveendran/AFT; *br* © PETER PARKS/AFP/Getty Images; **p.215** Stuart Freedman/Panos Pictures; **p.219** © Janine Wiedel Photolibrary/Alamy Stock Photo; **p.221** © Thomas Imo/Photothek via Getty Images; **p.222** © Simon Stirrup/Alamy Stock Photo; **p.224** © Everett Collection Historical/Alamy Stock Photo; **p.225** © Ulrich Doering/Alamy Stock Photo; **p.232** © epa european pressphoto agency b.v./Alamy Stock Photo; **p.233** © robertharding/Alamy Stock Photo; **p.234** © Charlotte Thege/Alamy Stock Photo; **p.239** © Joerg Boethling/Alamy Stock Photo; **p.240** © Bloomberg/Getty Images; **p.241** © Panos Pictures/Karen Robinson; **p.242** © Gary Whitton/Alamy Stock Photo; **p.243** *tl* © Ton Koene/VWPics/Alamy Stock Photo; *bl* © The International Women's Tribune Centre; **p.244** © Dieter Telemans/Panos Pictures; **p.249** © Friedrich Stark/Alamy Stock Photo; **p.251** © Desiree Martin/AFP/Getty Image; **p.253** © Shankar Mourya/Hindustan Times via Getty Images; **p.261** © Paul White - UK Industries/Alamy Stock Photo; **p.262** *t* © Panos Pictures/Christien Jaspars; *mr* © Colm Regan, Man thinking about a car and woman thinking about shoes, cartoon, Thin Black Lines: Political Cartoons & Development Education (Teachers in Development Education 1988); **p.268** © Pacific Press/LightRocket via Getty Images; **p.273** © epa european pressphoto agency b.v./Alamy Stock Photo; **p.275** © Horizons WWP/TRVL/Alamy Stock Photo; **p.279** © Panos Pictures/Alfredo Caliz; **p.281** © Jenny Matthews/Panos Pictures; **p.283** © UNMEER/Alamy Stock Photo; **p.285** © ZUMA Press, Inc./Alamy Stock Photo; **p.289** © Friedrich Stark/Alamy Stock Photo; **p.290** © Simon Price/Alamy Stock Photo; **p.293** Photo taken by Caroline Russell during fieldwork funded by Lancaster Environment Centre; **p.294** © YAY Media AS/Alamy Stock Photo; **p.295** *t* © Age Fotostock/Alamy Stock Photo; *m* © Greenpeace; **p.298** © WaterFrame/Alamy Stock Photo; **p.299** © A.P.S. (UK)/Alamy Stock Photo; **p.302** © cartoonstock.com; **p.303** © STEFAN HEUNIS/AFP/Getty Images; **p.307** *t* © ImageBroker/Alamy Stock Photo; *b* © Steffen Binke/Alamy Stock Photo; **p.308** © Lintao Zhang/Getty Images.